YO-CUI-267

Studies in Learning and Memory

Centennial Psychology Series
Charles D. Spielberger, *General Editor*

Anne Anastasi *Contributions to Differential Psychology*
William K. Estes *Models of Learning, Memory, and Choice*
Hans J. Eysenck *Personality, Genetics, and Behavior*
Irving L. Janis *Stress, Attitudes, and Decisions*
Neal Miller *Bridges Between Laboratory and Clinic*
Brenda Milner *Brain Function and Cognition*
O. Hobart Mowrer *Leaves from Many Seasons*
Charles E. Osgood *Psycholinguistics, Cross-Cultural Universals, and Prospects for Mankind*
Julian B. Rotter *The Development and Applications of Social Learning Theory*
Seymour B. Sarason *Psychology and Social Action*
Benton J. Underwood *Studies in Learning and Memory*

Studies in Learning and Memory
Selected Papers

Benton J. Underwood

PRAEGER

PRAEGER SPECIAL STUDIES • PRAEGER SCIENTIFIC

Library of Congress Cataloging in Publication Data

Underwood, Benton J., 1915–
  Studies in learning and memory.

  (Centennial psychology series)
  Bibliography: p.
  Includes indexes.
  1. Learning, Psychology of—Addresses, essays,
lectures. 2. Memory—Addresses, essays, lectures.
I. Title. II. Series.
BF318.U53   153.1   81-22694
ISBN 0-03-058976-2   AACR2

Published in 1982 by Praeger Publishers
CBS Educational and Professional Publishing
A Division of CBS, Inc.
521 Fifth Avenue, New York, New York 10017 U.S.A.

©1982 by Praeger Publishers

All rights reserved

23456789 145 987654321

Printed in the United States of America

Contents

	Editor's Introduction	vii
	Acknowledgments	xi
1	Historical Perspective	1
2	Proactive Interference	33
	Interference and Forgetting	34
	Proactive Inhibition in Short-Term Retention of Single Items	51
	Degree of Learning and the Measurement of Forgetting	67
3	Implicit Associative Responses	93
	Implicit Responses and the Role of Intralist Similarity in Verbal Learning by Normal and Retarded Subjects	94
	False Recognition Produced by Implicit Verbal Responses	106
	Implicit Responses and Conceptual Similarity	116
4	Frequency Theory	131
	A Frequency Theory of Verbal-Discrimination Learning	132
	Verbal-Discrimination Learning with Varying Numbers of Right and Wrong Terms	151
	Testing Effects in the Recognition of Words	157
	Recognition and Number of Incorrect Alternatives Presented During Learning	170
	The Syllable as a Source of Error in Multisyllable Word Recognition	181
	Individual Differences as a Crucible in Theory Construction	189

5	**Miscellaneous**	**201**
	An Orientation for Research on Thinking	202
	Effect of Distributed Practice on Paired-Associate Learning	218
	Attributes of Memory	252
6	**Current Perspectives**	**277**
7	**Biographical Sketch**	**309**
	Publications: A Comprehensive Bibliography	312
	Author Index	325
	Subject Index	329

Editor's Introduction

The founding of Wilhelm Wundt's laboratory at Leipzig in 1879 is widely acclaimed as the landmark event that provided the initial impetus for the development of psychology as an experimental science. To commemorate scientific psychology's one-hundredth anniversary, Praeger Publishers commissioned the Centennial Psychology Series. The general goals of the Series are to present, in both historical and contemporary perspective, the most important papers of distinguished contributors to psychological theory and research.

As psychology begins its second century, the Series proposes to examine the foundation on which scientific psychology is built. Each volume provides a unique opportunity for the reader to witness the emerging theoretical insights of eminent psychologists whose seminal work has served to define and shape their respective fields, and to share with them the excitement associated with the discovery of new scientific knowledge.

The selection of the Series authors was an extremely difficult task. Indexes of scientific citations and rosters of the recipients of prestigious awards for research contributions were examined. Nominations were invited from leading authorities in various fields of psychology. The opinions of experienced teachers of psychology and recent graduates of doctoral programs were solicited. There was, in addition, a self-selection factor: a few of the distinguished senior psychologists invited to participate in the Series were not able to do so, most often because of demanding commitments or ill health.

Each Series author was invited to develop a volume comprising five major parts: (1) an original introductory chapter; (2) previously published articles and original papers selected by the author; (3) a concluding chapter; (4) a brief autobiography; and (5) a complete bibliography of the author's publications. The main content of each volume consists of articles and papers especially selected for this Series by the author. These papers trace the historical development of the author's work over a period of forty to fifty years. Each volume also provides a cogent presentation of the author's current research and theoretical viewpoints.

In their introductory chapters, Series authors were asked to describe the intellectual climate that prevailed at the beginning of their scientific careers, and to examine the evolution of the ideas that led them from one study to another. They were also invited to comment on significant factors—both scientific and personal—that stimulated and motivated them to embark on their research programs and to consider special opportunities or constraints that influenced their work, including experimental failures and blind alleys only rarely reported in the literature.

In order to preserve the historical record, most of the articles reprinted in the Series volumes have been reproduced exactly as they appeared when they were first published. In some cases, however, the authors have abridged their original papers (but not altered the content), so that redundant materials could be eliminated and more papers could be included.

In the concluding chapters, the Series authors were asked to comment on their selected papers, to describe representative studies on which they are currently working, and to evaluate the status of their research. They were also asked to discuss major methodological issues encountered in their respective fields of interest and to identify contemporary trends that are considered most promising for future scientific investigation.

The biographical sketch that is included in each Series volume supplements the autobiographical information contained in the original and concluding chapters. Perhaps the most difficult task faced by the Series authors was selecting from the comprehensive bibliography a limited number of papers that they considered most representative of their life work.

Underwood's Contributions

Although general guidelines were suggested for each Series volume, the authors were encouraged to adapt the Series format to meet their individual needs. For this volume, Professor Underwood has selected fifteen papers that provide a comprehensive overview of his important contributions to theory and research on human learning and memory. Based on four decades of systematic work, these papers highlight the evolving theory and the empirical findings of a talented and dedicated investigator.

The lucid introductory chapter examines the historic context, describes the theoretical orientation that guided the research, and provides background information that will help the reader to more fully appreciate each reprinted paper and its special contribution to the research literature. Theoretical controversy and key studies by other investigators that have influenced Underwood's research are also cogently described. The reader will be especially rewarded in noting the subtle interplay between theoretical issues and innovations in methodology and experimental design.

The three papers on proactive interference that comprise Chapter 2 summarize Professor Underwood's seminal contributions to theory and research on this topic. His analysis of the role of interference, both within the laboratory and in the natural environment, leads him to conclude that proactive interference is responsible for most of the forgetting that takes place in long-term memory research. The research on proactive interference also points up the need to control the degree of original learning in studies of retention and forgetting.

In Chapter 3, Underwood examines classical association theory and the role of implicit associative responses (IARs) in learning, recognition, and recall. Chapter 4 consists of six papers related to frequency theory. These papers trace the development of the theory from its early articulation in a *Psychological Review* article in 1966 to the author's calling attention in 1975 to the importance of taking individual differences into account in theory construction.

The studies reprinted in Chapter 5 sample Professor Underwood's thought with regard to the higher mental processes involved in concept learning and thinking, the effects of massed versus distributed practice, and the structure of memory. His commentary on these topics in Chapter 6 serves to clarify the research results and their theoretical implications. This chapter also provides invaluable perspective regarding the current status of theory and research on proactive inhibition, the mechanisms that mediate the interference produced by implicit associative responses, and the strengths and shortcomings of frequency theory. A number of puzzles and problems that go beyond the topics discussed in this volume and that are targeted for future investigation are also discussed in Chapter 6.

The Centennial Psychology Series is especially designed for courses on the history of psychology. Individual volumes are also well suited for use as supplementary texts in those areas to which the authors have been major contributors. Students of psychology and related disciplines, as well as authorities in specialized fields, will find that each Series volume provides penetrating insight into the work of a significant contributor to the behavioral sciences. The Series also affords a unique perspective on psychological research as a living process.

The interest and enthusiasm of all with whom we have consulted concerning the establishment of the Series have been most gratifying, but I am especially grateful to Professors Anne Anastasi, Hans J. Eysenck, and Irving L. Janis for their many helpful comments and suggestions and for their early agreement to contribute to the Series. For his invaluable advice and consultation in the conception and planning of the Series, and for his dedicated and effective work in making it a reality, I am deeply indebted to Dr. George Zimmar, psychology editor for Praeger Publishers. The Series was initiated while I was a Fellow-In-Residence at the Netherlands Institute for Advanced Study, and I would like to express my appreciation to the director and staff of the institute and to my NIAS colleagues for their stimulation, encouragement, and strong support of this endeavor.

Charles D. Spielberger

Acknowledgments

I did not find it easy to select papers for this volume. At one time I considered drawing the papers randomly until the page limitation was reached. In the long run, however, order prevailed and I tried to build the papers around certain topics. I must acknowledge many debts in the selected papers and in the preparation of this volume. As will be seen in the footnotes to each paper, the Office of Naval Research has provided research support over the years. Graduate students who worked with me are coauthors for some of the papers and their contributions were substantial, not only for these papers but many others which I could not include. I am indebted to the American Psychological Association, Academic Press, and the University of Illinois Press for permission to reprint the papers. The selected papers are reprinted without change except for the figures. In the interests of greater uniformity, it was decided to redraw all of the figures. This was done with great care by Maureen Cannon, who also typed the manuscript. Dr. George P. Zimmar, senior editor of Praeger Scientific, and Dr. Charles D. Spielberger, Series editor, have been very helpful at all stages in the preparation of this volume.

Studies in Learning
and Memory

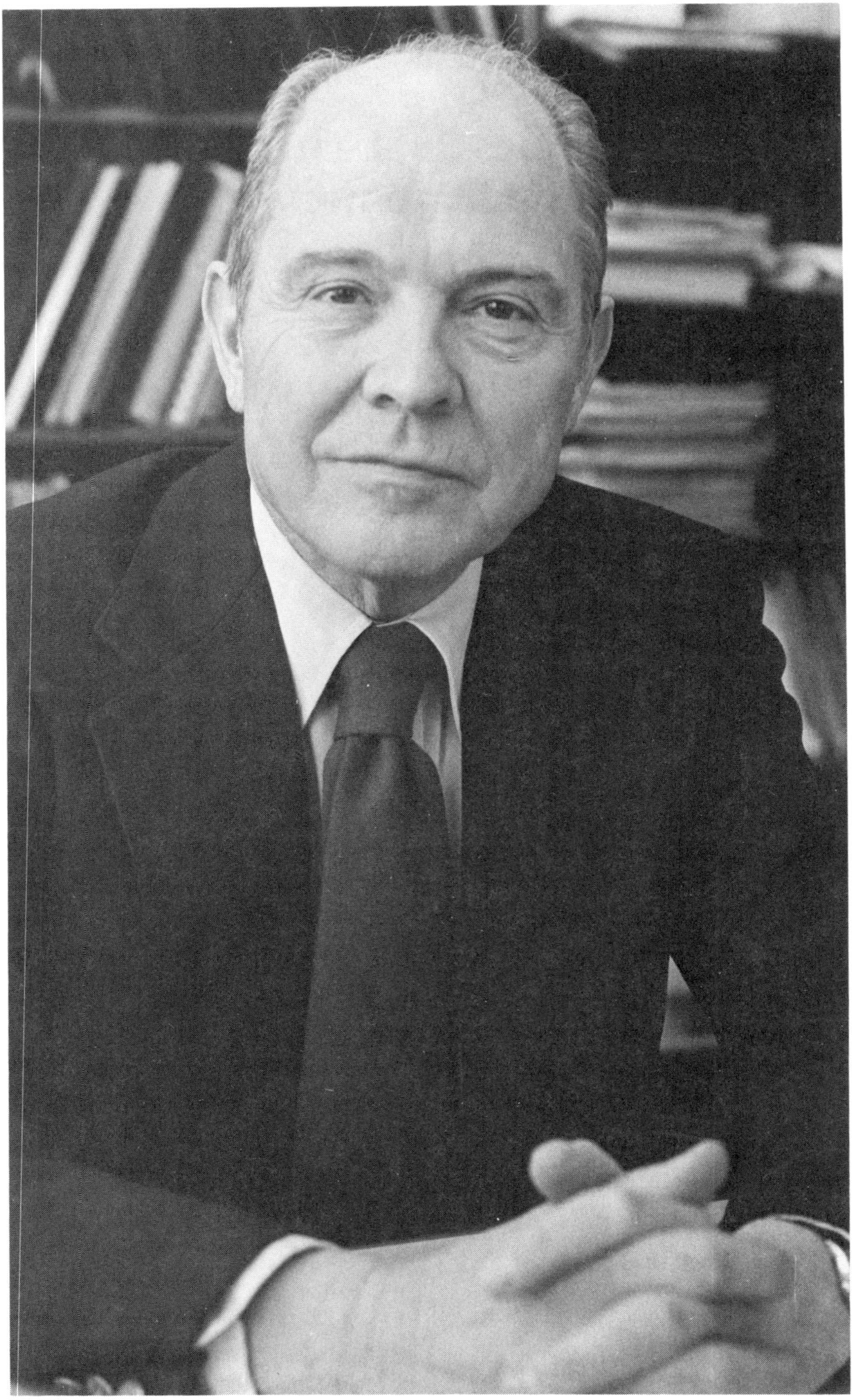

1
Historical Perspective

I entered graduate school at the University of Missouri in the fall of 1939 at about the time that Hitler invaded Poland. I did not see any causal link between the two events. Because Arthur W. Melton was chairman of the Department of Psychology, most of the research being done was in the area of verbal learning. Shortly after I arrived at Missouri I found myself conducting a study on the effect of social motivation on serial learning and on forgetting. This study was submitted as a master's thesis. In spite of the fact that the results of this first study were essentially negative, I found that experimental work gave me something that I had never experienced before; I was hooked. In 1940 I moved on to the University of Iowa to work with John McGeoch, perhaps the most eminent figure in verbal learning at that time.

Not only was I strongly attracted to experimentation, but also to the area of verbal learning. This area had its experimental roots in the work of Ebbinghaus (1913), and although Ebbinghaus believed that he was dealing with the higher mental processes, in more modern times many have referred to the area as rote learning. In the 1920s and 1930s verbal learning was associated with functionalism centered at the University of Chicago and with Woodworth's so-called dynamic psychology at Columbia University. In recent years the more imaginative researchers in the field have managed to get the area associated with the word "cognitive" or with "information processing." At both Missouri and the University of Iowa during the period 1939–1942 the research being done in the area was almost exclusively concerned with the forgetting of verbal materials. Of course, in order to study forgetting learning had to occur first, but I do not remember a single study in which the primary interest was on factors influencing the rate at which the list was learned.

So when I speak of my area of research as being verbal learning, it must be clear that it encompasses the work on the forgetting of verbal materials.

The situation in the Department of Psychology at Iowa in the immediate prewar years presented two contrasting research cultures in learning. One of these was the result of the presence of Kenneth W. Spence on the faculty. It was a time when the theories of Hull, Tolman, and Guthrie were preeminent, and Spence and his students were busily engaged in the animal laboratory as they sought out the crucial experiments to show that the Hull theory could predict better than the other theories. Those of us who were working in verbal learning with McGeoch were a little envious of the heady theoretical atmosphere associated with the animal laboratory. It was said to be characteristic of functionalism—of which McGeoch appeared to be a good representative—that formal theory was eschewed. Loose and general explanatory concepts were more in line with the functionalists' way of thinking, so in the verbal-learning laboratory at Iowa there were no identified bad guys and good guys as there were in the animal laboratory. Nevertheless McGeoch did entertain some quite specific theoretical ideas on some topics.

In 1932 McGeoch wrote an article that changed the whole course of theorizing about forgetting. Using logical tenets as well as empirical findings, McGeoch essentially destroyed decay or disuse as possible causes of forgetting; he substituted interference. Furthermore, in this article McGeoch noted that: "There are no warmly discussed theories of forgetting and there has been little research aimed directly at an explanation of the phenomenon" (p. 352). It seems beyond doubt that McGeoch was inviting theoretical discussion at some level, discussion that did not come, however, until 1940 when Melton and Irwin proposed the idea that retroactive inhibition had two factors involved in its production. Retroactive inhibition refers to the decrement in the recall of a list as a result of learning a second list. Melton and Irwin identified competition at the time of recall of the first list as being one of the factors, competition being an idea for which McGeoch was largely responsible. The new factor proposed by Melton and Irwin was unlearning, which meant that during the learning of the second of two lists the first-list items were weakened or unlearned, thus producing subsequent lowered recall. McGeoch quickly set us to work on experiments examining unlearning, but I never felt that he was warm toward this particular theoretical notion.

It came as a distinct surprise to me to discover that verbal-learning research was not an interest of many psychologists. I found that few of the major universities contained active groups of investigators of verbal learning. Iowa was simply an exception. To determine that my memory was correct on this matter, I recently went through the issues of the *Journal of Experimental Psychology* for the two calendar years 1940–1941 and counted the number of reports that dealt with verbal learning. There were 198 published articles in all, of which only 10 dealt with verbal learning. Furthermore, as the research trends began to stabilize following World War II, there was no evidence that the cataclysmic war had somehow produced a supercharged interest in verbal learning. I counted the number of articles printed each year in the *Journal of Experimental Psychology* during the years 1951 to 1971. The results of this count are plotted in Figure 1.1. Although the number of articles published each year in the 1950s was greater than the number published a decade earlier, in an absolute sense the number was quite small. Note, for example, that in 1955 only 10 articles on verbal learning were published. A clear increase in the number of reports in the area did not appear until 1959. All of this is to say that until about 1960 there were relatively few investigators working systematically in verbal learning. In my early years of research I could keep up with the literature in the field of verbal learning quite readily.

I joined the faculty at Northwestern University in January 1946. As is frequently the case, I suppose, the research I initiated represented an outgrowth of my Ph.D. dissertation. Included in the conditions of the experiments were several dealing with proactive inhibition or proactive interference (PI). Chapter 2 of this book consists of three reprinted articles dealing with PI.

PROACTIVE INTERFERENCE

Early History

Retroactive inhibition or interference (RI) was discovered about the turn of the century, and literally hundreds of investigations have been carried out in which this phenomenon was of major interest. It will be remembered that RI occurs when the first of two successively learned tasks is recalled. In contrast, PI involves the recall of the second of two successively learned tasks. When RI involves the use of interference paradigms (such as A-B, A-D, in which in two successive paired-associate lists the stimulus terms are the same but the response terms different), the amount of forgetting

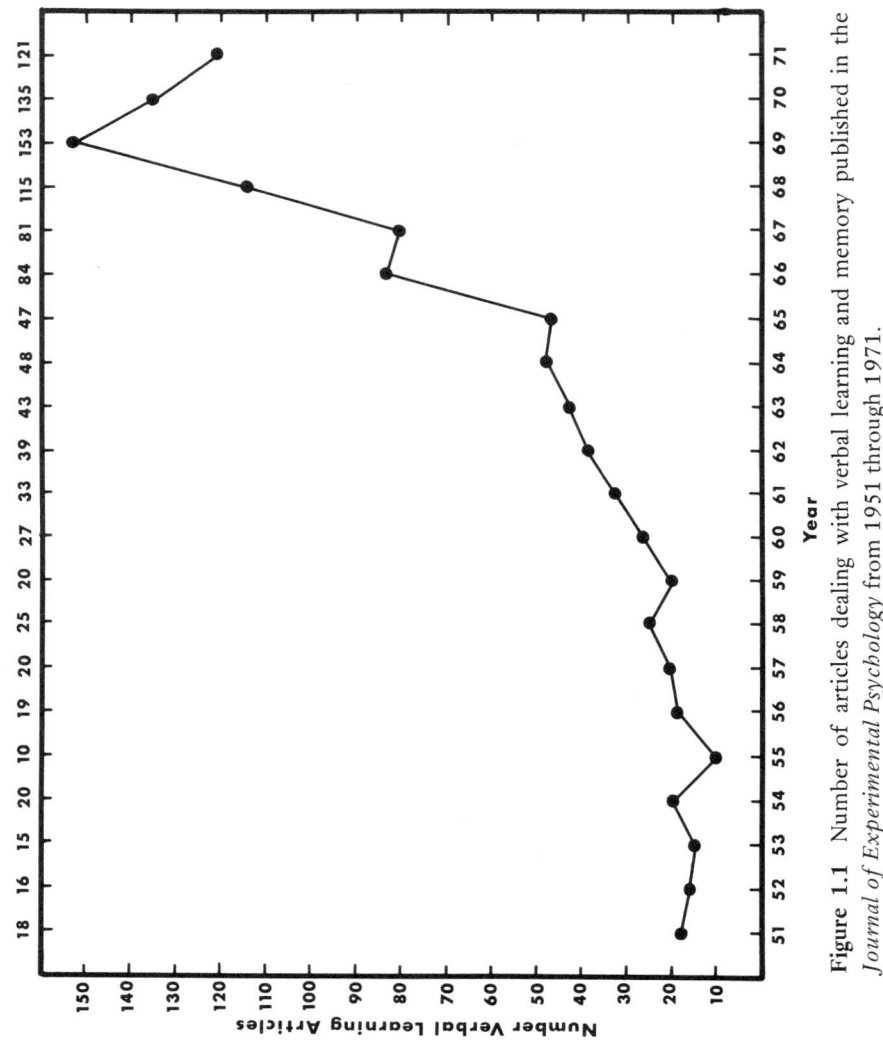

Figure 1.1 Number of articles dealing with verbal learning and memory published in the *Journal of Experimental Psychology* from 1951 through 1971.

of the first task produced by having learned a second task can be very great. It is no wonder that McGeoch (1932) used RI as a model for proposing that interference is the major cause of forgetting. Compared with RI, PI is a relatively recent discovery. Whitely (1927) received credit for the discovery of PI in an extensive series of studies (over 1000 subjects). The purpose of the experiments was to determine the effect on learning of intellectual activities occurring immediately before learning and the effect on recall of such activities inserted at various times before recall.

In Whitely's studies the central task was always an 18-item free-recall task consisting of words or phrases all dealing with the same topic. Thus, a list dealing with the Civil War might include Lincoln, Emancipation Proclamation, Secession, Bull Run, and so on. The potential interfering task—this is my phrase, not Whitely's—was one of two kinds. In one the subjects were given a two-page summary of a given field of knowledge. This summary was studied for a period of time, and then the subject answered questions about it. In the second method the subjects were required to try to answer a series of questions over a given field of knowledge, such as athletics or geography.

In one of the experiments, two conditions, among a series of conditions, defined PI. One group, the control group, was simply given the free-recall task for a single study and test trial, followed by a further test trial 48 hours later. The experimental group was given one of the potentially interfering tasks just prior to free-recall learning, with the retention of the free-recall task taken after 48 hours. The recall under the control condition was about 10 percent higher than the recall under the experimental condition. Most of the other conditions were concerned with RI. Whitely was able to conclude that the interfering tasks were "detrimental to recall, whether introduced prior to recall, prior to learning, or immediately following learning" (p. 506).

Whitely did not use the phrase *proactive inhibition* (or *proactive interference*) in the 1927 publication. It was nine years later that at the end of a report (Whitely & Blankenship, 1936) the following sentence occurred: "The term *proactive inhibition* (italicized in the original) may be employed to describe the phenomenon under consideration to differentiate it from retroactive inhibition" (p. 503). There were two experiments reported. In the first the central task was a free-recall list of 18 monosyllabic words. Again, an experimental and a control group were used, with another list of 18 monosyllabic words serving as the interfering task. The amount of PI in 48-hour recall was greater than in the earlier work, with the control group recalling 50 percent and the experimental group recalling 24 percent.

In a second experiment the central task consisted of stanzas of poetry, with the interfering task being other stanzas from the same poem. Without the interfering task, recall after 48 hours was 75 percent; with the interfering task, it was 46 percent. In short, this report contained two different experiments encompassing widely different materials, and both showed an appreciable amount of PI. Somewhat later (Blankenship & Whitely, 1941), it was demonstrated that PI was present in the memory for grocery-store advertisements. It is puzzling to me why McGeoch appeared to pay so little attention to PI. In his 1942 book he did not mention the phenomenon except as an alternative term for negative transfer.

It was not until well into the postwar years that PI began to be viewed as a powerful factor in forgetting. I published a study in 1948 that indicated that with the use of the A-B, A-D paradigm PI was just as large in amount as was RI after a 48-hour retention interval. Then, quite by chance, it was discovered that even with lists of unrelated words PI increased as the number of lists learned increased (Underwood, 1950, 4). Greenberg and I proposed to see if there was a phenomenon of learning-to-recall paralleling the phenomenon of learning-to-learn. What we found was just the opposite—the subjects forgot more and more with practice. The full implications of these findings finally struck me after several years, and I was led to do some library work that produced the paper "Interference and Forgetting," reprinted in Chapter 2 of this book.

PI in Short-Term Memory

Undoubtedly, the rapid increase in the interest in verbal learning in the 1960s (as seen in Figure 1.1) was in part due to the invention or discovery of short-term memory procedures by Brown (1958) and by Peterson and Peterson (1959). In the Peterson and Peterson study a subject was shown a consonant syllable, for example, CXJ, for perhaps a second or two, with recall requested after varying intervals of time up to 18 seconds. Recall of the syllable decreased sharply as the retention interval increased. Peterson and Peterson had used a within-subject design in which each subject was exposed to and tested on many different syllables during the single experimental session. This seemed like a miniaturized version of the studies using list learning and long-retention intervals—24 hours, for example—in which it appeared that PI was heavily involved (see "Interference and Forgetting"). Yet, the Petersons concluded from their analysis that PI was not responsible for the heavy forgetting occurring over their 18-second retention intervals. Geoffrey Keppel and I were skeptical of the conclusion that PI was not involved. We did some analyses on the Peterson and Peterson data and we thought we detected PI. It was apparent, however, that a different experimental design was needed to settle the matter. More particularly, we felt we needed to observe the forgetting of the very first few items given the subjects. We carried out three experiments and the results seemed to make a strong case for the conclusion that PI was responsible for most, if not all, of the forgetting observed by Peterson and Peterson. These three experiments are described in "Proactive Inhibition in Short-Term Retention of Single Items," reprinted in Chapter 2 of this book.

Measurement Problems

As the previous discussion has made manifest, the nature of the experimental design used was a critical factor in determining the absolute amount of forgetting measured. A within-subject design resulted in relatively low recall because of the PI produced by the other lists learned in the experiment. If one wanted an estimate of forgetting without PI from other lists being involved, a random-groups design was required. In fact, to obtain an estimate that was pure required that only subjects who had not previously served in any verbal-learning study be used.

As we were learning about the influence of type of design on retention, we were also living with a number of problems of method that were more specific in nature. These problems led us to consider the role of individual differences in retention. This started in 1954 when I published a report that demonstrated that there was no relationship between the rate of learning among subjects and the rate of forgetting. Basically, the idea was that if the level of learning achieved for fast-learning subjects and for slow-learning subjects was equivalent, there was no difference in amount forgotten over 24 hours. In various studies we had done and were to do, the generalized issue was that of determining differences in retention when there were differences in rate of learning. For example, if we had two lists learned, one of them being easy, the other difficult, how were we to determine whether the rate of forgetting of the two lists differed or not? The critical problem was to neutralize degree or level of learning as a differential factor in the forgetting. We also believed that the Peterson-Peterson method was confounding degree of learning with other variables, and thus we needed a solution to this problem also; the last paper in Chapter 2, "Degree of Learning and the Measurement of Forgetting," gives my solutions to this problem. It is also worth noting that in the process of working out methods to neutralize degree of learning we developed evidence that indicated to us that in these laboratory experiments there were no individual differences of consequence in long-term retention.

IMPLICIT ASSOCIATIVE RESPONSES

Associationism

I am an incurable associationist. Symptoms of this affliction are evident in almost everything I write. I do not know just how such doctrines became a firm part of my thinking, although there are some hints. One of the first books I read in graduate school was E. S. Robinson's *Association Theory Today,* published in 1932. I was impressed by this book; perhaps I was imprinted by it. Too, I had as mentors Melton, McGeoch, and Spence, and it is surely not unreasonable to assume that they did nothing to extinguish my attachment to associationism. It has seemed to me that it has been popular periodically to criticize associationist approaches. Such criticisms have usually led me to reexamine the tenets of associationism for the nth time with the result being that I become more firmly convinced of the necessity of the approach.

As I have observed human behavior it has always seemed to me that there are innumerable instances where it seems perfectly straightforward to say that associations are involved. When did Columbus discover America? Who is the current vice-president? What is a synonym for the word courageous? What is your name? What is the French word for window? To respond correctly to such questions requires a prior learning process that, according to my approach, establishes associations. That is, there is a domain of behavior implied by the above questions that can be thought of productively as involving associations between two events. I do not know of any reasonable alternatives that have been offered as substitutes for associations by those who do not like to think in associationist terms. To my knowledge there has not been a satisfactory substitute vocabulary offered as a replacement for the vocabulary of associationism. Rejections of the associationist doctrine usually mean the abandonment of an area of research. This is not always true. Sometimes it has meant the changing of the description of an association as has been done by Greeno, James, DaPolito, and Polson (1978). They say: ". . . we are led to a hypothesis that association is a form of cognitive organization, depending on relational ideas that the learner already has in cognitive structure" (p. 8). This type of vocabulary does not suit me.

It was noted earlier that there is a domain of behavior for which the classical associationist approach is judged to be singularly appropriate. How broad is this domain? To answer this question requires the consideration of two "dimensions." One of these refers to task dimensions, which may be identified by the names of various tasks used to study verbal learning. Certainly the paired-associate task represents the heart of the domain of associationism. Free-recall learning can probably also be analyzed in associationist terms. Strangely enough, the task that Ebbinghaus bequeathed us, the serial learning task, has been most resistant in modern times to analysis based on associations. The same problem arises when considering certain motor skills, such as tracking, but these tasks do not involve verbal units in the sense that serial learning does. At present, we have to acknowledge that an associationistic approach to serial learning has not been productive. This is not to say that a serial list cannot be learned as a sequence of associations between successive items, for the evidence clearly indicates that it can under special conditions. But, given the usual list of words, it appears that the average subject simply does not master the serial list by acquiring associations between successive words. The list may be mastered by forming associations between events that have not yet been identified, but it is surely not mastered in the usual case by acquiring a series of successive associations, each conceptualized as an association as in paired-associate learning. For the time being, therefore, the domain for which associationist analysis is appropriate seems limited by the nature of the tasks involved.

The second dimension needed in establishing the domain may be thought of as a vertical dimension. I have sometimes spoken of second-order habits or second-order associations. What I mean by this is that the second event in an association may be a class name that evolved because instances of the class or category had been associated with the first event. When a subject learns that event A is always followed by the name of an animal, the association between A and *animal* may develop even though there has never been an overt presentation of A and *animal*. As will be seen, such implicit associative responses may be used by the theoretician in trying to understand certain other phenomena.

I will repeat that I consider the use of associationist analysis to be appropriate for a relatively restricted domain of behavior. Future work may expand the domain or it might shrink it. No inference should be made that an association is necessarily useful in understanding more complicated verbal memories such as the memory for a sentence. In fact, as will be seen later, associations may develop between words in some tasks, such as the verbal-discrimination task, but these associations are judged to be quite irrelevant to the mastery of the task. To repeat, I think there is a restricted domain of behavior for which an associationist approach is quite useful.

Certain problems arise in characterizing an association. There seems to be a compelling tendency to view an association as representing a bond or connection that can vary in strength. To my mind, the most difficult issue we have in dealing with associations is how to rationalize data in which strength of the association seems to play only a minor role at best. Most of these puzzling cases occur in studies in which interference among associations is the central issue. The assumption is that the amount of interference between two competing or conflicting associations ought to be related in a systematic way to the strength of the competing associations. This seems not to be true. For example, negative transfer in the A-B, A-D paradigm is relatively independent of the strength of the competing associations beyond some minimal level (Postman, 1962). In certain contexts, however, the strength of the association seems to be a very useful way to describe outcomes. In learning a paired-associate list the likelihood of producing B given A increases gradually as the number of times that B has been given to A increases. And, a day or a week later, we find that recall is directly related to the number of times that B has occurred to A. To say this another way, the stronger the association the better the retention.

I do not know how, in the long run, these strength anomalies will be handled. Perhaps they might be conquered by holding firmly to a probabilistic notion of an association, by which it is possible to avoid having to refer to strength differences for the single item. I do not like such a solution for the very reason that it is offered. I would prefer for the time being to accept the anomalies of the strength position. Indeed, it might be concluded that if strength is eliminated as a characteristic of an association, a basic tenet of associationism is eliminated.

Theoretical Uses of Implicit Associative Responses

The human memory system—semantic memory, as it is sometimes called—consists of a large repertoire of words. Some have estimated that the young college student may know the meaning of as many as 75,000 words (Oldfield, 1966). Be that as it may, many associations exist among the words in the repertoire, and word-association studies show that there is considerable agreement across subjects as to the particular words that are associated. This is taken to mean that there is a rather high level of cultural constancy in the use of words across what may appear to be superficially different subcultures. Undoubtedly the common properties of the public school systems are to a large degree responsible. In this section I will give some background for the development of explanatory or theoretical notions in which culturally established associations represent the starting point. Explanatory attempts based on the occurrence of implicit associative responses (IARS) have a very simple but essential assumption. The basic assumption is that when a subject is given a learning task involving common words, these words will elicit implicitly other associated words. The theorist then asks what consequences these IARs have for performance on a given task. This is not a new theoretical approach. It has been and still is implicit in all situations in which interference occurs. If the association A-B, for example, tends to interfere with the learning of the association A-D, it can only mean that A-B is in some way occurring implicitly to slow down the learning of A-D.

Having said that words in a learning task will elicit implicitly other words not in the task, I must quickly add that there must be limitations on the extent of such activity, although at the present time we do not comprehend the mechanisms producing this limitation. Some have suggested that the subject can control IARs, producing them or not as the subject judges their usefulness in a particular situation. Some limitation must in some way be present or the task given the subjects would require enormous amounts of time to master because the IARS would keep getting in the way when they were inimical to the learning task. This matter is related to what has been called the *interference paradox* (Underwood, 1960, 3). The paradox is present if there is a strong association between A and B and if the subjects are now asked to learn D to A, between which there is minimal, initial associative connection. Why does the response B not persistently appear either as an overt or covert intrusion during the learning of A-D? There is some way by which we are able to set aside certain IARs or avoid them being elicited. In any event, it does not seem proper to take the position that there will be evocation of IARs without limit. Rather, the position must be that the words in the task to be learned will sometimes implicitly elicit associations. It is likely that if the IARs tend to aid learning they will occur more readily than if they tend to interfere with learning, but as previously noted the mechanisms underlying this control are not understood. I will have more to say about this in Chapter 6.

Three studies are reproduced in Chapter 3. The first paper in the chapter describes a study conducted by William P. Wallace as a master's thesis. The study was based on the assumption that retarded children do not spontaneously produce IARs. If this is true, then certain differences in the learning performances of retardates and normals follow. More particularly, if the IARs occur in a task in which learning is facilitated by them, the normals will perform better than the retardates. If the IARs occur in a task in which they normally inhibit learning, the retardates will perform better than the normals. A triple interaction, then, was the critical expectation from this experiment. This type of experiment, in which individual differences are examined only as they enter into interactions with manipulable variables, represents a strategy of research which I think will sharply reduce the number of inappropriate conclusions reached about characteristics of the subjects as causal factors. Incidentally, it may be noted that Wallace (1967) subsequently examined differences between normals and retardates on false alarms in recognition, and again the data led to the inference that retarded children produce few if any IARs in a learning situation.

The second paper in Chapter 3, "False Recognitions Produced by Implicit Verbal Responses," asks about the role of IARs in producing false alarms in running recognition. In running recognition a long series of items is presented and for each presentation the subject must decide whether the word had or had not occurred earlier in the list. If the idea is taken seriously that in a learning situation IARs are produced to the words in the list, then it would seem to follow that some of the false alarms observed in running recognition must be due to the subject confusing an IAR with a word actually presented in the list. I must confess that at the time I was thinking of carrying out such a study I was skeptical. To say that there may be confusion between words we produce covertly and those that are presented to us in the learning task did not seem to square with my personal experience. Furthermore, if in fact we cannot distinguish between covert mental events and external events it would seem that conditions would be chaotic in the sense discussed earlier. Still, perhaps we could handle a small amount of chaos. My skepticism was such, however, that I initially tested a rather large number of pilot subjects before reaching the conclusion that the theory might correctly predict the outcome, and so I proceeded with the full study.

Historical Perspective 13

I think it correct to say that the findings reported in "False Recognitions Produced by Implicit Verbal Responses" and in the many studies done subsequently using running recognition do indicate that by some unknown mechanism we can usually distinguish between words we implicitly produce and those shown us. As rough averages, the number of false alarms in running recognition produced by control items may be taken as 10 percent, those produced by experimental words, 20 percent. That is, the experimental variable produces a 10 percent effect. Sometimes the number of false alarms for the experimental items does not exceed that for the control items. This may assure us, then, that we are not insane; we can distinguish most of the time between words we produce implicitly to the words in the list and those that are shown to us in the list.

The last paper in the chapter, "Implicit Responses and Conceptual Similarity," concerns a study involving IARs carried out by Gordon Wood and myself, and it deals with the role of conceptual IARs in free recall. More particularly, it attempts to explain why lists of conceptually related words are learned more quickly than a list of unrelated words, and why learning is more rapid if the category instances are blocked in a list than if they are randomized to form the list. Again, IAR theory led us to certain predictions, including one concerning the relative recall of items occurring successively in a category. This prediction was not given unambiguous support, but subsequent work has been quite in line with the prediction (Underwood, 1969, 3; Greitzer, 1976).

Other Uses of IAR Theory

The use of IARs as theoretical tools is more widespread than suggested by the three articles reprinted in Chapter 3. Some of these uses may be briefly described. If we take several pairs of strong associates from word-association norms—needle-thread, for example—and re-pair them, the resulting paired associate list becomes more difficult to learn than a group of unrelated words (Underwood, 1968, 2). Thus, here is a case where there is no paradox in the interference because it seems beyond doubt that the cultural associations interfere with the learning of the re-paired pairs. In a sense, the presence of the words from the pairs that are strongly associated keep priming the culturally established associations to cause the interference to persist. But, of course, the subjects do learn the re-paired lists without severe problems.

In forced-choice recognition, IARs can be used to predict how both facilitation and interference will occur. Perhaps the most comprehensive study along these lines was performed by Bach (1974) in the Northwestern Laboratories. The particular "use" of IARs by Bach's subjects showed that one could make relatively sound predictions by adding inputs from an actual presentation of a word to that produced by an IAR.

Another use of IAR theory is to account for the fact that free recall is facilitated if directly associated words occur in the list. Still another use is to account for intrusions in free recall, such as those observed by Deese (1959). Deese showed that the more words in a list that elicited a common word as an associate, the greater the likelihood of an intrusion of that common word. Here, it seems, a high-frequency occurrence of an implicit response did leave the subject with the belief that the word had actually been shown as a word in the list.

FREQUENCY THEORY

Frequency theory was a major determinant of many of the studies conducted in our laboratory between 1965 and 1975. The theory was originally formulated to account for verbal-discrimination learning, but it soon became apparent that it could be applied to all forms or types of recognition memory. In a verbal-discrimination list pairs of words are used in which one member of each pair has been designated the correct word by the investigator. It is the subjects' task to learn which of the two words in each pair is the correct one. The basic idea of the theory is that subjects discriminate between right and wrong items by discriminating differences in the situational frequency of these items, that is, the number of times each has occurred in the experimental situation. The theory assumes that when subjects are faced with the task of discriminating between right and wrong items they will look for a rule that may be applied to the decisions to be made on all items. In the usual verbal-discrimination task or in other types of recognition tasks, the frequency rule is apparently the only one available. If better rules were available, for example, if all right words were printed in red ink and all wrong ones in black ink, the subject would surely abandon the frequency rule.

The details of the theory are given in the first paper in Chapter 4, "A Frequency Theory of Verbal Discrimination Learning." While still graduate students, Bruce Ekstrand and William Wallace had become intrigued with the idea that frequency might serve as a discriminative attribute for verbal-discrimination learning, and they took the initiative in setting the theory down in detail and in making some initial experimental tests, which are reported in the paper. Any good theory, of course, must suggest new experiments, and that proved to be one of the attractive features of the theory.

At the time the theory was formulated there was very little evidence on the ability of subjects to make frequency discriminations. We simply assumed that these discriminations could be made with a precision sufficient to mediate the learning of the verbal-discrimination task. As experimental work began on the theory, however, a parallel area of research developed that examined the ability of college students to make discriminations of the frequencies of words presented in the laboratory for varying frequencies. Such data encouraged the use of frequency as a theoretical tool because it was found that the level of frequency discrimination which subjects demonstrated was clearly in the range required for frequency theory to be applied to recognition performance.

The next three papers—"Verbal-Discrimination Learning with Varying Numbers of Right and Wrong Terms," "Testing Effects in the Recognition of Words," and "Recognition and Number of Incorrect Alternatives Presented during Learning"—were chosen for reprinting because they seemed to represent somewhat counterintuitive predictions from frequency theory, but predictions that were generally supported by the data. In the "Verbal-Discrimination Learning" paper, the number of right and wrong items in the list was varied independently. In the extreme case, for twelve pairs there were only two different right words, each occurring with six wrong responses. There was a parallel condition in which there were only two different wrong words, each occurring with six right responses. It would seem, perhaps, that both of these conditions would produce the same outcome. When there were only two right words, the subject could quickly learn that each pair would contain one of two words, and that these two were always correct. Likewise, when there were only two wrong words, the subjects would quickly learn that both these words were wrong words, and the rule was to choose the other word in all pairs. Thus, it might seem that learning would be very rapid and equal for both conditions. Frequency theory, however, made different predictions and the data supported them.

The next article, "Testing Effects in the Recognition of Words," represents a test of frequency theory using a forced-choice recognition procedure. Some rather unusual predictions were derived when it was assumed that frequency units accrue to words when they are being tested as well as when they are in a study list. This assumption led to certain predictions when some old (right) words were tested several times and when some wrong words (new words) were also tested several times. The "Recognition and Number" article was chosen because again the predictions mediated by frequency theory are rather unusual. We actually arrived at the particular conditions we used by asking about the relevance of frequency theory for multiple-choice tests, which are so frequently used in schools. As it turned out, the experiment was not directly germane to multiple-choice testing, but it was our belief that frequency theory did have some applications in the multiple-choice testing situation.

"The Syllable as a Source of Error in Multisyllable Word Recognition" paper describes an experiment that was arrived at by contemplating certain characteristics of background frequency. Background frequency means the frequency with which units have occurred in the real world and which have been "recorded" by the observer. In a relative way at least, subjects know quite precisely the frequency with which words occur in printed text, although they are somewhat surprised that they have this knowledge. They also know with some accuracy the frequencies with which letters occur in words, and the frequencies with which bigrams occur. All the above kinds of frequency knowledge have been abstracted from larger linguistic units. If this is what occurs outside the laboratory, it seemed that we might be able to devise a situation in the laboratory that would demonstrate the abstractive characteristics of background frequency. We asked if the syllables of multisyllable words had representation in memory after a single exposure of the list of words. Our results seemed to provide us with a positive answer.

The last paper in Chapter 4, "Individual Differences as a Crucible in Theory Construction," expresses some opinions about the ways in which individual differences may be used in making theoretical decisions. I have included this paper in the chapter dealing with frequency theory because this theory is a striking illustration of the type of theory for which the individual-differences approach is judged appropriate.

Other Uses or Tests of Frequency Theory

Many tests of frequency theory have been made, and it is most certainly not my goal to try to describe all of them. But there are a few applications that I will describe as a means of indicating the versatility of frequency theory. One of the more interesting predictions involves the double-function verbal-discrimination list. In such a list every item is used as a correct word in one pair and as an incorrect word in another pair. Thus, if the first letter represents the correct word, the second the incorrect word, a five-pair double-function list may be schematized as follows: A-B, B-C, C-D, D-E, E-A. Now, with each word being both a correct word and an incorrect word, there is no way that a frequency differential can develop. This would lead to the expectation that a double-function list cannot be learned. We have found that for most subjects this is true (Underwood, 1975, 4). Just how the few subjects that learn do learn is not known.

As mentioned earlier, frequency theory was not without relevance to multiple-choice testing. Nevertheless, under certain circumstances it can be predicted by the theory that the greater the number of alternatives in the verbal-discrimination task, the better the performance. This is just the opposite of what might be anticipated using the usual multiple-choice test. Nevertheless, the prediction has been supported (Radke and Jacoby, 1971).

Those who study the acquisition of concepts find that frequency theory fits well with their findings. "One might theorize that the development of a frequency differential among stimulus values over a series of encounters with positive and negative instances is the way people identify relevant attributes of a concept" (Bourne et al., 1976, p. 294). The evidence produced indicates that if the situation is not one that will allow the development of frequency differences among the attributes, the concept problem will not be solved. It is much like the effects found in the double-function verbal-discrimination list.

VERBAL LEARNING, CONCEPT LEARNING, AND THINKING

I have always had a secondary interest in research on the higher mental processes, which I usually describe as being represented in the studies said to be dealing with concept learning, reasoning, creativity, and thinking. My interest was never translated into a systematic research program, although I have published occasional studies on concept learning and concept recognition, and Jack Richardson and I (Underwood, 1956, 3) developed some materials for use in concept-learning experiments. Furthermore, as will be discussed in Chapter 6, there are some very strong relationships between certain verbal-learning paradigms and concept formation. But that is getting ahead of the plan; the question for the moment is why I was led to write a paper that purports to be an orientation for studying the higher mental processes; the paper "An Orientation for Research on Thinking," is the first paper in Chapter 5 of this book.

I suspect most would agree that the problems and materials that are a part of the experiments used to study the higher mental processes are intrinsically interesting. For the typical graduate student in experimental psychology the rote learning of a serial list does not have a chance in a paired comparison preference test when the Maier two-strong problem is the other member of the pair. Perhaps I also thought—subconsciously, of course—that by thinking about thinking one would be led to be a better thinker. I have no evidence that indicates this happened.

In the late 1940s, I completed a book called *Experimental Psychology* (Underwood, 1949, 1) and in the process of writing a chapter on thinking I had surveyed the literature rather comprehensively. I formed some fairly strong beliefs about the area and what was needed. I expressed the opinion that "our knowledge of the relationships between manipulable variables and thinking is meager and tentative" (p. 464). The solution? ". . . what is needed is vigorous and widely joined theoretical controversies centered around how people think. The current temper of scientific psychology is such that theoretical formulations point directly to potential experiments; if we had the theories they would certainly spawn research" (p. 464).

There are two observations I must make about the advice that I so unselfishly gave to the psychological world. First, the advice reflects my experiences at the University of Iowa where I had seen the role that strong theoretical positions could play in producing research. If the theories of Hull and Tolman and Spence could instigate so much research, why could not theories about thinking do the same? Second, having charted a path, I felt some responsibility for trying to enter into the travel.

There is one further matter that was not without influence in leading me to write this article on thinking. Generally, we all dislike to be associated with isolated and narrow areas of research. We prefer to reach out and bring under the umbrella of our concepts more than is obvious to the casual reader. I believed then that principles of association had a role to play in understanding how the higher mental processes work. This is quite apparent in the previously mentioned "Orientation for Research" article, and I will have more to say about this general issue in Chapter 6.

MASSED VERSUS DISTRIBUTED PRACTICE

The classical procedure for studying the effects of massed practice (MP) versus the effects of distributed practice (DP) was that of varying the length of the rest intervals between trials in learning lists of items. The independent variable, then, was the length of the intertrial interval. Rather arbitrarily, MP was said to be defined by intervals of perhaps two to four seconds, whereas DP was said to have longer intervals, perhaps fifteen seconds or longer, which in practice might be several minutes. These so-called classical procedures are to be distinguished from current ones in which MP is defined as the occurrence of the same item two or more times in adjacent positions within a list, and DP refers to the separation of two or more occurrences of the same item by one or more other items. Generally, this current MP-DP effect is studied within single-trial free recall. I will have more to say about this type of spacing in Chapter 6. For the time being the discussion will be centered around the classical MP-DP manipulations.

Between 1951 and 1967 my students and I published twenty-seven different reports concerned with the MP-DP effect. In the second article in Chapter 5, "Effect of Distributed Practice on Paired-Associate Learning," these reports are represented. Although this reprinted article may impart some of the affective flavor of the sixteen years of work, and although it contains somewhat of a summary of the work, there are many other matters that I must take up if I am to provide something of a balanced account of the work over the sixteen years. A certain amount of exasperation, or perhaps humiliation, attended the writing of our final report. After sixteen years we were not able to state empirical generalizations that we felt we could stand behind with confidence. In effect, this precluded any definitive theoretical attempt. Why, then, did I allow this series of studies to be prolonged over sixteen years and to absorb so much of our energies? There were three reasons, one philosophical, the other two more pragmatic.

A number of years ago I, along with several others, was asked to make a few remarks about centers of research, with the goal of identifying features of centers of research that might make them particularly successful. One of the qualities that I stated as being important was persistence in the research efforts. By this I meant that a series of investigations is undertaken all dealing with a particular phenomenon, with the intent being that of providing the phenomenon with a rather complete empirical description. Such research would also provide checks on the adequacy of various theoretical assertions that usually arise during such a series of experiments. The research may also involve resolution of conflicting findings both within the center and between laboratories. Conflicting findings usually signal the presence of a salient variable, and the task is to find out just what it might be. The activities proceed along these lines until some feeling of closure is reached, and this closure will ideally include a theoretical accounting of the empirical structure that had been built.

Of course, one never really solves all problems associated with a given phenomenon, but within the research culture of the moment it is possible to set aside the remaining few problems and call a halt. Therefore, the first reason why the MP-DP series went on for so many years in my laboratory is that I never reached that feeling of closure. I did not then, and I do not now, like hit-and-run experimentation; I do not think we should jump from problem to problem. This belief played a significant role in our 16-year saga.

A second reason that was in part responsible for continuing the work beyond a point where it might have been prudent to stop was that I frequently believed that we had found the key to the puzzles, or that we would find it in the next experiment. I remember at one point that we did a simple two-condition experiment in which the response terms in the paired-associate list were very difficult consonant syllables. One group of subjects learned the list under MP, the second group learned it under DP. The DP learning was much faster than the MP learning, with the statistical difference being huge. Several lines of research had pointed toward the degree of item integration as being a critical factor in producing the MP-DP effect, and the difficult consonant syllables represented a case of low initial integration of the letters in the units. We were, to say the least, ecstatic with our finding. We immediately set about to nail this discovery down by varying the degree of integration, length of intertrial interval, and so on. Included in the expanded experiment were two conditions that were exactly the same as in the previous experiment. The data showed a complete failure to replicate. This illustrates how data can lead one on; our data kept providing us with new hypotheses, or they kept suggesting why we had gotten contradictory effects in different experiments. The data were not entirely without value, but in the long run we found them quite intractable.

Failure to replicate within our own laboratory naturally raised questions about the adequacy of the methods of experimentation that we were employing. Of course we reviewed our methods continually, but perhaps the most comforting fact was that throughout the sixteen years we were also carrying out research on other verbal-learning phenomena and we never experienced the problems of replication to the degree that we did with the MP-DP experiments. It was as if a selective curse had descended on us.

A third reason for our persistence was the fact that in the process of trying to unravel the MP-DP puzzles we did produce a number of other findings or discoveries that seemed to move the field forward. For example, we found that intralist similarity, while producing enormous differences in learning, did not influence forgetting. Also, during our work on the MP-DP problems, we frequently took 24-hour recall measures, and it was as a consequence of these studies that we gradually worked through and corrected the techniques for neutralizing differences in degree of learning, eventually producing the paper reprinted in this book as the last paper in Chapter 2.

In spite of these rationalizations, in retrospect I would have difficulty denying that I persisted too long in the MP-DP series. Perhaps some of my clinical friends might be able to give better reasons for the persistence! Regardless, I now propose to turn to some of the issues and problems we confronted. It will be seen that in fact we did reach some fairly definitive conclusions about certain theories and about a few of the facts of the case. I will describe first the findings of the early studies and the implications we drew from them.

The Early Studies

In the first study (Underwood, 1951, 5) the task was the serial learning of 14 two-syllable adjectives. The adjectives within a list had low intralist similarity or high intralist similarity as determined by meaning. In the lists with high intralist similarity all of the words within the list had a common core of meaning. For example, one of the lists contained words such as *elated, gleeful, carefree, jolly, laughing,* and so on. The three intertrial intervals were 2, 15, and 30 seconds. The lists were learned to one perfect recitation by the anticipation method at a 2-second rate.

The results showed that although MP on the low-similarity lists resulted in more trials to learn than did DP, the difference did not reach acceptable levels of statistical significance. For the high-similarity lists, however, the difference between MP and DP was highly reliable statistically, with DP requiring fewer trials to learn. There was no difference of consequence between the two DP intervals. At that time we were not routinely using analysis of variance for statistical tests. The above statistical evaluations were made by *t* tests. The implication of the results was that there was an interaction, in that DP facilitated learning when intralist similarity was high, but not when it was low. It should be said that the high-similarity lists were more difficult to learn than were the low-similarity lists.

For reasons which will become clear shortly, measures were taken of the number of overt errors made during learning. The subjects did not differ in the number of errors in learning the low-similarity lists, but in learning the high-similarity lists the two DP conditions produced more errors than did the MP condition; that is, there was a *positive* relationship between number of overt errors and rate of learning, a seemingly bizarre state of affairs.

At the time we carried out this study there were two extant theories about the MP-DP effect. One of the theories was associated with McGeoch (1942) and indicates that he, a so-called functionalist, did not always behave in the atheoretical ways that functionalists were supposed to behave. Let me give the theory in McGeoch's own words:

> During the course of practice a subject learns not only the correct responses, but also incorrect and conflicting ones which retard the fixation of the correct responses. Since the conflicting associations may be expected to be less well fixed than the right ones, they should be forgotten sooner during the rest intervals of distributed practice. It is a reasonable hypothesis, then, that learning is more rapid under distributed practice than under massed, because the rest intervals give opportunity for this differential forgetting. [pp. 142-143]

Two features of this theory should be noted. First, it relied on the established fact that as degree of learning increased, rate of forgetting decreased. Second, it assumed that wrong responses were weaker than correct responses. At some point in learning, of course, the wrong responses must be weaker than the correct responses or learning would not occur. Thus, the theory carries no wild assumption; rather, it represents the clever union of two empirical laws. Unfortunately, the theory received no support in our series. If DP learning gains over MP learning because erroneous responses tendencies drop out over the DP intervals, the number of overt errors should be less with DP than with MP. The results of our first study showed quite the opposite. However, the interpretation of this finding was called into question by the results of a further study (Underwood, 1952, 2). It was discovered that the activity used to fill the rest intervals under DP was responsible for the greater error frequency under DP than under MP. A rest-interval activity is used to prevent rehearsal. The rest-interval activity consisted of naming the colors of many small squares of different colors pasted randomly in rows on a board. The subject named the color of the successive color patches row by row at a rate of from 60 to 80 per minute as paced by a metronome. As a result of the finding that more errors occurred with DP than with MP the rest-interval activity was changed to a symbol-cancellation task that did not increase error frequency for the DP conditions. Nevertheless, our conclusion did not change about the McGeoch theory. We never found support for the differential forgetting of correct and incorrect responses.

A second theory that had been offered for the MP-DP effect was associated with a group at Yale University (Hull et al., 1940), with most of the empirical work being done by Hovland. The critical part of the theory for our purposes was the assumption that under persistent and uninterrupted responding, as in MP, a performance inhibition develops that masks true learning. This inhibition dissipates rapidly with rests, thus allowing the true amount learned to be manifest in the performance scores. Even when this theory was written it had a problem. The theory must predict that long-term retention will be better following MP than following DP, but Hovland's (1940) work was in direct contradiction. Our first experiment was not critical one way or the other for a performance-inhibition type of theory. In fact, although we kept this type of theory in our thinking throughout the series we could not find evidence to give the theory support in a consistent fashion. Perhaps the best test of the theory consisted of examining retention over short intervals following massed practice. If the inhibition dissipates rapidly, reminiscence ought to be present after perhaps two or three minutes. As will be described later, we found that serial consonant lists produced a large MP-DP effect, but when a test for reminiscence was made (Underwood, 1957, 1) only forgetting was observed. The second paper in Chapter 5, "Effect of Distributed Practice on Paired-Associate Learning," also includes tests of the theory, but the same negative conclusions were required by the data.

A third theory occupied some of our attention during the early studies. This engaging theory was developed by Eleanor Gibson (1940), and because it was worked out at Yale it is not surprising that it leaned heavily on conditioning concepts. Roughly, the theory said that the learning of a paired-associate list involved the development of differentiation among the stimulus terms, these terms initially showing generalization. Thus, differentiation replaced generalization as learning occurred. A rest interval inserted after learning would allow spontaneous recovery of the generalization tendencies. A deduction from this idea was that overt errors (indices of generalization) should be greater during DP than during MP. It can be seen that the greater number of overt errors observed with the high-similarity lists for DP than for MP in the first study could be used to support the theory. Actually, the Gibson theory had nothing to say about the origins of the MP-DP effect. It was my idea to see if the theory might be extended in some way to include the effect. In the long run, however, I found that the theory was of no value for this purpose.

One more point should be made about the results of the first study. Although statistically speaking there was no MP-DP effect for the lists having low intralist similarity, we were to find over the years that, regardless of the material, there was a greater likelihood of demonstrating an MP-DP effect with serial learning than with paired-associate learning. This statement leads into the second study.

In this second study (Underwood, 1951, 2) paired-associate lists of adjectives were used, including lists of low intralist meaningful similarity and lists of high meaningful intralist similarity. The different levels of similarity produced large differences in learning, but there was no MP-DP effect. The failure to find an MP-DP effect was observed also in two later studies (Underwood, 1953, 3; 1954, 4) in which paired associates made up of adjectives constituted the learning task. The second study also tested retention over 24 hours. However, I am not going to be concerned here with the results for long-term retention following MP and DP. The facts of the effects of MP and DP on learning become sufficiently complex as to put a strain on memory; to talk also about the variety of effects found for long-term retention is more than any reader should have to bear.

One of the responsibilities I assumed in the series of studies under consideration was to try to resolve some of the contradictions between our results and those of other investigators. In the first study the MP-DP difference was not reliable statistically for the low-similarity lists, although the differences favored DP. Wilson (1949) had conducted a study using serial adjectives of low similarity that produced a significant MP-DP effect. Why should Wilson find this difference when we failed to do so? In studying the differences in the procedures of the two experiments it seemed likely that the critical differences were associated with the experimental designs. Wilson used independent groups for his conditions following a single practice session. Our experiment used a within-subject design, and the subjects served in eight different sessions. At about the time that we were studying the implications of differences in the design of the experiments we were in general becoming sensitized to the possibility that certain phenomena might be contingent upon between-list relationships. In fact, at the time I believed that a performance-inhibition theory might predict that the MP-DP effect would diminish as subjects became more and more practiced in learning lists. If this were true, it could account for the difference between Wilson's findings and ours.

The experiment I designed to get at the role of subject experience with learning on the MP-DP effect asked about the magnitude of the effect as a function of stage of practice (Underwood, 1951, 3). One group of subjects learned four successive lists under MP, another group learned the four lists under DP. One list was learned each day for four consecutive days. The lists of serial adjectives had low intralist similarity; three of the four lists were the same as those used in the first experiment. If stage of practice is a critical interacting variable as suggested above, the MP-DP difference would be expected to get smaller with each successive list learned. The results indicated nothing of the kind. The DP group exceeded the MP group but the difference remained constant across the four lists.

These results may have helped us somewhat in keeping the empirical facts consistent. In the first study the low-similarity lists did not yield an MP-DP effect that was reliable statistically. It is quite likely that the difference between the findings for the first experiment and the stage-of-practice experiment were not different statistically, and so I was led to conclude that Wilson's findings and the results for our two experiments indicated that serial lists of adjectives could be expected to produce a small MP-DP effect. In a later study (Underwood, 1953, 3), a small but reliable MP-DP difference was found in learning serial lists of adjectives of several levels of similarity, thus supporting the general conclusion just made.

At this point in the series it appeared that the experiments produced a clear difference in the MP-DP effect as a function of type of learning; the effect was present for serial lists but not for paired-associate lists. We also failed to find an MP-DP effect with verbal-discrimination lists (Underwood, 1951, 6; Underwood, 1955, 1). Further, we asked about the role of DP in concept learning using geometrical stimuli (Underwood, 1952, 5), and although the difference between MP and DP was not reliable statistically we concluded there was a small effect; I later withdrew this conclusion when a second study (Underwood, 1957, 4) failed to show an effect of DP, and when other investigators also found no influence of intertrial interval on concept learning. Thus it seemed that our initial studies limited the MP-DP effect to serial learning. It did not seem to me at the time that McGeoch's 1942 generalization was still appropriate. He said: "The experiments on distribution of practice have found that introduction of time intervals between practice periods . . . yields more rapid learning, under a wide range of conditions, than does continuous practice" (p. 147).

List Difficulty

A number of investigators had shown that the use of serial lists of nonsense syllables resulted in a superiority of DP over MP. As a rule of thumb it appeared that the amount of facilitation produced by DP was a direct function of list difficulty, however that difficulty was produced. I chose to test this rule by using nonsense syllables at a given level of meaningfulness, and by varying difficulty through manipulation of intralist formal similarity. Formal similarity is normally increased by reducing the number of different letters used in the syllables within a list. In the first experiment (Underwood, 1952, 2) serial learning was used with intertrial intervals of 2, 30, and 60 seconds. Intralist similarity produced large differences in the rate of learning, but there was no interaction with intertrial interval; DP facilitated the learning of all lists by about the same amount. In a further experiment (Underwood, 1953, 1), paired-associate lists of nonsense syllables were used with intralist similarity varied independently among response terms and among stimulus terms. Intralist similarity had a sizable influence on learning when manipulated among stimulus terms but not when varied among response terms. In neither case was there an MP-DP effect. It can be seen that at this stage of our work we were still clinging to a generalization to the effect that DP facilitated serial learning but not paired-associate learning. I was not happy with this generalization because Hovland (1949) had found a DP effect with nonsense syllables making up the paired-associate lists. I never did find a reason for this contradiction.

The difficulty hypothesis was not well supported by our work. However, when we turned to consonant syllables (CCCs) things began to happen. Generally speaking CCCs are far more difficult to learn than are nonsense syllables (CVCs). It was inevitable that sooner or later we would ask about the MP-DP effect with lists of consonant syllables. We found (Underwood, 1955, 2) that in learning serial lists of six consonant syllables the MP-DP difference was large. Some two years later we constructed paired-associate lists of four pairs of consonant syllables with fairly high intralist similarity (Underwood, 1957, 8). It was found that DP facilitated learning, and the finding was subsequently replicated (Underwood, 1958, 3).

We had lost our generalization that the MP-DP effect is limited to serial learning. What appeared to be the case was that the effect would also occur with paired-associate lists if the meaningfulness was low enough. This could be taken in support of the difficulty hypothesis, although such an hypothesis has very low theoretical potential. Greater difficulty might be associated with greater work and greater work might be linked to performance inhibition, but I had no confidence in such extrapolations.

Further Work

I have covered the early phases of our work on the MP-DP effect. Many more studies were to follow, although some were concerned primarily with retention following MP and DP. The work we did in the later years will be covered quite briefly here because a summary of certain aspects of this later work is included in the "Effects of Distributed Practice" paper in Chapter 5. Several factors directed our later work; these will be listed as a series of unrelated points.

1. As previously described, one of our earliest studies had shown that variation in intralist similarity in serial lists of nonsense syllables did not interact with intertrial interval. Still, one could abstract from our studies the idea that interference from formal similarity—and perhaps from meaningful similarity—was a necessary condition for the appearance of the MP-DP effect. There was also scattered evidence not entirely without exception that the MP-DP effect might result from interlist interference as a consequence of using within-subject designs. I felt that in order to clarify these matters we should start using random-groups designs. By so doing we might be able to learn more about the nature of the interference that seemed to be necessary for the appearance of the MP-DP effect.

Our first study using the random-groups design involved serial lists of nonsense syllables (Underwood, 1958, 2). The MP-DP effect occurred with high meaningfulness only with high intralist similarity, not with low intralist similarity. But we were greatly puzzled by the fact that with syllables of low meaningfulness there was no MP-DP effect with lists of either low or high intralist similarity. Further work (Underwood, 1959, 4) resulted in some understanding of the puzzle but it was never solved to my satisfaction. Nevertheless, I remain convinced that some minimal level of interference produced by incompatible response tendencies was necessary for the production of the MP-DP effect.

2. In the late 1950s the effects of certain variables on verbal-learning tasks began to be evaluated in terms of effects both on response integration or acquisition and on associative formation. It was natural, perhaps, that I began to wonder if the MP-DP effect

was tied to one of these two stages exclusively. Serial learning is not readily broken down for analytical purposes into the two stages, whereas the paired-associate task is. As noted earlier, we had found that we could get an MP-DP effect with paired-associate lists if we used consonant syllables. I set about to see if we could discover where the interference must be centered in order to produce the MP-DP effect. Our initial work supported the idea that the interference must lie in the response-integration phase if the DP-MP effect was to be manifest (Underwood, 1961, 4; 5). The full evidence was summarized in a paper read before the members of Division 3 of the American Psychological Association at the 1960 annual meetings (Underwood, 1961, 1). Sometime later the theoretical notions that I presented then were no longer tenable, because new empirical facts (for example, Underwood 1964, 5) forced me to adopt the position that interference within the response acquisition stage was not a critical element. I was trying to maintain my balance while standing in a barrel of eels.

3. Any flat statements about the necessity of interference for the MP-DP effect seemed to be called into question by some of our work that was primarily concerned with retention (Underwood, 1962, 6). We discovered that conditions of interference could be arranged so as to produce poorer learning by DP than by MP, although better retention was found following DP than following MP. Although it is a side issue, I would like to note that if widely spaced practice of lists is used, long-term retention will be markedly facilitated. Thus, Keppel (1967) had demonstrated that inserting twenty-four hours between blocks of two trials in learning produced an enormous facilitation in long-term retention, although the learning with DP was slower than with MP.

The preceding lengthy discussion gives some idea of the puzzles and problems that pestered me over a period of years. The research in the "Effect of Distributed Practice" paper (Chapter 5) represented the last gasp. I had tried to piece together an empirical story of the effects of intertrial interval in verbal learning as well as to try out certain theoretical notions. I was defeated in this enterprise; I could no longer develop sufficiently new ideas to justify the cost of further research.

In the early days of doing research I had an idealistic attitude toward it. This was that the empirical characterization of a phenomenon or a group of related phenomena had an inexorable quality about it. One experiment led logically to another, and after a period of time the laws relating the independent variables to the magnitude of the phenomena could be stated along with the interactions between variables. These facts plus some theory could be formed into a knowledge structure, a structure that would never crumble. My experience with the MP-DP effect was disturbing; my dedication to the experiment as a source of knowledge was not shaken seriously, but I was forced to recognize that the stability of that knowledge could not be taken for granted. Knowledge structures may be of poor quality, and it may take far longer than originally believed to establish a foundation that is something more than a quagmire. So-called experimental facts may seem to have an amoebic quality when replication is a goal. That we do stabilize, relatively speaking, an area of research in spite of our fallibilities must say something about unknown forces that view our enterprise with favor.

ATTRIBUTES OF MEMORY

Frequency theory proved to be a catalyst in my thinking, but a slow acting one. As data in support of frequency theory evolved in the mid-1960s I gradually became aware of a feeling of being a rebel or a turncoat. Here I was on the one hand writing experimental reports emphasizing the role of associations in accounting for certain phenomena of interest, and on the other I was preparing articles in which nothing was said about associations. Rather, the talk was of frequency discriminations and how such discriminations accounted for the learning. How could this happen to an avowed associationist?

My first idea for a rapprochement was tantamount to a word game disguised as "thinking," in which the association was to be maintained as basic. This is the way the reasoning went. Frequency theory asserted that the subject made decisions as to right or wrong or new or old by examining the situational frequency *associated* with each item. I did not see how such a statement could be denied, but if such a statement is accepted as being a theoretical statement in support of associationism then the concept of an association becomes so general as to lose its cutting edge.

The fact is that I reached a point where I did not see that it was necessary to resolve this word problem. I simply decided that it might be useful to see what the implications would be of proceeding as if associative information and frequency information might exist side by side, entering into memory functioning in different ways. From that point on my thinking has been geared to the separation of the two types of information.

Having taken this step I soon found myself saying that whether associationist or not, it may be of value to try to identify other types of information that go to make up a memory. I use this language to indicate that I soon reached the position that a memory qua memory did not exist; a memory was only a collection of information of different types. I set about to identify the types of information that might be said to be attributes of memory. This was a relatively simple task because the zeitgeist was appropriate and many studies were producing direct evidence about attributes of memory, or they came about as by-products. Thus there was evidence that memories might include temporal information, spatial information, frequency information, and so on. Having identified some of the different types of information that may be present as a memory, I viewed the next step as being that of formulating theories to show how each attribute contributed to memory functioning.

The last paper in Chapter 5 is "Attributes of Memory." It is a statement about the constituents of memories, but it is not a statement about the organization of the memory system.

REFERENCES

Bach, M. J. Implicit response frequency and recognition memory over time. *Journal of Experimental Psychology*, 1974, *103*, 675-679.

Blankenship, A. B., and Whitely, P. L. Proactive inhibition in the recall of advertising material. *The Journal of Social Psychology*, 1941, *13*, 311-322.

Bourne, L. E. Jr.; Ekstrand, B. R.; Lovallo, W. R.; Kellogg, R. T.; Hiew, C. C.; & Yaroush, R. A. Frequency analysis of attribute identification. *Journal of Experimental Psychology: General*, 1976, *105*, 294-312.

Brown, J. Some tests of the decay theory of immediate memory. *Quarterly Journal of Experimental Psychology*, 1958, *10*, 12-21.

Deese, J. On the prediction of occurrence of particular verbal instructions in immediate recall. *Journal of Experimental Psychology*, 1959, *58*, 17-22.

Ebbinghaus, H. *Memory: A contribution to experimental psychology.* Trans. by Ruger, H. A., and Bussenius, Clara E. New York: Teachers College, Columbia University, Bureau of Publications, 1913.

Gibson, E. J. A systematic application of the concepts of generalization and differentiation to verbal leaning. *Psychological Review*, 1940, *47*, 196-229.

Greeno, J. G.; James, C. T.; DaPolito, F. J.; and Polson, P. G. *Associative learning: A cognitive analysis.* Englewood Cliffs, N.J.: Prentice-Hall, 1978.

Greitzer, F. L. Intracategory rehearsal in list learning. *Journal of Verbal Learning and Verbal Behavior*, 1976, *15*, 641-654.

Hovland, C. I. Experimental studies in rote-learning theory: VI. Comparison of retention following learning to the same criterion by massed and distributed practice. *Journal of Experimental Psychology*, 1940, *26*, 568-587.

Hovland, C. I. Experimental studies in rote-learning theory: VIII. Distributed practice of paired-associates with varying rates of presentation. *Journal of Experimental Psychology*, 1949, *39*, 714-718.

Hull, C. L., Hovland, C. I.; Ross, R. T.; Hall, M.; Perkins, D. T.; & Fitch, F. B. *Mathematico-deductive theory of rote learning.* New Haven: Yale University Press, 1940.

Keppel, G. A reconsideration of the extinction-recovery theory. *Journal of Verbal Learning and Verbal Behavior,* 1967, *6,* 476–486.

McGeoch, J. A. Forgetting and the law of disuse. *Psychological Review,* 1932, *39,* 352–370.

McGeoch, J. A. *The psychology of human learning.* New York: Longmans & Green, 1942.

Melton, A. W., & Irwin, J. McQ. The influence of degree of interpolated learning on retroactive inhibition and the overt transfer of specific responses. *American Journal of Psychology,* 1940, *53,* 173–203.

Oldfield, R. C. Things, words and the brain. *Quarterly Journal of Experimental Psychology,* 1966, *18,* 340–353.

Peterson, L. R., & Peterson, M. J. Short-term retention of individual verbal items. *Journal of Experimental Psychology,* 1959, *58,* 193–198.

Postman, L. Transfer of training as a function of experimental paradigm and degree of first-list learning. *Journal of Verbal Learning and Verbal Behavior,* 1962, *1,* 109–118.

Radtke, R. C., and Jacoby, L. Pronunciation and number of alternatives in verbal-discrimination learning. *Journal of Verbal Learning and Verbal Behavior,* 1971, *10,* 262–265.

Robinson, E. S. *Association theory today.* New York: The Century Company, 1932.

Wallace, W. P. Implicit associative response occurrence in learning with retarded subjects: A supplementary report. *Journal of Educational Psychology,* 1967, *58,* 110–114.

Whitely, P. L. The dependence of learning and recall upon prior intellectual activities. *Journal of Experimental Psychology,* 1927, *10,* 489–508.

Whitely, P. L., & Blankenship, A. B. The influence of certain conditions prior to learning upon subsequent recall. *Journal of Experimental Psychology,* 1936, *19,* 496–504.

Wilson, J. T. The formation and retention of remote associations in rote learning. *Journal of Experimental Psychology,* 1949, *39,* 830–838.

2
Proactive Interference

Interference and Forgetting

I know of no one who seriously maintains that interference among tasks is of no consequence in the production of forgetting. Whether forgetting is conceptualized at a strict psychological level or at a neural level (e.g., neural memory trace), some provision is made for interference to account for at least some of the measured forgetting. The many studies on retroactive inhibition are probably responsible for this general agreement that interference among tasks must produce a sizable proportion of forgetting. By introducing an interpolated interfering task very marked decrements in recall can be produced in a few minutes in the laboratory. But there is a second generalization which has resulted from these studies, namely, that most forgetting must be a function of the learning of tasks which interfere with that which has already been learned (19). Thus, if a single task is learned in the laboratory and retention measured after a week, the loss has been attributed to the interference from activities learned outside the laboratory during the week. It is this generalization with which I am concerned in the initial portions of this paper.

Now, I cannot deny the data which show large amounts of forgetting produced by an interpolated list in a few minutes in the laboratory. Nor do I deny that this loss may be attributed to interference. But I will try to show that use of retroactive inhibition as a paradigm of forgetting (via interference) may be seriously questioned. To be more specific: if a subject learns a single task, such as a list of words, and retention of this task is measured after a day, a week, or a month, I will try to show that very little of the forgetting can be attributed to an interfering task learned outside the laboratory during the retention interval. Before pursuing this further, I must make some general comments by way of preparation.

Whether we like it or not, the experimental study of forgetting has been largely dominated by the Ebbinghaus tradition, both in

---

Benton, J. Underwood, "Interference and Forgetting," *Psychological Review* 64 (1957): 49–60. Reprinted with permission. Copyright 1957 by the American Psychological Association.

Most of the data from my own research referred to in this paper were obtained from work done under Contract N7 onr-45008, Project NR 154-057, between Northwestern University and The Office of Naval Research.

terms of methods and materials used. I do not think this is due to sheer perversity on the part of several generations of scientists interested in forgetting. It may be noted that much of our elementary knowledge can be obtained only by rote learning. To work with rote learning does not mean that we are thereby not concerning ourselves with phenomena that have no counterparts outside the laboratory. Furthermore, the investigation of these phenomena can be handled by methods which are acceptable to a science. As is well known, there are periodic verbal revolts against the Ebbinghaus tradition (e.g., 2, 15, 22). But for some reason nothing much ever happens in the laboratory as a consequence of these revolts. I mention these matters neither by way of apology nor of justification for having done some research in rote learning, but for two other reasons. First, it may very well be true, as some have suggested (e.g., 22), that studies of memory in the Ebbinghaus tradition are not getting at all of the important phenomena of memory. I think the same statement—that research has not got at all of the important processes—could be made about all areas in psychology; so that the criticism (even if just) should not be indigenous to the study of memory. Science does not deal at will with all natural events. Science deals with natural events only when ingenuity in developing methods and techniques of measurement allow these events to be brought within the scope of science. If, therefore, the studies of memory which meet scientific acceptability do not tap all-important memorial processes, all I can say is that this is the state of the science in the area at the moment. Secondly, because the bulk of the systematic data on forgetting has been obtained on rote-learned tasks, I must of necessity use such data in discussing interference and forgetting.

Returning to the experimental situation, let me again put in concrete form the problem with which I first wish to deal. A subject learns a single task, such as a list of syllables, nouns, or adjectives. After an interval of time, say, 24 hours, his retention of this list is measured. The explanatory problem is what is responsible for the forgetting which commonly occurs over the 24 hours. As indicated earlier, the studies of retroactive inhibition led to the theoretical generalization that this forgetting was due largely to interference from other tasks learned during the 24-hour retention interval. McGeoch (20) came to this conclusion, his last such statement being made in 1942. I would, therefore, like to look at the data which were available to McGeoch and others interested in this matter. I must repeat that the kind of data with which I am concerned is the retention of a list without formal interpolated learning introduced. The interval of retention with which I am going to deal in this, and several subsequent analyses, is 24 hours.

First, of course, Ebbinghaus' data were available and in a sense served as the reference point for many subsequent investigations. In terms of percentage saved in relearning, Ebbinghaus showed about 65 per cent loss over 24 hours (7). In terms of recall after 24 hours, the following studies are representative of the amount forgotten: Youtz, 88 per cent loss (37); Luh, 82 per cent (18); Krueger, 74 per cent (16); Hovland, 78 per cent (11); Cheng, 65 per cent and 84 per cent (6); Lester, 65 per cent (17). Let us assume as a rough average of these studies that 75 per cent forgetting was measured over 24 hours. In all of these studies the list was learned to one perfect trial. The percentage values were derived by dividing the total number of items in the list into the number lost and changing to a percentage. Thus, on the average in these studies, if the subject learned a 12-item list and recalled three of these items after 24 hours, nine items (75 per cent) were forgotten.

The theory of interference as advanced by McGeoch, and so far as I know never seriously challenged, was that during the 24-hour interval subjects learned something outside the laboratory which interfered with the list learned in the laboratory. Most of the materials involved in the investigations cited above were nonsense syllables, and the subjects were college students. While realizing that I am reviewing these results in the light of data which McGeoch and others did not have available, it seems to me to be an incredible stretch of an interference hypothesis to hold that this 75 per cent forgetting was caused by something which the subjects learned outside the laboratory during the 24-hour interval. Even if we agree with some educators that much of what we teach our students in college is nonsense, it does not seem to be the kind of learning that would interfere with nonsense syllables.

If, however, this forgetting was not due to interference from tasks learned outside the laboratory during the retention interval, to what was it due? I shall try to show that most of this forgetting was indeed produced by interference—not from tasks learned outside the laboratory, but from tasks learned previously in the laboratory. Following this I will show that when interference from laboratory tasks is removed, the amount of forgetting which occurs is relatively quite small. It then becomes more plausible that this amount could be produced by interference from tasks learned outside the laboratory, although, as I shall also point out, the interference very likely comes from prior, not interpolated, learning.

In 1950 a study was published by Mrs. Greenberg and myself

Proactive Interference 37

(10) on retention as a function of stage of practice. The orientation for this study was crassly empirical; we simply wanted to know if subjects learn how to recall in the same sense that they learn how to learn. In the conditions with which I am concerned, naive subjects learned a list of ten paired adjectives to a criterion of eight out of ten correct on a single trial. Forty-eight hours later this list was recalled. On the following day, these same subjects learned a new list to the same criterion and recalled it after 48 hours. This continued for two additional lists, so that the subjects had learned and recalled four lists, but the learning and recall of each list was complete before another list was learned. There was low similarity among these lists as far as conventional symptoms of similarity are concerned. No words were repeated and no obvious similarities existed, except for the fact that they were all adjectives and a certain amount of similarity among prefixes, suffixes, and so on must inevitably occur. The recall of these four successive lists is shown in Fig. 2.1.

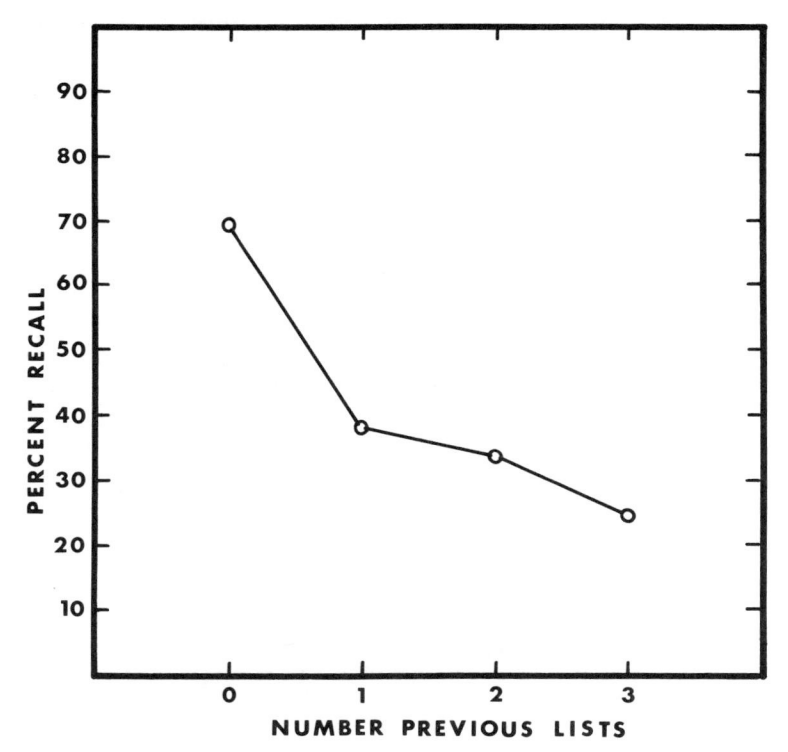

Figure 2.1 Recall of paired adjectives as a function of number of previous lists learned (10).

As can be seen, the more lists that are learned, the poorer the recall, from 69 per cent recall of the first list to 25 per cent recall of the fourth list. In examining errors at recall, we found a sufficient number of intrusion responses from previous lists to lead us to suggest that the increasing decrements in recall were a function of proactive interference from previous lists. And, while we pointed out that these results had implications for the design of experiments on retention, the relevance to an interference theory of forgetting was not mentioned.

Dr. E. J. Archer has made available to me certain data from an experiment which still is in progress and which deals with this issue. Subjects learned lists of 12 serial adjectives to one perfect trial and recalled them after 24 hours. The recall of a list always took place prior to learning the next list. The results for nine successive lists are shown in Fig. 2.2. Let me say again that there is no laboratory activity during the 24-hour interval; the subject learns a list, is dis-

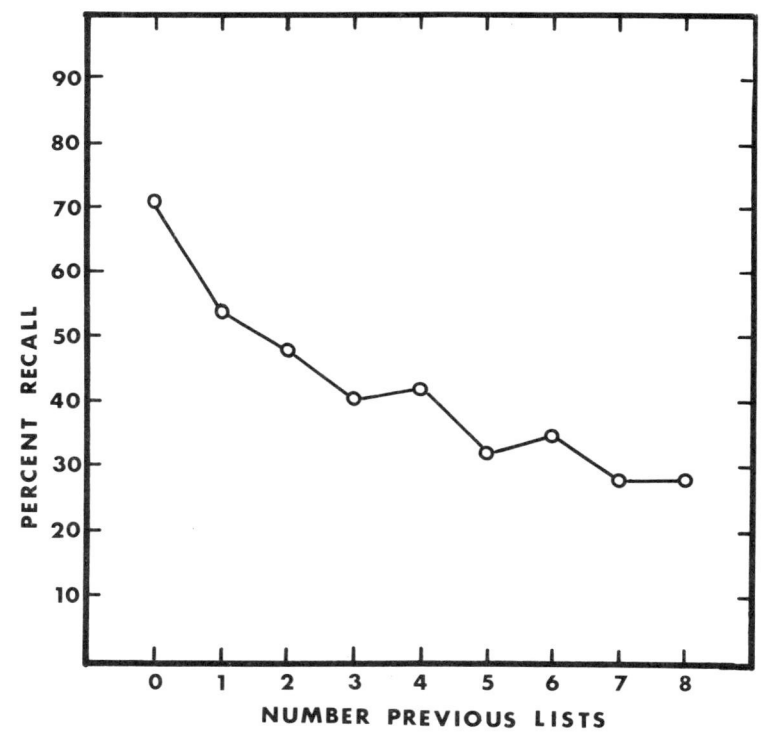

Figure 2.2 Recall of serial adjective lists as a function of number of previous lists learned. Unpublished data, courtesy of Dr. E. J. Archer.

missed from the laboratory, and returns after 24 hours to recall the list. The percentage of recall falls from 71 per cent for the first list to 27 per cent for the ninth.

In summarizing the more classical data on retention above, I indicated that a rough estimate showed that after 24 hours 75 per cent forgetting took place, or recall was about 25 per cent correct. In viewing these values in the light of Greenberg's and Archer's findings, the conclusion seemed inescapable that the classical studies must have been dealing with subjects who had learned many lists. That is to say, the subjects must have served in many conditions by use of counterbalancing and repeated cycles. To check on this I have made a search of the literature on the studies of retention to see if systematic data could be compiled on this matter. Preliminary work led me to establish certain criteria for inclusion in the summary to be presented. First, because degree of learning is such an important variable, I have included only those studies in which degree of learning was one perfect recitation of the list. Second, I have included only studies in which retention was measured after 24 hours. Third, I have included only studies in which recall measures were given. (Relearning measures add complexities with which I do not wish to deal in this paper.) Fourth, the summary includes only material learned by relatively massed practice. Finally, if an investigator had two or more conditions which met these criteria, I averaged the values for presentation in this paper. Except for these restrictions, I have used all studies I found (with an exception to be noted later), although I do not pretend to have made an exhaustive search. From each of these studies I got two facts: first, the percentage recalled after 24 hours, and second, the average number of previous lists the subjects had learned before learning the list on which recall after 24 hours was taken. Thus, if a subject had served in five experimental conditions via counterbalancing, and had been given two practice lists, the average number of lists learned before learning the list for which I tabulated the recall was four. This does not take into account any previous experiments in rote learning in which the subject might have served.

For each of these studies the two facts, average number of previous lists learned and percentage of recall, are related as in Fig. 2.3. For example, consider the study by Youtz. This study was concerned with Jost's law, and had several degrees of learning, several lengths of retention interval, and the subjects served in two cycles. Actually, there were 15 experimental conditions and each subject was given each condition twice. Also, each subject learned six practice lists before starting the experimental conditions. Among the

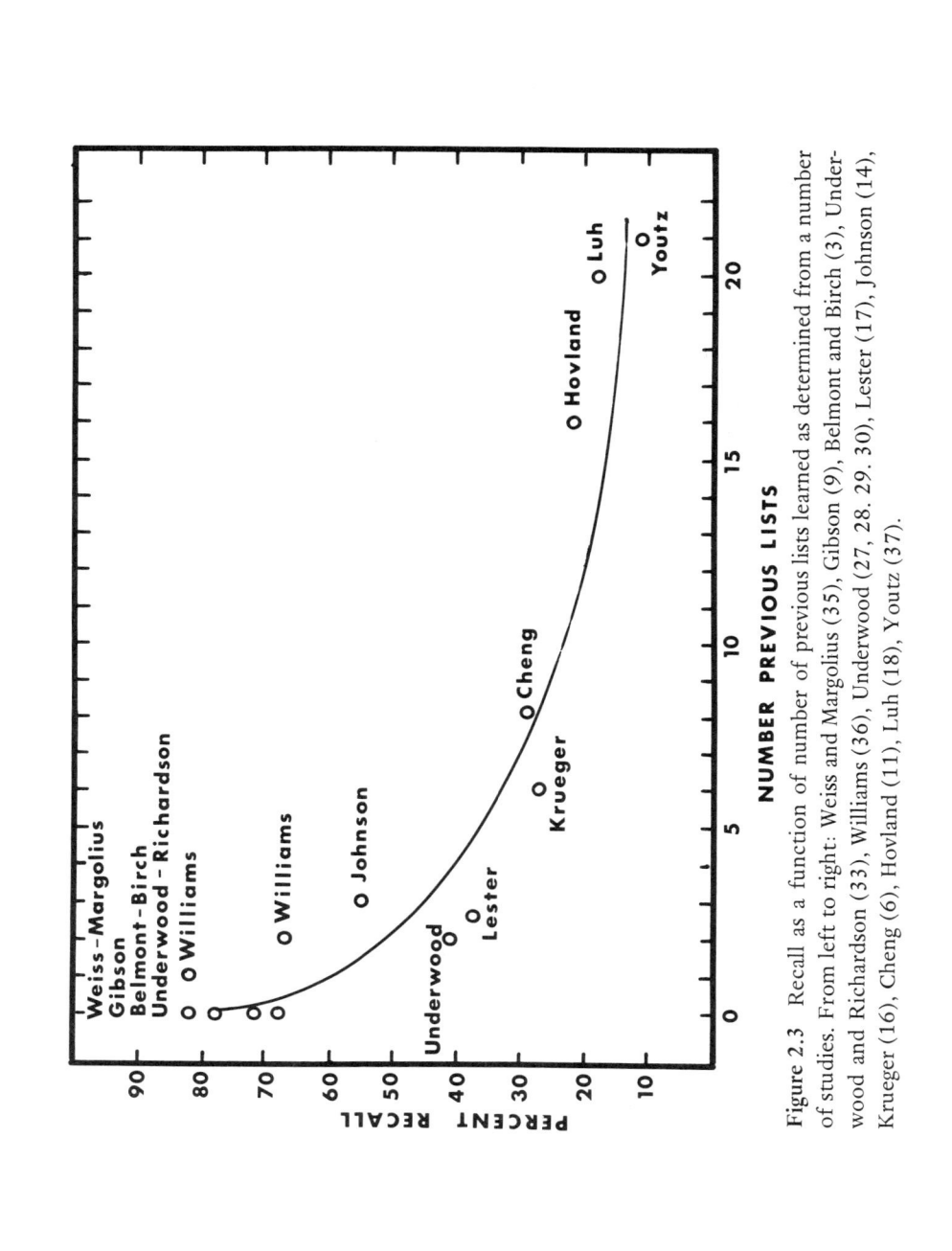

Figure 2.3 Recall as a function of number of previous lists learned as determined from a number of studies. From left to right: Weiss and Margolius (35), Gibson (9), Belmont and Birch (3), Underwood and Richardson (33), Williams (36), Underwood (27, 28. 29. 30), Lester (17), Johnson (14), Krueger (16), Cheng (6), Hovland (11), Luh (18), Youtz (37).

15 conditions was one in which the learning of the syllables was carried to one perfect recitation and recall was taken after 24 hours. It is this particular condition in which I am interested. On the average, this condition would have been given at the time when the subject had learned six practice lists and 15 experimental lists, for a total of 21 previous lists.

The studies included in Fig. 2.3 have several different kinds of materials, from geometric forms to nonsense syllables to nouns; they include both paired-associate and serial presentation, with different speeds of presentation and different lengths of lists. But I think the general relationship is clear. The greater the number of previous lists learned the greater the forgetting. I interpret this to mean that the greater the number of previous lists the greater the *proactive* interference. We know this to be true (26) for a formal proactive-inhibition paradigm; it seems a reasonable interpretation for the data of Fig. 2.3. That there are minor sources of variance still involved I do not deny. Some of the variation can be rationalized, but that is not the purpose of this report. The point I wish to make is the obvious one of the relationship between number of previous lists learned—lists which presumably had no intentionally built-in similarity—and amount of forgetting. If you like to think in correlational terms, the rank-order correlation between the two variables is −.91 for the 14 points of Fig. 2.3.

It may be of interest to the historian that, of the studies published before 1942 which met the criteria I imposed, I did not find a single one in which subjects had not been given at least one practice task before starting experimental conditions, and in most cases the subjects had several practice lists and several experimental conditions. Gibson's study (1942) was the first I found in which subjects served in only one condition and were not given practice tasks. I think it is apparent that the design proclivities of the 1920s and 1930s have been largely responsible for the exaggerated picture we have had of the rate of forgetting of rote-learned materials. On the basis of studies performed during the 1920s and 1930s, I have given a rough estimate of forgetting as being 75 per cent over 24 hours, recall being 25 per cent. On the basis of modern studies in which the subject has learned no previous lists—where there is no proactive inhibition from previous laboratory tasks—a rough estimate would be that forgetting is 25 per cent; recall is 75 per cent. The values are reversed. (If in the above and subsequent discussion my use of percentage values as if I were dealing with a cardinal or extensive scale is disturbing, I will say only that it makes the picture easier to grasp, and in my opinion no critical distortion results.)

Before taking the next major step, I would like to point out a few other observations which serve to support my general point that proactive inhibition from laboratory tasks has been the major cause of forgetting in the more classical studies. The first illustration I shall give exemplifies the point that when subjects have served in several conditions, forgetting after relatively short periods of time is greater than after 24 hours if the subject has served in only one condition. In the Youtz study to which I have already referred, other conditions were employed in which recall was taken after short intervals. After 20 minutes recall was 74 per cent, about what it is after 24 hours if the subject has not served in a series of conditions. After two hours recall was 32 per cent. In Ward's (34) well-known reminiscence experiment, subjects who on the average had learned ten previous lists showed a recall of only 64 per cent after 20 minutes.

In the famous Jenkins-Dallenbach (13) study on retention following sleep and following waking, two subjects were used. One subject learned a total of 61 lists and the other 62 in addition to several practice lists. Roughly, then, if the order of the conditions was randomized, approximately 30 lists had been learned prior to the learning of a list for a given experimental condition. Recall after eight waking hours for one subject was 4 per cent and for the other 14 per cent. Even after sleeping for eight hours the recall was only 55 per cent and 58 per cent.

I have said that an interpolated list can produce severe forgetting. However, in one study (1), using the A-B, A-C paradigm for original and interpolated learning, but using subjects who had never served in any previous conditions, recall of the original list was 46 per cent after 48 hours, and in another comparable study (24), 42 per cent. Thus, the loss is not nearly as great as in the classical studies I have cited where there was no interpolated learning in the laboratory.

My conclusion at this point is that, in terms of the gross analysis I have made, the amount of forgetting which might be attributed to interference from tasks learned outside the laboratory has been "reduced" from 75 per cent to about 25 per cent. I shall proceed in the next section to see if we have grounds for reducing this estimate still more. In passing on to this section, however, let me say that the study of factors which influence proactive inhibition in these counterbalanced studies is a perfectly legitimate and important area of study. I mention this because in the subsequent discussion I am going to deal only with the case where a subject has learned a single list in the laboratory, and I do not want to leave the impression that we should now and forevermore drop the study of interference produced by previous laboratory tasks. Indeed, as will be seen shortly, it is my opinion that we should increase these studies for the simple reason that the proactive paradigm provides a more realistic one than does the retroactive paradigm.

When the subject learns and recalls a single list in the laboratory, I have given an estimate of 25 per cent as being the amount forgotten over 24 hours. When, as shown above, we calculate percentage forgotten of lists learned to one perfect trial, the assumption is that had the subjects been given an immediate recall trial, the list would have been perfectly recalled. This, of course, is simply not true. The major factor determining how much error is introduced by this criterion-percentage method is probably the difficulty of the task. In general, the overestimation of forgetting by the percentage method will be directly related to the difficulty of the task. Thus, the more slowly the learning approaches a given criterion, the greater the drop on the trial immediately after the criterion trial. Data from a study by Runquist (24), using eight paired adjectives (a comparatively easy task), shows that amount of forgetting is overestimated by about 10 per cent. In a study (32) using very difficult consonant syllables, the overestimation was approximately 20 per cent. To be conservative, assume that on the average the percentage method of reporting recall overestimates the amount forgotten by 10 per cent. If we subtract this from the 25 per cent assumed above, the forgetting is now re-estimated as being 15 per cent over 24 hours. That is to say, an interference theory, or any other form of theory, has to account for a very small amount of forgetting as compared with the amount traditionally cited.

What are the implications of so greatly "reducing" the amount of forgetting? There are at least three implications which I feel are worth pointing out. First, if one wishes to hold to an interference theory of forgetting (as I do), it seems plausible to assert that this amount of forgetting could be produced from learning which has taken place outside of the laboratory. Furthermore, it seems likely that such interference must result primarily from proactive interference. This seems likely on a simple probability basis. A 20-year-old college student will more likely have learned something during his 20 years prior to coming to the laboratory that will interfere with his retention than he will during the 24 hours between the learning and retention test. However, the longer the retention interval the more important will retroactive interference become relative to proactive interferences.

The second implication is that these data may suggest greater homogeneity or continuity in memorial processes than hitherto supposed. Although no one has adequately solved the measurement problem of how to make comparisons of retention among conditioned responses, prose material, motor tasks, concept learning, and rote-learned tasks, the gross comparisons have indicated that rote-learned tasks were forgotten much more rapidly than these other tasks. But the rote-learning data used for comparison have been those derived with the classical design in which the forgetting over 24 hours is approximately 75 per cent. If we take the revised estimate of 15 per cent, the discrepancies among tasks become considerably less.

The third implication of the revised estimate of rate of forgetting is that the number of variables which appreciably influence rate of forgetting must be sharply limited. While this statement does not inevitably follow from the analyses I have made, the current evidence strongly supports the statement. I want to turn to the final section of this paper which will consist of a review of the influence of some of the variables which are or have been thought to be related to rate of forgetting. In considering these variables, it is well to keep in mind that a variable which produces only a small difference in forgetting is important if one is interested in accounting for the 15 per cent assumed now as the loss over 24 hours. If appropriate for a given variable, I will indicate where it fits into an interference theory, although in no case will I endeavor to handle the details of such a theory.

Time. Passage of time between learning and recall is the critical defining variable for forgetting. Manipulation of this variable provides the basic data for which a theory must account. Previously, our conception of rate of forgetting as a function of time has been tied to the Ebbinghaus curve. If the analysis made earlier is correct, this curve does not give us the basic data we need. In short, we must start all over and derive a retention curve over time when the subjects have learned no previous materials in the laboratory. It is apparent that I expect the fall in this curve over time to be relatively small.

In conjunction with time as an independent variable, we must, in explanations of forgetting, consider why sleep retards the processes responsible for forgetting. My conception, which does not really explain anything, is that since forgetting is largely produced by proactive interference, the amount of time which a subject spends in sleep is simply to be subtracted from the total retention interval when predicting the amount to be forgotten. It is known that proactive interference increases with passage of time (5); sleep, I believe, brings to a standstill whatever these processes are which produce this increase.

Degree of learning. We usually say that the better or stronger the learning the more or better the retention. Yet, we do not know whether or not the *rate* of forgetting differs for items of different strength. The experimental problem is a difficult one. What we need is to have a subject learn a single association and measure its decline in strength over time. But this is difficult to carry out with verbal material, since almost of necessity we must have the subject learn a series of associations, to make it a reasonable task. And, when a series of associations are learned, complications arise from interaction effects among associations of different strength. Nevertheless, we may expect, on the basis of evidence from a wide variety of studies, that given a constant degree of similarity, the effective interference varies as some function of the strength of associations.

Distribution of practice. It is a fact that distribution of practice during acquisition influences retention of verbal materials. The facts of the case seem to be as follows. If the subject has not learned previous lists in the laboratory, massed practice gives equal or better retention than does distributed practice. If, on the other hand, the subject has learned a number of previous lists, distributed practice will facilitate retention (32). We do not have the theoretical solution to these facts. The point I wish to make here is that whether or not distribution of learning inhibits or facilitates retention depends upon the amount of interference from previous learning. It is reasonable to expect, therefore, that the solution to the problem will come via principles handling interference in general. I might also say that a theoretical solution to this problem will also provide a solution for Jost's laws.

Similarity. Amount of interference from other tasks is closely tied to similarity. This similarity must be conceived of as similarity among materials as such and also situational similarity (4). When we turn to similarity within a task, the situation is not quite so clear. Empirically and theoretically (8) one would expect that intratask similarity would be a very relevant variable in forgetting. As discussed elsewhere (31), however, variation in intratask similarity almost inevitably leads to variations in intertask similarity. We do know from a recent study (33) that with material of low meaningfulness forgetting is significantly greater with high intralist similarity than with low. While the difference in magnitude is only about 8 per cent, when we are trying to account for a total loss of 15 per cent, this amount becomes a major matter.

Meaningfulness. The belief has long been held that the more meaningful the material the better the retention—the less the forgetting. Osgood (21) has pointed out that if this is true it is difficult for an interference theory to handle. So far as I know, the only direct test of the influence of this variable is a recent study in which retention of syllables of 100 per cent association value was compared with that of zero association value (33). There was no difference in the recall of these syllables. Other less precise evidence would support this finding when comparisons are made among syllables, adjectives, and nouns, as plotted in Fig. 2.3. However, there is some evidence that materials of very low meaningfulness are forgotten more rapidly than nonsense syllables of zero association value. Consonant syllables, both serial (32) and paired associates (unpublished), show about 50 per cent loss over 24 hours. The study using serial lists was the one mentioned earlier as knowingly omitted from Fig. 2.3. These syllables, being extremely difficult to learn, allow a correction of about 20 per cent due to criterion overestimation, but even with this much correction the forgetting (30 per cent) is still appreciably more than the estimate we have made for other materials. To invoke the interference theory to account for this discrepancy means that we must demonstrate how interference from other activities could be greater for these consonant syllables than for nonsense syllables, nouns, adjectives, and other materials. Our best guess at the present time is that the sequences of letters in consonant syllables are contrary to other well-established language habits. That is to say, letter sequences which commonly occur in our language are largely different from those in consonant syllables. As a consequence, not only are these consonant syllables very difficult to learn, but forgetting is accelerated by proactive interference from previously well-learned letter sequences. If subsequent research cannot demonstrate such a source of interference, or if some other source is not specified, an interference theory for this case will be in some trouble.

Affectivity. Another task dimension which has received extensive attention is the affective tone of the material. I would also include here the studies attaching unpleasant experiences to some items experimentally and not to others, and measuring retention of these two sets of items. Freud is to a large extent responsible for these studies, but he cannot be held responsible for the malformed methodology which characterizes so many of them. What can one say by way of summarizing these studies? The only conclusion that I can reach is a statistical one, namely, that the occasional positive result found among the scores of studies is about as frequent as one would expect by sampling error, using the 5 per cent level of confidence. Until a reliable body of fact is established for this variable and associated variables, no theoretical evaluation is possible.

Other variables. As I indicated earlier, I will not make an exhaustive survey of the variables which may influence rate of forgetting. I have limited myself to variables which have been rather extensively investigated, which have immediate relevance to the interference theory, or for which reliable relationships are available. Nevertheless, I would like to mention briefly some of these other variables. There is the matter of *warm-up* before recall; some investigators find that this reduces forgetting (12); others, under as nearly replicated conditions as is possible to obtain, do not (23). Some resolution must be found for these flat contradictions. It seems perfectly reasonable, however, that inadequate set or context differences could reduce recall. Indeed, an interference theory would predict this forgetting if the set or context stimuli are appreciably different from those prevailing at the time of learning. In our laboratory we try to reinstate the learning set by careful instructions, and we simply do not find decrements that might be attributed to inadequate set. For example, in a recent study (33) subjects were given a 24-hour recall of a serial list after learning to one perfect trial. I think we would expect that the first item in the list would suffer the greatest decrement due to inadequate set, yet this item showed only .7 per cent loss. But let it be clear that when we are attempting to account for the 15 per cent loss over 24 hours, we should not overlook any possible source for this loss.

Thus far I have not said anything about forgetting as a function of characteristics of the subject, that is, the personality or intellectual characteristics. As far as I have been able to determine, there is not a single valid study which shows that such variables have an appreciable influence on forgetting. Many studies have shown differences in learning as a function of these variables, but not differences in rate of forgetting. Surely there must be some such variables. We do know that if subjects are severely insulted, made to feel stupid, or generally led to believe that they have no justification for continued existence on the earth just before they are asked to recall, they will show losses (e.g., 25, 38), but even the influence of this kind of psychological beating is short lived. Somehow I have never felt that such findings need explanation by a theory used to explain the other facts of forgetting.

Concerning the causes of forgetting, let me sum up in a somewhat more dogmatic fashion than is probably justified. One of the assumptions of science is finite causality. Everything cannot influence everything else. To me, the most important implication of the work on forgetting during the last ten years is that this work has markedly *reduced* the number of variables related to forgetting. Correspondingly, I think the theoretical problem has become simpler. It is my belief that we can narrow down the cause of forgetting to interference from previously learned habits, from habits being currently learned, and from habits we have yet to learn. The amount of this interference is primarily a function of similarity and associative strength, the latter being important because it interacts with similarity.

SUMMARY

This paper deals with issues in the forgetting of rote-learned materials. An analysis of the current evidence suggests that the classical Ebbinghaus curve of forgetting is primarily a function of interference from materials learned previously in the laboratory. When this source of interference is removed, forgetting decreases from about 75 per cent over 24 hours to about 25 per cent. This latter figure can be reduced by at least 10 per cent by other methodological considerations, leaving 15 per cent as an estimate of forgetting over 24 hours. This estimate will vary somewhat as a function of intratask similarity, distributed practice, and with very low meaningful material. But the overall evidence suggests that similarity with other material and situational similarity are by far the most critical factors in forgetting. Such evidence is consonant with a general interference theory, although the details of such a theory were not presented here.

REFERENCES

1. Archer, E. J., & Underwood, B. J. Retroactive inhibition of verbal associations as a multiple function of temporal point of interpolation and degree of interpolated learning, *J. exp. Psychol.,* 1951, 42, 283–290.
2. Bartlett, F. C. *Remembering: a study in experimental and social psychology.* London: Cambridge Univer. Press, 1932.
3. Belmont, L., & Birch, H. G. Re-individualizing the repression hypothesis. *J. abnorm. soc. Psychol.,* 1951, 46, 226–235.
4. Bilodeau, I. McD., & Shlosberg, H. Similarity in stimulating conditions as a variable in retroactive inhibition. *J. exp. Psychol.,* 1951, 41, 199–204.
5. Briggs, G. E. Acquisition, extinction, and recovery functions in retroactive inhibition. *J. exp. Psychol.,* 1954, 47, 285–293.

6. Cheng, N. Y. Retroactive effect and degree of similarity. *J. exp. Psychol.*, 1929, 12, 444–458.
7. Ebbinghaus, H. *Memory: a contribution to experimental psychology.* (Trans. by H. A. Ruger, and C. E. Bussenius) New York: Bureau of Publications, Teachers College, Columbia Univer., 1913.
8. Gibson, Eleanor J. A systematic application of the concepts of generalization and differentiation to verbal learning. *Psychol. Rev.*, 1940, 47, 196–229.
9. Gibson, Eleanor J. Intra-list generalization as a factor in verbal learning. *J. exp. Psychol.*, 1942, 30, 185–200.
10. Greenberg, R., & Underwood, B. J. Retention as a function of stage of practice. *J. exp. Psychol.*, 1950, 40, 452–457.
11. Hovland, C. I. Experimental studies in rote-learning theory. VI. Comparison of retention following learning to same criterion by massed and distributed practice. *J. exp. Psychol.*, 1940, 26, 568–587.
12. Irion, A. L. The relation of "set" to retention. *Psychol. Rev.*, 1948, 55, 336–341.
13. Jenkins, J. G., & Dallenbach, K. M. Oblivescence during sleep and waking. *Amer. J. Psychol.*, 1924, 35, 605–612.
14. Johnson, L. M. The relative effect of a time interval upon learning and retention. *J. exp. Psychol.*, 1939, 24, 169–179.
15. Katona, G. *Organizing and memorizing: studies in the psychology of learning and teaching.* New York: Columbia Univer. Press, 1940.
16. Krueger, W. C. F. The effect of over-learning on retention. *J. exp. Psychol.*, 1929, 12, 71–78.
17. Lester, O. P. Mental set in relation to retroactive inhibition. *J. exp. Psychol.*, 1932, 15, 681–699.
18. Luh, C. W. The conditions of retention. *Psychol. Monogr.*, 1922, 31, No. 3 (Whole No. 142).
19. McGeoch, J. A. Forgetting and the law of disuse. *Psychol. Rev.*, 1932, 39, 352–370.
20. McGeoch, J. A. *The psychology of human learning.* New York: Longmans, Green, 1942.
21. Osgood, C. E. *Method and theory in experimental psychology.* New York: Oxford Univer. Press, 1953.
22. Rapaport, D. Emotions and memory. *Psychol. Rev.*, 1943, 50, 234–243.
23. Rockway, M. R., & Duncan, C. P. Pre-recall warming-up in verbal retention. *J. exp. Psychol.*, 1952, 43, 305–312.
24. Runquist, W. Retention of verbal associations as a function of interference and strength. Unpublished doctor's dissertation, Northwestern Univer., 1956.
25. Russell, W. A. Retention of verbal material as a function of motivating instructions and experimentally-induced failure. *J. exp. Psychol.*, 1952, 43, 207–216.
26. Underwood, B. J. The effect of successive interpolations of retroactive and proactive inhibition. *Psychol. Monogr.*, 1945, 59, No. 3 (Whole No. 273).
27. Underwood, B. J. Studies of distributed practice: VII. Learning and reten-

tion of serial nonsense lists as a function of intralist similarity. *J. exp. Psychol.,* 1952, 44, 80–87.
28. Underwood, B. J. Studies of distributed practice: VIII. Learning and retention of paired nonsense syllables as a function of intralist similarity. *J. exp. Psychol.,* 1953, 45, 133–142.
29. Underwood, B. J. Studies of distributed practice: IX. Learning and retention of paired adjectives as a function of intralist similarity. *J. exp. Psychol.,* 1953, 45, 143–149.
30. Underwood, B. J. Studies of distributed practice: X. The influence of intralist similarity on learning and retention of serial adjective lists. *J. exp. Psychol.,* 1953, 45, 253–259.
31. Underwood, B. J. Intralist similarity in verbal learning and retention. *Psychol. Rev.,* 1954, 3, 160–166.
32. Underwood, B. J., & Richardson, J. Studies of distributed practice: XIII. Interlist interference and the retention of serial nonsense lists. *J. exp. Psychol.,* 1955, 50, 39–46.
33. Underwood, B. J., & Richardson, J. The influence of meaningfulness, intralist similarity, and serial position on retention. *J. exp. Psychol.,* 1956, 52, 119–126.
34. Ward, L. B. Reminiscence and rote learning. *Psychol. Monogr.,* 1937, 49, No. 4 (Whole No. 220).
35. Weiss, W., & Margolius, G. The effect of content stimuli on learning and retention. *J. exp. Psychol.,* 1954, 48, 318–322.
36. Williams, M. The effects of experimentally induced needs upon retention. *J. exp. Psychol.,* 1950, 40, 139–151.
37. Youtz, Adella C. An experimental evaluation of Jost's laws. *Psychol. Monogr.,* 1941, 53, No. 1 (Whole No. 238).
38. Zeller, A. F. An experimental analogue of repression: III. The effect of induced failure and success on memory measured by recall. *J. exp. Psychol.,* 1951, 42, 32–38.

Proactive Inhibition in Short-Term Retention of Single Items

In 1959 Peterson and Peterson developed a technique whereby a single verbal item was presented to S for a learning trial of approximately .5-sec. duration, with retention being measured over intervals of up to 18 sec. These procedures produced a very systematic relationship between length of retention interval and percentage of items correct at recall, with 78% correct after 3 sec., and 8% after 18 sec. Thus, forgetting of the single item is nearly complete after 18 sec. The reliability of this forgetting curve is demonstrated by the fact that Murdock (1961) has repeated the Peterson-Peterson experiment and obtained nearly identical results.

The present experiments were designed to obtain data which would aid in interpreting theoretically the extraordinarily rapid forgetting of the single items which has been observed in the above experiments. The nature of the interpretative problem and how it arises, requires some background discussion.

The first distinction which must be made is between short-term retention procedures and long-term retention procedures. The short-term studies, as exemplified by Peterson and Peterson, involve retention of *single* items over very short intervals, say, 60 sec. or less. The long-term retention studies involve retention of *lists* of items over much longer intervals, such as 20 min., although usually hours or days are employed. Clearly no dichotomy is possible between the two types of studies based on length of retention interval, but in actual practice a working distinction between the two exists. We may identify the short-term studies as measuring short-term memory (STM) and the long-term studies as measuring long-term memory (LTM) with the understanding that the present usage also involves memory for singly presented items versus memory for lists of items.

The critical issue is whether or not LTM and STM will require fundamentally different interpretative principles. The resolution of

---

Geoffrey Keppel and Benton J. Underwood, "Proactive Inhibition in Short-Term Retention of Single Items," *Journal of Verbal Learning and Verbal Behavior* 1 (1962): 153–161. Reprinted with permission.

This work was supported by Contract Nonr-1228 (15), Project NR 154-057, between Northwestern University and the Office of Naval Research.

this issue rests primarily on determining the role which proactive inhibition (PI) plays in STM. Interference theories of LTM use PI as a cornerstone paradigm (e.g., Postman, 1961); associations learned prior to the learning of associations for which retention is being tested may interfere with recall. However, a secondary fact reported by Peterson and Peterson (1959) and by Peterson (1963) is that little or no evidence is found for PI in STM. In addition, since little or no retroactive inhibition (RI) is believed to be produced by the activity used to prevent rehearsal in the studies of STM, it would appear that an interference theory, based on PI and RI, is quite incapable of handling the extraordinarily rapid forgetting observed in the studies of STM. Thus, we are faced with a potential theoretical schism, with one set of propositions being used for LTM and another possibly wholly different set for STM. In the interests of theoretical continuity, such a schism should be avoided if possible.

As noted above, the critical issue involved is the role which PI plays in STM. If PI is operative in STM, the variables which govern magnitude of PI in LTM should also have counterparts in the laws of STM. Some of these more critical variables will now be discussed.

Number of Interfering Associations. In LTM the greater the number of previously acquired associations the greater the PI (Underwood, 1945; 1957). It is the reported failure to reproduce this law in studies of STM that has led to the conclusion that there is little, if any, PI in STM. Actually, the procedure used in these studies of STM would seem to be ideal for obtaining PI. For example, in the Peterson-Peterson study, a counterbalancing technique was used in which each S served eight times at each of six retention intervals. Thus, each S at the termination of his conditions had been presented 48 different items. The items presented late in the session should be subject to a greater number of potentially interfering associations than would those items presented early in the session. Yet there appears to be little difference in the retention of items presented early in the session and those presented late in the session (but see later discussion).

Degree of Learning. In LTM the higher the degree of learning of the list to be recalled the better the recall when the PI paradigm is used (Postman and Riley, 1959). This is not to say that the absolute PI is less with higher than with lower degree of learning (when evaluated against a control group) of the list to be recalled, for according to Postman and Riley this relationship is complex. But, given a high degree of learning of a list, its recall will be higher than will the recall of a list with a low degree of learning when the proactive interference is constant on both lists. This fact has been used by Melton (1963) indirectly to suggest that PI is indeterminate in the available studies of STM. His reasoning is that as S proceeds through a series of conditions the learning-to-learn will serve to increase the degree of learning of items presented. This higher degree of learning, in turn, will counteract a decrement in retention which should occur as a function of the increasing number of potentially interfering associations which have been established as practice proceeds.

There is evidence that learning-to-learn does occur in STM studies (Peterson and Peterson, 1959). That it does occur requires a distinction between learning and retention in STM, a distinction which has not, in fact, been carefully maintained in the studies to date. Normally, we may use an immediate test (say, after 1 sec.) as a measure of degree of learning. Retention for longer intervals are assessed against the scores on the immediate test to determine the retention function. However, when percentage correct for immediate retention is essentially 100%, there is no way to derive a meaningful retention function. For, in a manner of speaking, the true degree of learning may be more than 100%. Thus, if STM of common words is to be compared with that of consonant syllables, and if the immediate test for words shows 100% correct recall and that for syllables 85%, comparison of the retention of the two materials at longer intervals may be both a function of underestimated differences in degree of learning and of differences in material. Latency measures at recall might be used as subsidiary indices of forgetting which occurs when the percentage correct remains near 100% for retention intervals of increasing length, but the moment recall falls substantially below 100% we have subject selection (those who do not get an item correct are not included in the measures) which may distort the mean of the natural distribution of latencies based on all Ss.

Length of Retention Interval. The logic of the PI situation demands an increase in PI as a function of the length of the retention interval (Underwood, 1948). So far as is known, no completely satisfactory test of this relationship has been made for LTM. Theoretically the increase in PI with increase in length of the retention interval may be accounted for by the recovery of extinguished interfering associations. Several studies strongly suggest such recovery (e.g., Briggs, 1954).

Interaction of Variables. If the facts and theory of PI in LTM hold for STM, certain interactions among the above variables will be expected. Most critical among these is the interaction between the number of potentially interfering associations and the length of the retention interval. Theoretically it is assumed that the longer the retention interval the greater the recovery of interfering associations. If there are few or none such associations little or no decrement will be observed as a function of length of retention interval (i.e., forgetting will be very slow). If there are many potential associations which could interfere proactively, the longer the retention interval the greater the forgetting, since the longer the interval the greater the number of interfering associations which will have recovered.

We may now focus on the fact that PI is said not to be involved in the rapid forgetting in STM. In the Peterson-Peterson study Ss were tested on 48 successive items following two practice items. It has been suggested that PI reaches some maximum level rather quickly as a function of the number of previous items and that a constant amount of PI may occur thereafter. Thus, two practice items may "throw in" the maximum amount of PI and additional items may have no further decremental effects (Postman, 1962; Melton, 1963). While it seems apparent that there must be a limit to the number of previous items which will contribute to interference in STM, it does not seem reasonable that all potential interfering associations would be established with only two items—the two practice items. It seems more reasonable to look at the Peterson-Peterson data from another point of view. If it is assumed that there is a practice effect in learning successive items, degree of learning for each successive item will be higher and higher. By principles of PI in LTM, the recall should also be higher and higher if amount of interference remains constant. But, of course, interference does not remain constant; more and more potentially interfering associations are acquired as testing continues. As noted earlier in the discussion, the question is how the positive effects of increased degree of learning with successive stages of practice balance out against the increased interference which accompanies the higher degree of learning. Some indication of the direction the answer may take is available in the Peterson-Peterson data.

These investigators divided the 48 experimental items into successive blocks of 12 items each so that Blocks 1 through 4 may reflect increasing degrees of learning of the items to be recalled and, simultaneously, increasing numbers of potentially interfering items. The percentage correct at recall by blocks was determined separately for two short intervals (3 and 6 sec.) and for two long intervals (15 and 18 sec.). The results are presented in Fig. 2.4. For the short retention intervals there is a consistent increase in recall from Block

Proactive Interference

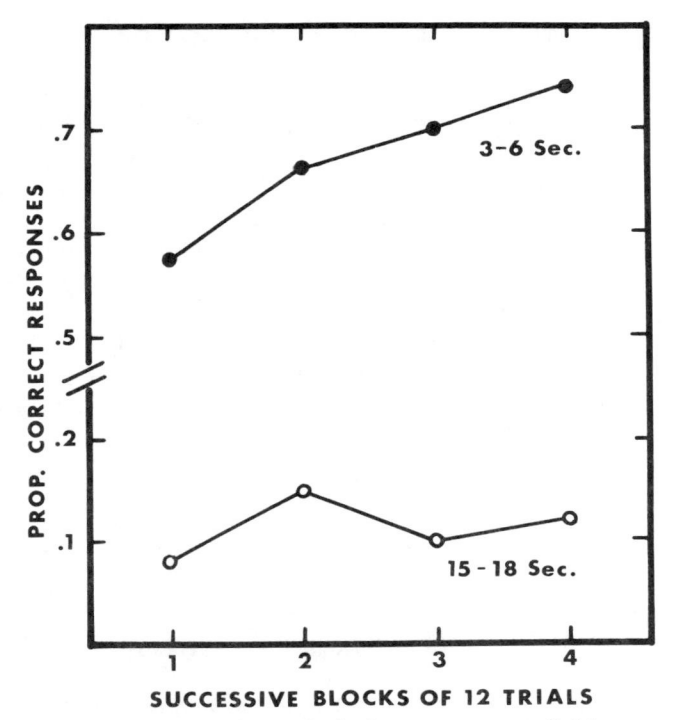

Figure 2.4 Retention of single consonant syllables over short (3-6 sec.) and long (15-18 sec.) retention intervals as a function of number of preceding items. From Peterson and Peterson (1959).

1 to Block 4, the difference between the recall for the two extreme blocks being significant at the .02 confidence level. Peterson and Peterson identified this as a practice effect. Since there is no reason to believe that the practice effect occurs in the recall process it must mean that the degree of learning attained in the constant exposure period increases as trials proceed. For the longer retention interval there is no increase in recall. If only practice effects are involved, this curve should rise in exactly the same manner as the curve for shorter intervals. That it does not may indicate an increase in amount of PI as trials proceed. Thus, Fig. 2.4 gives indirect evidence for the critical interaction discussed earlier; that is, the interaction between amount of interference and length of the retention interval. With short retention intervals the practice effects more than compensate for increased interference; with long retention

intervals the interference is of sufficient magnitude to mask the practice effects.

The evidence for the interaction between number of previous items and length of retention intervals as inferred from Fig. 2.4 is not entirely satisfactory. Not only is the magnitude of the interaction small, but the failure to find a change in retention over blocks for the longer retention intervals must be interpreted as due to a balance between practice and interference effects. We believe it is possible to devise situations which will destroy this balance and thus give more direct evidence for the role of PI. Furthermore, studies are needed in which STM is examined for Ss without prior practice so that the rate of onset of PI as a function of 0, 1, 2, 3, etc., previous items is observed. The present experiments were designed to study these two issues.

EXPERIMENT 1

Method

Subjects. A total of 108 Ss from introductory psychology classes at Northwestern University served in Exp. 1. Most Ss had served in one or more verbal-learning experiments but in no case did an S have prior experience with the specific materials of the present experiment.

Procedure. Three retention intervals were used, namely 3 sec., 9 sec., and 18 sec. A single consonant syllable was used for each retention interval. The procedure of Peterson and Peterson (1959) was followed, in which E spelled a syllable aloud and S attempted to recall it after the appropriate retention interval. The interval was timed from the moment the last letter of the syllable was spoken to the point at which S was instructed to recall. During the retention interval S counted backward by threes from a three-digit number spoken immediately after the presentation of the syllable, the rate of counting being one three-digit number per sec. Half the Ss were given a short practice period in counting backwards prior to being given the first syllable. However, since this practice had no discernible effect on the scores, the variable has not been maintained in presenting the results.

The three trigrams or consonant syllables were KQF, MHZ, and CXJ. Each has a 4% association value in the Witmer list (Underwood & Schulz, 1960). The retention for each S was measured over all three intervals with, of course, a different trigram being used for each interval. The three intervals were completely counterbalanced and three different orders of the trigrams were used such that each occurred equally often as the first, second, and third trigram presented. Thus 18 Ss are needed to fill the 18 different trigram-interval orders. Since 108 Ss were used, the design was replicated six times.

The design allows retention to be determined for the three retention inter-

Proactive Interference 57

vals after 0, 1, and 2 prior trigrams. Recall for the first trigram will be referred to as Test 1 (T-1), that of the second T-2, and the third, T-3.

Results

The results in terms of proportion of items correct for T-1, T-2, and T-3 for each retention interval are shown in Fig. 2.5. Each point is based on 36 Ss. Forgetting is apparent for all three tests. There is a large drop in proportion correct from T-1 to T-2, suggesting a severe proactive effect produced by a single prior item. There is no strong evidence that T-2 differs from T-3; thus, this may suggest a steady state or a constant amount of PI after the initial drop from T-1 to T-2. However, two facts relative to this point should be noted. First, at 3 sec. and at 18 sec., proportion correct is higher for T-2 than for T-3; only at 9 sec. is there a reversal. The fact that performance is better at 18 sec. than at 9 sec. (forgetting decreases between 9 and 18 sec.) suggests the possibility that for some unknown reason the 9 sec. T-2 estimate of retention is too low. Secondly, it is noted that the absolute number of Ss recalling correctly at T-2 and T-3 for the 9- and 18-sec. intervals is very low. At none

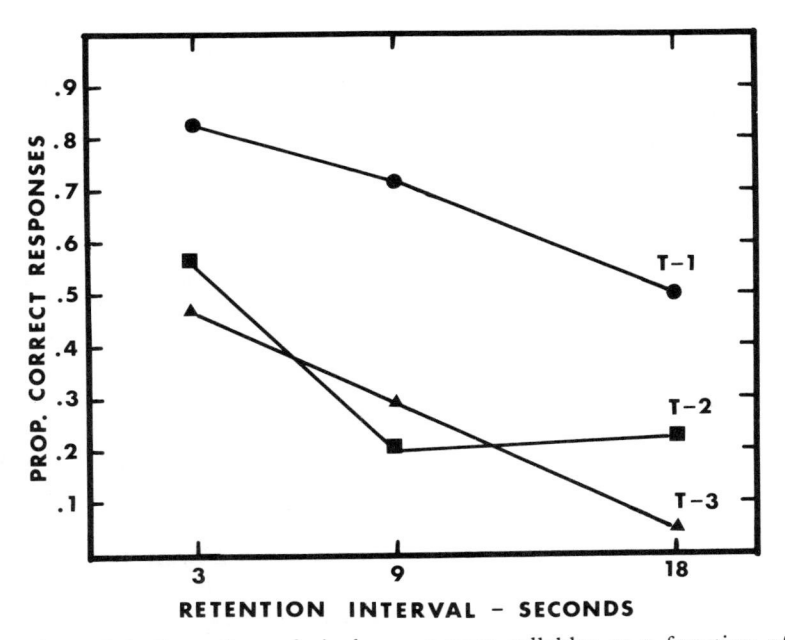

Figure 2.5 Retention of single consonant syllables as a function of length of interval and number of prior syllables. Experiment 1.

of these points is retention above 25% and on T-3 at 18 sec. forgetting is virtually complete. At these low levels of performance it may be very difficult to show consistent differences. Nevertheless, it must be concluded that there is no evidence for an increase in PI between T-2 and T-3. Furthermore, there is no evidence for an interaction between tests and retention intervals; the curves for T-1 and T-3 are essentially parallel, although here again it must be noted that on T-3 at 18 sec. forgetting is virtually complete, a situation which may preclude the appearance of an interaction. If, however, retention at 3 sec. is used as a base and if percentage of items lost between 3 sec. and 18 sec. is calculated, there is a 40% loss (from 30 items to 18 items) for T-1, and an 88% loss (from 17 to 2 items) for T-3. This method of evaluating the results clearly shows the expected interaction. While we do not believe that this response measure (proportion lost) can be judged inappropriate, it was our expectation that the interaction would be of such magnitude as to be measurable by the direct recall measures. Therefore, we will conclude only that the results are not unfavorable to the interaction hypothesis.

The retention exhibited on T-1 falls from 83% at 3 sec. to 50% at 18 sec. The difference between these two proportions is highly significant ($z = 3.00$). Only 83% of the Ss could correctly reproduce the trigram shown them 3 sec. later, and this was the first trigram shown. This suggests that degree of learning was low. However, to account for this we have no evidence to choose between failure to hear the letters and letter sequence correctly, as opposed to true forgetting over 3 sec. In any event, with a low degree of learning, STM should be easily interfered with. If interference via PI is responsible for the forgetting on T-1, it must come from associations acquired in previous laboratory experiments, from conflicting letter-sequence habits, or both.

EXPERIMENT 2

Except for one major change, Exp. 2 was very similar to Exp. 1. The change made was toward increasing the degree of initial learning by using a 2-sec. visual exposure of the items for learning. As previously noted in presenting the results for Exp. 1, recall was very poor for T-2 and T-3 for the 9- and 18-sec. retention intervals. With such low recall it is doubtful that any clear interaction between tests and intervals could have been observed. Therefore, it was believed that by increasing the degree of learning a greater range of forgetting could be observed for T-2 and T-3.

Method

A total of 216 Ss served in Exp. 2. Some had served in previous laboratory experiments on verbal learning and some had not. The three trigrams used in Exp. 1 also were employed in Exp. 2. However, each trigram was presented visually for a 2-sec. learning trial before the retention interval. Each trigram was printed with a lettering set on a 3 × 5-in. card, the letters being ½ in. high. Following the presentation of a card for 2 sec., E spoke a number as the card was removed and S counted backward by threes as in Exp. 1. Practice in number counting was given prior to presentation of the first trigram.

Each S again served in all three retention-interval conditions. Intervals were completely counterbalanced as were also the three trigrams; thus, 36 Ss were required for each possible interval-trigram order.

Results

The proportions correct at each test for the three retention intervals are shown in Fig. 2.6. Each proportion is based on 72 Ss. It is apparent that the level of recall is appreciably higher than in Exp. 1. This is due, we believe, to the longer exposure of the item on the learning trial. On T-1 only four responses (out of a possible 216)

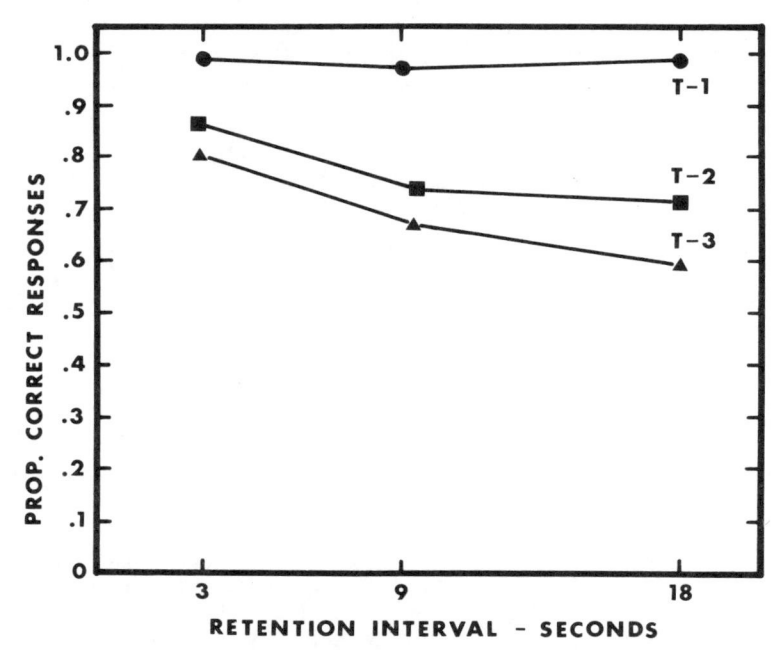

Figure 2.6 Retention of single consonant syllables as a function of length of interval and number of prior syllables. Experiment 2.

were incorrect; obviously, therefore, no forgetting is measurable across intervals on T-1. Proportion correct falls sharply from T-1 to T-2, with a continued but smaller decrease from T-2 to T-3. However, the drop from T-2 to T-3 is significant statistically. For each successive block of 18 Ss the interval order is perfectly balanced and each item has occurred equally often with each interval. Therefore, we may treat each group of 18 Ss as an independent experiment, thus giving 12 experiments. We may determine the total correct responses on T-2 and T-3 for each experiment separately, thus deriving two distributions of 12 entries each, one distribution representing number correct on T-2 and the other on T-3. The mean total items recalled per experiment for T-2 was 13.92, for T-3, 12.42. The mean difference (1.50 ± .54) gives a t of 2.78, which, with 11 df, is significant beyond the 5% level.

Although the forgetting over time for T-2 and T-3 is not as precipitous as in Exp. 1, it is clearly evident. Since there is no forgetting on T-1, it might appear that Fig. 2.6 shows the expected interaction between tests and intervals. However, such a conclusion is unwarranted. Whether or not forgetting "above" 100% correct occurred across intervals for T-1 is indeterminate from the correct-response measure. In recording the scores, note was made of all correct responses with latencies of 3 sec. or less. On T-1 almost all responses had latencies shorter than 3 sec. and there was no change in frequency of such responses with increasing intervals. This might be taken to indicate no forgetting across 18 sec. for T-1, hence that the interaction apparent in Fig. 2.6 is real. Experiment 3 would support such an interpretation.

The fact that Exp. 2 produced a difference between T-2 and T-3 in retention indicated that no "bottom" or steady state of PI had been reached. To test more fully the course of PI as a function of number of prior items, Ss in Exp. 3 were tested on six successive items.

EXPERIMENT 3

Method

A total of 96 Ss was used, divided into two subgroups of 48 each. Two retention intervals were employed, 3 sec. and 18 sec. One subgroup received the retention intervals in the order 3-18-3-18-3-18, and the other in the reverse order. This procedure permitted determination of retention after 3 sec. and after 18 sec. following 0, 1, 2, 3, 4, and 5 previous items.

Six new trigrams were chosen having a Witmer association value of 21%. This was the lowest association value from which six trigrams could be chosen so that no letter was duplicated among the 18 used. The six trigrams were: CXP, GQN, HJL, KBW, SFM, and ZTD. Six different orders of the trigrams were used such that each trigram occurred equally often on each successive test and, of course, equally often with each retention interval for each subgroup. None of the Ss used had served previously in laboratory experiments of verbal learning. The presentation procedures were exactly the same as in Exp. 2.

Results

The proportions of correct responses for both interval patterns are combined in Fig. 2.7. In this figure the six successive tests are given along the abscissa, with one curve representing retention after 3 sec. and the other retention after 18 sec. The trend of proactive interference which was initiated by the three tests in Exp. 2 is extended and clarified by Fig. 2.7. It may be noted that retention on T-1 is lower than in Exp. 2 for the 3-sec. interval. Since the procedures were identical in the two experiments, the differences must arise from the samples of Ss and from differences in materials.

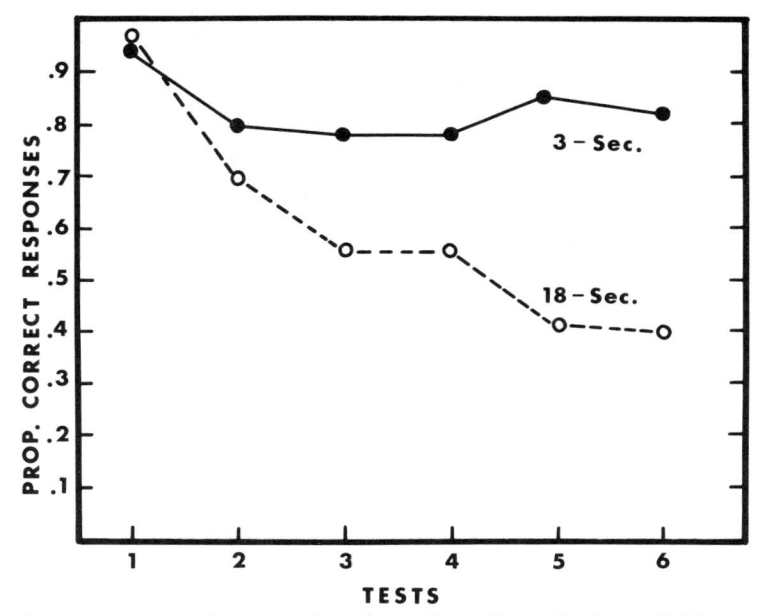

Figure 2.7 Retention as a function of number of prior syllables and length of retention interval. Experiment 3.

Actually, the trigrams of Exp. 2 had lower association value than those of Exp. 3. Whatever the cause, it is clear that degree of learning is lower in Exp. 3 than in Exp. 2. This unexpected turn of events, however, produces the very desirable effect of removing any problem of a "ceiling" effect in response measurement, at least for Tests 2 through 6.

It may be noted first that the recall on the very first item presented Ss does not differ for the 3-sec. and the 18-sec. retention intervals. However, with each successive test the differences increase, thus demonstrating the interaction between tests (number of prior interfering associations) and length of retention interval. Severe PI builds up over 18 sec. with successive tests but this does not happen over 3 sec. For T-1 through T-6, the z's for the difference between proportions for 3 and 18 sec. are: .47, 1.17, 2.17, 2.17, 4.51, and 4.23.

Significant forgetting is shown for the 3-sec. interval between T-1 and T-4 ($z = 2.33$). The rise between T-4 and T-5 is not significant statistically but may indicate that practice effects are more than counteracting interference effects produced by prior tests (see later).

The question as to whether a steady state of a constant amount of PI is being approached in the 18-sec. curve is not clearly answered by Fig. 2.7. The question can be more easily answered by replotting Fig. 2.7 to separate the two independent groups. That is, the 3-sec. curve in Fig. 2.7 is based on two different groups of Ss, one having the 3-18-3-18-3-18 order of intervals, the other the reverse. We may, therefore, plot the 3- and 18-sec. curves separately for each group. This is done in Fig. 2.8. The solid lines represent the group given the 3-18 etc. order, the dotted lines representing the group given the reverse order. The filled circles represent the 3-sec. retention, the open circles the 18-sec. retention.

For the 18-sec. curves, the 3-18 Group shows no evidence of leveling off and the 18-3 Group shows only slight evidence of negative acceleration. In short, it would appear that extrapolation of these curves beyond the six tests used would give further continued larger and larger decrements in recall over 18 sec. That this is not so apparent in Fig. 2.7 appears to be due to the fact that this figure combines two groups of slightly different ability levels. It also should be noted that for both groups there is a rise in retention between the second and the third tests for the 3-sec. interval. Although neither rise is significant statistically, the trend may be reliable in view of the Peterson-Peterson data shown in Fig. 2.4 where per-

Proactive Interference

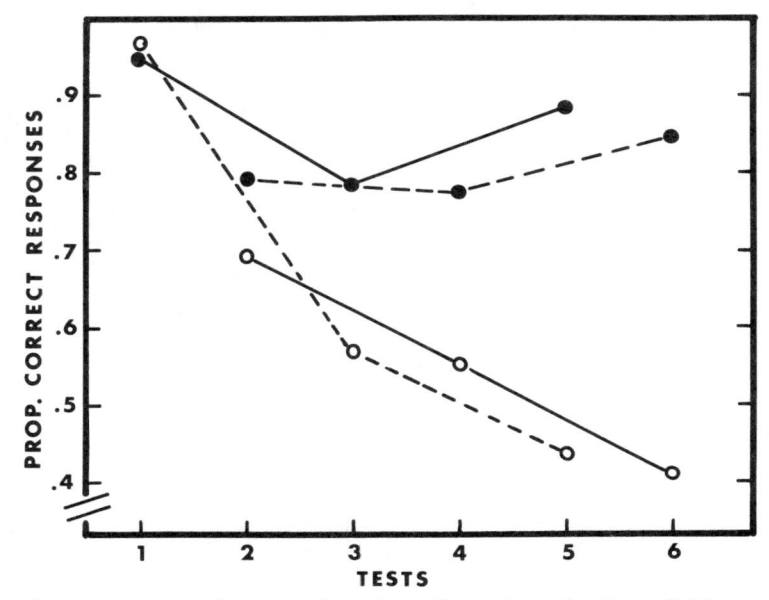

Figure 2.8 Retention as a function of number of prior syllables and length of retention interval (solid circles, 3 sec.; open circles, 18 sec.) for Ss having intervals in the order 3-18-3-18-3-18 (solid lines) and in the reverse order (dotted lines). Experiment 3.

formance does systematically improve as a function of successive tests for short retention intervals.

DISCUSSION

The results of the present experiments give strong support to the presumption that short-term retention of single items and long-term retention of lists of items are subject to the same laws of proactive inhibition. The parallelism of the results for STM and LTM when common variables are manipulated may be briefly summarized.

(1) In LTM, number of potential interfering associations and amount of PI are directly related. The same relationship occurred in Exps. 2 and 3; reasons for the failure of the evidence from Exp. 1 to support the principle were discussed earlier.

(2) Length of retention interval and magnitude of PI are directly related in LTM given a constant amount of interference. This relationship was observed in all experiments except for T-1 in Exps. 2

and 3, where interference was presumed to be low, and degree of learning high.

(3) In LTM, combining the effects of the above two variables leads to an interaction between number of potential interfering associations and length of retention interval. The interaction was clearly apparent in Exp. 3.

(4) In LTM, given constant interference, magnitude of PI decreases as degree of learning of list to be recalled increases. The degree of learning was not systematically manipulated in the present studies. However, since there is no reason to believe that auditory presentation intrinsically gives more PI than visual presentation, it may be inferred that the 2-sec. visual presentation in Exp. 2 produced a higher degree of learning than did the shorter auditory presentation in Exp. 1. Greater forgetting was observed in Exp. 1 than in Exps. 2 and 3. However, this is not a "clean" result, since the degree of learning of potentially interfering items in Exps. 2 and 3 would be higher than that of comparable items in Exp. 1. Nevertheless, the forgetting on T-1 over 18-sec. in Exp. 2 may be taken as an indication that the lower the degree of learning of the item to be recalled the more retention is influenced by proactive interference from sources outside the immediate experimental situation (associations developed in previous experiments or "natural" letter-sequence associations). It is a fact that on T-1 in Exp. 1 the intrusion of letters increased from 5% to 8% to 14% of all letters given for the 3-, 9-, and 18-sec. intervals, respectively. This suggests a recovery over time of interfering associations.

No data on letter intrusions occurring for tests beyond T-1 have been given. The reason for this is simply that by the nature of the designs used it is impossible to isolate variables which may be involved in producing intrusions. In the present studies, time between successive recalls differ; degree of learning of items given previously differ for different intervals; whether or not a previously presented item was correct or incorrect at recall should influence overt intrusions on subsequent items. If systematic laws concerning evocation of letter intrusions are to be derived, experiments must be explicitly designed for the purpose. For these reasons we have not presented intrusion data.

If the conclusion of the present experiments are sound, that is, the conclusion that the laws of proaction are the same for STM as for LTM, some economy in time may be gained by working out further laws of PI on STM rather than on LTM. For example, interitem similarity (e.g., letter duplication) should clearly influence STM. But there is reason to believe that this relationship may be complex. Specifically, in the present results it was noted that many intrusions consisted of a letter from a previous item replacing a letter at recall which occupied the same serial position, e.g., the middle letter. This suggests the operation of an A-B, A-C interference paradigm in which A is the common serial position. Such intrusions also represent the evidence needed to support the notion of spontaneous recovery of extinguished or partially extinguished associations over short intervals. If, however, serial position does constitute a common stimulus from item to item, identical letters in the same position for different items may produce a positive effect—i.e., proactive facilitation may result.

Finally, it may be noted that PI measured with a short recall interval (2 sec.) in LTM may disappear with longer intervals (Underwood, 1950). In all the STM studies reported thus far, recall intervals of from 10 sec. to 14 sec. have been used. A reduction in the time allowed for recall may increase the apparent PI, thus allowing work with higher degree of learning of single items than has been customary. With high degree of learning and long recall intervals (as in Exp. 2), no measurement of forgetting is possible for initial items tested. Very short recall intervals might produce systematic evidence for forgetting for such degrees of learning.

SUMMARY

Three experiments were performed to determine the relationship between certain variables influencing proactive inhibition in long-term retention of lists of verbal items and the influence of these variables on short-term retention of single items. More particularly, retention of single items over 18 sec. should, if the laws of long-term retention are applied, decrease with number of previous items to which S has been exposed. In addition, amount of forgetting should be a direct joint function of number of previous items and length of the retention interval.

In Exp. 1 each S was presented consonant syllables singly, with retention being measured after 3, 9, and 18 sec. Forgetting of the first item presented (T-1) was less than for the second (T-2) or third (T-3) item, but forgetting of the latter (T-2 vs. T-3) did not differ. On all three tests forgetting was directly related to length of retention interval, but no interaction was evident between number of previous items and length of retention interval.

In Exp. 2 a higher degree of initial learning of the items was achieved. Forgetting increased directly as a function of number of previous items presented. The predicted interaction was indeterminate since retention was essentially 100% on T-1 for all retention intervals.

Experiment 3 tested retention of six successive items over 3- and 18-sec. intervals. Retention after 3 sec. showed an initial drop and then a rise over the six tests, the rise suggesting a practice effect. Forgetting over 18 sec. increased directly from T-1 to T-6 and there was no indication that a constant amount of proactive interference had been reached. The interaction between length of retention interval and number of potential proactively interfering items was very evident.

The results were interpreted to mean that proactive inhibition in short-term memory of single items follows the same laws as proactive inhibition in long-term memory of lists of items.

REFERENCES

Briggs, G. E. Acquisition, extinction and recovery functions in retroactive inhibition. *J. exp. Psychol.,* 1954, 47, 285-293.

Melton, A. W. Discussion of Professor Peterson's paper. In C. N. Cofer (Ed.) *Problems and processes in verbal behavior and learning.* New York: McGraw-Hill, 1963.

Murdock, B. B., Jr. The retention of individual items. *J. exp. Psychol.,* 1961, 62, 618-625.

Peterson, L. R. Immediate memory: Data and theory. In C. N. Cofer (Ed.) *Problems and processes in verbal behavior and learning.* New York: McGraw-Hill, 1963.

Peterson, L. R., and Peterson, M. J. Short-term retention of individual verbal items. *J. exp. Psychol.,* 1959, 58, 193-198.

Postman, L. The present status of interference theory. In C. N. Cofer (Ed.) *Verbal learning and verbal behavior.* New York: McGraw-Hill, 1961.

Postman, L. Short-term memory and incidental learning. Paper read at ONR conference, Ann Arbor, Michigan, February, 1962.

Postman, L., and Riley, D. A. Degree of learning and interserial interference in retention. *Univer. Calif. Publ. Psychol.,* 1959, 8, 271-396.

Underwood, B. J. The effect of successive interpolations of retroactive and proactive inhibition. *Psychol. Monogr.,* 1945, 59, No. 3.

Underwood, B. J. Retroactive and proactive inhibition after five and forty-eight hours. *J. exp. Psychol.,* 1948, 38, 29-38.

Underwood, B. J. Proactive inhibition with increased recall time. *Amer. J. Psychol.,* 1950, 63, 594-599.

Underwood, B. J. Interference and forgetting. *Psychol. Rev.,* 1957, 64, 49-60.

Underwood, B. J. and Schulz, R. W. *Meaningfulness and verbal learning.* Philadelphia: Lippincott, 1960.

Degree of Learning and the Measurement of Forgetting

An experimental study of forgetting represents a two-stage experiment; the *S*s must learn a task (first stage) before an interval is introduced, following which retention is measured (second stage). Any two-stage experiment provides the unwary investigator with unusual opportunities for a confounding of the effects of independent variables. Very often in learning research an independent variable is introduced during the first stage to test some hypothesis about its influence on the second stage. For example, variations in the magnitude of food reward may be introduced during acquisition in any animal study to investigate the residual effects of this variable on the rate of extinction or of spontaneous recovery (third stage). If the variable introduced in the first stage influences the rate of change in performance in this stage, a warning about a potential confounding in later stages should be automatic. For in fact, if rate of learning in the first stage differs, final level of performance attained may differ. And, if measurements in the second stage are known to be influenced by the level of learning in the first stage (which is usually the case), differences in the second (or third) stage might be attributed either to level of performance at the end of the first stage or to some other residual effect of the independent variable. It is to this general problem in the study of forgetting that the present paper is addressed. The problem arises in the study of forgetting only if level or degree of learning *does* influence rate of forgetting. That such a relationship exists will be assumed without providing the extensive documentation which is available to support it. Furthermore, a by-product of the data to be presented makes it clear that a very strong positive relationship between degree of learning and retention does obtain.

Benton J. Underwood, "Degree of Learning and the Measurement of Forgetting," *Journal of Verbal Learning and Verbal Behavior* 3 (1964): 112-129. Reprinted with permission.

The present paper is an outgrowth of many discussions and many analyses over the past 10 years. Involved in these discussions have been E. J. Archer, Jack Richardson, R. W. Schulz, W. N. Runquist, Geoffrey Keppel, and Bruce Ekstrand. The latter two have critically read the manuscript and have contributed to the particular analyses presented.

This work was supported by Contract Nonr-1228 (15), Project NR 154-057, between Northwestern University and the Office of Naval Research.

A distinction must be drawn between learning and retention. It is misleading to say only that learning and retention are continuous processes. Of course, it is apparent that on any given trial in a verbal-learning experiment the performance measure includes the retention of the learning which had taken place on previous trials. But to say this, and no more, becomes somewhat absurd in view of the usual procedures for studying forgetting, in view of theories about forgetting, and in view of the facts available concerning the variables which influence forgetting. In studying forgetting, hours or days elapse between any two given trials; in studying learning, the interval between any two trials involves only a few seconds. Theories of forgetting make assertions about processes which occur slowly over time so that they have little if any influence during the short intervals between learning trials but may become of great importance when the interval is, say, 24 hours. Finally, the fact is that there are variables which produce marked differences in rate of learning which have no residual influence over a long retention interval. Thus, we may ask two questions. First, we may ask about the variables which influence the rate at which an association is learned, and second, given an association learned to a given level or degree, we may ask what variables will influence the subsequent performance of that association at a later point in time when no further practice intervenes.

The problem may now be stated more specifically. Suppose a variable is manipulated in a verbal-learning experiment with the intent of determining its influence on retention. Further, assume that the variable—a variable such as meaningfulness—produces a large difference in the rate at which the associations are formed. If an unambiguous answer to the experimental question is to be obtained, the degree of learning attained prior to the introduction of the retention interval must be equivalent for the associations of high and low meaningfulness. What solutions are available to this problem? How does one "make sure" that the differences in retention (if present) can be attributed to the effects of meaningfulness per se rather than to the degree of learning?

Some solutions to this problem have appeared in various sources over the past 10 years (Underwood, 1954; Underwood and Richardson, 1956; 1958; Underwood and Keppel, 1962). However, no single source exists which contains a complete discussion of the techniques available, and of the validity of these techniques. It is clear that an appreciation of the problem is not widespread, since research reports continue to appear which ignore the issues (e.g., Kothurkar, 1963). Furthermore, as theories of forgetting become more explicit, predictions are being made concerning small differences in retention, and it is in the experimental tests of such predictions that the potential confounding of the effects of degree of learning and the predicted effects of some other factor become most acute. There is yet one more reason for a discussion of the degree of learning and retention. There is reason to believe that certain studies in short-term retention are in fact confounding the effects of degree of learning and the effects of other variables. An elaboration of this issue will form the last section of the paper. Initially, attention will be focused on techniques of handling the degree-of-learning problem for studies in long-term memory.

The experimenter has available two alternative procedures for presenting the learning material prior to the introduction of the retention interval. He may present the task for successive trials until some specified criterion of performance is attained, or he may present the material for a constant number of trials (or for a constant period of time). In both cases, by the usual procedures, some continuous measure of learning is available (e.g., number correct on each successive trial). There is a third technique which is still used occasionally (e.g., Ausubel, 1960), but which is completely unanalytical and which disallows any statement as to whether the differences in retention are due to differences in learning or to differences in forgetting or to both. Thus, if two different passages of prose material are given to two different groups to study for an equal period of time, and then measurements are taken 24 hours later, to what are we to attribute differences in these scores? There is no way to analyze the results of such experiments productively; to do so requires both learning and retention measurements.

In the first section attention will be directed toward the results of the procedure wherein a constant number of learning trials is given before the retention interval is introduced.

CONSTANT NUMBER OF TRIALS

Assume a situation in which E gives a constant number of learning trials by the anticipation procedure. For expository purposes of the moment, it will be assumed that only a single list is involved, with the intent being that of measuring precisely the number of items or the percentage of items lost over the retention interval. The question concerns the base measure: exactly how much was learned? The number of items correct on the last anticipation trial is not the appropriate base, for such a measure does not include the learning which occurred on the last trial. The use of alternate study and test trials does not avoid this problem, for most assuredly some change in performance must occur as a consequence of a test trial even without knowledge of the correctness of performance. With either method, a determination needs to be made of the number of correct responses which would have been given had there been another trial.

One obvious solution to the problem is that of using a control group which is given the extra trial. The mean score for this group may then be used as an estimate of the immediate recall. However, such a procedure is wasteful of experimental time and subjects, and should be avoided if possible. Furthermore, the accuracy of the mean prediction by the control-group method is probably no greater than that which would be obtained by simple extrapolation of the acquisition curve for the experimental group. Fortunately, a technique is available by which one can, from the scores of a single group of Ss, predict with great accuracy not only the mean performance of the group on a hypothetical next trial, but also the scores for individual Ss. This latter is of considerable value for statistical purposes. The technique will be called the single-entry projection.

Single-Entry Projection. The objective of this technique is to project the learning curve for each S to the trial beyond the last one actually given, and to obtain, thereby, a score which may be used as an immediate retention score. The scores for an individual S may fluctuate rather widely from trial to trial so that an accurate projection based only on the individual S's data could be considerably in error. It is quite possible that an accurate estimate could be obtained by using the mean of a large number of judges' estimates as to the score to be expected for each S on the next trial, if the judges based these on the performance on all learning trials. We have not attempted this. Rather, scores for individual Ss are predicted from the pooled data of all Ss. At the risk of being pedantic, a detailed illustration will be given of the steps involved in single-entry projection.

The list learned consisted of six paired associates in which the stimulus terms were common words, the response terms low-meaningful trigrams. The 54 Ss were given a total of 15 trials, but to illustrate the method, it will be assumed that only six trials were given. Thus, predicting to a "next trial" in this case may then be checked against the actual scores attained on the seventh trial.

The logic of the procedure is simply that of using the first *five* trials to ascertain the history of the learning of individual items and to relate this history

Proactive Interference

Table 2.1 Results of the Initial Step in the Single-Entry Projection (see text for complete explanation)

Number Correct, Trials 1–5	Number Items	Number Correct on Trial 6	% Correct on Trial 6
0	204	18	8.8
1	46	27	58.7
2	22	13	59.1
3	23	20	87.0
4	18	17	94.4
5	11	10	90.9

to performance on the item for the sixth trial. A tally is made of the number of times each item was given correctly on the first five trials and whether or not it was correct on the sixth. In the present illustration there are 54 Ss and six items per S, or a total of 324 entries to be made. Each item becomes a single entry as opposed to a multiple entry, the latter procedure forming the basis for another technique to be discussed later.

Table 2.1 gives the results of the initial step. It will be noted that there were 204 instances in which an item had not been correctly anticipated at all on Trials 1–5. Of these, 18 became correct on the sixth trial, which is 8.8%. In only 11 instances was an item given correctly on all five trials and 90.9% of these were correct on the sixth.

The next step is to make predictions for the seventh trial, using the information obtained on Trials 1–6. The data of Table 2.1 indicate the increase in the probability that an item will be correct on a given trial (sixth) as a function of the number of times it has been given correctly prior to that trial. This relationship is assumed to be an orderly growth function. Therefore, a smooth curve is drawn by inspection, being guided in part by the number of cases (items) determining each empirical point. Such a curve is shown in Fig. 2.9, based on the data of Table 2.1. From this curve values are obtained to be used in predicting scores for the seventh trial. It should be noted that the data of Table 2.1 cannot give a value for an item given correctly six times on Trials 1–6. Since some items are likely to be given six times when Trial 6 is included, the value is obtained by projecting the growth curve as if there had been items having had six correct anticipations. From Fig. 2.9 we estimate that on the seventh trial 99% of the items having been given six correct times on Trials 1–6 would be correct on the seventh trial. Looking at the smooth curve, it may be expected that on Trial 7 the percentages would be 9, 49, 70, 82, 92, 96 and 99, for 0 through 6 correct anticipations, respectively.

In deriving predicted scores for individual Ss—estimates of the number of items each S would have gotten correct had there been a seventh trial—the assumption is made that the proportion of items correct on the seventh trial for each category (0, 1, 2, 3, 4, 5, and 6 correct anticipations) will be the same on

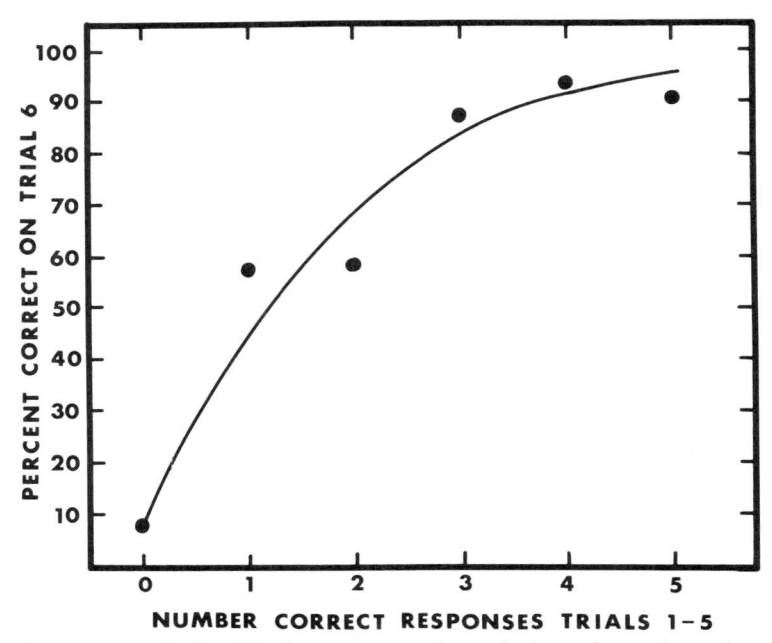

Figure 2.9 Relationship between number of times items have been correctly anticipated and the percentage correct on immediately succeeding trial.

this trial as it was on the sixth trial for each category. As will be pointed out later, this assumption will result in a slight error, but for the moment this may be ignored. By use of the method worked out by Richardson (Richardson and Underwood, 1957), obtaining the expected score for a single S may be illustrated. This S failed to give any correct responses during the first six trials for four of the six items. For each of these items the probability of being correct on Trial 7 is 0.09, so for the four items the summed probability is 0.36. One item was given once correctly on the first six trials; the probability of this item being correct on Trial 7 is 0.49. The sixth item was given correctly three times; the probability of this item being correct on Trial 7 is 0.82. Summing all the six probabilities, one for each item, gives a value of 1.67. This is to say that for this S a prediction is made that 1.67 items will be correct on the seventh trial (S actually got two correct). Since scoring is in fact done only by whole numbers (an item is either right or wrong), there may appear to be a certain amount of nonsense in making a prediction that 1.67 items will be correct. But, we may ignore this and see what in fact happened when predicted and obtained scores are evaluated for all Ss.

For these 54 Ss, the mean predicted score for Trial 7 was 2.21 items; the actual mean number obtained on Trial 7 was 2.26. Across the 54 Ss the product-moment correlation between predicted and obtained scores was 0.85. The method appears to work fairly well.

We may next examine the generality of the single-entry projection technique by testing it for three different learning tasks at three different points in learning for each. Also included will be the prediction for the trial beyond the last one actually given, together with the recall after 24 hours. Thus, an examination may be made of the correlation between predicted scores and the recall scores obtained after 24 hours.

The first set of data comes from the learning of the six-item paired-associate list used for the illustration above. Predictions were made for Trials 4, 7, 11, and for an hypothetical 16th trial. In Table 2.2 these data are labeled PA Trigrams. A second set of data was based on 48 Ss given eight paired associates consisting of nonsense syllables as stimuli and adjectives as responses, presented for 12 anticipation trials (Underwood and Schulz, 1961). Predictions were made for Trials 4, 6, 9, and the hypothetical 13 trial. These data are labeled PA Adjectives in Table 2.2. The third set of data comes from serial lists of 10 high meaningful-low similarity nonsense syllables (Underwood and Richardson, 1958). The list was presented for 30 trials to 50 Ss. Predictions have been made for Trials 7, 14, 24, and the hypothetical 31st trial. In Table 2.2 these data are labeled Serial.

Several characteristics of the data of Table 2.2 need examination, not only as a means of describing the outcome of single-entry

Table 2.2 Predicted and Obtained Values Obtained by the Single-Entry Projection Technique for Three Different Tasks at Three Points in the Course of Learning, and for Hypothetical Next Trial (in Quotation Marks) and Recall after 24 Hours

	Trial	Predicted M	Predicted σ	Obtained M	Obtained σ	$r_{pred.-obt.}$
PA trigrams	4	1.34	0.69	1.33	1.16	0.76
	7	2.21	1.06	2.26	1.51	0.85
	11	3.13	1.35	3.13	1.71	0.81
	"16"	4.03	1.25	3.24	1.72	0.74
PA adjectives	4	4.74	1.34	4.63	1.96	0.81
	6	5.64	1.39	5.48	2.13	0.91
	9	6.06	1.40	5.88	2.13	0.85
	"13"	6.66	1.33	5.58	1.65	0.81
Serial	7	5.68	1.38	5.42	1.95	0.69
	14	6.90	1.24	7.04	2.02	0.76
	24	9.07	0.80	8.74	1.82	0.68
	"31"	9.30	0.59	8.32	1.94	0.78

projection, but also as a means of pointing out certain characteristics of retention. First, how accurate are the predictions? For the PA Trigrams, the biggest discrepancy is 0.05 mean items, this being on Trial 7. For the PA Adjectives, the predicted values are consistently slightly higher than the obtained values, and although none of these approaches statistical significance, a bias is probably present. For the Serial, two of the three predicted means are higher than the obtained, but again none is significant statistically.

It will be noted that the variability of the predicted values is always less than that of the obtained. This is an inevitable consequence of the technique. Predictions for a given S can never be zero, but S may in fact obtain zero correct. It would be a rare situation in which the prediction would be made that a given S will get all items correct, but in fact this occurs. Thus the range of predicted scores must necessarily be less than the obtained.

The correlations between predicted and obtained scores are given in the last column. In view of the fact that in all tests many of the Ss had the same obtained scores, these correlations must be considered quite satisfactory. They are generally lower for the serial list than for the paired-associate lists, which probably reflects the greater variability in the obtained scores from trial to trial in this particular serial-learning task than in the paired-associate tasks used.

Finally, attention is directed to the last row for each set of material. The difference between the predicted and obtained scores indicates the mean number of items lost over 24 hours. For the three materials in order, these losses are 0.79, 1.08, and 0.98. In terms of percentages, the amounts retained are 80, 84, and 89%, respectively. The correlations represent the relationship between predicted and obtained scores, the latter being observed 24 hours following learning. Across all materials, these correlations are not appreciably lower than those obtained between predicted and obtained performance between successive learning trials. Thus, these correlations indicate a high relation between degree of learning attained on a constant number of trials and recall. This in turn must mean that characteristics of the S, other than those involved in producing differences in degree of learning, are of relatively minor importance in forgetting.

The Source of Bias. As indicated earlier, the single-entry projection technique may be expected to give a slight overestimation of the expected scores. The reason for this may be seen by following through the steps of the technique and their implications.

1. Items of equivalent difficulty are grouped together. Generally speaking, this grouping of items also groups Ss in terms of learning rate. Fast-learning Ss contribute more items to the categories consis-

ting of a high number of previously correct responses than do slow-learning Ss. Projections for a given S are made from data obtained from other Ss very much like him (but not identical) in learning ability.

2. Projections for a given item for a given S are based upon items which on the average are slightly less difficult than the item for which the prediction is being made and upon the performance of Ss who are slightly more rapid learners. For example, to return to the original illustration, we use the category of four correct responses obtained in five trials to predict for items which had received four correct responses in six trials when we predict to the seventh. An item gotten correctly four times in five trials must be slightly easier than one given four times in six trials; or, the former was obtained by slightly more rapid-learning Ss than the latter, or both. Thus, the projections will be expected to slightly overestimate the obtained.

In the data given in Table 2.2 these overestimations have not proven serious. However, it is known (Underwood and Keppel, 1962) that if the items within the list are very heterogeneous in difficulty, this overestimation can become serious. If this situation arises, it can be handled by doing a separate tally for each item and then using these values as the basis for predictions, rather than pooling all items together. If the question is asked as how one tells whether or not the heterogeneity of difficulty may produce trouble, the answer is that an analysis can be made on earlier trials to determine whether or not the projections are overestimating seriously. The most sensitive point at which to make such a test is early in learning (Underwood and Keppel, 1962), before many items have been correctly anticipated. If the problem does not prove serious at that point, it will not be serious at a later point in learning.

Asymptotic Probabilities. After a list is presented for learning for several trials, some or many of the items will reach an asymptote; the probability of being correct on each successive trial will be at 1.0 or slightly below. Some of the items may have just reached this level, others may have been at this level for several trials. The point to be made by these observations is that under such circumstances the predictions from trial to trial in learning will be equal for all such items (presumably indicating equal associative strength), but a test of retention will in fact show that they are not equal in recall probabilities. This point will be illustrated by using the PA Adjectives referred to in Table 2.2. The data of Table 2.2 are based on naive Ss learning their first list in a laboratory. In this experiment, they subsequently learned three additional lists with retention of the fourth list being taken after 24 hours, just as was the first list.

Since the lists were counterbalanced, the items reaching asymptote should be the same for the first and fourth list. In this study, interlist stimulus similarity built up across lists so that retention of the fourth list should be more influenced by proactive inhibition than should the first list.

In the upper part of Fig. 2.10 the probability of being correct on the next trial following 8, 9, 10, 11, and 12 correct anticipations is given. For 8 through 11 the values are empirical; for 12, it is estimated at 0.99. These two curves are considered asymptotic. The two lower curves show the per cent recalled after 24 hours for each list. It is quite clear that the learning measure does not differentiate the recall performance, whereas the number of times an item has been given at asymptote does. The point to be made by such data is that when learning performance is at or near asymptote, one cannot

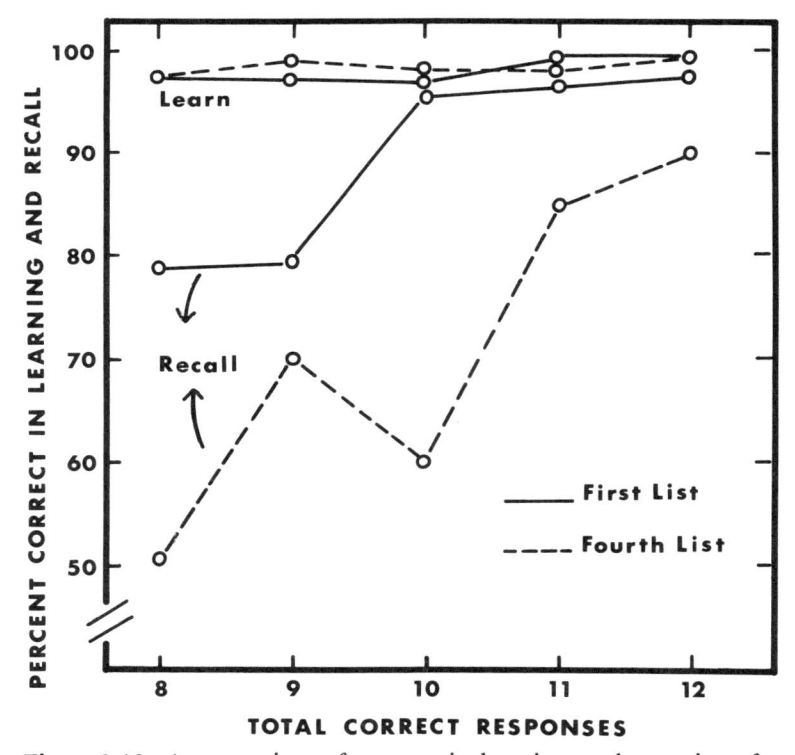

Figure 2.10 Asymptotic performance in learning, and retention after 24 hours as a function of number of correct anticipations after reaching asymptote for a list with low interlist interference (first list) and for one with high interlist interference (fourth list).

infer that effective recall strength after a period of time has elapsed is also equivalent. It is most reasonable to assume that the response measure for learning cannot reflect the increased strength of association which occurs with repetitions at or near a probability of 1.0, and that in effect "true" learning is greater than 1.0. For the present paper, the facts of Fig. 2.10 have two implications, one dealing with the use of the single-entry projection technique, and the other with short-term memory studies. The first implication will be discussed now, the second in a later section.

Comparison of Lists Learned at Different Rates. The problem stated in the introduction to the paper concerned the measurement of retention for materials or tasks learned at different rates. For example, if meaningfulness is manipulated, learning rate may be expected to vary. How, then, can we assure ourselves that degree of learning before the retention interval is equivalent so that retention measures can be compared without fear of confounding? For the present, the solution centers around the constant-trial method of presenting the learning materials.

Supposing that two lists of widely different difficulty were presented for learning for the same number of trials. For each list a single-entry projection could be made for each S, and we could test the difference in loss scores for the two groups over a retention interval. Or better, we might prefer to get a per cent loss for each S and test the significance of the difference of the two distributions of per cent losses. Is the interpretation clear? Can the differences in amount lost (if found) be attributed to differences in the material over and above differences in degree of learning? Probably not. In the first place, the average degree of learning for the two groups of Ss would differ markedly. If the group of Ss with the difficult list (showing the lower degree of learning) also forgot more than the Ss learning the other list, this might well be due to the fact that forgetting is greater with low degrees of learning than with high degrees. Secondly, very likely some of the items for the faster-learning Ss learning the less difficult list will have been at asymptote for several trials and we know that our measure of learning is insensitive to strength differences for such items.

One possible solution is to test retention for items in the two lists which had equivalent probabilities and these probabilities are below the asymptotic level. Thus, as had been done in some studies (e.g., Underwood and Richardson, 1958), double baselines on a graph could be constructed so that equal projected probabilities are equivalent for the items from the two lists. A graphical representation of the recall percentages will show whether or not there are systematic differences in retention. However, if the lists differ widely in difficulty, it seems clear that we are testing neither equivalent S samples nor a reasonable sample of the items in the two lists. For, we would in fact be comparing retention of slower learners of the difficult items in the easy list with the rapid learners of the easier items in the difficult list. Such a selective comparison does not give generality to the retention test.

The most adequate solution to the problem is that of giving a different number of trials on the two lists such that the mean level of learning attained is essentially equal for the two lists and with but few items attaining asymptote. The number of trials which needs to be given to produce this rough equation could be worked out in a pilot study. And it should be emphasized that the equation in terms of level attained need only be approximate. Under such circumstances, the mean projected values for the two groups should be roughly equivalent and any small mean difference in degree of learning cannot be of great concern. Given this situation, then, one may use the graphical solution with the dual baseline or statistically determine the percent loss for each S and thence the mean difference between the two distributions of losses. The graphical procedure gives evidence on the retention of items of the two lists at all degrees of learning within each list, but, as far as is known, there is no statistical test that can be applied. The loss-score technique gives a statistical test of the forgetting, but does not sort out the scores according to degree of learning.

It was noted above that the amount of learning given the easy and difficult list should be such that few if any items in either list attain asymptote. The reason for this is that at asymptote items in both lists will have equal probability values (although in fact the asymptote for the difficult list is likely to be a little lower than that for the easy list), but it is unlikely that they can be considered equal in associative strength (see Fig. 2.10). However, assume that we wished to study retention of items in the two lists which were overlearned. More particularly, assume that we give an item from the easy list five additional trials after reaching asymptote and do the same for a difficult item. Can we make a comparison of these two items at recall and conclude that any differences which occur are due to a factor other than differences in degree of learning? This does not seem possible, for the assumption is made that five trials at asymptote yield equivalent amounts of associative strength for the easy and difficult item. Since an equivalent number of correct anticipations below asymptote was not associated with an equal change in probability of being correct, there is no reason why the facts should change once asymptote is reached. In a manner of speaking, the easy item should grow more above the maximally measurable strength (100%) than should the difficult item. This may be conceptualized as in Fig. 2.11. Here, the associative growth is shown for an easy and a difficult item up to asymptote and then five additional trials are given beyond asymptote with the assumption that on these trials each item will be correctly anticipated essentially 100% of the time. The difference in the "true" associative growth, however, may be described by extrapolating the growth function which was observed below asymptote. When these curves are extrapolated for the five additional trials it becomes apparent that the strength of the two items are far from equal at the termination of the five trials beyond asymptote. While these projections are not measureable, it seems clear that something like this may occur.

We have no solution to this problem of measuring differences in retention for materials of wide differences in difficulty when the typical or average item in each list has been carried beyond asymptote. We have no solution because we do not have measuring techniques which tell us that the "true" associative strength of the items are equivalent. Only when these items are below asymptote can comparisons be made with confidence that degree of learning is equated.

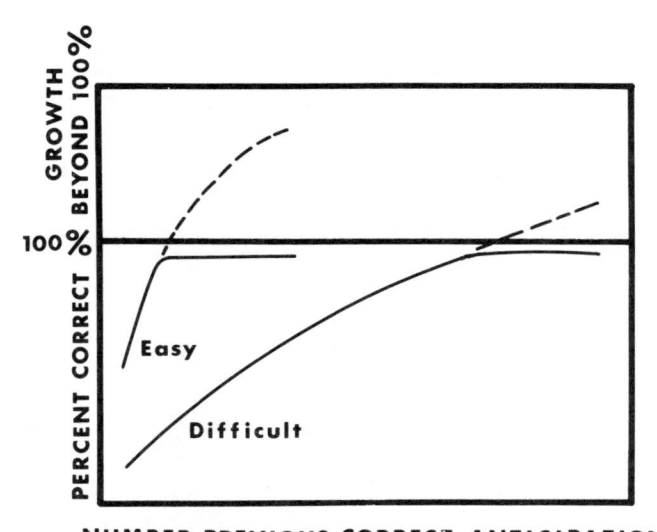

Figure 2.11 Hypothetical growth of degree of learning beyond 100% as a function of continued trials after reaching asymptote for easy and difficult items.

It should be pointed out that the failure of the present writer to recognize the seriousness of this problem probably led to an erroneous conclusion in an earlier article (Underwood and Richardson, 1955). In this study very difficult lists were learned by massed and by distributed practice. The group given distributed practice learned to a criterion a great deal more rapidly than did the group given massed practice (20 trials versus 33 trials). After 24 hours, retention of the list learned by massed practice was significantly better than that learned by distributed practice, with most of the effect being due to the high retention of the slow-learning Ss in the massed group. It seems highly probable that this difference is a product of the asymptotic artifact. The slow learning Ss, under massed practice, had some items which reached asymptote early in learning and these items were then repeated on trial after trial as S endeavored to learn the other items in the list. The Ss under distributed practice, learning in many fewer trials, would have few if any items which had been repeated at asymptote for many trials as had the slow-learning Ss given the massed practice. It should be clear that if the same list, learned under the same conditions by different groups, is given varying number of trials beyond asymptote, any differences in retention must be attributed to the differences in overlearning, and clearly the expected differences are found (e.g., Postman, 1962; Underwood and Keppel, 1963). The problem we have been unable to solve concerns analytical measurements of retention differences for materials carried beyond the asymptotic level when the rate of reaching the asymptote differs appreciably.

Possible Variations on Single-Entry Projections. The derivation of projected scores by the single-entry technique can be done without great labor. Although in our illustrations of the method given earlier we have used an appreciable number of Ss for each determination, fairly adequate stability can be achieved with as few as 20 Ss if the number of learning trials involved is not too great. Nevertheless, we might well ask if there are not easier methods to accomplish the same ends. We have not discovered such. One of the methods investigated was that of using total correct responses for each S as the entry, rather than an entry for each item. Thus, the basic plot relates total correct responses on a given number of trials to the number correct on the following trial. Several plots with different lists show that all produce a linear function between the two measures. However, when such a relationship is used to derive values to predict the following trial, overestimation occurs and is significant statistically. This is to say that the mean projected score for the group of Ss is significantly higher than the obtained. The correlations between predicted and obtained are only slightly lower than those found for the single-entry projection. Apparently, the predictive base is simply too gross and reflects a compounding of the bias discussed earlier for the single-entry technique. A comparison of the two methods applied to the same set of data will illustrate the above.

We had available data on 216 Ss learning a nine-item paired associate list for 10 trials. As a test, we derived projected scores for the sixth trial by the two methods (total correct and single entry). The single-entry technique predicted 4.63 mean items correct, the total-correct base predicted 5.03. The actual number attained was 4.53. The product-moment correlation between predicted and obtained was 0.79 for the single-entry, and 0.78 for the total correct as a predictive base. Tests on two other sets of data gave comparable results. We must conclude that the total-correct technique cannot be used if mean predictive accuracy is an objective.

The general conclusion is that the single-entry projection technique provides a highly accurate method of predicting performance beyond the trial actually given in learning. It may, therefore, be used as a method for predicting the amount of learning which occurred prior to the introduction of a retention interval. The method does not solve the problem of measuring retention following asymptotic performance of lists learned at different rates, if the intent is to separate effects due to degree of learning and effects attributable to other variables.

CRITERION PERFORMANCE

It has been quite common in studies of retention to present the learning material over and over until the S attains some given level of performance, such as one perfect trial. If lists of different difficulty are given to Ss until a common criterion of performance is reached, it has often been assumed that degree of learning was equivalent and that, therefore, differences in retention reflect the effect of some other variable. This assumption cannot be justified. Logically, we must expect that when acquisition curves approach a common criterion at different rates, and the learning is stopped at this criterion, the projection of the curves for one additional trial cannot result in equivalent performances. This will be illustrated by presenting the results of an experiment using the criterion technique.

An Experimental Illustration

Purpose. A test of an hypothesis about differential effects of extra-experimental sources of interference was recently published (Underwood and Keppel, 1963). More particularly, this experiment tested the letter-sequence hypothesis (Underwood and Postman, 1961). In devising this test, two paired-associate lists were constructed of single-letter stimuli and single-letter responses, the lists differing in terms of the initial associative strength of the letters of each pair. The hypothesis predicted that the list with the lower initial associative strength would show the most rapid forgetting.

The results of this experiment failed to confirm the hypothesis: no difference in retention of the two lists was observed. A perceptive critic pointed out that perhaps the hypothesis was not given a definitive test because the differences in the initial associative strength between the two lists was not high. The observation concerning the lack of large differences in initial associative strength was correct, and while highly significant differences in learning occurred, it remained a possibility that the hypothesis would receive some support with wider differences in initial associative strength. Our failure to use wider differences initially was determined by the criteria set for the lists, namely, no duplication of letters within a list and not to use pairs which formed two-letter words. In the present experiments, in order to have wide initial differences in the associations between the letters of a pair, two duplicated letters were used within each list.

Method. The high-association list (HA List) consisted of the following nine pairs: B-A, Q-U, X-I, J-P, U-T, E-N, W-O, V-D, and I-M. The low-association list (LA List) consisted of the following pairs: B-J, Q-C, X-F, J-H, U-A, E-Q, W-P, V-K, and I-G. It will be noted that the stimulus letters in both lists are identical. The letter-association norms (Underwood and Schulz, 1960) show a mean value of 0.4 for the LA List, and 37.9 for the HA List. In the previous study, the LA List was essentially the same as here but the HA List had a mean value of approximately 9. It is clear, therefore, that according to the norms, the present lists have a much wider difference in level of initial associative connection between the letters of each pair than had the previous lists. Two experimental groups (E Groups) and two control groups (C Groups) were used, each consisting of 20 Ss, naive to verbal learning except for five trials on a practice list as used in the previous study. One C Group and one E Group was given each list. Both E Groups learned their respective lists until a criterion of six correct responses on a single trial was achieved. These Ss returned 24-hours later and were given 5 relearning trials. The two C Groups were also presented the list until a criterion of six correct responses had been achieved on a single trial and then one additional trial was given. This additional trial was given without any intervening instructions (Underwood and Keppel, 1962) and the scores on this trial are, of course, to be used as an estimate of the amount which the E Groups would have gotten had another trial been given. Since the rate of presenting the pairs was 1.5:1 sec, the immediate recall interval was 2.5 sec.

Results. In learning to the criterion the C and E Groups did not differ for a given list. Combining the scores, therefore, gives a mean of 9.50 trials to learn the LA List and 2.55 trials to learn the HA List to the criterion of six correct. It is apparent that the differences in initial associative strength produced a very large difference in rate of learning. Of the 40 Ss presented the HA List, 14 reached the criterion on the first anticipation trial. It would seem therefore, that the situation is ideal for an extreme test of the letter-sequence hypothesis; for the hypothesis to receive support, there must be greater forgetting for the LA List than for the HA List.

Attention will first be directed to the recall scores for the two E Groups; 5.65 mean items were recalled for the HA List, and 4.30 for the LA List. The difference (1.35 ± 0.50) gives a t of 2.70, significant beyond the 1% level of significance. Thus, looking only at the scores for these two groups it might be concluded that the HA List has shown less rapid forgetting than the LA List and therefore, that the hypothesis being tested is given support. However, such a conclusion is incorrect. For, the recall of the E Groups can only be considered in conjunction with the immediate recall of the C Groups. The C Group having the LA List obtained 5.35 mean items on the trial after achieving the criterion, the C Group having the HA List obtained 7.20 mean items. This difference is also highly significant (t = 4.87), and indicates that the slopes of the acquisition curves differed so greatly that stopping both E Groups after achieving a common criterion did not result in an equal degree of learning.

Of course, the most appropriate analysis is to apply a 2 × 2 analysis of variance to the recall scores of the four groups, with C-E one variable, and LA and HA as the other. Figure 2.12 shows these scores. If there is differential forgetting, the interaction term must be significant. The F for interaction was 1.25, which is far from significant. It must be concluded that rate of forgetting of the two lists does not differ and that, as in the previous study, the letter-sequence hypothesis receives no support.

The above data indicate that when lists of different difficulty are carried to the same criterion, it cannot be assumed that degree of learning is equal. Generally speaking, the greater the difference in rate at which two lists approach a common criterion, the greater the difference in the inequality of degree of learning. In the above study we had "protected" ourselves against this contingency by using the C Groups given the extra trial. The question we now ask, however, is whether or not there is a technique by which one may project expected performance to a hypothetical next trial after a

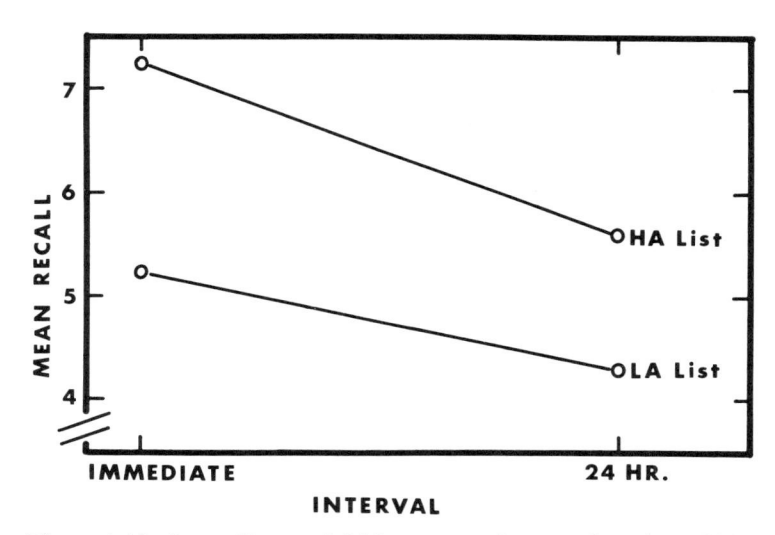

Figure 2.12 Immediate and 24-hour retention as a function of high (HA List) and low (LA List) initial associative connection between stimulus and response terms for lists carried to a criterion of six correct out of nine possible.

criterion is reached and thereby avoid the necessity of using control groups.

It should be first noted that the single-entry technique is quite inappropriate to the situation where all Ss are taken to the same criterion of performance. If the criterion of performance established is all items correct on a single trial, the single-entry technique must necessarily give an expected probability of 1.0 for all items regardless of number of times previously given correctly, since all items are correct on the criterial trial. If the criterion is less than all items correct, the single-entry technique must also produce overestimation to the subsequent trial, since criterion performance at any level represents atypical performance at the moment, atypical in the sense that the level of performance is greater than would be predicted by knowledge of the performance on either the previous or subsequent trial. Therefore, the single-entry technique must produce probability estimates for each item which are too high. For example, using the single-entry technique on the C Group given the LA List in the experiment above, produced a mean estimate for the postcriterial trial of 6.66 items, whereas in fact the mean obtained was 5.35, and the difference between these means is highly significant ($t = 3.45$). We see no way in which the single-entry technique can be adapted adequately for making projections when performance has been carried to a common criterion. However, another technique, to be called the multiple-entry technique, can be used.

Multiple-Entry Projections. This procedure was used in the first attempt to make projections (Underwood, 1954). Again, all Ss and items are pooled. Each item given more than once correctly produces multiple entries, the number of such entries always being one less than the total number of correct anticipations. Actually, the complete history of each item in learning for each S is entered on the tally sheet. The tallies indicate "what happened" (correct or incorrect) on the trial after the item was first correctly anticipated, what happened on the trial after it had been anticipated correctly twice, and so on. The histories of all items are then merged so that there is a composite percentage correct after the first correct anticipation, after two correct anticipations, after three, and so on. The number of instances on which successive percentages are based will decrease as the number of prior correct anticipations increase. For example, all items, except those first given correctly on the criterial trial, enter into the determination of the percentage correct on the trial after a single correct anticipation, but there will be fewer cases to determine what happened after two correct anticipations since those items correctly anticipated only once before the criterial trial will not enter into the determination. Finally, it may be noted that if the criterion of performance is less than all items correct, a percentage can be calculated for items not given correctly prior to the criterion level. However, for reasons noted earlier, this value is likely to be an overestimate of items never gotten correctly (including criterial trial) in projecting to the post-criterion trial, and should be given little weight in drawing the function relating number of correct anticipations and percentages correct.

The "growth" functions from such analyses, functions which relate the number of times items have been correctly anticipated and the probability of being correct on the immediately following trial, will differ as a function of the difficulty of the material. The rate of change per correct anticipation will be less for a difficult item (as a composite of a difficult list) than for an easy item. A further consideration of such a function will make it clear that all Ss are represented in the determinations for the early section of the curve (what happened after only a few correct anticipations) but that only the slow-learning Ss (those that require many trials to attain the criterion) will be represented in the latter portions of the function.

From the smoothed curve for the learning of any given list, we again may read off the expected values for one additional trial beyond the criterion trial for each category (once correct, twice correct, and so on). Thus, the probability of an item being given correctly on the post-criterial trial having been given correctly three times is determined from the curve for all items having been given at least three times correctly prior to the criterial trial. At this point we may handle the data in either of the two ways discussed for the single-entry technique. For two (or more) lists learned at different rates we may construct dual baselines so that expected probabilities are equivalent at any point along the baseline. The percentage recall for each category may then be plotted. Or, as the second method, we may get a projected score for each S in the manner described earlier and then use direct loss measures or percentage loss measures for each S.

We ask next about the accuracy of the predictions by the multiple-entry projection. Three different sets of data will be considered. First, in the experiment reported earlier, the multiple-entry technique has been used for the C group learning the LA List. Since these Ss had one trial beyond the criterial trial, the accuracy of the prediction can be assessed. The predicted score was 5.67 mean items, the obtained, 5.35. The difference (0.32 ± 0.41) gives a t of 0.78. The correlation between predicted scores and obtained scores for the 20 Ss was −0.51. This means that there is a tendency toward predicting that the slow-learning Ss will get more items correct on the post-criterial trial than will fast-learning Ss. It will be remembered that for the single-entry technique, correlations were high and positive. Therefore, it is clear that there is a difference in the outcome of the two techniques with regard to predicting individual scores. As will be seen, as a general finding the correlations do not differ appreciably from zero for the multiple-entry technique.

The reason for the failure of the multiple-entry technique to predict individual scores is fairly apparent. Predictions are made upon essentially an average probability of all Ss involved in a given category. By use of this average, probabilities for fast-learning Ss are lowered, those for slow-learning Ss raised.

A second set of data consisted of paired adjectives. These data were collected by Runquist (1957), and we used 50 of his control Ss. The list contained eight pairs; Runquist carried the learning two trials beyond the criterion of all items correct on a single trial. The first analysis was made for the trial following that on which all Ss first achieved four correct responses on a single trial. The predicted mean was 4.24, the obtained, 3.92. The overestimation is a little larger than usual but is not significant statistically (t = 1.51). The correlation between the 50 predicted scores and the 50 obtained was 0.07. The next analysis was made for the trial following that on which all terms were first anticipated correctly. The mean number predicted was 6.95, the mean number attained, 7.00. In this case the predicted mean was slightly lower than the obtained. The correlation between predicted and obtained was 0.12.

As a further test of the multiple-entry technique, projections were made for a five-item list in which the response terms were fairly difficult trigrams, the stimuli, names of colors. There were 35 Ss and predictions were made to the next trial following the trial on which all items were first correctly anticipated. The predicted mean was 4.06, the obtained 4.17, with the correlation between predicted and obtained being .10.

With another five-item list, in which response-term interference from a previously learned list was heavy, significant overestimations occurred for the 50 Ss. This was true for the trial after four items were first correct and for the trial after all five items were first correct. The overestimation appears to result from the wide differences in difficulty among the items, although this cannot be determined with certainty. In any event, when a separate function was derived for each item independently, the overestimation fell to a value that was far from significant. Thus, it appears that just as in the case of the single-entry technique, a prediction for the pooled items should be made initially at a lower level of learning than the level for which the next-trial prediction is critical, and thus assess the adequacy of the predictions for the particular material involved.

Generally speaking, the multiple-entry procedure produces predictions for mean performance with some accuracy. It is useless if individual predictions are of interest. The problem produced by asymptotic performance is the same as discussed for the single-entry technique. If a high criterion of performance is set, and if the intent is to compare retention of lists learned at different rates, the response measures at asymptote will not reflect differences in degree of learning although these may in fact exist. The expectation would be that the list learned most slowly will have some items which have been repeated at an asymptotic level many times. This will be less likely to occur with the easy list since the criterion is reached quickly. In such cases, the dual-baseline method of exhibiting the data has the advantage that comparisons can be made only for items which have not reached asymptote.

Evaluation of the Two Methods. It has been shown that both the single-entry technique and the multiple-entry technique predict with a fairly high accuracy the mean performance of a group of Ss beyond the trial at which learning was terminated. These values may then be used as the basis for determining amount forgotten. The advantage of the single-entry technique is that predictions for individual Ss have considerable accuracy. Indeed, all things considered, there seems to be little justification for using a criterion of performance to set the degree of learning before a retention interval. Rather, in all except special cases, it seems most reasonable to use the constant-trials procedure. If materials of appreciably different difficulty are to be compared for forgetting, the mean correct responses at the end of learning should be approximately equal. This can be determined roughly by the small number of pilot Ss to determine the acquisition curves for both types of material. Then a constant number of trials can be set, differing for each material, such that the mean number of items attained for both lists is roughly equivalent at the termination of learning. The equation need be only rough since the projected scores will be the critical learning measure, and any small difference in *mean* projected scores for the two tasks cannot produce any serious distortion in measures of retention, since the critical measure is the difference in the differences between the predicted and obtained for the two lists.

One final matter, relevant to both techniques, should be pointed out. Even if the projections overestimate for certain tasks, if the amount of overestimation is equivalent for the two or more tasks to be compared at recall, no bias will result. Of course, the absolute amount of forgetting will be overestimated, by as much as the projections overestimate.

The intent of the entire above discussion has been toward a refinement of measures of forgetting. Whenever materials differing in difficulty are to be compared for rate of forgetting, either such techniques as discussed here, or others which will accomplish the same end, seem mandatory if an adequate assessment is to be made of the variables which influence retention unconfounded by differences in degree of learning.

SHORT-TERM RETENTION AND DEGREE OF LEARNING

In the discussion above, it was pointed out that when percentages or probabilities are used as a measure of associative strength, these measures become insensitive to differences in true degree of learning when the performance is at or near asymptote. It was shown in Fig. 2.10 that items which were equal in strength by a probability or percentage measure at asymptote, differed very considerably in recall after 24 hours. When proactive interference was heavy, the discrepancy between the learning measure and the recall performance was most marked.

In concluding this paper the point will be made that very probably certain studies in short-term memory are confounding degree of learning with other variables and are reaching erroneous conclusions concerning the effects of these other variables. Two sets of data will be examined in order to give the problem a clear statement.

The first consists of two conditions from a study by Murdock (1961). Following the procedures of the original Peterson and Peterson (1959) study on retention of a single three-letter unit, Murdock presented either a single monosyllabic word or a triad of monosyllabic words, with retention being measured over several intervals up to 18 sec. In these procedures, just as in long-term retention studies using lists, there is a learning period prior to the introduction of the retention interval. For learning, Murdock apparently spoke the single word to S within a 1-sec interval, and also the triads within the same-length period so that learning time for both materials was constant. It is apparently assumed that degree of learning for the two materials is equivalent since the study time was equivalent. Therefore, the fact that retention tests showed wide differences (more rapid forgetting of the triads) was interpreted by Murdock to mean that something about the number of elements (words) making up the item is the significant variable producing the differences in forgetting over the retention interval.

As a second set of data, the results of a study by Melton, Crowder, and Wulff (as reported by Melton, 1963) will be considered. In five different conditions, either 1, 2, 3, 4, or 5 consonants were presented, with retention measurements taken after intervals up to 32 sec. Thus, the retention of a single consonant such as J, was compared with that of a unit such as JPRQS. The unit, regardless of size, was presented visually for 1 sec, and read aloud by S. The results show that rate of forgetting was directly related to the number of consonants in the unit. When the unit was a single consonant, only slight forgetting was obtained; when five consonants made up the unit, forgetting was essentially complete after 32 sec. Melton interprets these results as being due to intra-unit interference, this interference increasing as the number of elements increases. Intra-unit interference is said to be a major factor in short-term forgetting.

With great insistence it must be maintained that such studies confound degree of learning as a variable in retention with variables intrinsic to the differences in the materials (e.g., number of elements in the unit). To attribute differences in retention to these latter variables commits the same error as has been discussed in relation to studies of long-term retention above. This evaluation will be elaborated upon by a series of points.

(1) It was noted earlier that it seems necessary in studies of long-term memory to maintain a distinction between learning and retention, both operationally and theoretically. In Melton's paper referred to above, this distinction is clearly drawn.

(2) Degree of learning in short-term retention studies is commonly inferred, and appropriately so, from recall after zero seconds (which in practice may be a second or two). These studies report the percentage of Ss getting the item correct after zero seconds. These percentages are, in both studies reviewed above, near 100%. Indeed, Melton notes with some satisfaction that all the curves from his study have their origin very near to 100%.

(3) It has been pointed out earlier that it is quite impossible to determine differences in amount or degree of learning when a percentage measurement is used and when these are near 100%. Yet, in retention after 24 hours, wide differences in recall are found with items which were all or near the 100% level (Fig. 2.10). These differences in recall were particularly marked when proactive interference was heavy. Potential for proactive interference has been heavy in most studies of short-term retention, including the Melton and the Murdock studies reviewed above.

(4) It has been argued that we must accept the notion that when our response measure for learning for two lists of different materials is at or near 100% for both, and if rate of learning of the lists differed appreciably, differences in degree of learning "above 100%" exist. Furthermore, under these circumstances, it is impossible to make meaningful comparisons of these lists if the interest is in attributing the retention differences to a factor other than degree of learning.

(5) To present one word and three words for a constant period of time, or to present one consonant and five consonants for a constant period of study, and then assume that learning is equivalent because immediate recall is equal at 100% or slightly below, runs contrary to other facts. Surely, five consonants as a unit is more difficult to learn than a single consonant; the rate of acquisition per unit of time must differ. That both show an immediate recall of near 100% cannot be used as evidence that degree of learning is equivalent. This measure of learning is insensitive to differences at this point. Indeed, in the Murdock procedure, latencies were taken. At the zero recall interval the mean latency was 1.13 sec for the single word and 1.63 for the triads. Since the standard deviations are given, a t (without considering the correlation existing due to the same Ss serving under both conditions) was calculated by the present writer to be 5.56. If one wishes to accept latency differences as evidence of differences in degree of learning, then clearly Murdock's data show differences in degree of learning.

In summary, there is every reason to believe that differences in degree of learning existed for the different materials used in these experiments. Since degree of learning and rate of forgetting are related, it seems premature to be interpreting the differential rates of forgetting as being due to the action of some characteristic of the material (e.g., intra-item interference), an action which is said to occur following learning. Task variables in the long-term retention of lists have little if any influence on retention; if they do for short-term memory of single items, then the potential schism between short- and long-term memory, a schism which Melton so brilliantly argues against, may in fact exist. That is to say, further research may eventually show that factors such as number of units are indeed determinants of the rate of forgetting even when degree of learning is equated. Such research, it appears, can only be definitive when the level of learning attained prior to the introduction of the retention interval is equal for the different units and appreciably below 100%.

SUMMARY

This paper was directed toward problems involved in the measurement of forgetting uncontaminated by differences in degree of learning. More particularly, it was concerned with these measurements when some variable, such as a characteristic of the task, is being manipulated and when such a variable produces differences in rate of learning. If we are to assess properly the influences of these variables on retention, degree of learning must be equated, since degree of learning and retention are directly related.

The two basic situations considered were those in which a constant number of learning trials was given and those in which learning was carried to a specified criterion of performance. A technique (single-entry projections) was presented which allows projection of the expected performance on the trial after the last learning trial. Analysis of several different types of lists showed that not only were the mean projected scores highly accurate, but also that the predictions for individual *S*s were quite accurate. These predictions for individual *S*s were also correlated with 24-hr. recall, suggesting that individual differences in forgetting are of minor importance. It was further shown that if learning measures, expressed as percentages, are near 100%, differences in degree of learning cannot be measured but will nevertheless influence retention markedly. If learning measures are at or near this asymptote of 100%, and if rate of learning to this asymptote differs for two lists, there is no way known by which the items within the lists which have reached asymptote can be meaningful compared in retention without possible confounding by differences in degree of learning.

The single-entry technique is appropriate only when a constant number of learning trials is used. When a criterion of performance is set for learning another procedure (multiple-entry projection) may be used. Although the mean predictions are fairly accurate by this method, predictions for individual *S*s are not. In most studies of retention it seems most efficient to use a constant-trials procedure for learning.

Finally, it was pointed out that some studies of short-term retention of single items have probably confounded effects of degree of learning on retention with the effects of variables producing differences in rate of learning the items.

REFERENCES

Ausubel, D. P. The use of advance organizers in the learning and retention of meaningful verbal material. *J. educ. Psychol.,* 1960, 51, 267-272.

Kothurkar, V. K. Effect of stimulus-response meaningfulness on paired-associate learning and retention. *J. exp. Psychol.,* 1963, 65, 305-308.

Melton, A. W. Implications of short-term memory for a general theory of memory. *J. verb. Learn. verb. Behav.,* 1963, 2, 1-21.

Murdock, B. B., Jr. The retention of individual items. *J. exp. Psychol.,* 1961, 62, 618-625.

Peterson, L. R., and Peterson, M. J. Short-term retention of individual verbal items. *J. exp. Psychol.,* 1959, 58, 193-198.

Postman, L. Retention as a function of degree of overlearning. *Science,* 1962, 135, 666-667.

Richardson, J., and Underwood, B. J. Comparing retention of verbal lists after different rates of acquisition. *J. gen. Psychol.,* 1957, 56, 187-192.

Runquist, W. N. Retention of verbal associates as a function of strength. *J. exp. Psychol.,* 1957, 54, 369-375.

Underwood, B. J. Speed of learning and amount retained: A consideration of methodology. *Psychol. Bull.,* 1954, 51, 276-282.

Underwood, B. J., and Keppel, G. An evaluation of two problems of method in the study of retention. *Amer. J. Psychol.,* 1962, 75, 1-17.

Underwood, B. J., and Keppel, G. The effect of degree of learning and letter-sequence interference on retention. *Psychol. Monogr.,* 1963, 77, No. 4.

Underwood, B. J., and Postman, L. Extraexperimental sources of interference in forgetting. *Psychol. Rev.,* 1960, 67, 73-95.

Underwood, B. J., and Richardson, J. Studies of distributed practice: XIII. Interlist interference and the retention and serial nonsense lists. *J. exp. Psychol.,* 1955, 50, 39-46.

Underwood, B. J., and Richardson, J. The influence of meaningfulness, intralist similarity and serial position on retention. *J. exp. Psychol.,* 1956, 52, 119-126.

Underwood, B. J., and Richardson, J. Studies of distributed practice: XVIII. The influence of meaningfulness and intralist similarity of serial nonsense lists. *J. exp. Psychol.,* 1958, 56, 213-219.

Underwood, B. J., and Schulz, R. W. *Meaningfulness and verbal learning.* Philadelphia: Lippincott, 1960.

Underwood, B. J., and Schulz, R. W. Studies of distributed practice: XX. Sources of interference associated with differences in learning and retention. *J. exp. Psychol.,* 1961, 61, 228-235.

3
Implicit Associative Responses

Implicit Responses and the Role of Intralist Similarity in Verbal Learning by Normal and Retarded Subjects

When a common word is presented as a stimulus in a verbal learning task, two types of implicit responses which may be made to the word must be distinguished. There is first the response made to the word itself as the act of perceiving it. This implicit response has been called the *representational response* (RR) by Bousfield, Whitmarsh, and Danick (1958). A second type of implicit response may be produced by the stimulus properties of the RR and may often be an associate of it. This response will be called the *implicit associative response* (IAR). If the word presented is *dog,* the IAR may be *cat* or *animal*. In the present study an assumption is made about differences in the IARs produced by normal and retarded subjects. This assumption in turn leads to differential predictions of verbal learning for normals and retardates when intralist conceptual similarity is manipulated. We may first examine the role of IARs when such manipulations are carried out with normal subjects.

When two or more words elicit the same IAR, and when this IAR is a category or concept name, we may speak of the two or more words as having conceptual similarity. Thus, *dog, horse,* and *cow* may all elicit the IAR *animal* and are, therefore, conceptually related. When a list of such conceptually related words is used in verbal learning tasks with normals, facilitation or inhibition in learning may occur (as compared with a list of words which is not conceptually related) depending upon the type of learning task employed. In free learning (FL) a subject is presented a list of items for learning and may recall them in any order. If such a list contains conceptually related words, learning is facilitated (e.g., Bourne & Parker, 1964; Ekstrand & Underwood, 1963). Although a portion of this facilita-

---

William P. Wallace and Benton J. Underwood, "Implicit Responses and the Role of Intralist Similarity in Verbal Learning by Normal and Retarded Subjects," *Journal of Educational Psychology* 55 (1964): 362-370. Reprinted with permission. Copyright 1964 by the American Psychological Association.

tion may be attributed to direct associations among words within a category, the evidence indicates that the category name is also involved (Underwood, 1964). On the other hand, conceptual similarity among words within a paired-associate (PA) list may inhibit learning. The most extreme case of this is one in which a set of conceptually related words among stimulus terms is paired with a set of conceptually related words among response terms (Underwood & Schulz, 1961). For example, if three names of animals as stimulus terms in a PA list are paired with three names of birds as response terms, severe interference occurs. The subject learns quickly that animals and birds go together, but has great difficulty in associating a specific animal name with a specific bird name. For establishing these specific associations, the IARs (*animal* and *bird*) are nondifferentiating cues. However, they apparently continue to be elicited over many trials and appear to be responsible for the heavy interference. The above facts indicate that with normal subjects high conceptual similarity in FL will result in better performance than will low conceptual similarity, while the opposite holds true for PA. Thus, with normals, there is an interaction between the effects of conceptual similarity and type of task (FL versus PA).

Turning next to a consideration of mental retardates, we will assume that the tendency of an RR to elicit an IAR is much less strong than for normals. This is to assume that there is less likelihood that IARs will be elicited in retardates; and if they are elicited, they will be weaker than in normals. There are several studies which give indirect support to the assumption that retardates are "deficient" in IARs (Griffith, Spitz, & Lipman, 1959; Jensen & Rohwer, 1963; Rieber, 1964). The Jensen-Rohwer study in particular indicates that retardates do not spontaneously use mediators in associating stimulus and response terms in PA learning; and a mediator, of course, is an IAR to the RR to the stimulus term. We therefore arrive at a prediction concerning the role of conceptual similarity in verbal learning of retardates. We assume: (*a*) the primary effects of conceptual similarity on learning in normals are due to IARs, and (*b*) retardates do not spontaneously produce IARs to verbal stimuli (or, if so, they are weak). Therefore, conceptual similarity in the verbal learning of retardates should produce little or no effect for either FL or PA. It can be further seen that if the three variables (normals-retardates, FL-PA, and high and low similarity) are manipulated simultaneously, the triple interaction must be significant if the expectations concerning IARs are to be supported.

METHOD

The overall design called for four groups of normal subjects and four groups of mental retardates. Two of the four groups within each class were given FL; two were given PA. Within each type of task there was a list with high conceptual similarity and one with low. The initial phase of the investigation was conducted with retardates in order to develop materials and select appropriate subjects for the experiment.

Materials and Retarded Subjects

As outlined earlier, we assume that IARs leading to concept identification are less likely to be produced *spontaneously* by retarded than by normal subjects. Obviously, if the appropriate IAR is not available to the retarded subject, it cannot be produced, spontaneously or otherwise. Therefore, retarded subjects had to be selected who *could* produce the appropriate IAR when requested to do so. This selection was accomplished by a concept sorting task.

The concepts or categories and the instances of each were chosen from the materials derived by Cohen, Bousfield, and Whitmarsh (1957). These investigators asked 400 college students to give the first four instances they thought of when presented with a category name. Thus, if the category name was *animal*, the subjects wrote down the first four animal names that occurred to them. From the listings provided by these investigators, 24 concepts and three frequently given instances of each were selected for the concept sorting task used with the retardates. For procedural purposes, these were divided into six sets, each containing three instances of 4 concepts. Each item was printed in capital letters on a 4 × 6 inch card, so that a given set was represented by 12 cards.

A total of 115 residents of the Dixon State School, Illinois, participated in the sorting task.[1] All had reading ability at or above the second-grade level. Upon entering the experimental room, the subject was told that he would play a sorting game. The 12 cards within a set were shuffled and spread out before the subject, and he was asked to place items together that were alike or belonged together. He was further told that there were to be four groupings with three cards in each. The words *pen, pencil,* and *paper* were always included in the first set; and as the experimenter explained the task to the subject he illustrated the sorting by placing these three cards together and saying that these were three things used in school so they belong together. The subject was then instructed to sort the remaining 12 cards. If the subject made an error in sorting, those cards involved in the error were retained and the subject was asked to try and place them together in another way. If the cards were still not sorted appropriately, the experimenter moved on to the next set. Each subject sorted the cards in all six sets. The order of the sets was random and different for each subject with one exception: the concepts of one of the sets appeared appreciably more

---

[1] We are grateful to R. Metzger and the officials and residents of the Dixon State School for their aid in conducting this portion of the experiment.

difficult than those in the other five sets and therefore this set was never presented as a first set.

Using the results of the sorting task, eight concepts were chosen on which the fewest number of sorting errors was made. Also, 80 subjects who had made the fewest errors in sorting were identified for use in the verbal learning phase. In the process of running the verbal learning phase, 9 of these 80 subjects were lost for various reasons. They were replaced with the best sorters remaining in the original pool of 115 subjects. Of the 80 subjects who produced the final records for the verbal learning phase, 78 had correctly sorted all the cards for the eight concepts used in the lists. The other 2 subjects had correctly sorted the cards for seven of the eight concepts. We believe, therefore, that the retarded subjects used in the verbal learning phase had available the IARs which lead to concept recognition for the concepts in the lists used. The mean IQ of these final 80 subjects was 63.1, with a range of from 42 to 80. The mean reading level (grade) was 4.0, with a range of from 2.0 to 6.0. The average age was 20.4 years, with a range of from 13.5 to 26.5.

Lists

The nature of the lists used can be understood by examining the PA lists given the normal subjects (see Table 3.1). Each list consisted of 12 pairs. In the high-similarity list, the three instances of a given concept among the stimulus terms were paired with three instances of a concept among the response terms, e.g., the three male names were paired with the three colors. The eight concepts involved in this list were those for which the instances were most frequently sorted correctly by the retardates. The 24 words in the low-similarity list represented one word from each of the 24 concepts originally used in the sorting task.

Table 3.1 High- and Low-Similarity PA Lists Learned by Normal Subjects

High Similarity		Low Similarity	
Stimulus	Response	Stimulus	Response
Tom	Green	Fly	Wool
Jim	Blue	Bob	Red
Bob	Red	Saw	Leaf
Ocean	Tea	Snow	Box
Lake	Milk	Car	Inch
River	Coffee	Sun	Arm
Moon	Leg	Apple	Cat
Star	Head	Lake	Milk
Sun	Arm	Gas	Hat
Apple	Cat	Bed	Crow
Peach	Cow	Pork	Door
Pear	Dog	Day	House

The particular words were chosen to meet two criteria, namely: (a) rough equivalence of mean word frequency in the low- and high-similarity lists as determined by the Thorndike-Lorge (1944) word count, and (b) ability to read the words by the retardates as determined in the sorting task.

The FL lists given to the normal subjects consisted of 24 words. The high-similarity list consisted of the 24 words in the high-similarity PA list; the low-similarity list consisted of the 24 words of the low-similarity PA list.

The PA lists given the retarded subjects consisted of six pairs. For half the subjects within a given group the six pairs consisted of the first six as listed in Table 3.1, for the other half, the second six. The FL lists for the retardates consisted of 12 words. Again, for half the subjects within a group the 12 words consisted of those in the first six pairs of Table 3.1, for the other half, the 12 words of the second six pairs.

Procedure

The retarded subjects served in the verbal learning phase 2 weeks following the sorting task. They were told they were going to play a learning game. For FL, each of the 12 words occurred on a separate 4 × 6 inch card, and each card was exposed manually for 2 seconds. The subjects were instructed to try to see how many words they could remember after all the cards were presented to them. After all 12 cards had been shown, the subject was asked to recall orally and in any order as many of the words as he could. The experimenter recorded the responses as the subject spoke them, with a total of 90 seconds allowed for recall. The cards were then shuffled; and another study trial was given, followed by another recall trial, and so on, until six study-recall trials were completed.

The PA learning for retarded subjects was also handled by a manually operated card system. The cards were 5 × 8 inches. The stimulus term was printed on one side, with both the stimulus and response terms on the other, with the response term underlined. The subjects were instructed that they must learn and repeat the underlined word on the back of the card before the experimenter turned the card and exposed the word. The stimulus term appeared for 2 seconds, and the stimulus and response terms for 2 seconds. The cards were shuffffled between each trial. A total of 12 anticipation trials was given or five consecutive errorless trials, whichever occurred first.

The normal subjects were 80 college students, all of whom had had some previous experience in verbal learning experiments. The lists were presented on a memory drum. For FL, each item was exposed for study for 2 seconds after which a 90-second oral recall trial was given with the experimenter recording the responses. A total of six study-recall trials was given, and the words were arranged in four different orders for the study trials. The subjects were instructed that the words could be recalled in any order. For the PA lists, anticipation learning was used with a 2:2-second rate and a total of 12 anticipation trials. The pairs were arranged in four different orders.

The retarded subjects were run prior to the normal subjects. Since the length of the lists differed for normal and retarded subjects, pilot work was conducted with normal subjects to determine the number of trials to give so that the level of performance (percentage of correct responses) achieved at the termination of learning was roughly comparable to that achieved by the retarded subjects. Thus, the 6 FL trials and the 12 PA trials given the normal subjects were determined appropriate for producing the level of learning shown by the retarded subjects.

We may now summarize the design and general procedure. Four different lists were learned by four different groups of retarded subjects, there being 20 subjects per group. Four lists were also given to four groups of normals with each group consisting of 20 subjects. The four lists represent two types of learning (FL and PA) and low and high conceptual similarity for each type. The subjects within each class were assigned randomly to the lists based upon a prearranged schedule. In the case of the retardates, this random assignment also obtained for the two subgroups learning the two different lists of each type. When a subject was lost he was replaced by the next subject appearing.

RESULTS

Correct Responses

For the normal subjects, the mean numbers of total correct responses across all trials for the four lists are shown in Figure 3.1. The differences in the level of performance for FL and PA are not meaningful since the number of trials and number of items in the lists differed. The critical finding is represented in the differences in the slopes of the lines. Relative to low similarity, high similarity retards PA learning but facilitates FL. An analysis of variance shows this interaction to be significant far beyond the 1% significance level ($F = 32.44$, $df = 1/76$).

The results for the retarded subjects are shown in Figure 3.2. Again, the values are the mean total correct responses across all acquisition trials. The learning of the subgroups for each type of list did not differ significantly so the scores have been combined in Figure 3.2. If a subject was not given the full 12 PA trials (if he had 5 consecutive errorless trials before 12 trials), his score was calculated as being errorless beyond the 5 errorless trials. The marked interaction shown in Figure 3.1 is at best only suggested in Figure 3.2. The F for interaction between type of task and similarity is 3.07, with an F of 3.96 required for the 5% significance level. Thus, while the trend is in the same direction as that shown by normal subjects, it lacks statistical reliability. The results appear to support expectations derived from the assumption that retarded subjects are less likely to respond with IARs than are normals. It may be said that the acquisi-

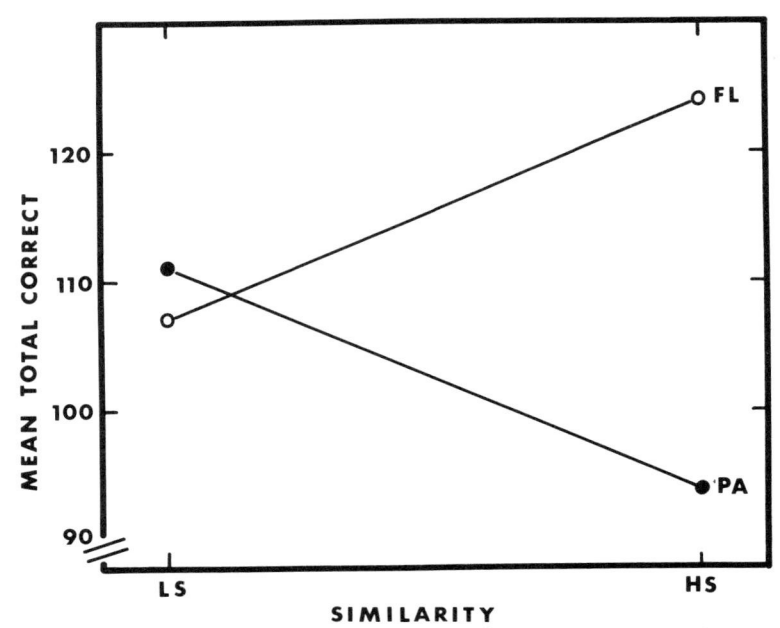

Figure 3.1 Mean total correct responses for FL and PA learning as a function of low (LS) and high (HS) conceptual similarity for normal subjects.

tion curves give no additional critical information, i.e., the differences shown in the two figures are present in essentially the same relative amounts over all acquisition trials.

The evidence in Figures 3.1 and 3.2 indicates that conceptual similarity influences normals more than retardates. However, we need to ask whether this influence is significantly greater for normals than for retardates. As noted in the introduction, this can only be assessed by examining the triple-interaction term if the scores for all eight groups are analyzed simultaneously. Such an analysis on the mean total correct responses does indeed show this interaction to be significant beyond the 1% level ($F = 7.95$). Nevertheless, it is not clear that this analysis is entirely appropriate in view of the fact that such widely different raw score levels are present due to differences in list lengths. Therefore, z scores were determined for each type of task for a given class of subjects separately. Thus, one set of z scores was based on the distribution of raw scores for the 40 normal subjects given FL (combining high and low similarity), another on the 40 given PA, and so on. This provides a mean z score for each

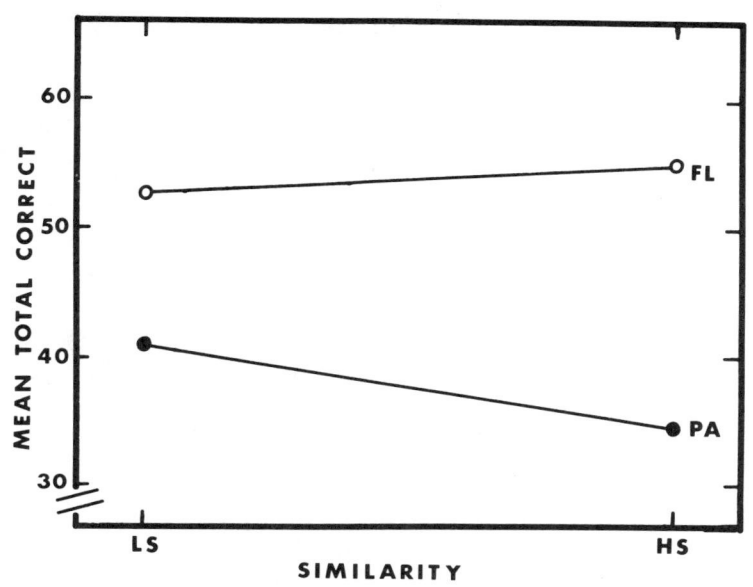

Figure 3.2 Mean total correct responses for FL and PA learning as a function of high (HS) and low (LS) conceptual similarity for retarded subjects.

of the original groups, but differences in these means are determined only by the effects of similarity on the learning. The main effects on the other two variables are "neutralized" by this procedure. An analysis of variance performed on these transformed scores yielded a significant Type of Task × Similarity interaction ($F = 26.86$) and an F of 6.67 for the triple interaction with 6.81 needed for the 1% level. We conclude that the differential effects of conceptual similarity on FL and PA is reliably greater for normal subjects than for retarded subjects.

Errors in PA Learning

Overt error rates were determined by the ratio between incorrectly placed response terms and total emissions (sum of correctly and incorrectly placed response terms). The mean ratios were higher for retardates than for normals for both lists, these ratios being .16 and .05 for the low-similarity list and .34 and .18 for the high-similarity list. An analysis of variance after arc sine transformations showed that both class of subjects and similarity were significant beyond the

1% level (Fs = 15.20 and 30.78, respectively), but the interaction was far from significant.

For support of the proposition concerning differences in strength and frequency of IARs between the two classes of subjects, within-concept overt errors must be more frequent for the normals than for the retardates in learning the high-similarity list. A within-concept error is one in which a response term is given to a stimulus term representing the appropriate category or concept, but which is incorrect to the particular stimulus. For example, in referring to the lists of Table 3.1, if the response term *green* is given to the stimulus term *Jim* it would be classed as a within-concept error. The within-concept errors must be more frequent for normals if their category IARs occur more frequently or are stronger than are those for the retardates. A similar expectation is present if the direct associations between instances of a concept are stronger for normals than for retardates. Either type of IAR must lead to more within-concept errors for normals than for retardates.

Since the number of paired concepts differed for the two classes of subjects (being four for the normals and two for the retardates as a result of there being 12 and 6 items in the lists, respectively), chance occurrence of what would be normally classed as a within-concept error differs for the two classes of subjects. For the normals, if a subject simply emitted a response from the list without regard to the stimulus present at the moment, the probability that it would be called a within-concept error is 2/11, or .18. This value is more appropriate than 3/12 because a randomly emitted response term has a certain probability of being correct (1/12). For the retardates, on the other hand, the probability of a chance within-concept error is 2/5, or .40. For each subject in the normal group the number of apparent within-concept errors was reduced by 18%; for the retardates it was reduced by 40%. These corrected values for each subject were divided by the total errors he made to obtain a within-concept error ratio. The mean of these proportions was .72 for the normals and .43 for the retardates. This is to say that following correction for chance occurrence of within-concept errors, the average normal subject's within-concept errors consisted of 72% of his total errors, while the corresponding value for the average retarded subject was 43%. An arc sine transformation was applied to each subject's proportion; the t for the difference between the means of the two distributions was 5.91. Clearly, normal subjects were making more within-concept errors than were retarded subjects as would be expected if their IARs are "behaving" as assumed.

Clustering in FL

The assumed difference in IARs for normals and retardates also leads to the prediction that clustering in FL of the high-similarity list will be greater for normals than for retardates. By clustering is meant the grouping of words from the same category during recall. The category IARs are assumed to be the mechanism producing the clustering. Cluster ratios were determined for each subject by the formula $r/(n - k)$, where r is the number of times a word was followed by another word from the same concept or category, n the total number of words recalled, and k the number of categories from which at least one word was recalled. By this formula, perfect clustering yields a ratio of 1.0. For normals, clustering was nearly perfect, averaging .96. Unfortunately, due to an experimental oversight, the recall data for only the last 8 retarded subjects learning the high-similarity list were recorded in a manner to allow determination of clustering ratios. However, the learning scores for these 8 subjects did not differ appreciably from the scores for the 12 other subjects in the group. It seems reasonable to assume, therefore, that the clustering scores for these 8 subjects are at least roughly representative of the group. The mean clustering ratio for these 8 subjects was .64, a value that differs significantly from that of the normals ($t = 7.12$). Clustering ratios to be expected by chance were determined from the low-similarity lists. Items were randomly assigned to form artificial clusters, and then recall performance was analyzed by the above formula for these artificial clusters. The values ranged between .25 and .35 across the six trials for both normals and retardates. Therefore, it is clear that although clustering for retardates is less than for normals, it is well above chance expectations.

DISCUSSION

All data (correct responses, within-concept errors, clustering) from the present study are consonant with the assumption that implicit associative responses (IARs) occur spontaneously with less frequency in mental retardates than in normals. Because of the inherent difficulty in drawing cause-effect conclusions from experiments in which subject variables are manipulated (Underwood, 1957), we should examine carefully the nature of the questions asked of the present experiment.

We may note that no questions pertaining to direct differences in learning rates of normals and retardates were asked. Indeed, such a question is not meaningful for the present study because the experimental conditions differed (intentionally) for the two classes of subjects. The lists, for example, differed in length. No direct questions were asked about differences in rate of free and PA learning, for such a comparison is also meaningless in the present study. Experimental control was imposed only for a given type of task within a given class of subjects, for here the question concerned the learning of this particular task by these particular subjects as a function of intralist similarity. This direct question can be asked four times (PA and FL for each class of subjects) of the present data and each answer stands by itself as an experimentally valid one. It is only when we start comparing the differences resulting from the four valid comparisons that caution must be exercised. For, at this point, the constancy of all variables except one no longer obtains. Thus, we either abandon making such comparisons or we try to "make sense" out of them by specifying theoretical variables whose action would produce the obtained results. It is obvious that we have chosen the latter course for the design of the study was dictated by the theoretical variable (differences in IARs between the two classes of subjects).

The critical finding for the present study was the triple interaction (Class of Subjects × Type of Task × Intralist Similarity). It is apparent that the two classes of subjects differ on many variables associated with diagnoses of retarded and normal. We have examined the experimental implications of assuming only one critical difference for the present tasks (amount of spontaneous occurrence of IARs). It is, therefore, quite reasonable to ask whether any one or more of the many other differences between the two classes of subjects could have produced the particular experimental relationships observed, particularly the triple interaction. We do not know how, but perhaps others will. Nevertheless, because we do not have and cannot have experimental control of all possible variables or differences between the two classes of subjects, we can never assert with finality that these other variables are not responsible for our experimental findings. We may only suggest that differences in spontaneous, implicit responding will incorporate the present findings; and it seems reasonable to assume that this variable is the critical one until an equally good or better accounting of the results is offered.

Finally, we should note that the results could be accounted for in part if it is assumed that the critical difference between normals and retardates is not in strength and frequency of IARs but rather in the nature of the IARs. It is possible that for some retarded subjects the IARs are indeed strong but simply are not "appropriate" to the concepts appearing in the lists. That is, these IARs may lead neither to the category name nor to other words within a category. We presume this is not the case, but only appropriate associative norms for retardates could settle the issue definitively.

REFERENCES

Bourne, L. E., Jr., & Parker, B. K. Inter-item relationships, list structure, and verbal learning. *Canad. J. Psychol.,* 1964, 18, 52-61.
Bousfield, W. A., Whitmarsh, G. A., & Danick, J. J. Partial response identities in verbal generalization. *Psychol. Rep.,* 1958, 4, 703-713.
Cohen, B. H., Bousfield, W. A., & Whitmarsh, G. A. Cultural norms for verbal items in 43 categories. Technical Report No. 22, 1957, University of Connecticut, Contract Nonr 631(00), Office of Naval Research.
Ekstrand, B., & Underwood, B. J. Paced versus unpaced recall in free learning. *J. verb. Learn. verb. Behav.,* 1963, 2, 288-290.
Griffith, B. C., Spitz, H. H., & Lipman, R. S. Verbal mediation and concept formation in retarded and normal subjects. *J. exp. Psychol.,* 1959, 58, 247-251.
Jensen, A. R., & Rohwer, W. D. Verbal mediation in paired-associate and serial learning. *J. verb. Learn. verb. Behav.,* 1963, 1, 346-352.
Rieber, M. Verbal mediation in normal and retarded children. *Amer. J. ment. Defic.,* 1964, 68, 634-641.
Thorndike, E. L., & Lorge, I. *The teacher's word book of 30,000 words.* New York: Columbia Univer. Press, 1944.
Underwood, B. J. *Psychological research.* New York: Appleton-Century-Crofts, 1957.
Underwood, B. J. The representativeness of rote verbal learning. In A. W. Melton (Ed.), *Categories of human learning.* New York: Academic Press, 1964.
Underwood, B. J., & Schulz, R. W. Studies of distributed practice: XXI. Effect of interference from language habits. *J. exp. Psychol.,* 1961, 62, 571-575.

False Recognition Produced by Implicit Verbal Responses

In the development of conceptual schemes to incorporate verbal-learning phenomena, implicit responses are being given more and more prominent roles. Two examples may be cited. The studies of mediation in transfer evolved from two basic assumptions, namely, that implicit responses to verbal stimuli occur and that these implicit responses will serve as mediators. When conceptual similarity within a paired-associate list is found to produce interference it seems appropriate to account for this in part by assuming that the instances of a category (e.g., *dog, cow, horse*) may all elicit the same implicit response (*animal*), which, in this situation, is a nondifferentiating response.

A distinction must be made between two kinds of implicit responses made to a verbal unit. There is first the response made to the unit itself as the act of perceiving it. This implicit response has been called the *representational response* by Bousfield, Whitmarsh, and Danick (1958), and will be abbreviated here as RR. The second kind of response, the one with theoretical relevance, is produced by the stimulus properties of the RR. This implicit response may be another word which is associated with the actual word presented and will be called the *implicit associative response* (IAR). The particular IAR to a given word is often assumed to be the most frequent associate produced to the word in word-association procedures. Or, as in a mediating transfer situation, the IAR is assumed to be the word which S had learned as a response to a given stimulus in a previous list. That other nonverbal implicit responses (such as affective responses) may occur to the RR cannot be denied, but for the present purposes, need not be considered.

It must be clear that IAR, in most theoretical formulations, is conceived of as actually occurring. This is to say, it is not a hypothetical construct. It is hypothetical only in the sense that it is as-

---

Benton J. Underwood, "False Recognition Produced by Implicit Verbal Responses," *Journal of Experimental Psychology* 70 (1965); 122–129. Reprinted with permission. Copyright 1965 by the American Psychological Association.

This work was done under Contract Nonr-1228 (15), Project NR 154–057, between Northwestern University and the Office of Naval Research.

sumed to occur in a particular situation where it cannot be observed directly, and this assumption is made because it *has* been observed to occur overtly with a certain frequency in other situations (e.g., word-association procedures). The validity of the assumption is tested by experimental procedures wherein a given phenomenon is predicted *if* specific IARs are occurring. The present study fits into this framework.

The rationale of the experiment may be understood by examining the task presented Ss. A total of 200 words was read to S at a 10-sec. rate. As each word was read, S made a decision as to whether or not the word had been read to him earlier in the list. Thus, the general procedure is that devised by Shepard and Teghtsoonian (1961) in their study of memory for 3-digit numbers. In the present list of 200 words were critical words assumed to elicit particular IARs. At a later point in the list, therefore, the words assumed to be IARs to earlier RRs were in fact presented to S. If S responded by saying that these words had been read earlier in the list we would conclude that the IARs had occurred to the critical words at the time these critical words were read. For example, if a critical stimulus word is *up,* and if later the assumed IAR (*down*) is presented and S indicates that *down* had occurred earlier in the list, we assume that *down* had occurred as an IAR to the RR to the word *up,* and that S subsequently confused an IAR with an RR.

METHOD

Words.—Four different types of words must be distinguished.

Critical Stimulus Words (CS Words): These words were assumed to elicit particular IARs.

Experimental Words (E Words): These were the words representing the assumed IARs to the CS Words.

Control Words (C Words): These words were used as controls for the E Words and were assumed not to have been preceded in the list by words for which they were IARs.

Filler Words (F Words): These words were presumed to be neutral with regard to the E Words and were used to build up a specific repetition frequency.

There were 20 E Words (hence, 20 C Words) as may be seen in Table 3.2. There were five different classes of CS Words, labeled A1, A3, CV, SO, and SI in Table 3.2. Each of these classes must be explained. Classes A1 and A3 consisted of words for which the E Word (assumed IAR) was an antonym of the CS Word. Thus, *top* is assumed to be the IAR to *bottom, take* to *give,* and so on. In forming A1 and A3, 16 pairs of antonyms were divided randomly into four subgroups of four pairs each. Two of these subgroups were then assigned randomly to A1 and A3 as CS Words and E Words, the second member of the pairs of the other two subgroups as C Words. However, for these C Words, no CS Word appeared earlier in the list. Thus, when S was confronted with the C Word *down*, this had not been preceded by *up*. On the other hand, when S was confronted with the E Word *top*, it had been preceded by the CS Word, *bottom*. The rationale of the study predicts that S will be more likely to say that *top* rather than *down* had occurred earlier in the list.

The CS Words for the A1 class were presented only once; those for the A3 class were each presented three times prior to the appearance of the E Word. A comparison between these two classes will provide evidence on the role of frequency of IARs.

The third class of CS Words in Table 3.2 is CV, an abbreviation for converging associations. Each of the CS Words on a line is known to elicit the E Word with appreciable frequency in word-association norms. Thus, *bread* is a frequent response to both *butter* and *crumb*, *sleep* a frequent response to both *bed* and *dream*, and so on. In selecting words for the first three classes in Table 3.2, major use was made of the Connecticut word-association norms as given by Bousfield, Cohen, Whitmarsh, and Kincaid (1961) with minor use of the Minnesota norms (Russell & Jenkins, 1954).

The fourth class of CS Words in Table 3.2 is labeled SO (superordinates). Each of the CS Words on a given line is a specific instance of the category which becomes the E Word. These words were taken from Cohen, Bousfield, and Whit-

Table 3.2 Critical Stimulus Words, Experimental Words, and Control Words

Class	Critical Stimulus Words	E Word	Position	C Word
A1	Bottom	Top	113	Down
	Give	Take	135	Good
	Day	Night	170	Low
	Man	Woman	188	Rich
A3	Rough	Smooth	154	Weak
	False	True	162	Dirty
	Hard	Soft	178	Short
	Slow	Fast	192	Girl
CV	Butter, Crumb	Bread	129	Bridge
	Bed, Dream	Sleep	155	Smile
	Sugar, Bitter, Candy	Sweet	147	Salt
	Animal, Cat, Bark	Dog	182	Horse
	Dark, Heavy, Lamp, Match	Light	175	Leg
	Warm, Chill, Freeze, Frigid, Hot, Ice	Cold	196	Cloud
SO	Maple, Oak, Elm, Birch	Tree	123	Fish
	Cotton, Wool, Silk, Rayon	Cloth	158	Fruit
	Robin, Sparrow, Bluejay, Canary	Bird	189	Flower
SI	Barrel, Doughnut, Dome, Globe, Spool	Round	146	Sharp
	Atom, Cabin, Germ, Gnat, Village	Small	165	Fat
	Bandage, Chalk, Milk, Rice, Snow	White	179	Red

marsh (1957). In actual fact these investigators asked *S*s to give specific instances to the category name. However, we are assuming that the instances will in turn elicit the category name as an IAR with appreciable frequency. Some justification for this assumption is found in word-association norms. For example, the Connecticut word-association norms show that 50% of the *S*s responded to the stimulus word *canary* with *bird*.

The final class in Table 3.2 is SI (sense impressions). Taken from Underwood and Richardson (1956), each word on a line is known to elicit the E Word with appreciable frequency when the associations are limited to sense impressions by instructions and training.

The CS Words on a given line are not completely without associates to E Words on other lines. There are two fairly obvious instances. The CS Word *doughnut* in the SI class also elicits the word *sweet* with appreciable frequency, *sweet* being an E Word in the CV class. So also *snow* leads to *cold*. Such "contamination" would, according to the notions in the introduction, tend to increase the number of false recognitions of the appropriate E Words.

The column labeled "Position" in Table 3.2 represents the position in the series of 200 words occupied by each E Word. The position of a given C Word was always two positions away from the position of its corresponding E Word. Thus, the C Word *down* occurred at Position 111. Taken as a whole, the C Words occurred after the E Words half the time and before the E Words half the time.

The CS Words were scattered throughout the positions with the last occurring at Position 151. However, it may be of value to indicate the number of positions between the last CS Words and the E Words of the classes. For A1, the range for the four words was from 86 to 104 positions, with a mean of 96. For A3, the range was 36–89, with a mean of 53; for CV, a range of 30–60, with a mean of 42; for SO, from 27–68, with a mean of 50, and finally, for SI, 27–73, with a mean of 53.

There were 47 F Words. Of these 42 occurred twice, 4 occurred three times, and 1 occurred only once. Therefore, the 200 positions are accounted for as follows: CS Words, 63; E Words, 20; C Words, 20; and F Words, 97. The actual repetition was arranged so that in the first quarter (first 50 words) 5 words had occurred earlier, with 19, 16, and 18 having occurred earlier in each of the remaining three quarters.

*Procedure and *S*s.*—The instructions and the words were presented by a magnetic tape recorder. The *S*s were given a single sheet of paper on which 200 numbered blanks occurred. The instructions required *S* to record a plus if he believed the word had occurred earlier in the list, a minus if he believed it had not. The instructions indicated that if *S* was in doubt a decision had to be made; a plus or minus had to be recorded for each blank. The words were read at a 10-sec. rate, each being spoken twice in immediate succession. The trial number was indicated after every tenth word to avoid any confusion as to the particular number of the word at the moment.

A total of 107 *S*s records was completed in four group sessions. All *S*s were college students taking introductory psychology courses at Northwestern. Seven of the records were eliminated on a random basis, so the data to be presented are based on 100 *S*s.

RESULTS

Table 3.3 shows the number of plusses (hence, percentage of Ss) recorded for each E Word and its corresponding C Word. Also shown are the subtotals for each class of words. Looking at these subtotals it may be quickly noted that for Classes A1 and SI, expectations are not supported but that for Classes A3, CV, and SO, frequency of plusses for the E Words is much greater than for the C Words. However, we may first make an overall statistical evaluation without regard to classes of words. For each S the total number of plusses made to the 20 E Words was determined and also the total number made

Table 3.3 Number of Plusses Given to Each E and C Word by 100 Ss with Subtotals for Each Class of Words

Class	E Word	No. of Plusses	C Word	No. of Plusses
A1	Top	9	Down	20
	Take	11	Good	5
	Night	24	Low	27
	Woman	5	Rich	10
	Total	49		62
A3	Smooth	28	Weak	9
	True	12	Dirty	9
	Soft	37	Short	25
	Fast	49	Girl	9
	Total	126		52
CV	Bread	21	Bridge	28
	Sleep	23	Smile	10
	Sweet	24	Salt	11
	Dog	20	Horse	7
	Light	42	Leg	13
	Cold	39	Cloud	15
	Total	169		84
SO	Tree	19	Fish	9
	Cloth	18	Fruit	11
	Bird	38	Flower	11
	Total	75		31
SI	Round	7	Sharp	9
	Small	14	Fat	7
	White	3	Red	8
	Total	24		24

to the 20 C Words. The E Words produced a mean of 4.43 plusses, the C Words a mean of 2.53. The difference (1.90 ± .23) gives a t of 8.26. It must be concluded that Ss responded more frequently to the E Words than to the C Words.

A statistical analysis of differences in frequency for E and C Words by classes of items is difficult by conventional methods since many Ss did not respond with a plus to any of the words within a class. Even in the above analysis there were 8 Ss with a zero entry for the 20 E Words and 24 Ss with a zero entry for the C Words. However, certain simple computations allow some fairly firm conclusions about the statistical significance of the responses by classes of words, a matter to which we will turn shortly.

We may ask about the frequency of plusses for all words except E words when they first occurred. This determination across the entire series of words provides a measure of the "false-alarm" or "false-positive" rate. The 200 words were divided into eighths and the number of false alarms determined for each of these eight sections. The number of words which first occurred (hence, could result in false alarms) in each successive eighth was 23, 22, 16, 15, 18, 9, 10, and 9. The mean numbers of plusses (false alarms) per word in each eighth are plotted as filled dots in Fig. 3.3 with a straight line

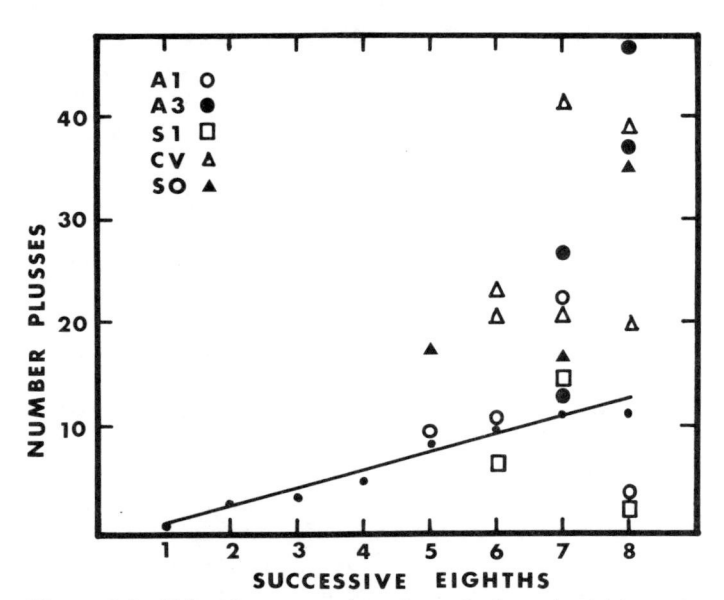

Figure 3.3 False-alarm rate (number of plusses) within each successive block of 25 positions across the 200 words and number of plusses for each of the 20 E Words.

drawn through them. It is clear that there is an increase in false alarms as the number of prior words increases; in the eighth section the 100 Ss averaged 11.2 false alarms for the nine words which first occurred in that section; in the first section the corresponding value was 0.5.

The plusses or false alarms for each E Word are also plotted in Fig. 3.3, above the eighth in which it occurred. The statistical question is whether or not the E Words of various classes can be considered to come from the population of words represented by the false-alarm rate of all non-E Words when they first occurred. Clearly, Classes A1 and SI could come from this population. It can be shown, however, that it is highly improbable that the E Words in each of the other three classes could have come from this population of false alarms for control words. The sum of the plusses for the three E Words in the SO class is 75; how probable is it that this sum would be equaled by any three control words used to derive the false-alarm rate in Fig. 3.3? To determine this the number of plusses for the 46 words used to derive the last half of the false-alarm curve were each listed. From this listing 100 samples of three each were drawn (using a table of random numbers) and the sum of the plusses for each sample determined. In drawing the samples, replacement was immediate; that is, the same value (representing the number of plusses for a given word) could have been drawn so as to constitute all three entries in a sample. The mean of this distribution of 100 sums was 30.71, with a standard deviation of 12.04. The maximum summed value obtained for any one sample was 71. Since the E Words in the SO class produced a sum of 75, we conclude that it is quite unlikely that these three E Words could come from the control population. This is to say, therefore, that the frequency of false alarms given to these E Words must have been influenced by the earlier presence of the CS Words. Or, to say this another way; S apparently confused the RR of the E Word with the IAR made earlier to the CS Word.

The above procedure could be repeated for the A3 and CV classes and the same conclusion would be reached. However, this is quite unnecessary. The maximum frequency of plusses for any word used in obtaining the control false-alarm rate was 28 (for *bridge*, a C Word). Multiplying this value by 4 (112) does not yield a frequency as high (126) as the frequency produced by the four E Words in the A3 class. Multiplying 28 by 6 does not result in a frequency as high as that produced by the six E Words in the CV class.

In summary, therefore, the evidence indicates that RRs were confused with IARs for three classes of words. Among the 13 E Word-C Word comparisons in these three classes there is only one instance in which the frequency of the plusses for the C Word was higher than for the E Word (Class CV, *bridge* vs. *bread*). The maximum frequency of false alarm for any E Word was 49; 49% of the Ss indicated that the word *fast* had occurred earlier in the list when in fact it had not. It is of some interest to compare this value with that of the lowest frequency of detection of a repeated word. The F Word *home* appeared in Position 13 and again in Position 118 at which time only 51% of the Ss indicated it had occurred earlier. Overall, however, the correct detection of repeated words was 85.0%. It is evident, therefore, that S is far more likely to recognize a repeated word than to give a false alarm to a nonrepeated word even when we attempt to confuse him.

Other relationships.—The Ss showed appreciable consistency in their tendency to report that a word had occurred earlier when in fact it had not. The product-moment correlation across the 100 Ss for number of plusses for the 20 E Words and for the 20 C Words was .62. A total of 102 of the 200 positions was held by CS Words and by the first occurrence of F Words. The correlation between the number of plusses made to these 102 words and the number made to the E Words was .60, and to the C Words, .67. On the other hand, the ability to detect a repetition is not related to the tendency to indicate that a word had occurred earlier when it had not. There were 58 positions held by repeated words. The correlation across the 100 Ss between the number of plusses assigned these 58 positions and the number of plusses assigned the 102 positions when words first occurred was -.02. A scatter plot gives no indication of curvilinearity.

DISCUSSION

Three of the classes of E Words produced results in conformance with the notion that RRs may be confused with IARs that occurred earlier; two classes did not. The fact that words in the A1 class did not produce false alarms beyond the control rate while those in A3 did, indicates that frequency of IARs is a critical variable. It would seem quite reasonable to presume that if an IAR occurs three times it has more of the properties of an RR than if it occurs only once. Indeed, it is precisely this fact which Deese (1959) has demonstrated by a sharp relationship between the appearance of an intrusion (a word which had not appeared in the list) in recall and the associative strength of the intruding word to the words actually in the list. However, in the case of the A1 words vs. the A3 words in the present study, another factor might be involved. As noted in the procedure section, on the average the number of words occurring between the CS Words and the E Words was greater for A1 than for A3. Perhaps the IARs to the

CS Words in A1 are, therefore, forgotten or interfered with more than those produced by the CS Words in A3. While this possibility cannot be ruled out entirely, there is evidence against it. In the A3 class a total of 89 words occurred between the last presentation of the CS Word *hard* and its E Word *soft*, yet 37% of the Ss indicated they had heard the word earlier. For two of the cases in the A1 class, 86 and 89 words occurred between the CS Word and the E Word, yet the E Words produced only 11% and 5% plusses. Furthermore, an examination of the results for the CV class indicates that those cases where four and five CS Words occurred (and were presumed to elicit a common associate) produced more false alarms than did the cases in the CV class where only two and three CS Words were used, and this occurred when the number of words between the last CS and the E Word was essentially the same for all cases. Thus, the evidence points strongly to frequency of IAR as a variable in producing confusion between IARs and RRs.

The SI class of words gave completely negative results; frequency of false alarms to the E Words in this class was no greater than for the C Words. As will be remembered, a given set of CS Words in the SI class will, under appropriate instructions and training, elicit the common response which was here used as the E Word. It is possible that within the context of the present series of words these sense-impression responses occur as IARs with low frequency. However, in the Connecticut word-association norms (Bousfield et al., 1961) four of the five CS Words presumed to elicit the E Word *round* do in fact elicit *round* with some frequency (10%, 9%, 9%, and 28%). Nevertheless, these frequencies are much lower than the frequencies in the other classes. We may tentatively conclude that the negative results in the SI class are due to the failure of the CS Words to elicit the common IARs with appreciable frequency.

The logic of the experiment was that the RR to the word of the moment would lead S to say that the word had occurred earlier if this RR was the same as an IAR produced by a word or words earlier in the list. This scheme might be reversed to say that the IAR to the word of the moment, if the same as an RR to an earlier word, would lead S to say that the present word had occurred earlier. Thus, if the word of the moment was *down*, and if it elicits the IAR *up*, and if *up* occurred earlier in the list, S might believe that *down* had occurred earlier. Such a mechanism might indeed handle the results for A3, for antonyms are bidirectionally associated. And, such a mechanism might account for the failure for the SI items, since the E Words do not elicit the CS Words with appreciable frequency in available norms. However, it cannot account for the results for the CV and SO classes. The positive effects produced in these classes must be due to the elicitation of the same IAR by two or more different CS Words, otherwise positive results would have been obtained in the A1 class. The IAR of the word of the moment cannot be confused with two or more different RRs of previous words such as would be necessary by the alternative scheme. Of course, it is possible that both mechanisms may be involved but until this is clearly demonstrated we will conclude that the original scheme presented is most appropriate; the RR to the word of the moment is confused with the common IAR produced by two or more previous words. This is essentially the same conclusion reached by Mink (1963) as a result of his studies on semantic generalization. And it should be noted that the present study could be classified as a study of secondary or semantic generalization.

Figure 3.3 showed that the frequency of false alarms increased throughout. Although this increase may be due to the same mechanisms presumed to operate for the E Words, another factor may be in part responsible. It is possible that the greater the number of words S heard the more likely he would believe that a repetition would occur. Thus, if in doubt late in the list he would be more likely to signify that a repetition had occurred than if in doubt early in the list. This could be true in spite of the fact that the objective repetition was held constant over the last three quarters of the list. Nevertheless, certain of the C Words produced false alarms with such high frequency that an examination of possible causes was made. Some may have been produced by high formal similarity of RRs. For example, *low* produced 27 false alarms. The word *law* occurred as an E Word earlier in the list. The high frequency for *short* may have been due to the appearance of *sharp* earlier in the list. The C Word which produced the highest number of false alarms was *bridge*. No previous word has high formal similarity and, when *bridge* is thought of as a structure spanning water, no previous word would seem to elicit it as an IAR. If these Ss are avid players and followers of the game of bridge, such words as *master* and *major* (which occurred three times) may have elicited *bridge* as an IAR. In any event, it is apparent that we were unsuccessful in the attempt to establish homogeneity in false-alarm rates to control words.

REFERENCES

Bousfield, W. A., Cohen, B. H., Whitmarsh, G. A., & Kincaid, W. D. The Connecticut free association norms. Technical Report No. 35, 1961, University of Connecticut, Contract Nonr-631 (00), Office of Naval Research.

Bousfield, W. A., Whitmarsh, G. A., & Danick, J. J. Partial response identities in verbal generalization. *Psychol. Rep.*, 1958, 4, 703-713.

Cohen, B. H., Bousfield, W. A., & Whitmarsh, G. A. Cultural norms for verbal items in 43 categories. Technical Report No. 22, 1957, University of Connecticut, Contract Nonr-631 (00), Office of Naval Research.

Deese, J. On the prediction of occurrence of particular verbal intrusions in immediate recall. *J. exp. Psychol.*, 1959, 58, 17-22.

Mink, W. D. Semantic generalization as related to word association. *Psychol. Rep.*, 1963, 12, 59-67.

Russell, W. A., & Jenkins, J. J. The complete Minnesota norms for responses to 100 words from the Kent-Rosanoff Word-Association Test. Technical Report, No. 11, 1954, University of Minnesota, Contract N8 onr-66216, Office of Naval Research.

Shepard, R. N., & Teghtsoonian, M. Retention of information under conditions approaching a steady state. *J. exp. Psychol.*, 1961, 62, 302-309.

Underwood, B. J., & Richardson, J. Some verbal materials for the study of concept formation. *Psychol. Bull.*, 1956, 53, 84-95.

Implicit Responses and Conceptual Similarity

It is necessary to distinguish between two kinds of implicit responses. The response made to the word itself as the act of perceiving it has been labeled the *representational response* (RR) by Bousfield, Whitmarsh, and Danick (1958). A word which is produced by the stimulus properties of the RR will be called the *implicit associational response* (IAR). When two or more words elicit the same IAR, they may be said to have conceptual similarity. For example, the words *apple, pear,* and *orange* are conceptually related because they all elicit the IAR *fruit.*

There is considerable evidence to indicate that free learning (FL) is facilitated if the words are conceptually related (e.g., Bourne and Parker, 1964; Ekstrand and Underwood, 1963). There appear to be at least two possible explanations for the superior FL of conceptually related words. The words may tend to elicit each other directly (e.g., *apple* may elicit *orange*) or the common IAR may be involved. The present study controls for direct associations among words in the FL list and assesses the role of the common IAR in FL. This was accomplished by using words which do not elicit common IARs unless an additional cue, a cue which would provide the appropriate IAR, is present. Thus, if a list of words is presented to one group with the additional cue, and to another without the cue, differences in learning must be attributed to common IARs which were elicited in the former case and not the latter. Direct interitem associations should be equivalent under both conditions and cannot, therefore, enter differentially in the learning.

How can common IARs facilitate acquisition? The assumption made here is that common IARs produce increased frequency of the appropriate RR via the backward association. This may be illustrated. Assume that two words, *forest* and *pine,* occur successively in a list, each eliciting the IAR *green.* When *pine* is presented, the implicit chain is assumed to be: *pine* to *green* to *forest,* the second association being a backward association. Thus, the RR to *forest*

Gordon Wood and Benton J. Underwood, "Implicit Responses and Conceptual Similarity," *Journal of Verbal Learning and Verbal Behavior* 6 (1967): 1–10. Reprinted with permission. Copyright © 1967 by Academic Press Inc.

occurs twice, once when *forest* is presented and once when *pine* is presented. On the assumption that frequency of RRs is directly related to learning, a list in which common IARs are elicited should produce faster learning than one in which common IARs are not elicited. Furthermore, by the reasoning indicated, it must follow that in a series of conceptually related words those presented first in the series will be better recalled than those presented later, since the first ones will have a greater opportunity of being elicited by backward associations from the common IAR than will the latter ones.

Three variables are manipulated in the present study. The first is the cue variable. In one case the additional cue, in effect, provided S with the appropriate (common) IAR. In a second case a cue other than the relevant cue was presented. In a third case no cue was presented. The second variable was the number of instances within a concept (I/C). This variable was manipulated to determine if the presence of the common IAR had a differential effect depending on whether there were 3, 5, or 8 instances in each concept. The order of presentation of the items (constrained vs. random) was the final variable. In the constrained lists all the instances of one concept are presented, then all the instances of a second concept, etc. In the random lists, instances of the same concept do not necessarily appear consecutively. Other investigators (e.g., Bourne and Parker, 1964) have shown the constrained condition to be superior to the random. In the present study it is expected that the difference between constrained and random presentation will be absent or minimal when the common IAR is not elicited (irrelevant and no-cue conditions), and will be maximal under the relevant cue conditions.

EXPERIMENT I

Method

Design and Lists. The design can best be understood by referring to the lists in Table 3.4. Each of the five rows contains words which elicit a common sensory-impression response (Underwood and Richardson, 1956). That is, the eight words in row one all elicit *black* as a sensory impression. Similarly, the words in rows 2, 3, 4, and 5 elicit *red, green, yellow,* and *white,* respectively, as sensory impressions. The words in column one were used in the three instances/concept (I/C) list. The words in columns one and two were used in the five I/C list. All 40 words in Table 3.4 were used in the eight I/C list. The mean Thorndike-Lorge frequency and Underwood and Richardson dominance levels were approximately equal for the three lists.

Table 3.4 Words which Elicit a Common Color-Sense Impression According to the Underwood and Richardson Norms

Common Sense-Impression	Column I	Column II	Column III
Black	derby coal asphalt	coffee tar	telephone pot skunk
Red	brick lips measles	beet freckle	flannel cranberry tongue
Green	forest moss seaweed	grasshopper bean	pine spinach lizard
Yellow	canary custard sulphur	corn bracelet	moon pollen straw
White	chalk sheep diaper	frost napkin	cigarette hospital rice

The relevant cue for any of the rows of words in Table 3.4 was the IAR (sensory impression) common to these words. For the relevant-cue condition a rectangle of the appropriate color followed each stimulus word. For example, a black rectangle followed the stimulus word *tar*. In the irrelevant-cue condition, the five colors were randomly paired with the words from the list, with the restriction that a word was not paired with its relevant color cue. Thus, for the irrelevant-cue groups, a yellow, red, green or white square followed the stimulus word *tar*. For the no-cue condition, a non-colored rectangle followed each word.

The cue presented with the Underwood and Richardson sense-impression words was a manipulation of the presence of the common IAR because these words do not tend to elicit sensory-impression responses unless Ss are told to restrict themselves to sense impressions (Underwood and Richardson, 1956). Also, Underwood (1965) found no evidence that these words, when presented without any cue or special instructions, elicited sense-impression IARs.

Materials. The words were presented in booklets (4¼" by 5½") having a total of 15, 25, or 40 pages, depending upon the number of words presented, plus a cover page on which was written the booklet number. One word followed by a rectangle, either colored or blank, appeared in the middle of each page. In the nine constrained conditions, all the instances with the same IAR appeared consecutively in the lists. Eight different random orders of the five sense-impressions and the instances within each sense-impression were used. In the random conditions, eight random orders of the words were used with the restric-

Implicit Associative Responses 119

tion that the first five, second five, third five, etc., block of words contained one word from each of the five concepts. There were 144 booklets in all (eight random orders of each of 18 conditions).

Procedure. A total of 360 Northwestern University students in undergraduate psychology courses served as Ss, being run in groups of 5 to 25. All Ss in any one experimental session received lists of the same length. All 48 booklets representing a given length list were thoroughly shuffled prior to the experimental session and then passed out to the Ss according to their seating arrangement. Once a booklet was used, it was not used again until the other seven booklets of the same conditions had been used. The number of items/list was changed with each session (i.e., the first group of Ss was given the 40-item list, the second, third, fourth, etc., group was given the 25, 15, 40, etc., item list, respectively). The above procedure was continued until 20 Ss had served in each condition.

Each S received an answer sheet, with 48 blank spaces on which to write the words, and a booklet of words. The Ss were told to put the number of his or her booklet on the answer sheet. This identified the condition for each S. The Ss were instructed that they would have 5 sec to look at each word in the booklet, and that they would be told when to turn each page in the booklet. In addition, they were informed that there was "something" else on each page besides the word, which might or might not help them recall the word. It was stressed that Ss would only be asked to recall the words, order of recall being unimportant. An unlimited amount of time was allowed for Ss to recall the words that were in their booklet.

Results

The mean number of words recalled correctly for the 18 conditions is given in Table 3.5. An examination of Table 3.5 reveals that the relevant-cue groups were superior to both the irrelevant- and no-cue groups, and that the performance of the irrelevant- and no-cue groups was essentially equivalent. An analysis of variance demonstrated the cue variable to be significant, $F(2, 342) = 10.44, p < .001$. Although the order-of-presentation variable was not significant statistically, $F(1, 342) = 3.42, p > .05$, the anticipated superiority of the constrained conditions was partially supported in that eight of the nine groups receiving constrained presentation were superior to the corresponding groups receiving random presentation. The number of I/C was a significant source of variation, $F(2, 342) = 207.01, p < .001$, but this is not meaningful since the total number of items presented and, consequently, the total presentation time differed for the three levels of this variable. None of the interactions was significant.

It should be noted that the irrelevant-cue condition could be considered an interference paradigm in that the cue would produce an implicit response which was inappropriate to the word with which it

Table 3.5 Mean Correct Recall and *SD* for Each Experimental Condition

		\multicolumn{3}{c}{Constrained I/C}	\multicolumn{3}{c}{Random I/C}
		3	5	8	3	5	8
Relevant	M	12.60	15.50	20.15	11.15	15.20	19.90
	SD	1.93	2.69	4.05	1.77	2.94	4.26
Irrelevant	M	10.75	15.00	18.20	9.75	13.55	18.80
	SD	1.71	2.82	4.14	1.31	3.42	3.78
None	M	10.00	14.16	18.70	9.86	13.65	17.70
	SD	1.70	2.40	3.90	1.56	2.46	4.74

was paired. However, we have found no evidence of any kind (correct responses; clustering) that performance under the irrelevant-cue conditions differed from the performance shown when no cue was present.

Since the total presentation time has been shown to be an effective predictor of FL (Murdock, 1960), it was necessary to equate the number of correct responses recalled for total presentation time before considering the variable of number of I/C. This was done by using Murdock's formula to compute a k-score for each S, where $k = (R - m/t)$. In this formula R is the total number of correct responses, m is a constant, and t is the total presentation time in seconds. Since Murdock obtained the median m value of 6.1 over a series of experiments, this value was used as the constant in the above formula.

Figure 3.4 shows the mean k-scores for the 18 conditions. Except for the effect of the order of presentation and the number of I/C, the statistical analysis of the k-scores is consistent with the analysis made on the number of words recalled correctly (Table 3.5). The failure of the number of I/C to influence performance, which has been equated for total presentation time, $F(2, 342) = 2.04$, $p > .05$, supports Murdock's (1960) position that the number of items recalled after one presentation is a linear function of the total presentation time. The constrained groups were superior to the random groups, $F(1, 342) = 6.66$, $p < .01$. This variable appears significant in this analysis and not the earlier analysis because the correction for total presentation time decreased the variances for the various conditions differentially. Since the significance of the random

Implicit Associative Responses 121

vs. constrained variable depends on which score is considered, there is little choice but to accept the ambiguity. Nevertheless, the lack of a significant interaction between this variable and cue conditions does not support the expectation that constrained presentation would influence learning more under the relevant-cue conditions than under the irrelevant- and no-cue conditions.

Clustering in Recall. A cluster score was obtained for each S by counting the number of times two instances of the same concept (IAR) occurred consecutively in each recall protocol. In the irrelevant-cue condition the recall protocols could be scored according to the IAR that is assumed to be elicited, or the cue given. That is, are the words which are followed by a common irrelevant cue clustered in recall? Since there was slightly more clustering when scoring was done on the basis of the IAR that was assumed to occur, these cluster scores are reported. Dallett (1964) reported a procedure for calculating the number of

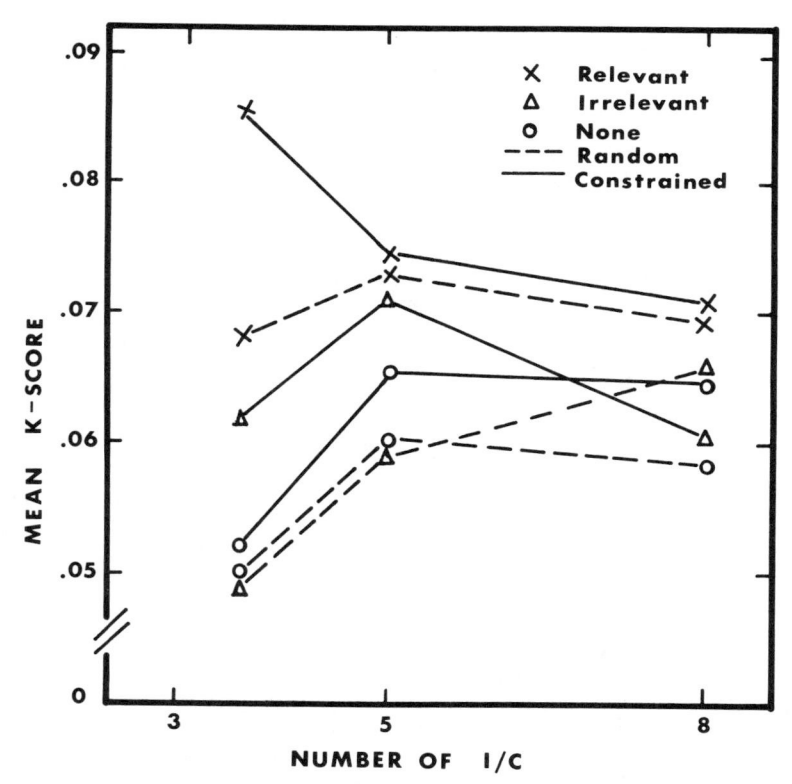

Figure 3.4 Mean *k*-scores for the 18 conditions.

clusters which would be expected if the recall protocol was randomly determined. The expected number of clusters is given by the formula

$$E(c) = \frac{\sum_{i=1}^{k} m_i^2}{\Sigma m_i} - 1$$

where m_i ($i = 1, 2, \ldots k$) is the number of words recalled in one of the k categories (concepts). For each S the expected number of clusters was subtracted from the obtained number of clusters to yield a score which should be independent of the number of I/C. This score will be called the deviation from expected (DE) score. Figure 3.5 shows the mean DE cluster score for each of the 18 conditions.

The analysis of the DE cluster scores indicated that cue, order of

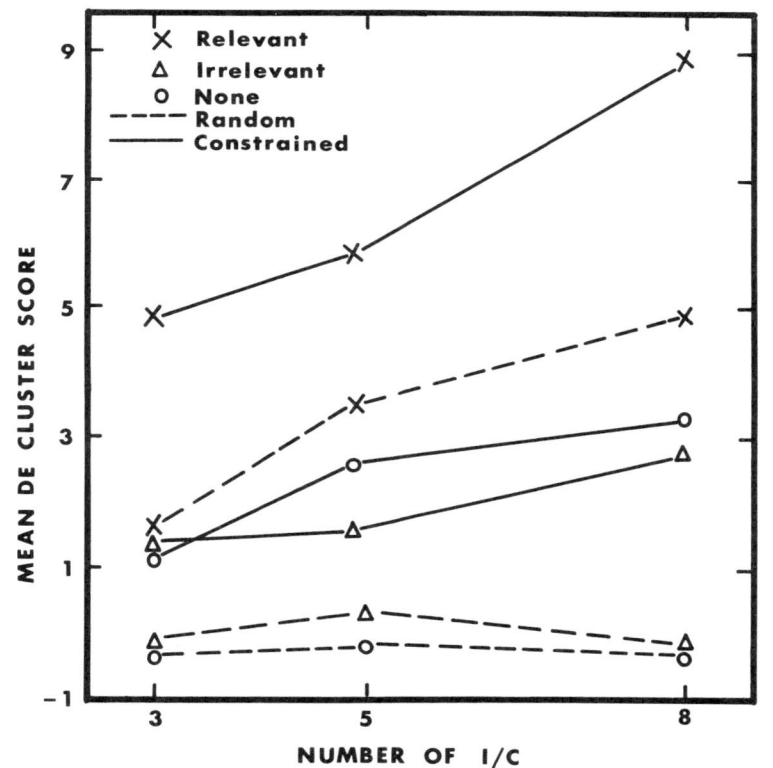

Figure 3.5 Mean DE cluster scores for the 18 conditions.

presentation, and number of I/C were all significant ($p < .001$) sources of variance yielding Fs of 120.44 (df = 2, 342), 132.86 (df = 1, 342), and 18.57 (df = 2, 342), respectively. The superior clustering in the relevant-cue groups indicates that the presence of the common IAR influenced the order of word recall. Also, the absence of clustering for the groups receiving random presentation and irrelevant- or no-cue supports the earlier assertion that the words used would not elicit sense-impression responses unless an appropriate cue was provided. The superior clustering as the number of I/C increases in the relevant-cue condition is consistent with the notion that the greater number of times a common IAR is elicited, the more the IAR should influence order of recall. Cue × Number of I/C, $F(4, 342)$ = 5.33, $p < .05$, and Order of Presentation × Number of I/C, $F(2, 342)$ = 5.02, $p < .05$, were the only significant interactions.

An analysis was made of the clustering according to serial position of the no-cue random presentation groups to determine if the superior clustering for the constrained presentation conditions resulted from Ss clustering according to serial position. That is, in both the random and constrained presentation conditions, Ss may cluster words in recall which are presented together during learning, but, when clustering is scored according to concepts, only the cluster scores of the constrained groups reflect this tendency. The protocols were scored to ascertain if the words presented in the first fifth, second fifth, etc., of the list were clustered in recall. The analysis revealed that approximately one half of the difference between the DE cluster scores for the constrained and random presentation, no-cue conditions can be attributed to clustering according to serial position. The superior clustering with constrained presentation, above that which can be attributed to clustering according to serial position in the no-cue condition, may result from the fact that for an occasional concept common IARs were elicited. However, the data on learning (previously presented) show that if this is true, it did not influence overall learning. It should also be noted that clustering scores in the other constrained conditions may also be in small part due to clustering by serial position.

Position of Instance within the Concept

The prediction was made that the first words in a series of conceptually related words should be better recalled than those presented later since the first ones have a greater opportunity of being elicited by backward associations from the common IAR. For the 20 Ss in each condition an analysis was made of correct recall as a function of the position of the instance within the concept for all five concepts taken together. Since eight random orders were used, at most only three Ss in any one condition received the same word orders, but the same words and word orders were used for all of the conditions of any given length of list. Thus, differences in the recall of words presented at the different positions within the concept, for conditions receiving the same length of list, may be attributable to the presence of the common IAR. Figure 3.6 gives the percentage correct recall for the positions of the instances within the concept for the six groups having constrained presentation; relevant- or no-cue; and 3, 5, or 8 I/C. Although the data for the groups receiving random presentation are not presented, they are consistent with the data presented in Fig. 3.6 in that the instances having an earlier position in the concept, in general, were recalled better than the later items for the relevant-cue conditions, but not for the no-cue conditions.

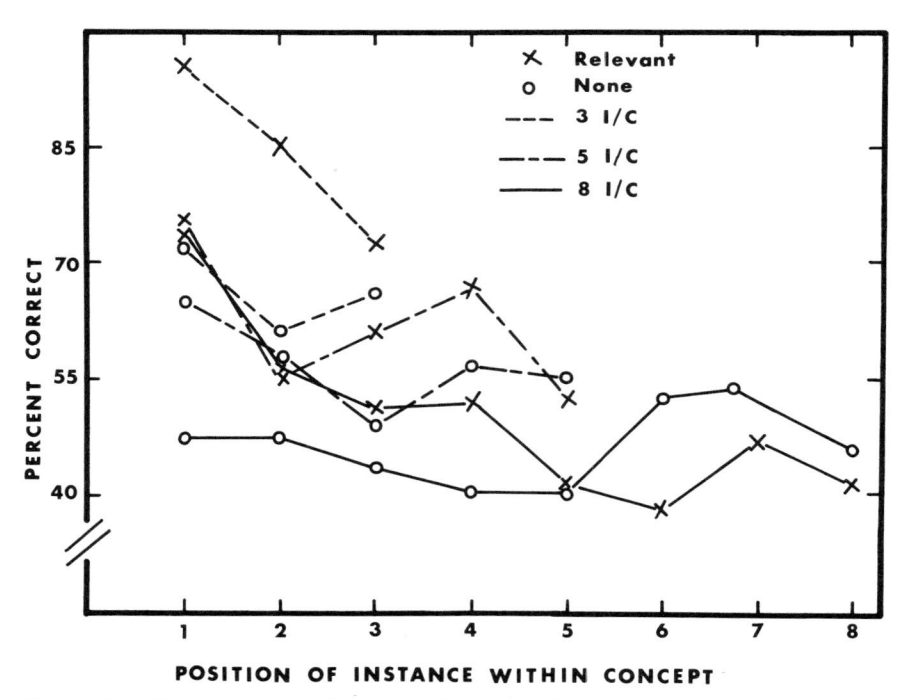

Figure 3.6 Percent correct for each of the positions of the instance within the concept for the groups receiving the constrained-presentation, relevant- and no-cue conditions.

A trend analysis of the data in Fig. 3.6 demonstrated that the position of the instance in the concept influenced recall for the 3, 5, and 8 I/C lists. However, the critical comparisons are the interactions between the cue variable and position of the instance within the concept since the earlier instances of a concept were predicted to be superior to the later instances for the relevant-cue condition but not for the no-cue conditions. An examination of the three I/C in Fig. 3.6 reveals that the differences between the relevant-cue and no-cue condition are greater for the first two instances than for the last instance, but this interaction, although it is in the predicted direction, failed to reach significance, $F(2, 76) = 2.83$, $p > .05$. There is no clear relationship between position and cue condition for the five I/C conditions. For the eight I/C lists, the interaction between position and condition was significant, $F(7, 266) = 3.59$, $p < .01$. It appears that in the eight I/C relevant-cue groups, the facilitation of the earlier items of a concept tends to be offset by a decrement in the later items. That is, Ss making a backward association to earlier items in the concept, in effect, are taking time away from the later items and spending it on the earlier items. However, since this crossover in the performance of the eight I/C relevant-cue and no-cue groups is not as clear in Exp. II, the matter will not be pursued further.

To rule out the possibility that the position of the concept within the list was, in part, responsible for the superior recall of the earlier instances of the concept for the relevant-cue groups, the five concepts were considered individually for each of the conditions of Fig. 3.6. This analysis demonstrated that the relationships existing in Fig. 3.6 were also present in each of the individual concepts. That is, the position of the concept within the list was not responsible for the superior recall of the earlier instances of the concept for the relevant-cue groups.

The superior recall of instances having an early position within the concept for the relevant-cue, constrained-presentation conditions, is consonant with the hypothesis that there is a backward association from the IAR to the RRs. Yet there still remains the possibility that the facilitation took place in the recall phase and not in the learning phase. That is, if during learning Ss were presented the items without the common IARs, and then presented the common IARs at recall, they might (for some unknown reason) be able to recall the earlier items of each concept better than the later items. Experiment II was designed to test this possibility.

EXPERIMENT II

Method

The relevant-cue, constrained-presentation, eight-I/C condition ($N = 13$) and no-cue, constrained-presentation, eight-I/C condition ($N = 16$) were run in an attempt to determine if the superior recall of earlier instances of a concept could be a recall phenomenon. Except for the nature of the answer sheet, the materials and procedure was identical to that of Exp. I. The following was written in all capital letters on the answer sheet: "Each word in your booklet could be grouped under one of the five colors given below. Write the words under the 'color' to which they belong." Each of the words *black, red, green, yellow,* and *white* was given as a column heading. There were eight blank spaces under each heading. For the relevant-cue group, the *S*s were given the answer sheets prior to receiving the booklets. The *S*s in the no-cue condition were given their answer sheets immediately after they had been allowed to look at the words in the booklet. Thus, the common IARs were not available for the *S*s in the no-cue condition until after the learning had taken place. That these *S*s were able to cluster their responses correctly is indicated by the fact that their mean number of incorrect word placement was only 1.06.

Results

Figure 3.7 shows the percentage of the total possible words that each group had correct for each of the eight positions of the instances. A trend analysis on these data demonstrated that: the relevant-cue condition was superior to the no-cue condition, $F(1, 27) = 9.96$, $p < .001$. The position of the instance within the concept was a significant source of variance, $F(7, 189) = 2.78$, $p < .01$, and the interaction between position and cue condition was significant, $F(7, 189) = 2.14$, $p < .05$. In short, the results of Exp. II are essentially identical to those for the corresponding groups in Exp. I. The failure of the no-cue group of Exp. II to perform differently from the no-cue group of Exp. I, as a result of being given the common IARs at recall, demonstrates rather conclusively that the facilitation of the earlier words in each concept in the relevant-cue conditions is a learning rather than a recall phenomenon. Also, since Underwood, Schwenn, and Keppel (1964) have demonstrated that there are no systematic trends in the performance of Northwestern *S*s over the school term, it would seem permissible to compare the mean performance of the no-cue group of Exp. II (16.38) with the corresponding group of Exp. I (18.70). The fact that performance is poorer in the condition in which *S*s were given the common IAR at recall would seem to

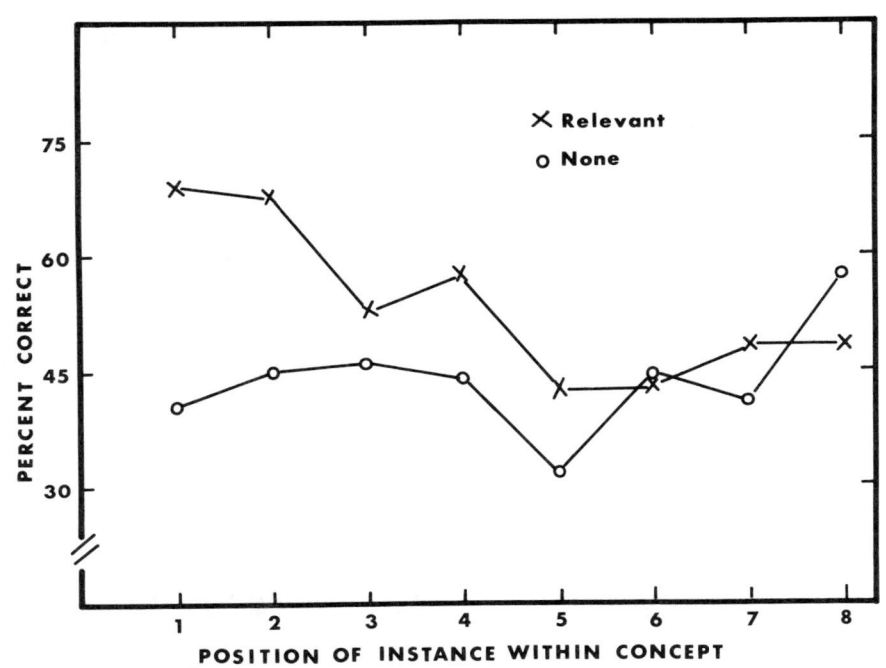

Figure 3.7 Percent correct for each of the eight positions of the instance within the concept for the two groups receiving the eight-I/C, constrained-presentation, relevant- and no-cue conditions.

rule out the possibility that the presence of the common IAR at recall facilitates performance.

DISCUSSION

Several points require comment. First, the predicted interaction between the order of presentation (constrained vs. random) and the cue variable was not obtained for the k-scores. That is, there was not a significantly greater difference between constrained and random presentation in the relevant-cue condition than in the irrelevant- and no-cue conditions. If one accepts the theory that the facilitation of learning in the relevant-cue conditions resulted from Ss making a backward association from the common IARs to the appropriate RRs, the failure to find the predicted interaction indicates that Ss can produce this backward association as well under random presentation as under constrained. In addition, the finding that the recall of words as a function of their position in the concept did not differ as a function of order of presentation, and the equivocal finding regarding the random vs. constrained variable, support the view that making backward associations from the IAR to the appropriate RRs is not affected by order of presentation.

Secondly, the recall of words as a function of the position of the instance within the concept was not in perfect accord with the predictions made for the relevant-cue, five-I/C conditions. Yet, this minor ambiguity should not be allowed to obscure the principal finding that the instances of a concept that are presented first are in general learned better than later instances when the common IAR is available. This finding strongly supports the hypothesis that the common IAR elicits earlier presented instances as backward associates. In effect, the earlier instances of a concept are given more "trials" than are the later instances.

Finally, the results of Exp. II indicate that Ss given the IAR at the time of recall did not perform better on items having an earlier position in the concept, verifying the view that the facilitation of the earlier instances of each concept takes place during the presentation of the words, i.e., during the learning trial. Also, a comparison of recall as a function of the position of the instance within the concept for the no-cue and relevant-cue groups supports the notion that the overall facilitation of the performance of the relevant-cue groups takes place during the learning trial. That is, these data are consistent with the notion that the superior learning of words that are conceptually related may be produced by a backward association from the common IAR to the appropriate RRs during the learning trial.

REFERENCES

Bourne, L. E., Jr., and Parker, B. K. Inter-item relationships, list structure, and verbal learning. *Canad. J. Psychol.,* 1964, 18, 52–61.

Bousfield, W. A., Whitmarsh, G. A., and Danick, J. J. Partial response identities in verbal generalization. *Psychol. Rep.,* 1958, 4, 703–713.

Dallett, K. M. Number of categories and category information in free recall. *J. exp. Psychol.,* 1964, 68, 1–12.

Ekstrand, B., and Underwood, B. J. Paced versus unpaced recall in free learning. *J. verb. Learn, verb. Behav.,* 1963, 2, 288–290.

Murdock, B. B. The immediate retention of unrelated words. *J. exp. Psychol.,* 1960, 60, 222–234.

Underwood, B. J. False recognition produced by implicit verbal responses. *J exp. Psychol.,* 1965, 70, 122–129.

Underwood, B. J., and Richardson, J. Some verbal materials for the study of concept formation. *Psychol. Bull.,* 1956, 53, 84–95.

Underwood, B. J., Schwenn, E., and Keppel, G. Verbal learning as related to point of time in the school term. *J. verb. Learn. verb. Behav.,* 1964, 3, 222–225.

4
Frequency Theory

A Frequency Theory of Verbal-Discrimination Learning

The present paper deals with the processes involved in verbal-discrimination (VD) learning. In VD learning, pairs of verbal units are presented to the subject (S), and his task is to discover which unit in each pair has been arbitrarily designated by the experimenter (E) as being the correct unit. The correct alternative shall be referred to as the C unit and the incorrect alternative as the I unit. Normally a list consisting of several VD pairs is presented on a memory drum, and S must pronounce the correct response within a prescribed time limit. In a typical VD list, the C and I items are presented to S one above the other. (Half the time the C unit is presented above the I unit, and half the time the two are reversed.) The S is requested to choose one of the two units and pronounce it, after which E informs S as to the correctness of his choice. This information has been given verbally—E says "right" or "wrong"—or visually—the memory drum is programmed to indicate the C item after S's choice is made. It has also been typical of VD procedures to omit a study trial at the beginning of learning; since there are only two alternatives (although more alternatives could be employed), S has a 50:50 chance of being correct without any learning taking place.

The theory to be presented here was first developed to explain the results of an experiment on transfer from one VD list to another VD list, but it became apparent that it could be used to interpret the manner in which a single VD list is learned. It will be useful to review first the results of that transfer experiment (Underwood, Jesse, & Ekstrand, 1964) and the manner in which the results were interpreted. The extension of the interpretation to single-list VD learning will then be considered.

Bruce R. Ekstrand, William P. Wallace, and Benton J. Underwood, "A Frequency Theory of Verbal-Discrimination Learning," *Psychological Review* 73 (1966): 566–578. Reprinted with permission. Copyright 1966 by the American Psychological Association.

This work was supported in part by Contract Nonr-1228 (15), Project NR 154-057, between Northwestern University and the Office of Naval Research. Reproduction in whole or in part is permitted for any purpose by the United States Government.

TRANSFER EXPERIMENT

The Underwood et al. (1964) experiment employed three conditions. The control condition involved the learning of two unrelated VD lists. In the wrong condition (W), Ss learned one VD list to criterion and then transferred to a second VD list in which the I item in each pair in List 1 remained the I item in List 2, but the C items of List 1 were replaced with new C items in List 2. Condition R (right) was the reverse of Condition W; the C items of List 2 were the same C items that were in List 1, but all of the I items were changed from List 1 to List 2.

The results indicated that Condition R showed essentially 100% transfer. Transfer was initially almost as high in Condition W, but these Ss showed a strange inability to improve their performance across trials. Indeed, the control group managed to reach criterion on List 2 before the W group.

Underwood et al. offered the following interpretation for their results. The basis for the discrimination in List 2 was the subjective difference in frequency of occurrence between the C and I items within a pair. In Condition R all of the I items were "new" items in List 2, and all of the C items were "old"—they had been in List 1. By always selecting the old items Ss could perform perfectly, which they essentially did. Always selecting the more frequent of the two units in a pair is a "rule" for VD learning which shall be referred to as Rule 1. The term rule shall be used for convenience of discussion; this usage should not be construed as necessarily meaning that S consciously applies a rule in the literal sense of the word. In the W condition, all of the I items were old, and all of the C items were new. Therefore, the appropriate rule would be always to guess the less frequent of the two units in a pair (Rule 2). Since Ss were fully informed about the relation between List 1 and List 2, and since at the start of learning of List 2 it should be very easy to tell new items from old, initial transfer would be high in both groups, and indeed it was.

It can be seen, however, that as trials continued on List 2 the new items would start to get old, and the old items would get older. Underwood et al. reasoned that C items get older faster than I items because the C items are pronounced once in the act of anticipation as well as seen once on the memory drum. The I items, on the other hand, are only seen on the drum and are not pronounced. Thus, each trial adds two frequency "units" to the C items and one unit to the I items. This is the basic postulate of the present theory.

Assuming this 2:1 frequency difference in favor of the C items, the failure of the W groups to improve with practice is understandable. The new C items get two units on each trial whereas the old I items are getting older, but only at the rate of one unit on each trial. At some later point in learning, the new C items will be as old as the I items, and beyond that point they will be older than the I items. Application of Rule 2 from this point on will result in an incorrect response because Rule 1 is now appropriate. For any given VD pair, Rule 1 or Rule 2 may be the appropriate one, depending upon the age of the C and I items. Neither rule could be applied with success until all of the C items had become older than their corresponding I items; therefore, the performance should suffer.

SINGLE-LIST VD SITUATION

The purpose of the present paper is to extend the basic hypothesis of Underwood et al., designed to explain transfer results, to the single-list VD situation. It is assumed that in learning a single VD list, the cue for discrimination is the subjective difference in frequency of occurrence between the C and I item in each VD pair. More particularly, it is asserted that as trials proceed there is built up at least a 2:1 frequency difference in favor of the C item, and that this difference can serve as the discriminative cue so that application of Rule 1 will result in the correct response.

Let us trace the sequence of events in the learning of a VD list and indicate the critical events assumed by the theory. On the guessing trial, a pair of items is presented, and S reads each one. This act of perception of each alternative has been referred to as a representational response (RR) by Bousfield, Whitmarsh, and Danick (1958). The RR to each item, according to the present theory, adds one frequency unit to the C item and one to the I item. After the two RRs have been made, S chooses one of the two items and pronounces it; this is his guess as to the correct one. This pronuniciation response shall be referred to as the PR. It is assumed that the PR adds another frequency unit to whichever item is pronounced. If S made his PR to the C item, there would be a 2:1 difference in favor of the C item. If S chose the I item, there would be a 2:1 difference in favor of the I item.

Now, by chance, half the PRs would be I items and half would be C items, so that if no frequency units other than the RR and PR were involved, the frequency-difference cue would be useless. The more frequent item in each pair would be correct in half the pairs (those pairs for which S guessed the C item) and incorrect in half the pairs (those for which S guessed the I item). Rule 1 would be appropriate for the former type of pair, and Rule 2 would be appropriate for the latter type of pair. In order to learn on this basis, S would have to learn which pairs go with Rule 1 and which go with Rule 2. For this reason, it is believed that a third type of response is occurring, namely, a rehearsal-of-the-correct-alternative-response (RCR). This RCR may be thought of as a pronouncing of the C item implicitly or explicitly, and it may occur more than once immediately after E supplies the information about the correctness of S's response.

The nature of the hypothesized processes in VD learning can now be more explicitly stated. In general, it is asserted that the single VD list of unrelated items is learned by application of Rule 1; namely, select the more frequent alternative. In order for this to be adaptive, Rule 1 must be appropriate for all the pairs; that is, the unit with greater frequency must be the correct one. Pairs for which S guesses the C item on the first trial will have a 2:1 difference in favor of the C item, so Rule 1 will be appropriate. Pairs for which S guesses the I item, as pointed out, would have a 2:1 difference in favor of the I item, so Rule 1 would be inappropriate. However, if S makes one RCR after having been informed that his guess was incorrect, the difference in frequency would be eliminated. Such pairs would now have 2:2 ratios, and on the next trial if S guessed and this time chose the C item, there would then be a 4:3 frequency ratio in favor of the C item. Now Rule 1 would be appropriate for this item. If S makes more than one RCR after choosing the I item, the pair would immediately become appropriate for Rule 1. Implicit in this discussion is the prediction that if the guessing trial were eliminated (thus eliminating some of the PRs to the I items), performance would be enhanced.

The extent to which these RCRs are made by Ss is not known, but for frequency to be the appropriate cue and for Rule 1 to be the appropriate rule for every pair, it is only necessary to postulate that one RCR is made, and that it is made only when S guesses the I item. In other words, the frequency unit that is added by the RCR just offsets the frequency unit that the I item received as a result of the PR. This returns the pair to a "neutral" state (2:2) so that there is a 50:50 chance that S will make his PR to the C item on the next trial. If Ss make RCRs more than once for any given pair, and if they make RCRs when they have chosen the C item, the frequency cue would only be further enhanced. For example, if S makes a correct choice on the guessing trial, it has been postulated that there is a 2:1 difference in favor of the C item. But if, in addition, S makes one RCR, there would be a 3:1 difference.

As trials continue, there will be a buildup in frequency units for the C and I items, but this buildup will always tend to favor the C item. As a result, the difference in frequency units between the C and I items will increase, making the discrimination between the more and less frequent items easier. Note that the interpretation states that the number of frequency units for each item can be determined by counting the RRs, PRs, and RCRs that have been made to that item. It also is apparent from the above discussion that it has been assumed that one RR adds as much to the subjective frequency of an item as does one PR, or RCR; that is, the equality of RRs, PRs, and RCRs has been assumed. Both of these assumptions are merely working hypotheses. It is quite possible that the three postulated responses are unequal, that an RCR is "worth more" than an RR, or that a PR of the C item (a correct response) is somehow qualitatively different than a PR of the I item (an error) in terms of the consequences for frequency units. For simplicity's sake it has been assumed that these responses are equal in terms of frequency units added.

A fourth way in which frequency units may be added to VD items is through an implicit associative response (IAR). Bousfield et al. (1958) hypothesized that the presentation of a verbal unit elicits IARs related to the given verbal unit. Thus, if the word *dog* is presented, an IAR of *cat* (or some other related item) is presumed to occur. In a VD list the frequency of a given unit may be increased if that unit has occurred elsewhere in the list as an IAR. For example, if the word *cat* appears in the list, it will attain a certain frequency value after one presentation based on RRs, PRs, and RCRs. The appearance of the word *dog* in the same list may increase the frequency value of the word *cat* to the degree that *dog* elicits *cat* as an IAR. To the extent that the associations are bidirectional, the appearance of *cat* may add frequency units to *dog*. In other words, S may "confuse" an IAR with an RR, so that these IARs may add frequency units in the same sense that an RR does. This frequency alteration by an IAR mechanism is assumed to occur only in specific instances (e.g., VD lists containing associatively related words).

Another major process postulated here is that Ss can and do discriminate items on the basis of their frequency of occurrence. That they can make accurate judgments of the frequency of an item in the language has been shown by Underwood (1966). The Underwood et al. (1964) transfer study shows that when frequency differences are extremely large, performance is essentially perfect; a fact which strongly suggests that the cue for discrimination in that study was the frequency difference. It has also been stated that Ss learn single VD lists by application of Rule 1; however, there is no reason to believe that when the frequency difference is reversed (i.e., the less frequent member of each pair is correct), Ss cannot operate using Rule 2. The W condition of the Underwood et al. (1964) study shows that they can. Thus, either Rule 1 or 2 can be applied depending on the appropriateness of the situation. In the single-list VD situation where S is required to pronounce the C item, there is a built-in difference in frequency, due to this PR, which makes Rule 1 more appropriate.

THE EXPERIMENT

The frequency theory, first developed to explain the transfer results in the Underwood et al. (1964) experiment, was admittedly postulated after the data were collected and analyzed. As such, the theory requires verification under other situations, and this was the purpose of the present experiment. More particularly, it was desired that the theory as applied to the single-list VD situation be tested.

It was reasoned that if the discriminative cue is the relative frequency of the two units in a pair, increasing the difference in frequency should facilitate performance (a difference of 4:1 should be easier than 2:1), and decreasing the difference should inhibit performance (a "difference" of 2:2 should be more difficult than 2:1). The method decided upon to produce these increases or decreases was to have an item occur in two pairs; therefore, the repeated item would be doubled in frequency, receiving two RRs per trial instead of one. For the moment, let us consider only the frequency units added by RRs and PRs, and let us assume that the frequency ratio is normally 2:1 when there are no repeated items in the list.

In the first condition, the same item occurs in two pairs, and it is correct in both pairs; this will be referred to as the same-right condition (SR). Since the repeated item is the C item in the two pairs in which it occurs, it will have four frequency units added to it on each trial (two RRs and two PRs, assuming S guesses the C item). The I item in each of those pairs will have only one unit added on each trial (an RR). Thus, for each pair there will be a 4:1 ratio in favor of the more frequent item, and application of Rule 1 will result in the correct response. If a 4:1 ratio makes for easier discrimination than a 2:1 ratio, Condition SR should surpass a control condition in which there are no repeated items in the list.

In the second condition, the same item occurs in two pairs, but it is incorrect in both pairs; this was called the same-wrong condition (SW). Since the I item gets only one unit per trial (an RR), the repeated item in this condition will now have only two units added to it on each trial (one RR for each pair in which it occurs). The C item in each of these pairs will also get two units added per trial (one RR and one PR). Thus, the ratio is 2:2 when only RRs and PRs are considered. This should be considerably more difficult than the SR condition where the ratio is 4:1 and also more difficult than the control condition (2:1).

The third condition investigated was designed to produce maximum interference by making the frequency cue very difficult to use. In this condition the repeated item is the C item in one of the two pairs in which it occurs and the I item in the other pair; this shall be referred to as the same-both condition (SB). Consider the pair in which the repeated item is correct; it receives two units for being correct (one RR and one PR) and one unit from the fact that it is repeated in another pair (an RR). The I item in this pair receives only one unit, an RR. The resultant ratio is 3:1 with the more frequent one being correct. However, in the pair in which the repeated item is incorrect, the situation is reversed. The repeated item has a frequency of three (an RR and a PR from the other pair, and an RR from this pair), and the C item in this pair has a frequency of two (one RR and one PR). The resultant ratio is 2:3 with the *less* frequent item being correct. As a result, Rule 1 would be appropriate for the pair in which the repeated item is correct, but Rule 2 would apply to the pair in which the repeated item was incorrect. Such an arrangement should produce considerable interference, so the SB group should be inferior to the other three conditions, SW, SR, and the control. In summary, the frequency theory predicts that the SR group should surpass the control condition which should surpass the SW condition. Finally, the SB group should do poorest.

As a second method of increasing or decreasing the frequency ratios within a VD pair, strong associates of some of the items in other pairs were inserted. Thus, one pair might be *Queen-Fast* and another pair, *King-Pepper.* Instead of repeating *Queen* to add to its frequency, we reasoned that presentation of *King* would lead to an IAR which would most likely be the word *Queen.* Of course, to the extent that the associations are bidirectional, presentation of *Queen* would also lead to an IAR of *King.* Underwood (1965) had in-

Frequency Theory 139

Table 4.1 Sample Pairs

Control	Same Right (SR)	Same Wrong (SW)
Queen[a]-Fast Door[a]-Pepper	Queen[a]-Fast Queen[a]-Pepper	Queen-Fast[a] Queen-Pepper[a]
Same Both (SB)	Associate Right (AR)	Associate Wrong (AW)
Queen[a]-Fast Queen-Pepper[a]	Queen[a]-Fast King[a]-Pepper	Queen-Fast[a] King-Pepper[a]
	Associate Both (AB)	
	Queen[a]-Fast King-Pepper[a]	

[a]Denotes the correct item in each pair.

dependent evidence that Ss may confuse the RR to an item with the same response given as an IAR to a strong associate of that item. For example, if *King* were actually presented, but *Queen* was never presented, Ss would indicate, nevertheless, that *Queen* (the IAR to *King*) had actually been presented. The present manipulations were designed to explore the possibility, mentioned earlier, that IARs may contribute frequency units in the same sense that RRs, PRs, and RCRs are hypothesized to increase frequency.

Using strong associates, the three experimental conditions described above were repeated. In Condition associate right (AR), the strong associates were the C items in their respective pairs; in Condition associate wrong (AW), the associated items were the I items in their respective pairs; in Condition associate both (AB), one item would be the C item in its pair, and the associate of that item would be the I item in its pair. To the extent that Ss make IARS that are words in other pairs, the predictions for these associated (A) conditions are the same as those for the conditions in which an item is actually repeated (S conditions). The AR condition should produce facilitation, the AB condition should produce interference, and the AW condition should fall in between AR and AB, and below the control condition. Examples of the seven types of pairs are presented in Table 4.1.

Design

The design was a 3 × 2 factorial, with 2 types of interpair relationships (S or A) and 3 types of lists (R, W, or B). This produces the 6 experimental groups described above: SR, SW, SB, AR, AW, and AB. In addition, a control group was run. The Ss in this group learned a VD list in which there were no formal interpair relationships.

The frequency theory predicts a main effect of type of list—the R conditions should surpass the W conditions, both of which should surpass the B conditions—and an interaction of type of List × type of Interpair Relationship. This interaction is predicted because the effect of type of list (R, W, or B) should be greater when the same item occurs in two pairs (S conditions) than when strong associates occur in different pairs (A conditions). Repeating the same item will always add one frequency unit, but presentation of a strong associate will add a frequency unit only if S makes the appropriate IAR.

Lists

Each of the seven lists contained 20 VD pairs. The items were selected from the Russell and Jenkins (1954) and the Palermo and Jenkins (1964) word-association norms. From these norms 40 pairs of associated items were selected; it was attempted in the process to keep interpair associations at a minimum. By selecting at random one word from each pair, the 40 presumably unrelated words

Table 4.2 Lists Used

Control list	S list	A list
Cold-Sickness	Cold-Sickness[a]	Cold-Sickness[a]
Boy-Woman	Cold-Woman	Hot-Woman
Chair-Head	Chair-Head	Chair-Head
Carpet-Foot	Chair-Foot[a]	Table-Foot[a]
House-Rough	House-Rough[a]	House-Rough[a]
Dark-Bread	House-Bread	Home-Bread
Tiger-Wool	Tiger-Wool	Tiger-Wool
Nail-Short	Tiger-Short[a]	Lion-Short[a]
Queen-Fast	Queen-Fast	Queen-Fast
Door-Pepper	Queen-Pepper[a]	King-Pepper[a]
Needle-Sweet	Needle-Sweet[a]	Needle-Sweet[a]
Ugly-Shallow	Needle-Shallow	Thread-Shallow
Road-Web	Road-Web	Road-Web
Round-Doctor	Road-Doctor[a]	Street-Doctor[a]
Hill-Smoke	Hill-Smoke	Hill-Smoke
White-Baby	Hill-Baby[a]	Mountain-Baby[a]
Steal-Soft	Steal-Soft[a]	Steal-Soft[a]
Loud-Apple	Steal-Apple	Thief-Apple
Town-Low	Town-Low[a]	Town-Low[a]
Bed-Cat	Town-Cat	City-Cat

Note—In the Control list, the pairs are given in the order: C item—I item; Cold was correct, Sickness was incorrect. In the A and S lists, both of the associated or repeated items were correct in conditions AR and SR, incorrect in AW and SW, and one was correct, one incorrect in AB and SB.

[a]Indicates those pairs in which the associated or repeated item was incorrect in the AB or SB conditions, respectively.

Frequency Theory 141

for the control list were obtained. These 40 words were paired randomly to make the 20 VD pairs, and within each pair one word was randomly designated as the C item for that pair; the remaining item, of course, became the I item.

In order to construct the experimental lists 10 pairs were chosen at random from the 20 control pairs. In addition, the 10 I items from the remaining 10 control pairs were used. This provided a pool of 10 pairs and 10 single items. From each of the 10 pairs chosen from the control list, two pairs for use in the experimental lists were constructed. For example, one control pair was *Queen-Fast;* in the S list this became two pairs, *Queen-Fast* and *Queen-Pepper, Pepper* having been an I item in one of the 10 control pairs not used. In the A list, the pair *Queen-Fast* also was used to make up two pairs, *Queen-Fast* and *King-Pepper*. By using the 10 control pairs and the 10 I items selected from the control list, 20 experimental pairs were constructed with maximum overlap between S, A, and control lists. The pairings for the S, A, and control lists are presented in Table 4.2.

Once the pairs were determined, the right and wrong members were designated as follows: In the AR list, the two associated items (e.g., *Queen* and *King*) were both correct in their respective pairs; in the AW list, the pairs were simply "turned over" so that the two associated items were wrong in their respective pairs (i.e., *Fast* and *Pepper* were correct). In the AB list, one of the two related pairs (chosen at random) was turned over so that the I item in one pair was a strong associate of a C item in another pair (e.g., *Queen-Fast, Queen* is correct; *King-Pepper, Pepper* is correct). For the S lists the procedure was identical; in SR, the repeated item was correct in both pairs in which it occurred; in SW, the list was turned over so that the repeated item was incorrect in both pairs; in SB, the repeated item was correct in one pair but incorrect in the other pair in which it appeared.

Procedure

The procedure employed group learning sessions with the materials being presented via a tape recorder. The learning method was alternate study and test trials with a modified anticipation procedure on the test trials. Four study and four test trials were administered to each of the seven groups. No guessing trial was used. The presentation rate was 3 seconds for both study and test trials.

On study trials, the two items in each pair were read, and then the voice on the tape repeated the correct one; for example, "*Queen-Fast, Queen* is correct." Both the reading of the pair and the saying of the C item took place within the 3-second interval. This procedure insured that a frequency difference in favor of the correct alternative existed, because the C item was said twice on the study trials. On test trials, the pairs were again read at a 3-second rate, but the voice did not indicate correctness. The *S*s recorded their responses on IBM answer sheets numbered from 1 to 80, with two alternatives for each of the 80 numbers. As each pair was read, *S*s indicated in the corresponding place on their answer sheets which member of the pair (first or second) was correct. Since the nature of this procedure does not allow *S* to make a PR, the frequency unit for the PR is eliminated. Instead, the voice on the tape spoke the

C item twice on study trials to insure the 2:1 ratio postulated by the theory. Across the four study and four test trials, the C item of each pair was read first four times and second four times. Within a trial, the ordering of the C and I items was random. Eight random orders of the 20 pairs were used for the eight presentations.

Subjects and Instructions

The Ss were college students from introductory psychology courses at Northwestern University; there were 20 in each of the seven groups. The seven conditions were each run twice, so a total of 14 group sessions were administered. These 14 sessions were run at either 1:00 P.M. or 1:30 P.M. on 7 consecutive school days. The Ss made an appointment for one of the 14 sessions at their convenience. The seven conditions were assigned at random to the 14 different sessions, subject to the restriction that each condition occur once before any condition received its second session. The result was that there were 20, 21, or 22 Ss in each of the seven groups. IBM sheets were randomly discarded until each group consisted of 20 Ss.

The Ss were read ordinary instructions for VD learning with the necessary modifications for the group procedure. No mention was made of the possibility of repeated or associated items.

RESULTS

The results (mean number of total errors) are shown in Figure 4.1—acquisition curves revealed no interactions with trials. The base line in Figure 4.1 represents an assumed continuum of similarity of implicit responses ranging from unrelated items (control) to associated items (A) to identical or same items (S). The plotting parameter is the type of list, either R, W, or B. In addition, for convenience of comparison, a dotted line representing the control mean is included.

An initial analysis of variance was performed on all seven groups. This produced an F (6, 133) of 25.68 which is highly significant. This indicates that the different treatments did produce differences in learning. Next a 3 × 2 analysis of variance was performed on the six experimental groups. The results indicated that both main effects and the interaction were significant at better than the .01 level. The main effect of A versus S interpair relationship produced an F (1, 133) of 18.48, that of type of list (R, W, or B) and F (2, 133) of 52.78. The interaction gave an F (2, 133) of 8.83. It can be seen from the df that these Fs are based on the within-groups term for all seven groups combined.

The results indicate that the A lists were easier than the S lists. Second, the type of list (R, W, or B) is important: the R conditions

Frequency Theory 143

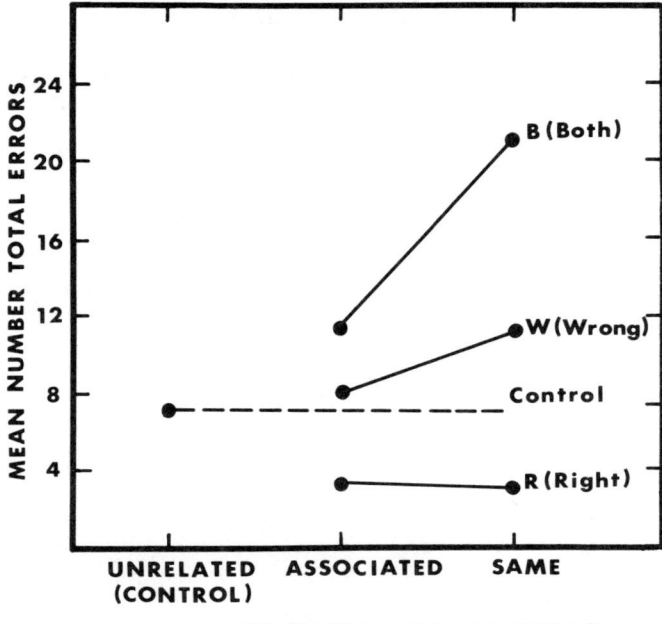

Figure 4.1 Mean total errors in four trials of VD learning for the six experimental groups and the control group. (The dotted line represents the control mean and is presented for the convenience of comparison.)

are clearly superior to the W conditions which, in turn, are superior to the B conditions. The interaction indicates that, as predicted, these differences between R, W, and B lists are more pronounced with the S interpair relationship than with the A relationship.

The control-group mean falls exactly as predicted, between the R and W conditions. Thus, numerically, the W and B conditions show interference, and the R conditions show facilitation. To evaluate the differences among the seven groups, a Duncan multiple-range test was performed using the .05 level of significance (Edwards, 1960). The results are shown in Table 4.3 where the seven means are given.

Within the S conditions, SR is significantly superior to the control condition whereas SW and SB are significantly inferior to the control. These four groups are thus ordered and differ significantly as predicted by the theory. Furthermore, since the SW group differs from the control group, interference in this group has apparently been produced by repeating an I item in another pair.

Table 4.3 Mean Total Errors for the Seven Groups and Results of the Duncan Multiple-Range Test

SB	SW	AB	AW	Control	AR	SR
21.50	11.35	11.30	8.00	6.90	3.05	2.80

Note.—Any two means underlined by the same line are not significantly different (Edwards, 1960).

Within the A conditions, the results are not as conclusive as for the S conditions. The four groups (including the control) are ordered in the same way as in the S conditions, but, as expected, the differences among them are considerably smaller. The AR group is significantly superior to the control group, and AB is significantly inferior to the control, indicating facilitation and interference, respectively. The AW group, however, is only slightly and insignificantly inferior to the control group, which may indicate that there is no interference from a strong associate being in the list when both associated items are I items.

DISCUSSION

The results of this experiment provide substantial support for the frequency theory. Both main effects and the interaction in the 3 × 2 design were significant at the .01 level in the predicted direction. Within the A conditions and within the S conditions, the groups were ordered exactly as predicted. By increasing the difference in frequency between the C and I items (R conditions), performance was improved, and by decreasing this difference (W conditions), interference, although small in amount, was apparent. Much more striking inhibition was apparent in the B conditions which were designed to produce maximum difficulty for frequency discrimination.

The results would also tend to support the idea that these frequencies can be manipulated by presenting associates of some items in other pairs. However, due to the small effects of this operation, a strong conclusion is not indicated. Nevertheless, it appears that under optimal conditions, the perceived frequency of the word *Queen* can be increased by presenting the word *King.* This is taken as further support for the operation of an implicit associative-response process in *S*s as they respond to verbal stimuli.

GENERAL DISCUSSION

The above experiment has put the frequency theory to a rather severe test, and it has survived. In view of this success, other predictions of the theory and related evidence in the literature shall be examined.

Similarity

Increasing intralist similarity should interfere with VD learning (the similarity existing between correct and incorrect alternatives). The more similar two items are, the more likely an RR, PR, or RCR made to one item will be confused with an RR, PR, or RCR made to another item. The SB condition from the experiment reported here is just an extreme case of this similarity (identity), and SB was shown to be an interference condition. Both Underwood and Archer (1955) and Battig and Bracket (1963) have shown that increasing formal intralist similarity in a VD list can produce interference.

Underwood and Viterna (1951) compared VD lists of high and medium meaningful similarity manipulated within a pair, keeping interpair similarity low. Thus, the two adjectives within a pair were either of high or medium synonymity. Their results indicated a small but significant difference in favor of the medium-similarity group. Although the interference in the present experiment was entirely interpair interference, with intrapair similarity at a minimum, the frequency theory would predict interference in either case. If *King* and *Queen* are in the same pair, the IAR to *King* would tend to increase the frequency of *Queen,* and vice versa, just as if *King* and *Queen* were in two different pairs. Thus, the Underwood-Viterna conditions were quite similar to the AB condition which showed evidence of interference.

Meaningfulness

The theory would seem to require the prediction that, with integrated units, meaningfulness of the units (in terms of frequency) should have no effect. If the two units in a VD pair are of equal frequency, whether that frequency is high or low on an absolute scale, adding an additional frequency unit to either item should make the pair more discriminable. The theory might even predict (according to Weber's law) that adding one unit to an item already high in frequency should be less noticeable than adding one frequency unit to an item low in frequency. This would mean that VD pairs of very-high-frequency units would be more difficult than pairs of low-frequency units. Assuming that frequency units established outside the laboratory are comparable to frequency units established by RRs, PRs, and RCRs in the laboratory, one might then predict that VD pairs of high-frequency words would be more difficult than pairs of low-frequency words. However, the applicability of Weber's law in this situation has not been demonstrated, and neither has the equality of experimental and extraexperimental frequency units.

There is some evidence that VD learning is not strongly affected by the meaningfulness of the items. Keppel (1966) found no difference in trials to criterion between a VD list of nonsense syllables and a list of words. Postman (1962) found that VD pairs of high-frequency words were more difficult than pairs composed of either low- or medium-frequency words. It should be pointed out, however, that the difficulty of the high-frequency list may be a result of a greater number of interitem associations in that list (Deese, 1960). To the extent that there are interitem associations in Postman's high-frequency list, it is similar to the AB list of the present experiment (an interference condition) which may explain why it was more difficult than the medium- and low-frequency lists.

If a detrimental effect of low meaningfulness is found for VD learning, the theory would predict that this would be with nonintegrated units in which the RRs, PRs, and RCRs are letter responses, instead of responses to the entire unit. To the extent that there are repeated letters in the list, the frequency theory would predict interference, since the RR to a nonintegrated unit could easily be confused with the RR to another unit with similar letters (e.g., Underwood & Archer, 1955). Moreover, the lower the integration, the less reliable the RR is likely to be; that is, the less similar two RRs to the *same* unit will be. Until the unit is integrated sufficiently for RRs to be reliable, we cannot expect a buildup of a particular PR that can be used as a frequency cue.

The theory need not necessarily predict a difference in VD learning as a function of meaningfulness or frequency of occurrence of words in the language since extraexperimental frequency may not be comparable to experimentally induced frequency. However, if frequency differences are induced entirely within the experiment (possibly by familiarization training), it is possible that a VD pair of two high-frequency units will be more difficult than a VD pair of two low-frequency units. Other things being equal (interitem associations in particular), an extra frequency unit added to a member of a high-frequency pair should not be "worth as much" in terms of cue value as a frequency unit added to a member of a low-frequency pair.

Presentation Rate

The theory makes a rather unusual prediction with regard to the effects of anticipation time. A large increase in anticipation time, with study time held constant, should have no effect on VD performance, or perhaps even an inhibitory effect. If S is forced to spend extra time studying the two units in a VD pair before he is allowed to make his choice, performance could suffer. This additional time should result in additional RRs being made to the C and I items. If the same number of RRs is added to the C and I items by this extra time, the relative frequency difference can only decrease, making the discrimination more difficult (again assuming the applicability of Weber's law). An analogy can be made with the strategy often suggested for taking multiple-choice examinations; namely, "stick with your first choice." Continued study of the alternative answers should tend to reduce their discriminability. On the other hand, if the study time after reinforcement is increased, the theory predicts better performance, on the assumption that this time will be spent mainly in the act of making RCRs. Increasing the study time after reinforcement should increase the number of RCRs relative to the number of RRs to the I item; any such increase should result in a more discriminable frequency difference.

Forgetting

If one subscribes to a strict interference theory of forgetting and applies it to the frequency theory, one would have to predict no forgetting of a VD pair unless there were "occurrences" of the C and I items during the retention interval. Such occurrences would add frequency units to both items and reduce the discriminability of the pair. By appropriate manipulations in a second VD list, it should be possible to produce a variety of positive or negative transfer effects (e.g., Underwood et al., 1964) and either retroactive inhibition or facilitation when recall of the first list is measured. Of course, in addition to the interference effects, there may be some loss of frequency cue due to a decay process.

From the standpoint of a strict interference interpretation, the theory must predict that increasing the number of pairs in a VD list will have no effect on the number of trials required to learn that list. This prediction, however, will hold only if it is possible to increase list length without also increasing the number of interitem associations. Such an increase in interitem associations would tend to make the longer lists analogous to the AB list of the present experiment and would result in poorer performance.

Further Implications

Some predictions based on the frequency theory and some findings of other investigators which may be interpreted within the framework of the theory have been noted. The fact that other theoretical approaches may be developed which will give an equally good accounting of the data available is fully recognized. At the same time, however, it must be emphasized that there is a critical finding which must be handled by any alternative theoretical approach. This finding, predicted by the frequency theory, showed a large difference in learning between a list in which repeated items were correct and a list in which repeated items were incorrect. That learning of the latter list resulted in some interference (when compared with a control) only adds to the problem with which other theories must cope.

The assumption that differences in frequency of events provide a discriminative cue should have applicability to phenomena beyond those associated with VD learning. Some possibilities for such extensions of the theory may be mentioned briefly. It has often been noted that in tasks where verbal units must be recalled (paired associates, free learning) it is a rare occurrence for S to produce a unit that is not in the list. Even if the response units are 10 single letters drawn randomly from the 26 letters, S will rarely produce one of the 16 letters not in the list. It is as if some selector mechanism (Underwood & Schulz, 1960) quickly and effectively differentiates between the appropriate and inappropriate pool of responses. A frequency discrimination may be responsible for this selective capacity. The letters in the list have a situational frequency of at least one each, those not in the list have none, thereby providing the discriminative cue. Even if S cannot recall response terms which are in a list, he is able to reject response terms which are not in the list.

In learning the second list of certain transfer paradigms (e.g., A-B, A-B'), an appreciable number of intrusions from the first list may be observed in learning the second list (Postman & Stark, 1964). Furthermore, many of these intrusions appear after several trials on the second list (Schwenn & Underwood, 1965). This might be interpreted to mean that intrusions are most likely to occur when the associative strengths of two responses elicited by the same stimulus become equivalent. However, the frequency-discrimination theory would predict this phenomenon on the grounds that after the second-list responses have occurred several times the frequency discrimination between first- and second-list responses breaks down as the frequency of the second-list responses approximates that of the first.

Intrusions at recall in retroactive-inhibition studies decrease sharply in frequency as the degree of interpolated learning increases beyond the level of original learning (Melton & Irwin, 1940), although amount of retroactive inhibition does not. The reduction in intrusions would be expected from the frequency-discrimination theory since the higher degrees of interpolated learning make the frequency discrimination between first- and second-list responses easier.

REFERENCES

Battig, W. F., & Brackett, H. R. Transfer from verbal-discrimination to paired-associate learning: II. Effects of intralist similarity, method, and percentage occurrence of response members. *Journal of Experimental Psychology,* 1963, 65, 507–514.

Bousfield, W. A., Whitmarsh, G. A., & Danick, J. J. Partial response identities in verbal generalization. *Psychological Reports,* 1958, 4, 703–713.

Deese, J. Frequency of usage and number of words in free recall: The role of association. *Psychological Reports,* 1960, 7, 337–344.

Edwards, A. L. *Experimental design in psychological research.* New York: Holt, Rinehart & Winston, 1960.

Keppel, G. Association by contiguity: Role of response availability. *Journal of Experimental Psychology,* 1966, 71, 624–628.

Melton, A. W., & Irwin, J. McQ. The influence of degree of interpolated learning on retroactive inhibition and the overt transfer of specific responses. *American Journal of Psychology,* 1940, 53, 173–203.

Palermo, D. S., & Jenkins, J. J. *Word association norms grade school through college.* Minneapolis: University of Minnesota Press, 1964.

Postman, L. The effects of language habits on the acquisition and retention of verbal associations. *Journal of Experimental Psychology,* 1962, 64, 7–19.

Postman, L., & Stark, K. Proactive inhibition as a function of the conditions of transfer. *Journal of Verbal Learning and Verbal Behavior,* 1964, 3, 249–259.

Russell, W. A., & Jenkins, J. J. The complete Minnesota norms for responses to 100 words from the Kent-Rosanoff word association test. Technical Report No. 11, 1954, University of Minnesota, Contract N8 onr-66216, Office of Naval Research.

Schwenn, E., & Underwood, B. J. Simulated similarity and mediation time in transfer. *Journal of Verbal Learning and Verbal Behavior,* 1965, 4, 476–483.

Underwood, B. J. False recognition produced by implicit verbal responses. *Journal of Experimental Psychology,* 1965, 70, 122–129.

Underwood, B. J. *Experimental psychology.* (2nd ed.) New York: Appleton-Century-Crofts, 1966.

Underwood, B. J., & Archer, E. J. Studies of distributed practice: XIV. Intralist similarity and presentation rate in verbal-discrimination learning of consonant syllables. *Journal of Experimental Psychology,* 1955, 50, 120–124.

Underwood, B. J., Jesse, F., & Ekstrand, B. R. Knowledge of rights and wrongs in verbal-discrimination learning. *Journal of Verbal Learning and Verbal Behavior,* 1964, 3, 183–186.

Underwood, B. J., & Schulz, R. W. *Meaningfulness and verbal learning.* Philadelphia: Lippincott, 1960.

Underwood, B. J., & Viterna, R. O. Studies of distributed practice: IV. The effect of similarity and rate of presentation in verbal-discrimination learning. *Journal of Experimental Psychology,* 1951, 42, 296–299.

Verbal-Discrimination Learning with Varying Numbers of Right and Wrong Terms

When words are presented S in a verbal-learning task, several characteristics or attributes of each word may become a part of the memory for the word. One of these attributes is the frequency of presentation in the experimental situation, for it is known that judgments of differential frequency of presentation are quite accurate even when S is not anticipating that such judgments will be called for.[1] This ability to make rather fine discriminations of frequency provides a plausible basis for the assumption that in verbal-discrimination learning the detection of frequency differences is a basic mechanism in the acquisition.[2] In the usual verbal-discrimination task, pairs of words are presented, one word in each pair being arbitrarily designated as the correct or right (R) word, the other as the wrong (W) word. When presented for learning by the anticipation method, the pair is shown briefly followed by the appearance of the R word only. As a working assumption, it is presumed that as a consequence of these procedures the R word gains two frequency units on each trial; the W word, one unit. If this difference in frequency is sufficient for a discrimination, S will be correct in choosing the higher-frequency word after a single trial.

A test of one of the more counter-intuitive predictions which stems from the theory was reported in an earlier article.[3] This prediction stated that if one R word was paired with two different W words, learning would be more rapid than if one W word was paired with two different R words. Assuming the accretion of frequency

---

Benton J. Underwood and Joel S. Freund, "Verbal-Discrimination Learning with Varying Numbers of Right and Wrong Terms," *American Journal of Psychology* 82 (1969): 198-202. Reprinted with permission.

This work was supported by Contract Nonr-1228 (15), Project NR 154-057, between Northwestern University and the Office of Naval Research. Reproduction in whole or in part is permitted for any purpose by the United States Government.

[1] B. J. Underwood, Some correlates of item repetition in free-recall learning, *J. verb. Learn. verb. Behav.*, 1969, in press.

[2] B. R. Ekstrand, W. P. Wallace, and B. J. Underwood, A frequency theory of verbal-discrimination learning, *Psychol. Rev.*, 73, 1966, 566-578.

[3] Ekstrand, Wallace, and Underwood, *op. cit.*, 566-578.

units as noted above, in the former paradigm the ratio should be 4:1 in favor of the R word after a single trial, while in the latter paradigm both the W word and the R words should gain two units. In fact, if these values are correct, learning based upon a frequency difference should be impossible in the second paradigm. However, the basic notion of the theory was assumed to be supported when it was shown that the 1R-2W paradigm was a much easier task than that produced by the 1W-2R paradigm.

As a followup, the present study was a systematic exploration of the influence of varying numbers of R and W words. The list length here was always 12 pairs. In one set of four conditions, there were either 2, 4, 6, or 12 different R words, with the number of different W words constant at 12. The frequency theory clearly predicts that learning rate should be inversely related to number of R words. When there were only two R words, each was paired with six different W words. After a single study trial the frequency differential would be 12:1 in favor of the R words; learning should occur after a single study trial. As the number of R words increases from 2 to 12, the frequency differential between R and W words would decrease and the learning rate should be retarded correspondingly.

In a comparable set of four conditions, the number of different R words was held constant at 12, with the number of different W words being 2, 4, 6, or 12. With only two W words, the frequency differential for a pair after a single trial would be 6:2 in favor of the W word. If this difference were sufficient for a frequency discrimination, and if S followed a rule of choosing the least frequent member of the pair, learning should occur on a single trial. However, it can be seen that the frequency difference (2:6—here reversed for R:W comparison) was appreciably less than in the parallel 2R list (12:1). With four different W words, the R:W ratio was 2:3, with six W words, 2:2. Therefore, the difficulty in learning should increase as the number of W words increases from two to six, difficulty being maximal at six. With 12 different W words, the task should become easier, for with 12 W words and 12 R words (the typical task), the ratio after a single trial should be 2:1 in favor of the R word.

METHOD

Lists. All lists contained 12 pairs of moderate-frequency, two-syllable nouns. In List 2R, two different R words were used as correct words, each being paired with six different W words. Exactly the same list was used as List 2W except that the two words which were correct words in List 2R were incorrect in List 2W; thus, each W word was paired with six different R words. In List 4R, four different R words were used (the two appearing in List 2R plus two more), each being paired with three different W words. The roles of the words (*i.e.* whether correct or incorrect) were reversed in List 4W. List 6R contained six different R words (those four used in 4R plus two more), each paired with two different W words; for List 6W, the roles were reversed. Lists 12R and 12W were exactly the same, but with 12 of the words correct in one version, and the other 12 correct in the other version.

Procedure and subjects. Learning was by the anticipation method. The pair occurred together for 1.5 sec., after which the shutter of the memory drum lifted to expose the correct word alone for 0.5 sec. The intertrial interval was 2 sec. On the first trial S did not guess. Following this study trial, four anticipation trials were given, S being instructed to respond to each pair by calling out the word he believed correct. During the 1.5-sec. exposure period one word occurred above the other, these positions being varied randomly across trials.

A total of 20 Ss was assigned to each of the eight lists. Lists were randomized within each of 20 blocks, and S was assigned to a given list in order of his appearance at the laboratory. All Ss were college students.

RESULTS

Since all Ss responded to each pair on each anticipation trial, correct responses and errors were complimentary. For presentation here, mean errors are used as the response measure. A plot of mean errors on (anticipation) Trial 1 and a plot of mean total errors across Trials 1–4 showed essentially the same relationships. Mean errors on Trial 1 are plotted in Fig. 4.2.

Looking first at the results for the R lists, it can be seen that the mean numbers of errors increased directly as number of different R words increased. Of the 20 Ss given List 2R, 16 showed perfect performance on Trial 1; the remaining four Ss produced a total of five errors. A total of two errors occurred on Trial 2, none on Trials 3 and 4. Thus, a single study trial produced nearly perfect learning. On List 4R, eight Ss made at least one error on Trial 1; 10 Ss did so on Trial 1 for List 6R; and all 20 Ss made at least one error on List 12R.

On List 2W, 15 Ss made at least one error on Trial 1; and on Lists 4W and 6W, all Ss made at least one error on this trial. Performance on Lists 4W and 6W was better than chance (six errors), but this was not statistically better than chance for List 4W ($t = 1.67$). The mean number of errors for List 4W on Trial 4 was 1.75, and for List 6W,

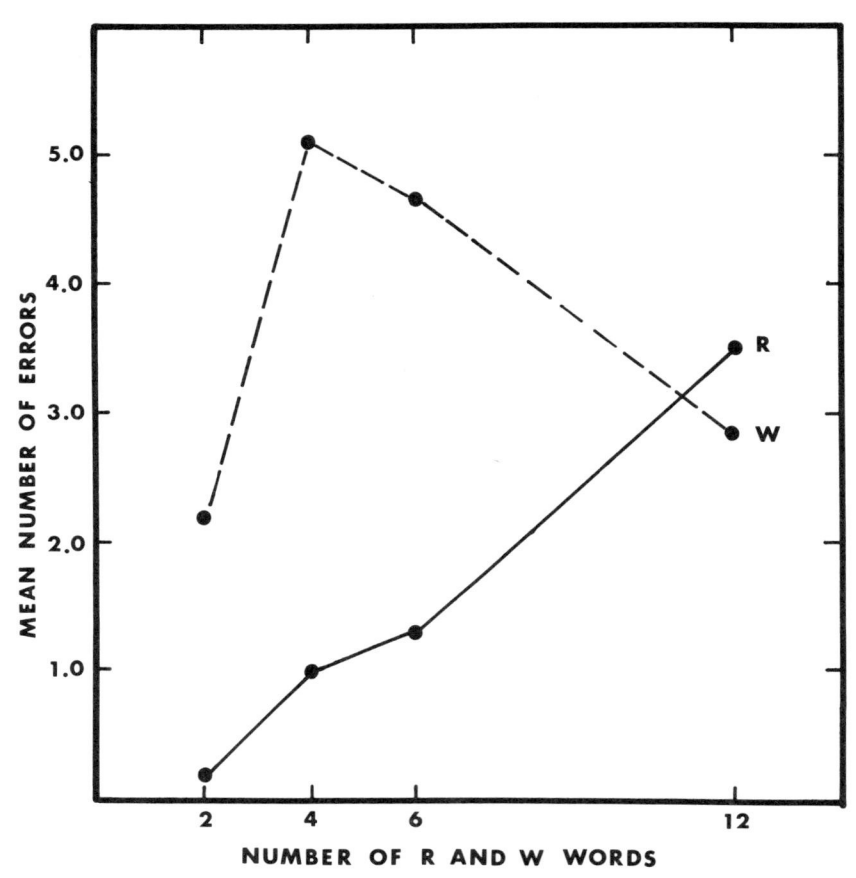

Figure 4.2 Mean errors in learning as a function of number of R and W words.

1.90. Clearly, these two lists provided a difficult learning task in comparison with the other lists.

An overall statistical analysis showed that R vs. W, number of R and W words, and the interaction of these two variables were highly significant statistically. However, with so many zero scores for the R lists, the appropriateness of the analysis may be questioned. The results for the R lists appear clear from the plot in Fig. 4.2. Therefore, a separate analysis was performed on the scores for the four W lists. The $F(3,76) = 8.84$, $p < .01$, indicates that it is very unlikely that these four means came from the same population. The nonmonotonic nature of the function is indicated by the fact that the means for Lists 2W and 6W differed significantly ($t = 3.48$), as did those for Lists 6W and 12W ($t = 2.80$).

DISCUSSION

A commonsense approach to an interpretation of the nearly perfect performance for the Ss given List 2R could be that S learns on the study trial that there are only two correct words and instructs himself to respond *always* with them. There is no evidence to deny this possibility. However, to be consistent, such an interpretation must also be applied to the Ss given List 2W: it should be equally plausible for S to instruct himself *never* to respond with the two W words. Yet, performance on List 2W was appreciably poorer than that on List 2R. On the other hand, the frequency difference for R and W words was less for List 2W than List 2R, which, according to the theory, *would* make List 2W a more difficult task than List 2R.

The results for the R lists were quite in accord with the expectation from the theory that as number of R words increases the frequency differential between R and W words decreases, thus making the discrimination more and more difficult. The results for the W lists also conformed in general to expectations from the theory, but one detail did not. The theory predicts that as number of W words increases, difficulty in learning first increases and then decreases, and this was found. However, the point of maximum difficulty, according to the theory, should have been for List 6W, where the frequency units should be equivalent for the R and W words. The results showed that List 4W was slightly more difficult than 6W. How seriously this failure of the theory should be taken is not clear. It is possible, perhaps, that when a frequency differential is initially indiscriminate (as it might have been for both lists), S turns to other characteristics or attributes of the words to establish the discrimination.

SUMMARY

The frequency theory of verbal-discrimination learning makes two predictions concerning learning difficulty as number of correct words and number of incorrect words are varied, holding total numbers of pairs in the lists constant. First, as number of correct words increases, list difficulty should increase correspondingly. Second, as number of incorrect words increases, difficulty should first increase and then decrease. Eight lists were used, each consisting of 12 pairs. In four lists the number of correct words was 2, 4, 6, or 12, with 12 incorrect words for each list. In four other lists the number of incorrect words was 2, 4, 6, or 12, with 12 correct words for each list. Both predictions were confirmed, but the theory failed to account for the point of maximum difficulty as number of incorrect words was varied.

Testing Effects in the Recognition of Words

A memory may be viewed as consisting of attributes which discriminate one memory from another and act as retrieval cues. The dominance of an attribute may change depending upon the type of memory test employed. In recognition memory it is assumed that a frequency differential is the dominant attribute. In the simplest recognition procedure, units are presented once for study and then are mixed with new units and S is requested to identify those shown him for study. Frequency theory assumes that the discrimination between the old and new is made on the basis of a frequency differential, the old units having a situational frequency of one, the new ones a frequency of zero. The three experiments reported here are concerned with an evaluation of this application of the theory, an evaluation that is made by manipulating frequency during the test of recognition learning. The basic logic, in light of the theory, may now be examined.

Assume that three words, A, B, and C, are presented once for study. Then, for the recognition test by the usual method, each is paired with a new word (A-X, B-Y, C-Z) and S is requested to choose the old one in each pair. The theory assumes that S will choose the word in each pair with the greatest situational frequency. Now, consider the case in which the same new word is used for all three tests in the order A-X, B-X, C-X, with many other pairs falling between the successive tests. As noted, when A-X is presented, A is chosen because it has a higher frequency than X. When this test is made, however, X gains a frequency unit of one in the process of testing. If it is assumed for the time being that the magnitude of this unit is the same as the magnitude occurring from a single presentation on the study trial, then, when B-X is presented to S the frequency is equivalent for B and X. If frequency is the dominant discriminative attribute, performance should fall (from performance

---

Benton J. Underwood and Joel S. Freund, "Testing Effects in the Recognition of Words," *Journal of Verbal Learning and Verbal Behavior* 9 (1970): 117–125. Reprinted with permission.

This work was supported by Contract N0014-67-A-0356-0010, Project NR 154-057, between Northwestern University and the Office of Naval Research. Reproduction in whole or in part is permitted for any purpose by the United States Government.

on the A-X test). Indeed, if frequency is the only discriminative attribute involved, performance should fall to a chance level. When the test for B-X is made, X gains an additional frequency unit. Therefore, when C-X is tested, X should be chosen for it now has a higher frequency than C. This is the general reasoning lying behind all of the experiments.

It can be seen by the above description that the retention interval increases with each successive test. Performance might be expected to decline from test to test for this reason alone. There are no data available on this matter for recognition experiments in which many words are presented for study and many tests are made. Therefore, it will be necessary to evaluate changes in performance across the test period for items which are not paired with repeated wrong words during the test.

EXPERIMENT 1

Method

The S was presented 200 different words on a single study trial with full instructions concerning the nature of the recognition test. On the test, each of the 200 correct words (R words) was paired with a new or wrong word (W word). In each case S was to choose the word which had been presented on the study trial. A given W word was used once, twice, or three times. The experimental question concerns the relationship between frequency of use of a W word and recognition performance.

Words. A pool of 416 words was formed from the Thorndike-Lorge (1944) tables by choosing the first two-syllable word from each column on each page which had a frequency of 10 or less in the general count. Proper nouns were not included. From this pool, 200 words were drawn randomly and used as R words, and 140 further words used as W words. From the 140 W words, 100 were selected randomly and were used once on the test; 20 were used twice; and 20 were used three times. Obviously, a W word occurring three times provides evidence on a W word occurring once and also occurring twice. However, as noted earlier, position in the test series was of concern over and above effects of repeated W words. Further, it seemed wise to have many nonrepeated W words to prevent S from easily learning that words were being repeated.

Procedure. The college-student Ss were tested in groups of from 20–30 until a total of 100 records was available. At the beginning of the session Ss were told that they would be presented a very long list of words and that they were to remember as many of them as possible. Each of the 200 words was presented for 5 sec. each by lantern slides. Immediately following the last slide, the test booklets were distributed. The cover sheet of the booklet included a restatement of the test instructions plus the requirement that S was to proceed through the test booklet in order, i.e., he must complete all items on the first page before going to the second, all on the second before going to the third, and so on, and he must never return to a page once it was completed. The test was unpaced; S encircled the word in each pair which he believed had been shown on a slide.

Test booklet. There were 20 pages in the booklet, each containing 10 pairs. The 200 R words were ordered randomly, and this order was different from the random order in which the slides were presented. There were 10 R words on each page; five of the 100 W words noted earlier were paired randomly with five of the R words on each page. These will be called 1W pairs. There were 20 W words used twice (2W). Two rules were established with regard to a 2W word. First, its initial occurrence would be within pages 1-10, its second within pages 11-20. Second, two 2W words were assigned to each page. The first rule was carried out by twice pairing pages 1-10 randomly with pages 11-20, thus determining the pages on which each of the 20 2W words were to occur. The 2W words for each page were paired randomly with two of the remaining R words.

There were 20 W words used three times (3W). The pages for these were determined by randomly drawing three page numbers 20 times subject to the restriction that each page number occur three times. The remaining three R words on each page were then paired randomly with the three 3W words assigned to the page. The left and right positions of the R and W words was determined randomly across the 200 pairs. The order of the pairs on each page was also random.

Results

Single tests. There were 100 words tested under typical recognition procedures, that is, each with a different W word (1W). Five such words occurred on each page of the booklet. For presentation here, the results for successive tenths (two pages) of the testing period were used, and the percent correct for each tenth is shown in Figure 4.3. In spite of the fact that 10 different words and 100 Ss are represented at each point, there is considerable irregularity. Overall, there appears to be a small decline in performance across the testing period. A statistical test was made by determining for each S the number correct for the first half (50 pairs) and the number correct for the second half (also 50 pairs) and evaluating the difference. The t was 2.93 ($p < .01$). Fifty-three Ss showed a decline, 37 an increase, and 10 no change between the two halves. In the first half there were 81.8% correct responses; in the second half, 79.2%, for a decline of 2.6%.

No records were kept of the time to complete the test booklet, but an estimate of 7 min. for the average S is probably reasonable. Thus, differences in performance as a function of the length of the retention interval within the range of 7 min., or differences due

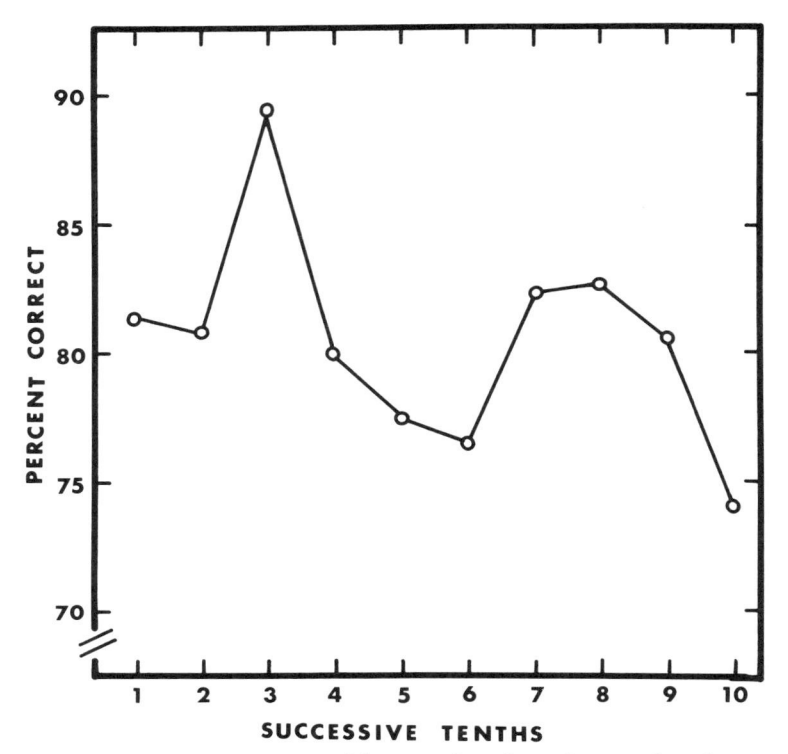

Figure 4.3 Correct recognition as a function of stage of testing.

to any type of internal interference, or both, are minimal. This is in marked contrast to the severe testing effects found with relatively nonintegrated units such as nonsense syllables (e.g., Peixotto, 1947). The present results are also in marked contrast to results reported by Norman and Waugh (1968), but the differences in procedures are so numerous that no attempt will be made here to identify the critical factors involved.

Repeated W words. There were 20 2W words and 20 3W words. The position of each successive test was identified in terms of mean page number and the results are shown in Figure 4.4. Both types of items showed a sharp drop from the first test to the second test as anticipated by frequency theory. However, the theory also predicts that a further fall will occur for 3W words on the third test and this obviously did not happen. Statistically, the difference between the two points for the 2W words is highly reliable ($F = 86.68$), as are the differences among the three points for the 3W words ($F = 53.59$). By comparing Figure 4.3 with Figure 4.4 it can be seen that the

Frequency Theory 161

drop involved between the first two tests was far more than would be anticipated by a simple testing effect. Clearly, the repeated W words were influencing performance. The difference in the level of the 2W and 3W lines, particularly on the first test, can only be attributed to differences in the samples of the words used.

It might appear that an analysis in terms of conditional probabilities from test to test would be useful. However, such an analysis involves not only item-selection artifacts, but also S-selection artifacts. It is, therefore, judged to be inappropriate. However, the 100 Ss were separated into three groups on the basis of number of errors committed on the first test of the 3W words, and then performance on tests two and three was observed. There was no apparent difference in the amount of the fall from the first to the second test, and all three subgroups showed a slight increase in performance from the second to the third test.

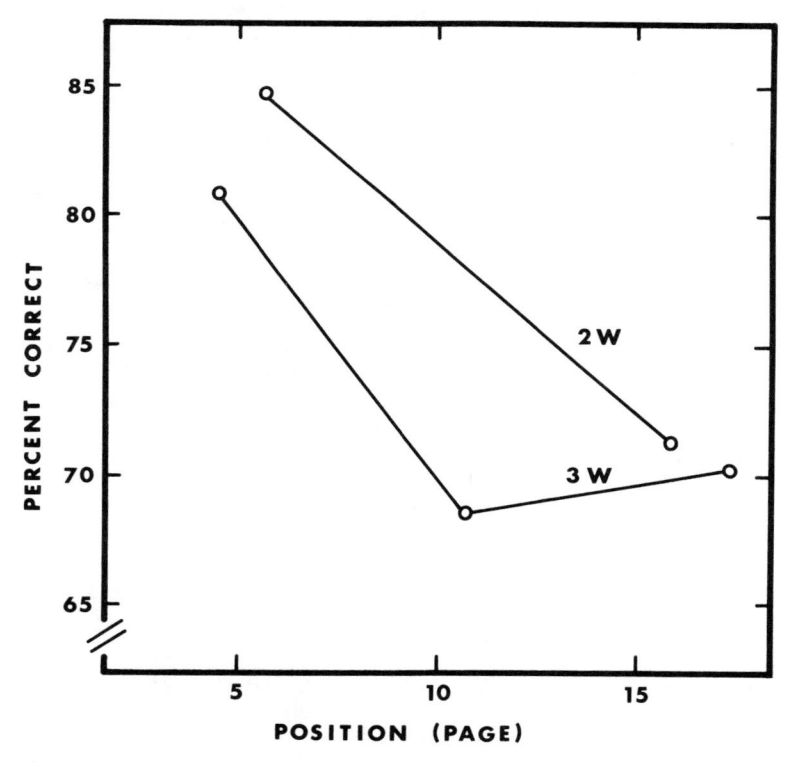

Figure 4.4 Correct recognition when the same wrong (W) word is used twice (2W) and three times (3W) during the testing phase.

EXPERIMENT 2

The first purpose of Exp. 2 was to repeat the 3W conditions of Exp. 1. In Exp. 1, no words were repeated on the study trial. If, during the test, S recognized that a given word had occurred more than once, this might have led him to choose the other word in the pair on the grounds that no word had been repeated during the study phase. Therefore, to exclude this possibility, words occurred with varying frequencies on the study trial of Exp. 2.

The second purpose of Exp. 2 was to test another deduction from the theory which assumes that frequency information is a dominant attribute in recognition memory. If, according to the theory, a repeated W word should produce a decrement in performance, it must also be true that successive testing of an R word, each time with a different W word, should produce an increment in performance.[1] Thus, if A is the R word, three tests of A-X, A-Y, and A-Z should produce successive increases in the freqency of A and a parallel increase in the ease with which the frequency discrimination can be made.

Method

The basic procedures were the same as in Exp. 1, so only the differences need to be described. During the study trial 100 words were presented once, 10 twice, 10 three times, 10 four times, and 2 five times. There were 132 different words, with 200 slides needed to handle the presentations on the study trial. The words serving the various functions were drawn randomly from the basic pool.

The following tests for recognition were made. There were 100 words presented once on the study trial. On the test 20 were used in 1W pairs, that is, each was tested once as in the usual recognition procedure. Sixty of the 100 words presented once for study were used in 3W pairs just as in Exp. 1, that is, a given W word was used three times, each time with a different R word. The remaining 20 words presented once on the study trial were tested three times each (3R words), each time with a different W word. All words having multiple occurrences on the study trial were tested once, as in the normal recognition procedures, except the two words presented five times. These two words were not tested.

A total of 170 pairs was required for the test; these were given in a 12-page booklet, with 14 pairs on the first 11 pages, and 16 on the last page. Ten pairs on each page involved repeated test words (3R words and 3W words); successive occurrences of a word never occupied adjacent pages. Aside from these two

---

[1] We wish to thank Professor Leo Postman for calling our attention to this prediction from frequency theory.

restrictions, page location was random. Nonrepeated test words filled the remaining positions on each page, each type being about equally represented on each page. There were 44 Ss, all tested in a single session.

Results

The findings for the 3R and 3W pairs are summarized in Figure 4.5. Since Exp. 1 showed that any decrement across the testing period was slight, the baseline in Figure 4.5 simply identifies the three successive tests. For the 3W pairs there was again a sharp drop (nearly 20%) from the first test to the second, but no further loss from the second to the third. The F was 65.13. Except for the some-

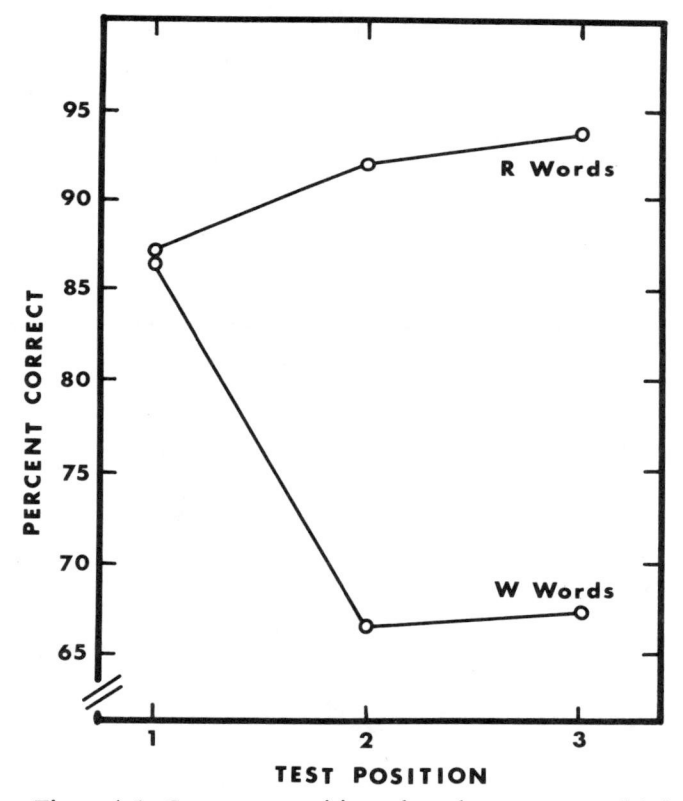

Figure 4.5 Correct recognition when the correct word (R) is used three times, each time with a different W word, and when the W word is used three times, each time with a different R word.

what greater magnitude of the initial drop, therefore, the results are quite comparable to those of Exp. 1. The results for the 3R pairs conform quite well to expectations from the frequency theory. Thus, when the same R word was tested three times, each time with a different W word, performance increased as if there had been learning occurring during the act of testing. The increase is highly reliable, $F(2,86) = 14.16, p < .01$.

It will be remembered that there were 20 words presented once for study and tested once. Performance on these words was appreciably higher than in Exp. 1, and higher than the performance on other types of items when first tested. The reason for this is unknown. A small testing effect was again found. The percent correct for the first 10 words tested was 95.9%, and for the second 10 tested, 92.0%, a change of 4% which is reliable, $F(1,43) = 5.29, p < .05$.

Ten words were presented twice, 10 three times, and 10 four times during the study trial. As would be expected, recognition performance increased directly as study frequency increased. It is of some interest to compare this increase with the increase shown by the 3R words during testing. The plot is shown in Figure 4.6. The deviance of the results for the words presented once for study (as noted above) is quite apparent; performance is better for these

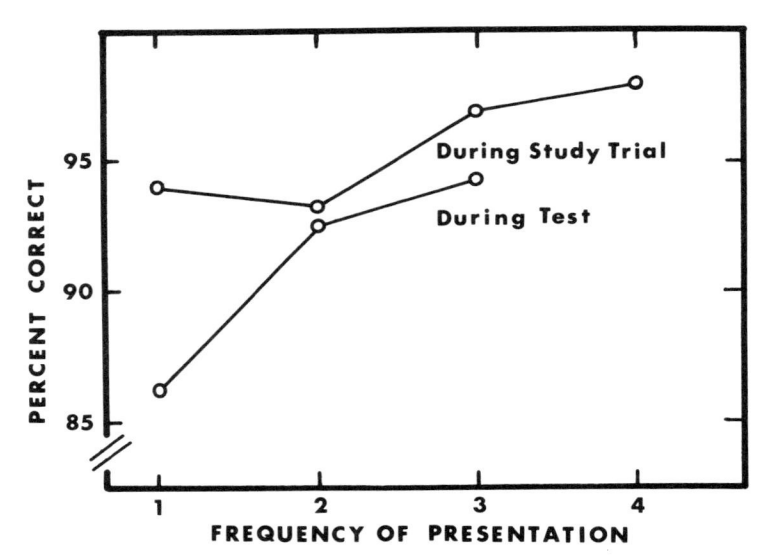

Figure 4.6 The comparative effects of a repetition of a word during the study trial and during the testing phase.

words than for words presented twice. Allowing for this variance, it can be seen that the improvement in performance as a function of frequency of presentation is nearly as great for the R words occurring two and three times during the test trial as for words occurring two and three times on the study trial.

EXPERIMENT 3

The results for the first two experiments provide some support for the frequency theory (a more complete discussion will be delayed). However, the failure of a decrease to occur between the second and third tests for the 3W pairs is a concern for the theory. Contextual attributes may be a part of a memory in the sense that a given word may be associated with the context in which it was learned. In Exp. 1 and 2 the words were projected on a screen on slides with a blue background in a semidarkened room. The test was conducted by S going through a booklet in a fully lighted room. Not only might the contextual attribute per se serve as a discriminative cue for some words, but it might also facilitate the temporal discrimination between the old and new words. The main purpose of Exp. 3 was to examine this perhaps somewhat remote possibility. This was done by using slides to conduct the recognition test.

In Exp. 1 and 2 only three tests were conducted with the W pairs. On the second test the theory assumes equal frequency between the R and W word, with S's choice being based on other attributes of the memory. On the third test it was assumed that the W word had greater frequency than the R word and that again the frequency information would enter into the decisions. However, it may be that on the third test the frequency difference, although greater for the W word than for the R word, was insufficient for a discrimination and therefore did not enter into it. If this were true, a fourth and fifth test would increase the frequency of the W word far enough beyond that of the R word so that it would be clearly discriminable and would again influence the decision. In Exp. 3, therefore, 5W pairs were used (the same W word was used five times, each time with a different R word). Also used were 5R pairs; the same R word was tested five times, each time with a different W word.

Method

A total of 125 words was presented once for study; 10 words were presented three times, and 10 words, five times. Thus, 205 slide presentations were required. Words in positions 1-3, and 204-205, all presented once, were not used in the test series. Also, none of the words given multiple presentations on the study trial was used in the test series. The only words presented for study which also appeared on the test were the 120 words which had been presented once each. Twenty of these were used for the 5R pairs; each was tested five times, each time with a different W word. The remaining 100 words were used in 5W pairs; five R words were tested with the same W and there were 20 different W words. The 5R and 5W pairs required 200 test positions.

During the test, each pair was projected on the screen for 5 sec. and S made his choice by marking a prepared data sheet. The two words on the slide appeared one above the other, and S encircled T or B (top or bottom) to indicate his choice for the word that had occurred on the study trial. At least 20 slides occurred between the successive occurrences of an R or W word. As was true in the previous experiments, words serving a given function were chosen randomly from the pool of 416 words. A total of 65 Ss served in the experiment.

Results

The results for the two types of items tested, 5R and 5W, are shown in Figure 4.7. Performance on the W pairs shows a continuous decline for the first three tests with an apparent asymptote reached by the third test ($F = 64.45$). The maximum amount of the decrement is 27%. At the lowest level (56%), performance is not greatly above chance. As was true in Exp. 2, performance on the R pairs increases ($F = 21.20$), although apparently a top level is reached by the fourth test at about 94%. The maximum increase is 10%.

Suppose that S adopted a simple strategy of responding positively to any word he recognized as having occurred earlier in the test series. Such a strategy should produce an increase in the frequency with which the R words were chosen in the R pairs and a decrease in the frequency with which the R words were chosen in the W pairs. This is to say, therefore, that the general effects in Figure 4.7 would be produced. There are two facts which make it seem unlikely that such a responding strategy was adopted. First, the strategy should cause the performance on the W pairs to fall close to zero correct. Second, and perhaps more convincing, if this strategy were employed by any sizeable proportion of the Ss, there should be a high negative correlation between the number correct for the two types of words. The number correct on the 4th and 5th tests was determined for the R pairs and for the W pairs for each S and a product-moment correlation calculated between the two arrays. The correlation was −0.01, or essentially zero.

Frequency Theory 167

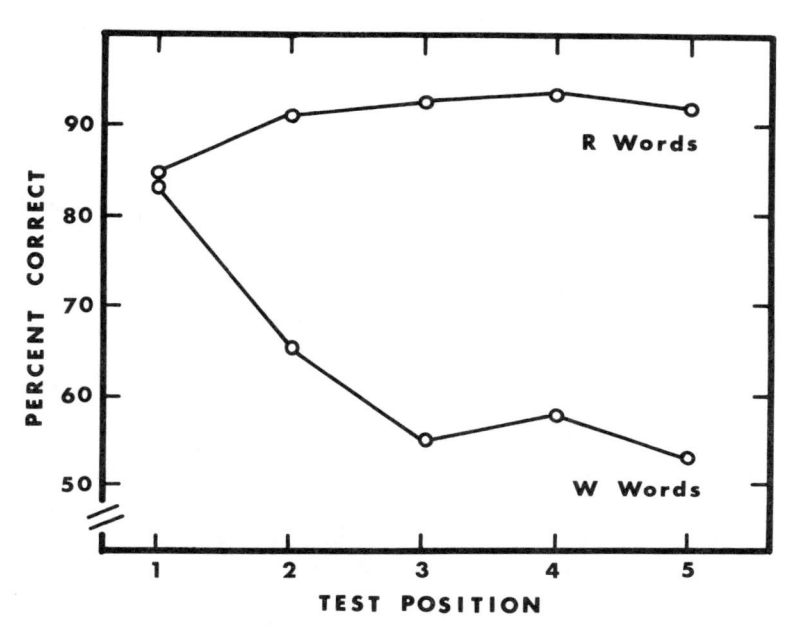

Figure 4.7 Correct recognition when an R word and W word are used for five tests.

The decrement shown in the W pairs over the first three tests was greater for the present experiment than for the first two experiments. This may be due to context constancy in Exp. 3, but this cannot be concluded with confidence. Each test slide was shown for 5 sec. The estimate (given earlier) of the duration of the test period for the average S with a 200-pair booklet was 7 min., and the average time to complete the 3W pairs would be about 6 min. For the paced test, the time to complete the pairs for the first three tests would be 10 min. on the average for all items. Therefore, the duration of the retention interval for the first three tests does not differ appreciably for the paced and unpaced tests across the experiments. However, when slides were used on the test they remained in front of S for the full 5 sec., and it is possible that the frequency input was greater than under the unpaced test where our observations suggested that in some cases S did not even perceive the W word if the R word held the first position. The conclusion is that we cannot tell precisely the causal factor involved which produced the greater decrement in the W pairs of the present experiment as compared with the earlier experiments.

DISCUSSION

The results of the three experiments are taken as support for the theory that in recognition memory a discrimination based upon a frequency difference is a dominant determinant of performance. At the same time, however, it is quite evident that other attributes of the memory may support a discrimination based on frequency and, when frequency becomes invalid, determine performance. That under certain conditions performance can be reduced to a near chance level by making the frequency differential favor the incorrect word is taken as evidence for the power of the frequency attribute in the Ss' decisions. But, of course, if frequency were the only attribute involved, performance should fall to a zero level when the incorrect word has the discriminably higher frequency.

The experiments have not identified the other attributes which enter into recognition performance. As noted earlier, it is possible that a temporal discrimination may be involved although the cues involved are not known. The most probably candidates for supporting attributes in recognition are characteristics of the words as such. It is known from other works that the characteristics of words influence apparent frequency appreciably (Underwood & Freund, 1970). This is to say that two words given equivalent input frequencies may not be judged to have the same apparent frequency. The precise characteristics contributing to this variance have not been identified, but they may reflect other attributes of memory which become dominant when a frequency discrimination is lost.

The pool of words used for the present studies had only two restrictions placed upon it, namely, all words had low background frequency and two syllables. They vary enormously (by inspection) on a number of other attributes such as length (four to eleven letters), affectivity, abstractness, and so on. The use of a random pool of words has certain obvious advantages for research. However, since apparent frequency differs as a function of word characteristics, it will probably be necessary to develop a group of words in which subjective frequency differences are minimal with constant input frequencies. The removal of attributes which produce differences in apparent frequency (and which may, at the same time, serve as supporting attributes for frequency in recognition) should provide a much cleaner test of the theory which assumes the dominance of the frequency attribute in recognition memory.

REFERENCES

Norman, D. A., & Waugh, N. C. Stimulus and response interference in recognition-memory experiments. *Journal of Experimental Psychology,* 1968, 78, 551-559.
Peixotto, H. E. Proactive inhibition in the recognition of nonsense syllables. *Journal of Experimental Psychology.* 1947, 37, 81-91.
Thorndike, E. L., & Lorge, I. *The teacher's word book of 30,000 words.* Teachers College, Columbia University, Bureau of Publication, 1944.
Underwood, B. J., and Freund, J. S. Relative frequency judgments and verbal-discrimination learning. *Journal of Experimental Psychology,* 1970, in press.

Recognition and Number of Incorrect Alternatives Presented During Learning

A theory of recognition memory has been advanced which assumes that in the usual or typical recognition task with verbal units, performance is largely determined by a frequency differential (Underwood & Freund, 1970). In a typical experiment, a subject is given a series of units for a single study trial following which testing is accomplished by mixing these old units with a series of new units and the subject is asked to identify the old. The theory assumes that old units have a situational frequency of 1, the new units a situational frequency of 0. The degree to which a subject can discriminate this frequency difference will determine his performance. The implication of the theory is, perhaps, most clearly seen in the multiple-choice type of recognition test. If each old item is paired with a new item, the subject may make a direct frequency comparison of the two. Of course, there may be two or more new items accompanying each old item. With three or four such items present, the test structure for each old word is much the same as for multiple-choice tests used so frequently to assess academic performance. Indeed, the present experiments came about as a consequence of viewing multiple-choice tests from the perspective of frequency theory, albeit the final procedure adopted was not intended to simulate these tests.

The learning task consisted of 50 unrelated words. The test for recognition memory consisted of 50 sets of five words each with each set containing one correct word and four incorrect words. The experimental variable was the number of these incorrect words which had been present at the time the subject was attempting to learn the correct word. Let the five words in a given test set be identified as A, B, C, D, and E, with A the correct word and the others incorrect. The variable, then, was the number of the four incorrect responses

---

Benton J. Underwood, Miles Patterson, and Joel S. Freund, "Recognition and Number of Incorrect Alternatives Presented During Learning," *Journal of Educational Psychology* 63 (1972): 1–7. Reprinted with permission. Copyright 1972 by the American Psychological Association.

This work was supported by Contract N00014-67-A-0356-0010, Project NR 154-057, between Northwestern University and the Office of Naval Research. Reproduction in whole or in part is permitted for any purpose of the United States Government.

which were also present during the learning stage. In Condition 0, none of the incorrect alternatives was presented during learning, hence, A was presented alone. In Condition 1, one of the alternatives was presented during learning, and so on. For Condition 4, it can be seen, all incorrect alternatives were presented during learning. All five words in a set always occurred during the test phase.

The expectations from frequency theory may now be considered. Suppose that during learning, the subject has two incorrect responses (B and C) presented along with the correct word (A). These are presented successively as follows: B, A, C, $\underline{A}$. As each word appears, the subject pronounces it and the appearance of A the second time (it is also underlined at its second presentation) provides the information that A is correct. At the time of the test, the subject is shown A, B, C, D, and E and is asked to select the correct word. For this particular case, three different frequency levels exist at the time of the test. The correct word, A, has had two frequency inputs or units, B and C have each had one, and D and E are new, hence have zero situational frequencies. If the subject can discriminate between frequency values of 2 and 1, he will be correct by choosing the unit with the higher frequency. If he cannot discriminate between 2 and 1, but still uses the frequency attribute to determine his selection, the error is more likely to result from a choice of B or C, rather than D or E, since the former two each have one unit of situational frequency. To say this in more general terms: If an error is made, it is most likely to be made by choosing a word which was present during the learning phase in spite of the fact that the subject was given indirect information that it was not correct.

Consider next the case where A is presented alone during the learning phase. The subject sees A, $\underline{A}$, and, therefore, the frequency is 2. At the time of the test, A will occur with four additional words all of which have a frequency of 0. If recognition is based on a frequency differential, the discrimination will be 2 versus 0. The prediction must follow then that recognition performance will be better when no incorrect alternatives are presented during learning than when one or more incorrect alternatives are presented.

As examined thus far, the theory leads to two rather direct predictions, namely, Condition 0 will result in performance that is superior to the performance of the other four conditions, and that for these latter four conditions, when an error is made it is far more likely to result from the choice of an alternative presented during learning than from the choice of an alternative not presented. The final prediction to be considered deals with possible differences in performance among the four conditions in which from one to four incorrect alternatives were presented during learning. The reasoning is somewhat indirect and requires three steps.

As the first step, it is necessary to consider the possible outcome of an experiment in which no incorrect alternatives are presented during learning (as in Condition 0) but in which testing takes place by having one, two, three, or four alternatives. With one new alternative, the subject is faced with a choice between an old item (presented twice) and one new item. From Hintzman's (1969) work it is known that a subject will choose the old item approximately 90% of the time when asked to choose the word with the highest frequency. This means that for a small proportion of the pairs, the subjects cannot discriminate between the old and new on the basis of frequency. When an error is made it must mean that the apparent frequency of the item presented twice is far less than two (perhaps zero), that the apparent frequency of the new item is above zero, or some combination of these two events. That a new word could have an apparent frequency greater than zero could result from a number of factors which need not be of concern here. The critical point is that the apparent frequency of an item presented twice will occasionally be less than the apparent frequency of a word not presented (a new word). As noted, this is to be expected when a single new word is tested with an old word. Now, if the apparent frequency of a single new word will sometimes be greater than that of a word presented twice, what will happen as two, three, or four new words are used? It seems proper to assume that the addition of each new alternative will increase the probability that the apparent frequency of one of the new words will be greater than the apparent frequency of the old word (presented twice). Thus, although Hintzman (1969) found that the subject chose the most frequent word 90% of the time when a single new alternative was presented on the test, this value should be appreciably lower in the present Condition 0 since four new alternatives are used on the test.

As the second step, the effect of adding from one to four incorrect alternatives during the learning must be evaluated. Suppose that a subject is presented one incorrect alternative during learning and is tested by presenting only this incorrect alternative and the correct word. Hintzman's (1969) data show that a subject will be correct 67% of the time when he is asked to choose the word with the highest frequency. This is far less than when the incorrect alternative is new (as described above). If more than one incorrect alternative is presented during learning (and also used on the test), the number of errors should increase directly as the number of incorrect alternatives increases. This is to say that as the number of incorrect alternatives increases, there is an increase in the likelihood that the apparent frequency of one of these will be greater than the apparent frequency of the correct word. Thus, an expectation of change in performance as alternatives are added is the same whether new items (not previously presented) are added, or whether items presented once are added. The difference lies only in the base error rate produced by a single wrong alternative that had or had not been presented during the learning phase. Given this base difference, an increase in errors produced by having two, three, or four incorrect alternatives should occur whether the additions consist of new items or whether they consist of items presented once.

As the final step, the conditions of the present experiment may be examined in the light of the above assumptions. The five conditions as they are presumed to differ at the time of the test are as follows:

	Frequency of Five Alternatives				
Condition 0	2	0	0	0	0
Condition 1	2	1	0	0	0
Condition 2	2	1	1	0	0
Condition 3	2	1	1	1	0
Condition 4	2	1	1	1	1

The value of 2 represents the frequency of the correct item, 1 the frequency of incorrect items presented during learning, and 0 the frequency of incorrect items not presented during learning. As described earlier, it is expected that Condition 0 will be superior to Conditions 1–4. On the surface it may appear that performance would deteriorate as the number of ones increases. However, with each increase in the number of ones, there is a reciprocal decrease in number of zeros. Therefore, in proceeding from Condition 1 to Condition 4 there is an increase in one source of error but a corresponding decrease in errors from another source. If the rates of increase and decrease are equal, total errors should not differ among the four conditions, although the theory doesn't specify such equality.

It should be noted that the theoretical expectations were reached by assuming that recognition is mediated primarily by a frequency discrimination. Evidence from frequency discrimination studies was used in arriving at the predictions. These predictions appear to have been confirmed in an experiment done by Kaess and Zeaman (1960). The subjects in the Kaess-Zeaman experiment were given a 30-item multiple-choice test dealing with definitions of psychological terms. On the first trial there were zero to four incorrect alternatives present. The subject discovered the correct response by inserting a punch into the answer sheet. On the second trial, all questions had five alternatives. The results show that performance was best if no incorrect alternatives were present on the first trial, but there was little difference for the conditions having one to four incorrect alternatives. Furthermore, the investigators showed that the errors made on the second trial were most likely to be made by choosing an alternative that had also been chosen on the first trial. Thus, these results seem quite in line with the theoretical expectations from frequency theory. However, precise knowledge of the input frequency of the correct and incorrect responses on the first trial is lacking. Also, since a given subject had only one condition for all 30 items, the total number of different terms to which subjects were exposed differed across conditions. These two points are not criticisms of the Kaess-Zeaman study, per se, but they are points which cause doubts as to whether the data can be taken as adequate tests of the frequency theory as applied to multiple-choice learning.

The experiments to be reported examined one further variable. Disregarding frequency theory for the moment, it may be asked how much the information about right and wrong items is dependent upon the particular items constituting a set, that is, the items forming each multiple-choice question. Does knowledge of a correct item depend upon a contrast of "wrongness" for the other items in the set? Or to ask the question in more general terms: Is knowledge of right and wrong contingent upon the context of each set? Frequency theory makes no assumption about this issue. The theory asserts that frequency differentials are dominant in mediating recognition performance, and this would be true regardless of a change in the context as defined by a set of words. In Experiment I, the context of a set remained constant between learning and testing. In Experiment II, the context changed in that incorrect alternatives occurring with a given correct word during learning appeared with a different correct word during testing.

METHOD

Experiment I

Materials

A total of 250 two-syllable words with frequencies between 1 and 10 were chosen from Thorndike and Lorge (1944). This pool was divided randomly into 50 sets of five words each. As a further step, one of the five words was randomly chosen to be the correct word and it remained correct for all conditions. The 50 items for a given subject consisted of 10 fitting each of the five conditions, namely, zero, one, two, three, or four incorrect alternatives presented during learning. However, five forms were used, so that across all five forms each of the 50 correct items occurred once under each of the five conditions. The position of a given item in the learning series was the same across all forms; it differed only in terms of the number of incorrect alternatives presented. The order of the 50 items was random subject to the restriction that an item in each condition occur in each five-item block. A different random order was used on the test form, this test form being exactly the same for all subjects. A test item always consisted of the correct word and four incorrect words randomly ordered.

Procedure and Subjects

The subjects were fully informed concerning the nature of the learning phase and how they were to be tested. The instructions included the use of a sample card to illustrate how the items would be presented and how the number of items in the sets would differ during the learning phase. Presentation was by a memory drum at a 2-second rate. Each word was presented individually at this rate and the subject was required to pronounce each word aloud as it appeared. After the last alternative appeared, the correct alternative was shown again, underlined, and the subject pronounced it for the second time. At this point it was assumed that all incorrect alternatives had frequencies of 1, and the correct alternative a frequency of 2. If no incorrect alternative was presented (Condition 0), the correct word followed itself, and the subject pronounced it for the second time. Following the second appearance of the correct item for a given set, an asterisk was shown for 2 seconds signifying that the words from a new set would appear next.

On the unpaced recognition test, a subject went through the 50 sets of five words each, circling the correct word in each set. No omissions were allowed. There were 25 sets on each of two pages and the subject was required to complete the first page before going to the second.

A total of 100 college students was used as subjects, 20 being assigned to each form by a block-randomized schedule.

Experiment II

One change was made in Experiment II. The test form was modified so that incorrect alternatives appearing with a given correct word during learning never occurred with that correct word on the recognition test. Rather, they appeared with a different correct word. Five different test forms were used although the list presented for learning was the same as for Experiment I. The interchange between items was always made for items having the same number of incorrect alternatives during learning. Condition 0, in which no correct alternatives were used during learning, was exactly the same in both experiments. Again, 100 subjects were used, 20 for each of the five forms.

RESULTS

Number of Errors

The mean numbers of errors (out of 10 possible) as a function of number of incorrect alternatives presented during learning are shown in Figure 4.8. Both experiments show a sharp increase in error frequency between 0 and 1 incorrect alternatives, with little change thereafter. For Experiment I, $F = 17.39$, $df = 4/380$, $p < .01$; for Experiment II, $F = 15.69$, $p < .01$. Between one and four incorrect alternatives for Experiment I, there is a slight upward slope to the error curve. However, a test of these four points does not allow rejection of the hypothesis that the slope is zero ($F < 1$). The first theoretical expectation, therefore, appears confirmed; best performance was observed for an item when no incorrect alternatives were present during learning. The data also indicate that given at least one incorrect alternative during learning, performance does not change as the number is increased.

There is consistently greater number of errors for Experiment II than for Experiment I. However, statistically the overall difference does not reach significance ($F = 2.68$, $df = 1/198$, $p > .05$). It seems appropriate to conclude that whether an incorrect item had or had

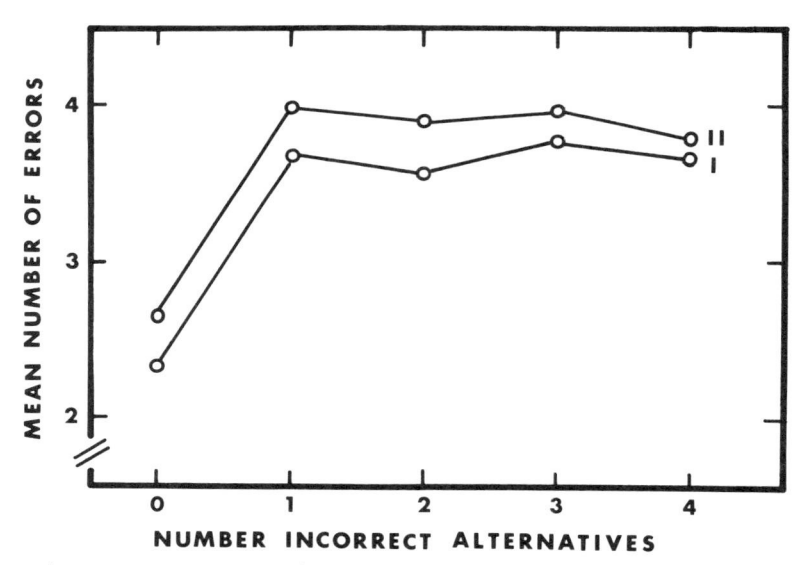

Figure 4.8 Mean errors in recognition as a function of the number of incorrect alternatives presented during learning.

Source of Errors

The percentages of errors from each of two sources are plotted in Figure 4.9 for the two experiments combined. The two sources are: (a) those alternatives presented during learning, and (b) those not presented. Of course, with zero incorrect alternatives presented during learning, all must arise from alternatives not presented. And, when four incorrect alternatives were presented during learning, all must arise from among those four. Therefore, to evaluate the expectation from the theory (that errors will arise largely from items presented during learning) attention must be directed to the three conditions in which one, two, or three incorrect alternatives were presented. When one incorrect alternative was presented during learning, 70% of the errors were the result of subjects choosing that alternative and 30% were the result of choosing one of the three alternatives not presented during learning. As may further be seen,

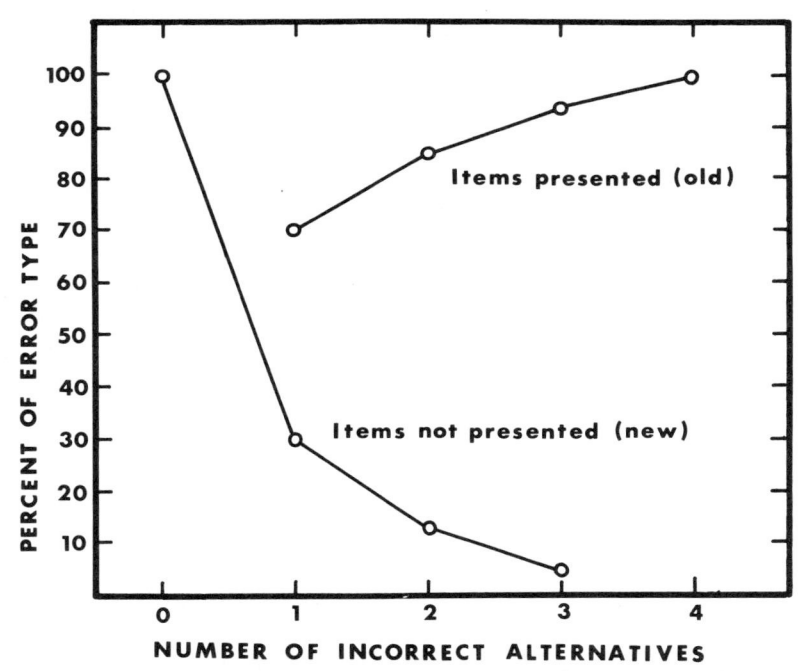

Figure 4.9 Percentage of error types for old and new alternatives.

when two incorrect alternatives were presented during learning, 85% of the errors resulted from a choice of one of these two alternatives. The chance likelihood of choosing an incorrect alternative presented during learning given an error is 25%, 50%, and 75% for one, two, and three alternatives, respectively. As can be seen, the empirical percentages are far above the chance percentages.

The above data give strong support to the theoretical expectation that an error is more likely to be made by choosing an item presented during learning than by choosing one not presented. Yet, it is apparent that an item not presented during learning has some small probability of being chosen when an error is committed. As explained in the introduction, this is believed to be due to variations in apparent frequency which occur with constant input frequency. The source of these variations are not understood at this time.

DISCUSSION

The present results are in substantial accord with the theory that word recognition memory is dominated by frequency information. To say that recognition memory is dominated by a frequency attribute does not deny that other attributes may enter into certain of the decisions subjects must make on a recognition test. Indeed, it is possible that the subject sometimes chooses a new word (not presented during learning) because of an overlap of other attributes between this word and some correct word in the list. The data show that errors do not increase as the number of incorrect alternatives presented during learning increases (Figure 4.8). This could be accounted for if it is assumed that there are only two sources of error, namely, from new items and from items presented during learning. In the present experiment the numbers of items of each type were reciprocal. Therefore, it appears that the increase in errors produced by adding items that had been presented during learning was counteracted by a decrease in errors resulting from the dropping out of items that had not occurred on the learning trial. If these two curves had the same slope (one positive and one negative) it would result in the performance showing no increase in error frequency as number of alternatives presented during learning increased beyond one. That the slopes of these two curves could be the same may seem intuitively unreasonable since neither an additive nor a strict probabilistic model would lead to this outcome. So, in detail the assumption may be wrong, although it seems to handle the present data. Obviously, to clarify this matter, data are needed on error increases as number of new alternatives increases and as number of alternatives presented during learning increases, but without mixing the two types at the time of the test.

The findings are quite consistent with those reported by Kaess and Zeaman (1960) as described in the introduction. On the other hand, the results of a recent study by Sturges (1969) would seem to be at odds with frequency theory. In the Sturges study, subjects were given a multiple-choice test covering certain facts from the social sciences. There were four alternatives. Following the initial testing, one group was shown the stem and only the correct alternative, while another group was shown the stem, the correct alternative and the three incorrect alternatives. A further testing showed that the two groups did not differ. According to frequency theory, the group shown only the correct alternative should have been superior. However, if the subjects in the group shown the correct and incorrect alternatives ignored the latter and studied only the correct alternative, the conditions for the two groups were effectively not different. If a subject had been forced to read the incorrect alternatives it seems highly probable that the findings would have been different.

The above discussion implies that frequency theory may have some applicability to multiple-choice testing as commonly carried out in schools. Murdock (1963) analyzed recognition performance on a multiple-choice test of general information. He reached the conclusion that a subject appears to eliminate incorrect alternatives and then (if more than one alternative remains) chooses randomly from among the remaining. This conclusion is not necessarily at odds with frequency theory. Frequency theory specifies the attribute of memory which allows a subject to distinguish between correct and incorrect alternatives. Perfect recognition occurs when the apparent frequency of the correct alternative is greater than the apparent frequency of each incorrect alternative. Errors occur when apparent frequency of one or more incorrect alternatives is indistinguishable from the apparent frequency of the correct alternative. In these instances, it is believed, performance will be above chance only insofar as other attributes of the memory will reliably distinguish between the correct item and incorrect alternatives.

The items in the present experiment did not include a "stem" or premise as is the usual case for multiple-choice items. Frequency theory is applicable to the more usual case if it is assumed that the frequencies of the alternatives have some degree of specificity to the stem. Or, to say this another way, the apparent frequencies are to some degree, at least, contingent frequencies. The lack of this contingency in the present studies allowed shifting of incorrect alternatives from one item to another with no appreciable influence on performance. However, there is no reason to believe that frequency theory will not apply to the more usual case where contingent frequencies are established.

One final conjecture will be made. Apparent frequency of alternatives may change during the process of testing (Underwood & Freund, 1970). Consider a case in which the frequency of the correct alternative is marginally distinguishable from one or more incorrect alternatives. The subject may, at this point, "study" the various alternatives carefully in order to get additional information to help reach a decision. However, the act of gathering this information may increase the frequency of the alternatives to the point that they are no longer distinguishable from the correct alternative. Therefore, unless the additional information clearly leads to a correct decision, the decision can no longer be based upon a frequency differential. In short, poorer performance may result if too much time is spent in trying to arrive at a decision.

REFERENCES

Hintzman, D. L. Apparent frequency as a function of frequency and the spacing of repetitions. *Journal of Experimental Psychology,* 1969, 80, 139-145.

Kaess, W., & Zeaman, D. Positive and negative knowledge of results on a Pressey-type punch-board. *Journal of Experimental Psychology,* 1960, 60, 12-17.

Murdock, B. B., Jr. An analysis of the recognition process. In C. N. Cofer and B.S. Musgrave (Eds.), *Verbal behavior and learning: Problems and processes.* New York: McGraw-Hill, 1963.

Sturges, P. T. Verbal retention as a function of the informativeness and delay of informative feedback. *Journal of Educational Psychology,* 1969, 60, 11-14.

Thorndike, E. L., & Lorge, I. *The teacher's word book of 30,000 words.* New York: Teachers College, Columbia University, Bureau of Publications, 1944.

Underwood, B. J., & Freund, J. S. Testing effects in the recognition of words. *Journal of Verbal Learning and Verbal Behavior,* 1970, 9, 117-125.

The Syllable as a Source of Error in Multisyllable Word Recognition

When the frequency information which is a part of the memory for words presented for learning is juxtaposed against recognition decisions on those words the resulting relationship strongly suggests that the frequency knowledge is critically involved in the recognition decisions (Underwood, 1972). To infer a causal relationship from such facts is not to assert that semantic or meaning responses to the words are of no consequence for recognition. It is quite possible that the perceptual representational response to a word and the semantic responses are both represented, perhaps independently, in the frequency information about each word. In the present study the inquiry concerns the syllable as a unit in multisyllable words. Essentially, the question is whether recognition errors are predictable when it is assumed that the frequency of a syllable has representation in the memory for a word.

To propose that a syllable of a word has frequency representation in memory is to assume that the subject may abstract a smaller unit (syllable) from a larger unit (word) and that this smaller unit is given some degree of independence in memory. On the surface, such an assumption may seem preposterous. Yet, it is known that this type of abstraction has occurred in the developmental history of the subject. Subjects have a good knowledge of the frequency with which individual letters occur in words (Attneave, 1953). This knowledge could only arise by abstracting letter frequencies from larger units (words), since it is unlikely that a subject experiences letters in isolation with frequencies that correspond to the frequencies with which the letters occur in words. Subjects also have a good knowledge of the relative frequencies with which words occur in printed discourse (e.g., Shapiro, 1969), and this could come about only by abstracting their frequencies from a broader context (sen-

---

Benton J. Underwood and Joel Zimmerman, "The Syllable as a Source of Error in Multisyllable Word Recognition," *Journal of Verbal Learning and Verbal Behavior* 12 (1973): 701–706. Reprinted with permission.

This research was supported by the Personnel and Training Research Programs, Psychological Sciences Division, Office of Naval Research, under Contract No. N00014-67-A-0356-0010, Contract Authority Identification No. NR 154-321. Reproduction in whole or in part is permitted for any purpose of the United States Government.

tences). Although less precise than frequency information about letters and words, the subject does carry reliable information about the frequencies of bigrams in words (Underwood, 1971).

The above evidence indicates that information about the frequencies of units appearing as parts of larger units has been assimilated over many years by the usual subject. However, it may be quite another matter to expect that the subject would abstract syllable frequencies from words in a single presentation of a list of words in the laboratory. Nevertheless, if this does occur, it has a number of implications for the study of recognition. An elaboration of this point will be delayed to the discussion section.

The rationale of the experiment may now be examined. The subject was presented a list of two-syllable words singly for study. These words were chosen so that when a pair of words was considered, a new word could be formed by combining the first syllable of one of the words with the second syllable of the other. For example, two of the words presented were *instruct* and *consult.* By combining the first and second syllables of the two words in order, the word *insult* was formed. This word was used as a new or distractor word on the recognition test. The test consisted of a series of two-alternative forced-choice items. Thus, on test, *insult* occurred as a new word, being paired with an old word but never one of the old words from which it was derived. On the test, in fact, *insult* was paired with *reptile,* an old word which, along with *fervent,* was used to produce the word *fertile* by merging *fer* and *tile.* It is important to understand the nature of these pairings because formal similarity between the two alternatives at the time of test was eliminated as a source of error. Had, for example, *insult* been paired with *consult* on the test, the interpretation would be ambiguous. The method also would seem to have eliminated semantic factors as a source of error in recognition decisions. Since the word *insult* had never occurred on the study, nor did any word which had a meaning similar to its meaning, there appears to be no reason why *insult* should have been chosen instead of *reptile* if the decision was based on semantic information. In short, if *insult* were chosen, the interpretation based on a frequency input to each syllable independently during study seems reasonably clean.

The experiment was designed to test three predictions. Two of these were positive in the sense that if syllabic frequency is a source of error, more errors would be expected to occur for experimental pairings than for control pairings. The third prediction was of a null outcome. Each of these three will be considered in order.

On the test, half of the pairs consisted of an old word and a merged or induced word (I word), whereas the other half consisted of an old word and a neutral new word (C word). The theory predicts more errors for the former pairs than for the latter.

The second prediction has to do with testing effects. It is known that if a new word on a forced-choice test is used more than once (in two or more pairs), errors may increase with each successive use (Underwood & Freund, 1970). This suggests that frequency induced during testing will influence decisions on pairs occurring later in the test series. It seems quite possible, then, that syllabic frequency can be increased during testing. For example, if the words *instruct* and *consult* are tested prior to the testing of *insult*, more errors should result (the syllables of *insult* gain additional frequency) than if *insult* is tested prior to the testing of *instruct* and *consult*. Conditions were arranged to test this by having half the I words tested before their inducing words were tested, and half after their inducing words were tested.

It might be argued that words resulting from the merging of two syllables of other words have some special or unusual characteristic which makes them good lures on a forced-choice test. To eliminate this possibility, the I words were used as new words on the test without the inducing words (e.g., *consult* and *instruct*) having occurred on the study list. If there is something peculiar about the I words, more errors should occur for these items than for the C words. The theory that syllabic frequency is induced during study (when appropiate words are used) would predict no difference between pairs containing I and C words under these circumstances.

METHOD

Design and Materials

The three predictions can be tested by two groups of subjects, one being used for the first two predictions, the second for the third. However, in order to study the testing effects for all induced (I) words, two forms were required, hence there were four groups of subjects. The two involved in the first two predictions will be called the inducing groups, I-1 and I-2, those in the third, the control groups, C-1 and C-2. The description of the arrangement of the materials for these four groups essentially describes the conditions of the experiment.

Group I-1. The study list consisted of 48 two-syllable words varying in Thorndike-Lorge frequency between 1 and AA. Although the 48 words were presented singly, they may be thought of as 24 pairs of inducing study words in that from each pair a critical test word was derived (I word) by combining the first syllable of one of the words with the second syllable of the other. Only five of the 96 syllables occurred more than once and only three of these occurred as parts of the critical test words. Essentially, then, each I word would have one frequency input for each of the syllables. The 48 words were randomized in the study list subject only to the restriction that any two words used to produce an I word could not occupy adjacent positions in the list.

For the test list the 24 critical words were used as new words along with 24 additional neutral words (C words). These 24 neutral words were matched on first letters and Thorndike-Lorge frequencies with the 24 I words. Of the 48 syllables represented by these 24 C words, only nine were represented among the 48 words used in the study list. The 48 new words were paired randomly with the 48 study words for the test with two restrictions. One I word and one C word were paired with the two words constituting an inducing pair, and an I word was never paired with one of the members of its inducing pair.

One restriction was applied to the ordering of the test pairs. In order to study testing effects, it was necessary to have pairs containing I words tested prior to the testing of the two study words from which each was derived, and the reverse order must also obtain. Twelve I words were chosen arbitrarily and placed in the first half of the test sequence, with their inducing items tested in the second half. The remaining I words occurred in pairs tested in the second half, with their inducing items being tested in the first half. Within each half the ordering was random.

Group I-2. For this group the procedure was exactly the same as for Group I-1. The only difference was that the test halves were reversed. Thus, by summing across the tests for Groups I-1 and I-2, each I word occurred in a pair in the first half of the test (not being preceded by tests of the two inducing items) and once in a pair in the second half (having been preceded by tests of the two inducing words).

Group C-1. The study list for this group was composed of 48 words matched on first letters and on Thorndike-Lorge frequencies with the 48 study words shown to Groups I-1 and I-2. These were chosen to have minimum duplication of syllables with the critical test items. Of the 96 syllables, eight matched a syllable in the I words, but in no case were both syllables of an I word represented by syllables of the study words. The test series was exactly the same as for Group I-1 except that the neutral study words replaced the 48 inducing study words of Group I-1.

Group C-2. This group had exactly the same materials as Group C-1. The only difference was the reversal of the test halves.

Procedure and Subjects

The study lists were presented once at a 1-sec rate. The subjects were told that they would be given a recognition test but its nature was not specified. Immediately after the presentation of the last word, instructions were given for the forced-choice recognition test. The subjects were informed that each pair contained a word shown to them during study and one which had not been shown, and they were to call out the correct word. Each pair was presented for 3 sec and the subject was told that he must choose one of the words within this interval, guessing if necessary. The right-left positions of the correct words in the pairs were determined randomly.

Thirty college students were assigned to each of the four groups by a block-randomized schedule. It should be noted again that Groups I-1 and I-2 were used only to allow each I word to occur once in the first half of the test series, and once in the second half, so that any testing effects which occurred would be measured for pairs containing all 24 I words. The same is true for Groups C-1 and C-2, although there was no reason to anticipate unusual testing effects for these groups since neutral items were used in both study and test as correct items.

RESULTS

I Groups

The results for the I Groups will be examined first. On the test for these groups there were 12 pairs containing I words on the first half of the test, and also 12 pairs containing neutral or C words. The same was true for the second half. The numbers of errors for each class of items for each half were determined. These were combined for Groups I-1 and I-2 and presented as percentages in the left panel of Figure 4.10. The number of errors was greater for the pairs containing I words than for the pairs containing C words in both halves as would be anticipated if frequency information about the syllables is a part of the memory for a word. For both types of items the errors increased from the first half to the second half, but the increase was greater for the I words.

The statistical analysis supports the differences seen in the figure. The difference between the I and C words was reliable ($F = 43.53$) as was test halves, $F(1, 174) = 19.61$. In addition, the interaction between item type and test halves was significant, $F(1, 174) = 5.68$, $p < .05$. Of the 60 subjects, 45 made more errors on I words than on C words during the first half of the test. The corresponding number for the second half was 56. The difference between the I and C pairs on the first half was also reliable, $t(58) = 3.39$, $p < .01$. This, taken in conjunction with the interaction between item type and halves, suggested (according to theory) that syllabic frequency was induced during the study phase and further incremented during the test phase.

Finally, the statistical tests showed a substantial interaction, $F(1, 174) = 10.01$, between word type and groups (the I-C differ-

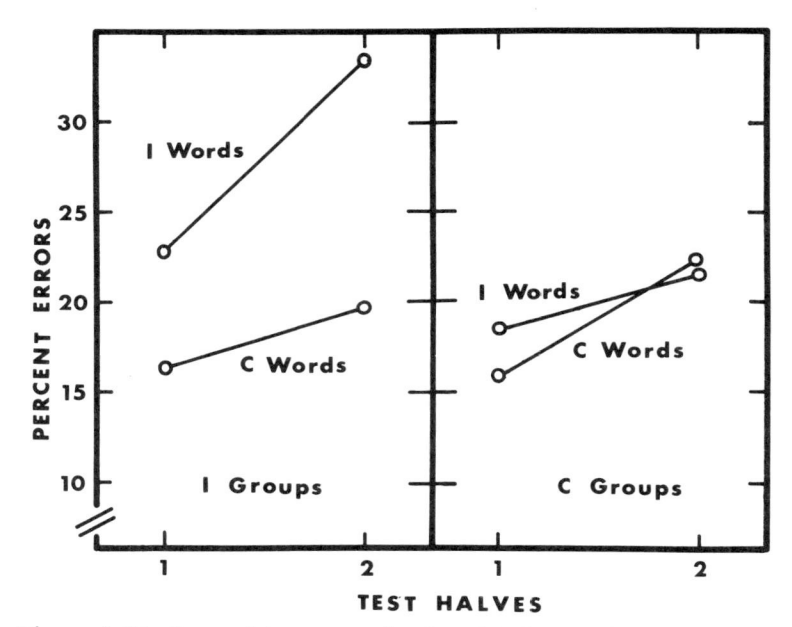

[Figure 4.10: Percent errors plotted against Test Halves (1, 2) for I Groups (left panel) and C Groups (right panel), showing curves for I Words and C Words.]

Figure 4.10 Recognition errors for I and C items when appropriate inducing words were used in the study list (I Groups) and when inappropriate words were used (C Groups).

ence was greater for Group I-2 than for Group I-1). This was produced by there being fewer errors for the C words for Group I-2 than for Group I-1. Errors on the I words were essentially equivalent for both groups. It is not known why the C words should differ in difficulty for the two groups. However, the interaction between groups and test halves was not reliable, $F(1, 174) = 1.84$, nor was the triple interaction, $F < 1$.

Groups C-1 and C-2

It will be remembered that the test for these groups included the critical test items (I words), but the study list consisted of neutral words in that the syllable overlap between them and the I words was minimal. Theoretically, therefore, the prediction was of a null result for the I-C difference. The right-hand panel of Figure 4.10 shows the outcome. The only significant source of variance was test halves, $F(1, 174) = 17.44$. It should be noted that the slopes of the two curves correspond quite closely to the slope of the curve for the C items for Groups I-1 and I-2. That there is a positive slope indicates that there are other unidentified sources of testing effects; perhaps forgetting increases as the retention interval gets longer during testing, or there might be other factors involved.

DISCUSSION

The results were consonant with three expectations from frequency theory. A word on the test consisting of two syllables, each having appeared in a different word on the study list, "drew" more errors than did a control word. Based upon the assumption that when the two syllables each gain a unit of frequency, the word as a unit possesses some level of frequency greater than the control word, the results would be anticipated. Frequency theory, as thus far developed, does not specify the composition rules whereby the phenomenal frequency of a larger unit can be predicted knowing the input frequency on subunits. Therefore, the present study has proceeded on the assumption that the apparent frequency of the larger unit would be greater than that of a control unit; how much greater is not known. The prediction that the syllable frequency would be further incremented during testing was also supported. Finally, it was shown that the first two findings were not due to a peculiarity of the critical words per se, since omitting the words used to induce syllable frequency during study had no influence on recognition errors produced by the critical words.

The positive effects observed, while highly reliable statistically, were not large in an absolute sense. Certainly the effect was much less than would be expected had the critical word been presented during study. There are many possibilities as to why this outcome might be expected. For example, a syllable may not gain frequency unless pronounced, implicitly or explicitly. However, the present study does not elucidate such mechanisms.

Alternative explanations must be considered. It seems that the choice of the I word, thereby producing an error, was not based on its semantic characteristics. The word had not occurred during study and words with similar meanings were not presented during study. The I word was a composite of the two parts of two words, each having different meaning, and neither of which was similar to the meaning of the I word. In one way of viewing the procedures they are in correspondence to those used in a study of recognition memory for sentences by Bransford and Franks (1971). If parts of complex sentences were presented for study, parts which in themselves constituted sentences, the subject had a high probability of identifying the complex sentence as one which had been presented when in fact it had not. An interpretation in terms of synthesis of meaning may be appropriate for that effect but it clearly will not fit the present results. On the other hand, it is not beyond possibility that the Bransford-Franks finding may yield to a frequency interpretation. The work of Reitman and Bower (1973) makes such an interpretation plausible.

The present results might be interpreted in terms of formal similarity. That is, the I word was necessarily formally similar to words presented for study. Two remarks seem appropriate. First, the formal similarity did not obtain at the time of the test in that the two words in each test pair were not formally similar. Thus, there could not have been a perceptual discrimination failure at the time of the test. Second, it might be argued that when the subject was in doubt about the correct word in a pair he made his decision by saying, in effect, "there was a word or two like this in the list." However, formal similarity is an independent variable and how it influences behavior requires interpretation. It is our belief that formal similarity influences recognition performance (when it does) because of the induced frequency of the components or elements of the larger units. With poorly integrated units, such as consonant syllables, the individual letters or bigrams may be the critical elements in the frequency accrual and by which formal similarity produces its effect. With words, we have assumed that the syllable is a "natural" element which could have frequency representation independent of the frequency of the larger unit. In short, the effects of formal similarity may be interpreted by referring to frequency inputs on elements of larger units.

REFERENCES

Attneave, F. Psychological probability as a function of experienced frequency. *Journal of Experimental Psychology,* 1953, 46, 81–86.

Bransford, J. D., & Franks, J. J. The abstraction of linguistic ideas. *Cognitive Psychology,* 1971, 2, 331–350.

Reitman, J. S., & Bower, G. H. Storage and later recognition of exemplars of concepts. *Cognitive Psychology,* 1973, 4, 194–206.

Shapiro, B. J. The subjective estimate of relative word frequency. *Journal of Verbal Learning and Verbal Behavior,* 1969, 8, 248–251.

Underwood, B. J. Recognition memory. In H. H. Kendler & J. T. Spence (Eds.), *Essays in neobehaviorism.* New York: Appleton-Century-Crofts, 1971.

Underwood, B. J. Word recognition memory and frequency information. *Journal of Experimental Psychology,* 1972, 94, 276–283.

Underwood, B. J., & Freund, J. S. Testing effects in the recognition of words. *Journal of Verbal Learning and Verbal Behavior,* 1970, 9, 117–125.

Individual Differences as a Crucible in Theory Construction

My proposal is that we should formulate our nomothetic theories in a way that will allow an immediate individual-differences test. I am proposing this because, among other benefits, I believe this approach will make individual differences a crucible in theory construction. The argument I advance is applicable to theory construction in all areas of experimental psychology, but my illustrations come largely from the areas of learning and memory. I feel impelled initially to reconstruct as best I can the reasons that led me to compose an article dealing with theory construction. It has resulted from a professional uneasiness that has grown over the past few years. These pinpricks of uneasiness seemed to say that our profession needed to open a discussion of theory construction in psychology, a discussion led by psychologists, for psychologists. When the uneasy feelings were articulated in this manner, I was able to identify three developments that had been responsible for the pinpricks. And then a fourth development took place which led me to presume I might have something to say that could just possibly initiate the discussion.

The first source of uneasiness was quite an unlikely one, namely, *the undergraduate student.* On occasion, a perceptive one will ask me, "How do you get a theory?" How does one answer this question? I found myself answering with a few pieces of trivia of the kind that any experienced teacher has ready for such moments. My lack of a guiding answer was demonstrated most blatantly when I found myself turning to anecdotes to shunt the question aside. Thus, I would tell the student that one great theoretical insight in the history of science is alleged to have occurred during a bath. So, perhaps, taking a bath would be a way to get a theory. But, of course (I told him), if you really want to develop a majestic theory, the only avenue open is to learn to play the violin and go to Princeton.

The question remained unanswered, but I did set about to see if

---

Benton J. Underwood, "Individual Differences as a Crucible in Theory Construction," *American Psychologist* 30 (1975): 128–134. Reprinted with permission. Copyright 1975 by the American Psychological Association.

This article was a Distinguished Scientific Contribution Award address presented at the meeting of the American Psychological Association, New Orleans, August 1974. It was supported by the Psychological Sciences Division, Office of Naval Research under Contract N00014-67-A-0356-0010, Contract Authority Identification NR 154-321.

I could put something down on paper of a systematic nature that might be given to a student who would be so brazen as to ask such a question. To some extent, what I say here was prepared for such a student.

The second stimulus I can identify as being involved in my uneasiness relates to developments in the area of memory, including the offshoot now called information processing. In particular, I refer to *structural model building.* Certainly, in the last dozen years, the favorite after-class occupation of many college professors has been that of building models of memory. Just what is responsible for this furious activity is not entirely apparent to me. One might guess that the flow diagram presented by our English colleague, Donald Broadbent, in his 1958 book *Perception and Communication* was involved, but I choose not to saddle him with this reverse lend-lease if he doesn't want to take the responsibility for it. The fact remains that we have models running out of our ears, and there seems to be no surcease.

This may be quite healthy; at least lots of people are getting skilled in drawing boxes, arrows, and circular nodes. But all of these models cannot be right, or even useful or believable, and evaluation seems to be rather low on the priority list. It seems to be easier to formulate a new model than to test an old one, and one never gets pinned down that way. I am being unfair, of course, and this is particularly troublesome because the model builders are very friendly people; many are my friends. All I ask of the builders is please, sooner or later, come up for breath and see what you have wrought. Is this really the way we want theory development to occur?

A third stimulus was a book published in 1967 called *Learning and Individual Differences.* It represents the thinking of a number of investigators brought together by Robert Gagné for a conference at the University of Pittsburgh. Reading this book gave me a small intellectual abrasion that has continued to fester over the years. I was unable to get rid of it by saying to myself that the problem of individual differences is someone else's responsibility. I finally came to accept the notion that individual differences ought to be considered central in theory construction, not peripheral. How can we make individual differences of central focus in our theories? This volume contains ideas, and I suspect that if one were to juxtapose what was said at that conference with some of my later comments, the similarity would be found to be more than coincidental.

And finally, certain events which occurred in our laboratory served as the catalyst for the final step, namely, that of *trying to bring individual differences into the mainstream of theory construc-*

tion. Some background is necessary. In 1966 an article was published (Ekstrand, Wallace, & Underwood) which proposed that verbal-discrimination learning (which is a special kind of a recognition task) is mediated by the subject discriminating the apparent frequency differences between the right and wrong words in each pair. The idea was subsequently extended to the more classical recognition procedures. The theory, commonly called *frequency theory,* has had some success in predicting the consequences of manipulating a number of independent variables. A severe critic might argue about the use of the word "success," but that is unimportant for the present paper. But it is important to understand the basic nature of the theory.

As I understand the strict use of the term *model,* it means that a set of empirical relationships developed in one area of discourse is applied to another area of research as a possible explanatory system. As an extreme case, if the laws and relationships among the functions of the organs of the digestive system were applied to memory as an explanatory system, this would be an illustration of the true meaning of the word *model.* This transfer from one area to another need not be across disciplines; it can be within a discipline. If the laws of learning are used to try to account for bizarre behaviors, it would be a form of modeling. Frequency theory, in the language of modeling, is a within-discipline model of an unusual kind. The theory asserts that the laws and relationships that hold for frequency discrimination (as viewed, perhaps, in the classical psychophysical sense) will determine the performance in the usual recognition-memory study. The unusual nature of the theory lies in the fact that when the theory was formulated there wasn't a body of laws and relationships concerning frequency discriminations. It has been necessary, therefore, to develop both areas simultaneously. Nevertheless, the theory is quite explicit on the central point; the facts of frequency discrimination must hold for the recognition situation or the theory is in trouble.

The theory as stated is a nomothetic theory, since the thinking was geared entirely to mean performances and mean frequency discriminations. This form of thinking can be blinding. But finally (and there were a number of developments that were responsible but that will not be set down here) the time came when a now obvious implication forced itself into our thinking. The whole fabric of the theory, quite by accident, rests on a postulate that is in fact an individual-differences postulate. However we might have stirred uncomfortably when we realized this and however we might have tried to find some escape, the implication would not go away. A subject who demonstrated fine or precise frequency discriminations must show good recognition memory; a subject who demonstrated poor or imprecise frequency discriminations must show poor recognition memory. What a devastating relationship to contemplate so late in the development of the theory, particularly so since we knew that both frequency discriminations and recognition memory yielded quite reliable scores. In this case, when the belated tests were made, the outcomes showed the prerequisite relationships. But suppose this had not been the outcome? Suppose we had found a zero correlation between measures of frequency discrimination and measures of recognition memory? The theory would simply have to be dropped. That we had demonstrated the necessary relationships on the fiftieth study, was, perhaps, a stroke of luck. The point is that, had we been so wise as to perceive it, the fiftieth study should have been the first study. If the data from this first study did not approve of the individual-differences relationship inherent in the theory, there would have been no theory, no 50 studies.

Let me now state the generalized case. If we include in our nomothetic theories a process or mechanism that can be measured reliably outside of the situation for which it is serving its theoretical purpose, we have an immediate test of the validity of the theoretical formulation, at least a test of this aspect of the formulation. The assumed theoretical process will necessarily have a tie with performance which reflects (in theory) the magnitude of the process. Individuals will vary in the amount of this characteristic or skill they "possess." A prediction concerning differences in the performance of the individuals must follow. A test of this prediction can yield two outcomes. If the correlation is substantial, the theory has a go-ahead signal, that and no more; the usual positive correlations across subjects on various skills and aptitudes allow no conclusion concerning the validity of the theory per se. If the relationship between the individual-differences measurements and the performance is essentially zero, there is no alternative but to drop the line of theoretical thinking. It is this form of reasoning that has led to the title of this article; individual differences may indeed be used as a crucible in nomothetic theory construction. The approach, I believe, provides a critical test of theories as they are being born; if they fail to pass the test, they should neither see the light of day nor the pages of the *Psychological Review.*

I now must turn to a broader perspective of theory construction and show how the individual-differences approach fits into this perspective. In effect, I am going to try to give the student an answer to his inquiry, albeit an indirect and an incomplete one. What I want to tell the student is that there seems to be a common way in which theoretical thinking gets started, and then I will provide him with some guidelines with which he should be concerned if he wants his theory to be disciplined in the sense that it can be discredited as well as affirmed.

A behavioral phenomenon is defined by the relationship between some independent variable and measured behavior. As research develops, certain key phenomena are identified and a body of empirical knowledge builds up around them. Thus, we have such key phenomena as extinction, retroactive inhibition, altruism, motivation, space perception, and so on. Now, even in the definition of such phenomena we may tend to allow an internalization of a process. It is not a great leap to recognize that the independent variable produces an influence only because it did something to the "workings" of the subject. When, over successive trials, we observe an increase in the number of correct responses given by a subject, we say that learning has occurred, although learning is neither the number of correct responses nor the trials. Learning is a term we use to represent the relationship between the two, and frequently also to represent the implicit belief that something has "gone on" in the subject. It is almost impossible to think of a term such as *motivation* without thinking of it at the same time as being changes in the organism.

The above illustrations suggest that it is difficult to avoid thinking about intervening processes even when thinking about the definition of so-called empirical phenomena. Theoretical efforts merely make the thinking about intervening processes more formal and more deliberate. The basis of theorizing is that of proposing intervening processes (some prefer the term *mechanisms*) that will mediate the observed empirical relationships between various independent variables and the key phenomenon of interest. I will not entertain the question of whether we should or should not be theorizing; not many can avoid it. But it is reasonable to ask what we propose to achieve by a theory. From one point of view, theorizing is simply one of the later steps along the chain of steps known as data reduction. We try to comprehend the scores of 100 subjects by getting a statistical description of the scores. We try to comprehend the scores of five groups given different levels of an independent variable by plotting the mean scores above the five levels of the variable. We try to summarize a number of different experiments in an area by trying to extract the commonalities and stating the empirical generalizations. We try, by theorizing, to state basic processes that could underlie the behavior and produce the several laws within the area of interest. Theorizing is always reductive in the sense that we try to propose processes more elementary (but more general) or basic than the phenomena for which we are trying to account. In all of the steps of data reduction, including theoretical speculation, we are trying to produce the ultimate in economy of thought.

Now (still speaking to the student), what guidelines can be used in proposing the intervening process? There are many obvious ones, such as explicitness and testability, but these are generally necessary consequences of others. I propose three guidelines.

The first guideline is a compound one: The theory must assume at least two intervening processes, and these processes must interact in some way to relate the independent variables to the dependent variable. This statement needs to be unpacked. Why must we have two processes? A single-process theory must always be isomorphic to empirical relationships. If I assume that interference as a theoretical process is responsible for forgetting, assuming that and no more, the empirical relationships give the complete story, since interference must vary in magnitude as forgetting varies in magnitude. As a theoretical concept, it is superfluous and has no predictive power. It can also be seen that if two intervening processes are assumed, but which vary in magnitude in exactly the same way for all independent variables, it reduces essentially to a single-process theory.

The moment we propose two intervening processes that, for at least one independent variable, have different functions and hence interact, we begin to get predictive power. This guideline seems to have been followed for many years, as witness the many different theoretical approaches including an excitatory and an inhibitory process (by whatever names) which are assigned differential functions for certain independent variables. The interaction can be "inserted" at two different points. It is probably most common to provide the interaction by having different functional relationships between the two assumed processes and the independent variables. But it would be quite possible to have the theoretical relationships be the same for the independent variable but differ with regard to their influence on the dependent variable.

I emphasize the necessity of the interaction between the intervening processes for at least one independent variable because I do not believe it has been clearly enunciated in recent years. I emphasize it also for quite a different reason. Those of us who teach undergraduates know that teaching them how to see, verbalize, and become generally facile in thinking about empirical interactions in data know that it is adventurous, to say the least. But it seems necessary for them to develop this skill if we want them also to grasp the nature of predictive theory.

In the statement of this guideline it was indicated that there must be at least two intervening processes. The complexity of a theory increases directly as the number of postulated processes increase. Obviously we try to keep the number of processes to a minimum, but if it becomes necessary to add, we must add. In so doing we recognize that a problem in understanding will necessarily arise. Some idea of the magnitude of the problem of understanding can be obtained by trying to comprehend, for example, an empirical interaction among four variables. The complexity may be necessary and, if it is necessary, I believe we will find it imperative to represent the theoretical processes in strict mathematical terms so that the derivations can be unambiguous.

A second guideline I would suggest to my student is implicit in a number of previous statements. It is that any assumed process must be tied to at least one independent variable. I would point out to the student that not all would agree with this guideline, but also I would feel impelled to tell him that if he doesn't abide by this guideline he is likely to find himself in a pack of trouble. Nothing is more conducive to the infection of a theory by ploglies and homunculi than a free-floating intervening process. I read or heard (from a source that I have not been able to identify) that the idea that an intervening process must be tied to at least one independent variable is no longer considered essential and should be abandoned as an unnecessary stricture on the imagination needed for theorizing. It seems to me that it doesn't take much imagination to realize that to abandon this rule is to invite chaos.

The third guideline is concerned with the nature of the intervening processes to be postulated. I think we must allow great latitude, perhaps along several different dimensions, in proposed intervening processes. At one extreme, they may be strictly abstract mathematical propositions that disclaim any correspondence or relationship to a psychological process with which we might identify intuitively. Although we might not be able to resonate personally to such abstract, impalpable processes, they do have the very distinct advantage of avoiding misinterpretations that may occur when common psychological terms are used for identifying the processes. In any event, some of my subsequent comments cannot, it will be seen, be germane to the completely abstract intervening process.

At the other extreme, we may assume an intervening process that is more or less given by an empirical relationship in another area of psychological inquiry. Earlier I described the basic idea of frequency theory; it is a good illustration of this low-level form of theorizing. In between the two extremes there are various steps, and in fact many theories represent a mixed bag with regard to placement along the dimension of abstractness.

Now obviously, under this guideline, I have one specific proposal in mind, namely, that in choosing theoretical processes if at all possible choose at least one which has some possibility of yielding an individual-differences interpretation, as has been described. The illustration I gave from frequency theory may seem obvious and atypical. In fact, however, after I worked on the matter with other theoretical notions, I began to form the opinion that the individual-differences approach could in principle be implemented with any but the more abstract propositions. Let me give three illustrations.

If a free-recall list includes words occurring more than once, the recall of the words given spaced repetition will be superior to those given massed repetitions. Our theoretical thinking emphasized a reduced processing of the items when they were massed. Some indirect tests showed this to have some support. In thinking about this theory in light of the guideline under discussion, it seemed beyond doubt that subjects must differ in their propensity to attenuate processing. Now, if we could measure this tendency independently, and if it is a reliable individual-differences variable, we could make a test to tell us whether the theory should be dropped or whether we had a license to continue its development. Such a test now seems possible, and we will undertake it in the fall. My only regret is that we did not formulate this approach several years ago when the theory first came into being.

Assume that a theory is proposed for serial learning which includes a process identified as generalization along a spatial dimension. We have the techniques for measuring generalization outside the serial learning task. The role that generalization is assigned in serial learning must surely be in some way predictably different for subjects having different generalization gradients.

My skimming of abstracts has suggested that some investigators studying the skills involved very early in the process of learning to read are suggesting that the subject's ability to develop an internal schemata of each of the letters is important. The schemata will allow a "match" even though some distortion is present in the visually presented letters. At the same time, the schemata should not be too broad or it will accept wrong letters as a match. Would it be possible to get an independent measure of the characteristics of the schemata without visual inputs of letters? Adults can identify very accurately individual letters when "printed" on the skin of the back with the index finger (wielded by another person, of course). Would this be useful for measuring schemata in pure form in children? And, then, would this predict errors in identification of visually presented letters?

These three illustrations are sufficient to see the direction I think this approach might take. By this time, objections may be cropping up. I hope these can be anticipated in the three possible objections I will now discuss. Two of the objections can be handled quite satisfactorily, I believe; one is a little more difficult. We will start with the difficult one.

I used frequency theory to illustrate a basic application of the individual-differences approach. The theory, in addition to assuming that a frequency discrimination is critical, also assumes that the subject applies a rule to cover all pairs in a verbal-discrimination task, namely, the rule to choose the word with the highest apparent frequency in each pair. Suppose that frequency discrimination and the rapidity of rule discovery are correlated. That subjects with good frequency discrimination are also good verbal-discrimination learners might then be due to the fact that they learn rules quickly and that some rule other than the frequency rule is mediating the performance. In this particular case, there are several auxiliary facts (which will not be detailed here) that rule out this possibility, but it may not be possible to do this in other situations. The generalized issue concerns the correlative relationship between the performance produced by the intervening process being evaluated as an individual-differences variable, and the performance produced by other processes in the theory. The solution is to make sure that only the symptoms of the individual-differences variable are being measured in the case in which the other processes may also be operating to influence performance. If this cannot be done it may produce a positive conclusion concerning the individual-differences variable when in fact the evidence producing the positive conclusion results from a correlation with the consequences of the other theoretical process. To avoid this, we must in some way neutralize the effects of the other variable. Experimental ingenuity should find a way to accomplish this. But even if a solution is not found, it should be clear that we are no worse off than we are at present when this approach is not used. However, the most important function of the individual-differences approach is that of nipping an inappropriate theoretical notion in the bud, and this is indicated when a zero correlation is found. So, the first objection is by no means a lethal one.

The second objection is quite a different one. I think it a certainty that the individual-differences approach described here will be most applicable when the process used theoretically has more or less empirical status in another area of research within psychology. What constitutes another or different area? Behavior is behavior, some might say. I can illustrate the question in as stark a manner as possible. Suppose there is an empirical relationship derived from the learning of two-syllable words. Now, we say, we are going to use this relationship theoretically as a part of a theoretical system to explain the learning of three-syllable words. We go through the individual-difference routine and find a high positive correlation that, according to the argument which has been advanced, gives us license to proceed with the development of the theory. There isn't a good name for such thinking; around our laboratory we speak of this by the rather crude but descriptive word *incest*. We must be sure that when we use the approach I am advocating we are dealing with no more than kissin' cousins. I suppose that good judgment must be imposed, or that the union is acceptable when it is not intuitively obvious that they should be related. And further, we are always transferring what appears to be a simple process for use as a theoretical concept (along with the use of at least one other) in attempting to account for performance on a more complex task than the one used to measure the simple process directly.

A third objection that may be raised is not directed necessarily toward the individual-differences approach but toward the use of a relationship discovered in one area as an explanatory concept in another. It might be insisted that this approach doesn't explain anything. As an illustration: if frequency discrimination can be used to account for recognition memory, it is fine and good, but what has been gained? It merely means that to understand recognition memory, we must understand the processes involved in frequency discriminations. This objection is without validity and can be raised about any theoretical approach using behavioral constructs (as opposed to the use of physiological constructs). The whole idea behind behavioral theory is to reduce the number of independent processes to a minimum; to find that performance on two apparently diverse tasks is mediated at least in part by a single, more elementary, process is a step toward this long-range goal.

There is one further point that should be made, relative to the third guideline, the discussion of which has largely consisted of trumpets being blown in support of the individual-differences approach. There is nothing in this approach that prevents the use of mathematical expressions for the theoretical processes. Indeed, they should be used by all who have the skills and the wills. All that is being proposed is that when possible, one of the theoretical processes be identified in such a way that it is at least remotely feasible that it could be measured as an individual-differences variable.

It should be apparent that the more traditional attempts to relate nomothetic theories to individual differences by using standardized tests, for example, paper-and-pencil tests, are quite in line with the approach proposed here. Thus, tests of manifest anxiety, introversion–extroversion, ego strength, and so on, have been used to identify individual differences that are in turn said to be identifiable with assumed processes in nomothetic theories. If there are differences in the approaches, they lie in the indirectness of the measurements and the types of conclusions drawn when the theoretical tests are made. A positive correlation is to be responded to in the way discussed earlier. A zero correlation, however, is frequently not used in a critical, decisive manner. The investigator far too frequently puts the blame on the paper-and-pencil test for not measuring what it is said to measure, rather than putting the blame on the assumed theoretical relationship. Under these circumstances, the individual-differences variable is not a crucible in theory construction. Rather, it is an interesting adjunct of theoretical development.

As a final point, I would like to suggest an implication of the approach advocated here for the understanding of individual differences in general. As many have pointed out in the past, we cannot deal constructively with individual differences when we identify the important variables as age, sex, grade, IQ, social status, and so on. The critical variables are process variables. The approach proposed here, the approach which makes individual-differences variables crucibles in theory construction, will identify the process variables as a fallout from nomothetic theory construction if, of course, the nomothetic theories are dealing with fundamental processes of behavior.

Now that the article is completed, I find that I have exorcised the uneasy feelings that led to it. I had not hoped merely for therapy, but rather for a discussion of theory construction in the coming years. But even if this discussion does not ensue, you may be sure that the next student who asks me that question is likely to be severely imprinted.

REFERENCES

Broadbent, D. E. *Perception and communication.* New York: Pergamon Press, 1958.

Ekstrand, B. R., Wallace, W. P., & Underwood, B. J. A frequency theory of verbal-discrimination learning. *Psychological Review,* 1966, 73, 566–578.

Gagné, R. M. (Ed.). *Learning and individual differences.* Columbus, Ohio: Charles E. Merrill, 1967.

5
Miscellaneous

An Orientation for Research on Thinking

I

This paper is an exposition of an orientation around which certain research on thinking can be carried out. It is not to be considered a formal theory of thinking although, as will be seen, there are certain assumptions which clearly underlie the framework. And, even though testable problems are generated by the orientation, it will be recognized that the expected results from the tests could be accounted for largely on the basis of extant concepts. Finally, by way of introduction, it will be obvious that the orientation does not provide a framework for all recognized problems about thinking.

There is no general agreement on what problems, when presented to a subject, do or do not study behavior which can be called thinking. The behavior with which this paper is concerned is that reported in the literature under such names as *problem solving, reasoning, concept formation,* and *creativity.* For convenience, all of these modifications of behavior will be called thinking. An examination of various tasks in these areas shows that, for solution of the task, the subject is required to learn or recognize perceptual or functional relationships among objects (or properties thereof), among symbols, or among both. By perceptual relationships are meant similarities or identities (depending upon the experimenter) in form, color, or size.[1] By a functional relationship will be meant either of two kinds of relationships: (1) a cause-effect relationship, since variation in X produces reliable variation in Y. Any known lawful relationship existing in nature is of this kind. (2) The second form of relationship is man-made, and may be thought of as mechanical. Such relationships are those obtaining between a wrench and a nut, a ball and a bat, and a horse and a cart.

It has been said above that these tasks require the subject to learn or recognize relationships. Both of the terms, *learning* and

---

Benton J. Underwood, "An Orientation for Research on Thinking," *Psychological Review* 59 (1952): 209–220. Reprinted with permission. Copyright 1952 by the American Psychological Association.

[1] Attributes of stimuli in other sense modalities could likewise be specified.

recognition, must be used because in some tasks the subject must discover only which one of several already known relationships is required or is appropriate for solution. That is to say, for a particular problem the subject need only recognize which one of several known relationships is pertinent. In other tasks the subject is required to learn relationships which during the normal course of his life he would never have acquired. Thus, if the task requires the subject to show that automobiles, horses, and trains are related (all are methods of transportation), it would be the recognition of a relationship. But, the subject might be required to learn that all blue triangles represent the concept DIT, while all red triangles represent REC. Such relationships would not normally have been acquired in our culture. These are man-made relationships for purposes of research only.

It is recognized, of course, that thinking may also require the recognition or learning of relationships among relationships. Such problems approximate what is sometimes referred to as creative thinking (8), and are, descriptively, more complex than the tasks described above. Several of Maier's problems (15) meet these requirements as do some of those given by Duncker (5) and Wertheimer (29). Syllogisms are problems in which two relationships are given and the subject is to decide what third relationship is based on the two given. Yet, the basic requirement is still that of perceiving relationships.

II

Behavior changes called thinking meet all the definitional requirements of learning. This does not mean, of course, that the inferred processes which are said to produce behavior changes (also called learning) resulting from conditioning techniques are the same as those which produce the behavior changes called thinking. Nor does it mean that there is *not* a high degree of communality among these processes. It will be the working assumption here that there is communality among the processes producing all behavior changes which fit the definitional requirements of learning. While such an assumption is not essential for the development of the orientation it will be seen that it is implied and may therefore be stated flatly. It is the sense of the present paper that the greatest need at present for understanding thinking is a set of empirically well-established laws between stimulus dimensions and response variables. Such laws might destroy some of the chronic problems which show themselves in arguments of insight vs. trial and error, single vs. multiple learning processes, learning by understanding vs. learning by rote, etc. On the basis of present data it is impossible to give convincing arguments concerning the reality or irreality of these demarcations; the data on thinking at the human level are far too meager. But, we may ask: What data are needed to help dissipate some of the disagreements?

There are at least three ways by which we might focus more definite answers to questions concerning the amount of overlapping of basic processes responsible for the wide variety of behavior changes from those called conditioning through those called thinking. One of these methods is that of correlation analysis. If a subject does well on a rote learning task and poorly on a thinking task, there would be some basis for inferring the lack of similarity among the processes needed to perform the two tasks. No serious attempts have been made with this approach. Maier (16) reports some data on rats which suggest low communality among various processes. Billings (1) shows a moderate relationship between what might be called rote learning and thinking. Nevertheless, it is a fair guess that the results of even a thorough-going factor analysis of behavior on a wide variety of tasks, from conditioning through thinking, would demand the postulation of many different processes if the lack of inter-correlation is the basis for such postulation. It is known, for example, that in the area of motor behavior, where apparently simple skills *seem* to be highly similar, correlations may be quite low (23). Thus, if we require the postulation of different processes whenever correlations are low, we will likely have scores of processes. This may be necessary, but it is no premise on which to proceed at the moment. Correlations may be low for a variety of reasons; they may reflect operation of secondary factors or processes which are masking the influence of processes which in effect are common to the performance of a wide variety of tasks. Or, all processes may be common to all learning but the amount of each required may vary widely. In short, factor analysis would probably lead to the postulation of a number of processes which might not actually be required by theory.

A second method of unifying data at various levels of learning is in terms of theory directly. If theoretical concepts derived from one area of discourse are shown to be capable of accounting for phenomena at another level, one may feel some confidence in bringing the two areas together. Some progress in this direction has been made with conditioning and rote learning (7, 11). It cannot be given an adequate tryout with, say, thinking and rote learning, because of the paucity of data on thinking. Certain attempts to relate concept formation and less complex forms of learning have not been without some success (7, 27), but the lack of systematic laws about concept formation does not allow a definitive evaluative attempt.

The third method is that of determining the functional relationships between manipulable variables and behavior for various levels of behavior which meet the definitional requirements of learning. If these lawful relationships turn out to be similar for an appreciable number of independent variables then again we have a strong basis for inferring common processes.

Actually, of course, there is no incompatibility between the second and third approach; they should be carried out simultaneously. A program of research based on the third approach could proceed without theory, but it is my belief that in the long run it would become sterile. However, it should be stated again that the ultimate fruitfulness of the second approach (theory) cannot be determined until some empirical laws (third approach) are obtained against which the theory can be checked, verified, modified, thrown out, etc. The conclusion is that a great deal of the future development in thinking rests squarely on filling the hiatus representing lack of empirical relationships between stimulus variables and response changes for tasks said to be measuring thinking. The purpose of the present orientation is to set up simple hypotheses about the influence which some of the environmental and task variables should have on rate or efficiency of thinking.

III

In this section the basic assumption on which this orientation rests will be stated. In behavior called thinking the subject is motivated to solve a problem—reach a goal—and the solution depends upon his learning or recognizing certain relationships among symbols, objects, or among relationships themselves (as discussed above). For simplicity of exposition, in future references these symbols, objects, and relationships will all be called stimuli. *Stimuli*, therefore, will be used in a general sense to mean any of the following: (1) objects *per se;* (2) physical properties of those objects; (3) symbols which may stand for a functional relationship, for an object, or for a property thereof; (4) functional relationships which become cues by virtue of being responses to objects, properties of those objects, or symbols;[2] and at times (5) memorial representation of any of these stimuli.

For the perception of relationships among stimuli the needed assumption is that the *appropriate responses to those stimuli be contiguous.* By appropriate is meant the perceptual, ideational, or motor response which defines the stimulus property demanded by the relationship. To illustrate with a simple case: If a concept to be evolved is "blueness," and the subject is presented with blue triangles and blue circles, the common property can be perceived only if the two responses "blue" occur contiguously.[3]

The orientation may be made more clear if a mechanical model is used. Assume that there are six capsules in a bowl, each capsule representing a single stimulus. The solution to the problem requires that the relationship among three of the six stimuli be perceived. Assume further that the subject is an automaton set to draw three capsules at a time. After each draw the capsules are returned to the bowl. When the three appropriate capsules are drawn simultaneously, *when they appear contiguously,* the problem is solved. For such a situation the time of solution can be calculated on a straight probability basis. On a single draw of three capsules the probabilities are .05 that the correct three will be drawn.

$$(n^c r = \frac{n}{(n-r!)\,(r!)},$$

where $n^c r$ is the number of combinations of n things taken r at a time.) There are two essential points to be made by this mechanical analogy. (1) Drawing three at a time is the mechanical analogy of achieving maximum contiguity of responses to stimuli. Thus, if the appropriate concept is "blue" and the subject responds spontaneously with such a response to the three stimuli in rapid order, we would be achieving maximum contiguity. (2) The second point is that human subjects are *not* automatons set to draw on a random

---

[2] Response-produced stimuli have been discussed in detail by Miller and Dollard (18) and Dollard and Miller (4). It is their belief that stimuli-producing responses are largely verbal (4, p. 101). It should also be clear that these events may extend into a series of relatively implicit stimulus-response units.

[3] No new assumptions are needed concerning matters of reinforcement. In rote learning it is known (25) that the anticipation of the correct response to a given stimulus strengthens the stimulus response connection, i.e., increases the probability that the stimulus will elicit the response. It shall be assumed that the same process operates in thinking. When appropriate responses occur contiguously (and are in some way known to be correct) there is an increase in the probability that the stimuli will elicit the response.

basis. The human subject has a memory by which contiguity of responses may be produced even though the physical stimuli for those responses are not present. Furthermore, the human subject need not draw three stimuli at a time. He brings past experiences to the situation which might allow him to discard one or more of the stimuli as irrelevant before he starts drawing. But, because problem solvers are human does not necessarily mean that they would be superior to the automaton at solving problems. For they have biases and sets and prejudices which may retard as well as enhance solutions. Thus, the problem of manipulable variables in studying thinking might be thought of as the study of factors which enhance or decrease probabilities of solution over those offered by a straight mechanical analogy. The main problem, then, is to suggest factors which are likely to increase or decrease the probabilities that pertinent responses will become contiguous.[4] This will be accomplished in the following section.

IV

Contiguity. The basic assumption is that in order for relationships among stimuli to be perceived and acquired, responses to those stimuli must be contiguous. As with most basic assumptions, there is no way to make a direct test of the validity of this one. But, conditions may be set up in which temporal contiguity among relevant stimuli is varied and thereby show an inverse relationship between actual time among these stimuli and rate of solution. It is assumed that contiguity operates in the manner specified because the greater the interval between pertinent stimuli the greater the subject must rely on memory; hence, the less the probability that pertinent responses will be contiguous.

As an illustration, let us consider a concept-learning situation. Twelve stimulus objects of some complexity are presented to the subject in a series. Four of the objects represent one concept, four another, and the other four still another. Each stimulus is presented for, say, five seconds for the subject to study, and then the subject is told the response which goes with that particular concept. The subject must, in each case, determine what the relevant stimulus dimensions of the various objects are. According to the mechanical analogy, if all four stimuli of a set were placed in front of the subject, and

---

[4] It is quite possible, of course, that pertinent stimuli may be contiguous without the pertinent responses to those stimuli being made or being contiguous. This is largely a problem of individual differences.

if he put a capsule for each dimension of all stimuli in the bowl, successive drawings would allow him to discover the common dimension running through all four. But, in serial presentation he cannot do this. He must "draw" by (ideally) stating hypotheses and testing them on each item until rejected or confirmed. To reject or confirm an hypothesis at any given moment, he must rely on his memory for the dimensions of the subjects not physically present. Because of the fallibility of memory we would expect that the greater the time between pertinent stimuli the slower the rate of acquiring a concept. Assuming that retention is inversely related to time, putting the four stimulus objects in close temporal contiguity should enhance solution; separating them by other stimulus objects (irrelevant) should retard solution.

There has been no adequate test of this hypothesis. Gagné (6) has shown that temporal closeness of highly similar stimuli leads to more rapid discrimination in rote learning, but where thinking as described in this paper is involved, no data are available. The test proposed above would not be entirely unambiguous, for by varying temporal contiguity of stimuli one is also varying the degree of massing and distribution of those stimuli. Furthermore, if the concepts appeared in close contiguity the subject could use some abilities of logical elimination which he could not use if the samples of a set were randomly distributed among samples of other sets. It is possible, however, to overcome both of these difficulties either by design or by interpretation (see later discussion).

In summary, it should be reiterated that insofar as can be told at present, there is no way by which we can test the proposition that contiguity of pertinent responses is necessary for solution.[5] But it does seem possible to demonstrate that time separating stimuli to which the pertinent responses must be made (for solution) would be an important variable influencing thinking.

Perceptual vs. symbolic presentation of stimuli. These two terms, perceptual and symbolic, may not carry the exact meaning intended. However, an illustration should clarify the distinction. Presenting an object or a picture of an object will here be called a perceptual presentation of a stimulus; presenting the object name will be called a symbolic presentation. Thus, a picture of a fish is perceptual presentation; presenting the word "fish," a symbolic presentation.[6]

---

[5] Maier (16) hints strongly that contiguity in experience is not essential for problem solution. Obviously, this idea is rejected in the present formulation.

[6] No clear-cut dichotomy is possible. The barest outline of a fish may be equivalent (in our predictions) to the word fish. The problem is obviously amenable to experimental attack. In the present paper, however, we will be concerned only with the extremes of the perceptual-symbolic dimension.

In dealing with this manipulable variable, the basis for prediction again concerns the fallibility and incompleteness of memory. However, no overall prediction can be made concerning rate of solution. We shall be concerned with two particular situations which will indicate the factors which need to be considered in making predictions.

1. Properties (stimuli) of objects may not be remembered when the stimuli are symbolic, and if these properties are germane to the solution of a given problem, solution will not be achieved. To return again to the mechanical analogy, failure of memory would mean that some of the pertinent capsules would not be in the bowl. To illustrate: If we ask a child what relationship exists between a table and a sheep, it is likely that the common four-leg property will be discovered more readily if the sheep and table are presented perceptually (real or by pictures) than if the child must depend upon memory as he searches for common properties.

2. On the other hand, if the forgotten properties of the symbolized object are irrelevant and the remembered properties relevant, solution might be more rapid for symbolic presentation than for perceptual presentation. For, in the case of perceptually-presented objects, properties which were forgotten for the symbolized objects may actually serve as potent distracting stimuli. In the mechanical analogy, all pertinent capsules are in the bowl but fewer irrelevant capsules are present when the symbol is presented than when the object itself is presented.

The above considerations make it clear that in order to derive unambiguous predictions concerning problem solution for perceptual vs. symbolic presentation of stimuli, it is necessary to know the location of the pertinent response or responses in the hierarchy of responses to the two kinds of stimuli. To bring this variable under adequate experimental control, two approaches will be mentioned.

The first approach provides a limitation on the number of stimuli. Thus, we might use simple stimuli for which the number of possible responses is very limited. Simple geometric forms provide such materials. For complex stimuli, a limitation on the number of dimensions to be considered by the subject could be afforded by proper instruction or pretraining. For example, we might have the subject first learn that this object (for which a symbol stands) has, say, ten characteristics, one of which is pertinent to solution. We could likewise point out to subjects in another group that this perceptually-presented object has the same ten characteristics and that one of these is pertinent to solution. It would then be predicted that in an actual problem-solving situation the perceptual stimuli would produce more rapid solution since the ten characteristics of the object indicated by the symbol would be less available because of forgetting.[7]

A second approach requires first that materials be calibrated. We would need to know, for example, the dominant responses to a perceptual stimulus and to the corresponding symbolic stimulus. For example, if a photograph of a fish is presented to the subject and he ia asked to "tell all you can about a fish," how will the responses compare with those when he is merely presented the word "fish" and given the same instructions? Knowing how the response hierarchies are arranged in the two cases, we could choose the pertinent (correct) characteristics for concept formation studies which have greater, less, or equal probabilities of being elicited by either method of presentation, and predictions of solution rates made accordingly.

This particular variable cannot be manipulated for problems which require the perception of relationships among relationships for solution. That is, it cannot be varied unless it be said that graphical or algebraic representation is perceptual representation of a functional relationship.

There is some experimental evidence to support the expected relationship between efficiency in problem solution and perceptual representation of pertinent stimuli. Maier (17) has shown that if a model is set up to solve one problem, and this model possesses properties essential for solving a subsequent problem, solution will be more rapid if the model remains in the immediate perceptual field. This is not a cleancut verification of the proposition, however, since the presence of the mechanical model may have tended to limit the subject's search more than if the model were not present. But it may mean that certain properties or functional relationships suggested by the model were less available on a recall basis than on a perceptual basis.

Number of stimuli. The greater the number of stimuli involved the slower will be the rate of solution. The stimuli may be relevant, irrelevant, or both, and the proposition still holds.[8] For, with an increase in the number of stimuli goes a decrease in the probabilities that the pertinent responses to stimuli will become contiguous. The greater the number of capsules we put in the bowl the less the

---

[7] It is possible that the speed with which perceptual stimuli can be "drawn" and "rejected" is greater than with recall "drawing." If this is true, predictions will have to be modified accordingly.

[8] One of my students, Ross L. Morgan, has pointed out that it may be necessary in future developments not to speak merely of number of stimuli, but of the ratio between the number of relevant and irrelevant stimuli.

probabilities that the pertinent ones will be drawn simultaneously so that the responses to them are contiguous. Confirmation of this principle may be accepted tentatively from the results of a study by Reed (22). In this study the appropriate concept word was placed among four irrelevant words in one condition and among six irrelevant words in a second condition. Concept formation was more rapid in the first instance.

This proposition has a great deal of face validity and is probably not one which requires urgent experimental work.

Similarity among stimuli. No categorical prediction can be made concerning the influence of similarity among stimuli on rate of thinking. It must first be recognized that the similarity which is often dealt with in thinking is learned similarity, and thus is itself a relationship. Physical similarity, as among tones, colors, sizes, has sometimes entered into stimuli used in concept studies and does, of course, provide a basis for careful quantification of similarity dimensions.

The influence of similarity can be most carefully analyzed in concept-formation studies. Welch (28, p. 236) has indicated two basic relationships which appear adequate for this situation. If, in the concept formation study, the similarity obtains either among the positive (relevant) stimulus dimensions, or among the negative (irrelevant), concept formation will be most rapid. If the similarity holds both among the positive and negative instances, solution will be slow. Welch also presents some confirming evidence (28, p. 255 f.).

Gibson's theory (7) of verbal learning, which she also indicates may handle concept formation (at least certain aspects of it), stresses generalization as the process which would account for the influence of similarity in concept-formation studies. Recent studies by Buss (3) and Oseas (21) have shown that it is possible to derive gradients of stimulus generalization from the errors made in learning concepts. Thus, on at least this one basic explanatory concept, we do have a rapprochement of conditioning, rote learning, and tasks which fall within the category of thinking.

We have said that similarity may retard or enhance thinking depending upon the particular stimuli among which the similarity obtains. From analyses of transfer in verbal learning it is known that if one response is to be attached to two similar stimuli, high positive transfer will be measured; if a different response must be made to these two stimuli, negative transfer will occur. It can be seen that this is essentially the situation we have in concept learning as described above. From another point of view, it can be shown that among verbal stimuli at least, similarity (scaled synonymity) is almost perfectly correlated with associative connection (as defined also by scaling). Haagen's work (9) shows this clearly. Thus similarity acts as a biasing agent so that in the mechanical model certain capsules have a greater probability of being drawn than do others. More specifically, if the capsules were of different size with the large ones representing similar stimuli, the large ones would have the highest probability of being drawn. Responses to these stimuli thus have a high probability of occurring contiguously. If a common response is to be made to these similar stimuli, facilitation will occur; if different responses, inhibition will occur.

In more complex thinking in which solution demands the perception of relationships among relationships there is every reason to believe that the above principles of similarity obtain. Syllogistic reasoning would fall into this category as would analogistic reasoning. Anyone who has taken some of the more difficult analogies tests can be easily convinced of the major role played by similarity. All factors considered, it would appear that we can have high confidence in the importance of similarity as a variable, and, furthermore, that we know fairly well the direction of its influence in various situations.

Biases. It was mentioned previously that one of the major factors which prevents the mechanical analogy from being accurate is that living organisms have memories. A second major factor which further prevents the direct analogy is that subjects have response biases. It has been shown that the influence of similarity might be deduced by considering the biasing effect which it has. Any bias produces a selection of responses to stimuli, or in some instances may select stimuli; thus all stimuli (and all possible responses to a particular stimulus) do not have equal probabilities of being drawn. And it is patent that these biases may enhance or retard thinking. If the subject is biased toward irrelevant stimuli, rate of solution will be slow; if biased toward relevant stimuli, rate of solution will be fast. Furthermore, the subject may cast aside capsules on a rational basis; that is to say, he may believe that some capsules are irrelevant to solution. This process is in itself thinking and should, according to the present orientation, be subject to the same laws as the solution toward which the elimination of capsules was directed.

Over a period of years the literature has developed a rather sizable catalogue of stimulus-response biases. For the present we need only list some of the more prominent ones.

1. Woodworth and Sells (30) have demonstrated clearly that in syllogistic reasoning the negative or positive atmosphere of the premises produces response bias. This "atmosphere effect" tends to produce negative conclusions if the premises are negative and

positive conclusions if the premises are positive. Prejudices will also tend to cloud straightforward solution of syllogisms when the premises contain ideas which tend to elicit emotional responses. This has been shown clearly by Morton (20), Thistlethwaite (24), and Lefford (12).

2. Heidbreder's long series of studies (10) have shown consistently that in concept formation we tend to respond first on the basis of objects, then form, then number. Thus, an object such as a house will be more quickly categorized than will a wreath representing a circle.

3. Luchins, in his studies of set or *Einstellung* (13, 14), has shown the great potency which past success in solving problems in a given fashion has on the solution of subsequent problems. In line with this, Maier (15) presents some evidence that one of the primary causes of failure is that the subject persists in trying solutions of a very restricted nature. Explicit instructions to vary attacks on problems tends to decrease routine and unsuccessful attempts.

4. Morgan (19) has demonstrated that in a situation where several stimulus properties have equal logical priority as critical properties, size and position will predominate over form and pattern.

5. The many observations made by the Gestalt psychologists demonstrate that the initial stimuli attended to in the visual field are by no means on a chance basis. Closure, good figures, etc., all tend to bias perceptions, thus voiding the possibility that all stimuli have the same probability of being responded to, i.e., of being drawn from the bowl. And we are just beginning to realize that motivation may have a selective influence on responses.

The above is not an attempt to list all biases; they have been given as illustrations of the basic fact with which we must deal, namely, that all stimuli in a given situation do not have equal probabilities of being responded to. It is believed that the study of these biases is an extremely important one for obtaining an overall set of principles which will determine efficiency in thinking. Indeed, these biases are in themselves so important that we may expect miniature theories to develop around them. A great many studies will be needed to determine the influence of manipulable variables on these biases.

V

In this section mention will be made of the more obvious problems associated with the study of thinking which are not considered in the present orientation.

First, it is recognized that there are logical tools used in thinking which commonly develop in all people in our culture. These tools are those which are necessary in order to discriminate among stimuli. Relationships such as big-little, up-down, under-over, etc. are necessary knowledge if differences among stimuli are to be responded to. So also are the tools which lead us to conclude that if A is greater than B and B greater than C, then A is greater than C. Which tools or methods are going to be most successful in solving problems will certainly be important variables to investigate, but the present orientation develops no specific prediction concerning these matters. It is clear, however, that a particular method is in effect a biasing agent and whether or not it will be successful depends upon the nature of the task. Some evidence is available which supports this contention (2). A specific method restricts the range of responses, and depending upon the problem, may facilitate or inhibit solution.

Does the orientation outlined here imply that the best way to solve problems is to put all seemingly relevant stimuli into a bowl and keep drawing and drawing different combinations of stimuli, each time searching for common properties? It would appear that such a procedure would have some advantages in that it should eliminate many biases. And it is possible that many new relationships might emerge from such a procedure. It is obvious also that such a recommendation removes all vestige of the psychic from thinking. But the method has certain evident limitations. If all relevant stimuli are not in the bowl, solution to the particular problem would be impossible, although unexpected relationships might emerge. The orientation outined here requires that pertinent responses to stimuli become contiguous. Therefore, even though the appropriate stimuli are drawn contiguously, there is no assurance that the appropriate responses to those stimuli will be made, that is to say, appropriate in the sense that they would provide solution. Why one subject may respond with the appropriate response and another may not is a problem—and an important one—not handled in the present paper. It is a fair possibility, however, that these differences in behavior represent in part differences in the magnitude of influence of the variables here said to be important for subjects at large.

Another matter of importance is the influence of practice in thinking on thinking. We know that in less complicated forms of learning, practice effects may be very large. We need likewise to know if the practice effect in thinking is large or small. No systematic data are available on this matter at the present time.

There are also problems related to productive thinking (29). Particular problems can be solved without the subject also acquiring a general principle by which other problems can be solved. The present orientation makes no prediction concerning this matter; that is to say, no prediction is made concerning the transfer effects following solution. It is clear, however, that many relationships are useful in solving other problems regardless of whether that relationship is understood or learned by rote. There is no reason to disbelieve the general idea that learning with understanding will lead to more adaptive behavior in other situations; likewise, there is no reason to doubt the usefulness of rote-learned relationships for thinking.

The basic assumption of response contiguity presented here may be interpreted to give a prediction that spaced practice would be inferior to massed practice in thinking. Spaced practice would reduce the likelihood of response contiguity because of forgetting which takes place during the spacing interval. And even though spaced practice is usually defined in terms of time between trials and not the time between stimuli representing the same concept, the prediction should still hold. The published data on massing vs. distribution in thinking tend to show that massing does result in better performance. Such data support the basic assumption of the present paper. It has been maintained (26, p. 439), however, that these studies have not adequately explored the time dimension of distribution and that no inclusive generalizations are possible. A recent study on concept formation (21) has shown that distributed practice up to one minute between trials produced slightly superior performance to the massing of trials. In short, it is possible that for certain kinds of tasks involving thinking, e.g., concept formation, where stimuli may be presented fairly rapidly, other processes may operate to such an extent as to obscure the differences produced by variation in response contiguity *per se*. All evidence of rote learning points to the fact that distribution of practice will facilitate only when the subject is required to respond rapidly. There is no reason to believe that the factor or factors which operate in these cases will not also operate in thinking if the speed is comparable to that of rote learning.

Other variables, such as subject variables (sex, age, intelligence) are also ignored and will need to be evaluated before any theory of thinking reaches a point that could be called comprehensive. Before such a theory can be developed, many empirical laws must be determined. The present framework is to be thought of as a device for directing the research for obtaining some of these laws.

VI

Summary. A point of view concerning thinking was developed for the sole purpose of giving direction to research on certain variables which appear to influence efficiency in thinking. The one essential assumption made was that for new relationships to be acquired the pertinent responses to stimuli must be contiguous. With this assumption, predictions concerning the influence of certain manipulable variables on thinking were made. Some admittedly important problems are not handled by the orientation as it now stands.

REFERENCES

1. Billings, M. L. Problem-solving in different fields of endeavor. *Amer. J. Psychol.,* 1934, 46, 259-292.
2. Burack, B. The nature and efficiency of methods of attack on reasoning problems. *Psychol. Monogr.,* 1950, 64, No. 7.
3. Buss, A. H. A study of concept formation as a function of reinforcement and stimulus generalization. *J. exp. Psychol.,* 1950, 40, 494-503.
4. Dollard, J., & Miller, N. E. *Personality and psychotherapy.* New York: McGraw-Hill, 1950.
5. Duncker, K. On problem-solving. *Psychol. Monogr.,* 1945, 58, No. 5.
6. Gagné, R. M. The effect of sequence of presentation of similar items on the learning of paired associates. *J. exp. Psychol.,* 1950, 40, 61-73.
7. Gibson, Eleanor J. A systematic application of the concepts of generalization and differentiation to verbal learning. *Psychol. Rev.,* 1940, 47, 196-229.
8. Guilford, J. P. Creativity. *Amer. Psychol.,* 1950, 5, 444-454.
9. Haagen, C. H. Synonymity, vividness, familiarity, and association-value ratings of 400 pairs of common adjectives. *J. Psychol.,* 1949, 27, 453-464.
10. Heidbreder, Edna. The attainment of concepts: II. The problem. *J. gen. Psychol.,* 1946, 35, 191-223.
11. Hull, C. L., et al. *Mathematico-deductive theory of rote learning.* New Haven: Yale University Press, 1940.
12. Lefford, A. The influence of emotional subject matter on logical reasoning. *J. gen. Psychol.,* 1946, 34, 127-151.
13. Luchins, A. S. Mechanization in problem solving. *Psychol. Monogr.,* 1942, 54, No. 6.
14. ———, & Luchins, Edith H. New experimental attempts at preventing mechanization in problem solving. *J. gen. Psychol.,* 1950, 42, 279-298.
15. Maier, N. R. F. An aspect of human reasoning. *Brit. J. Psychol.,* 1933, 24, 144-155.
16. ———. The behavior mechanisms concerned with problem solving. *Psychol. Rev.,* 1940, 47, 43-58.

17. ——. Reasoning in humans. III. The mechanisms of equivalent stimuli and of reasoning. *J. exp. Psychol.*, 1945, 35, 349-360.
18. Miller, N. E., & Dollard, J. *Social learning and imitation.* New Haven: Yale University Press, 1941.
19. Morgan, J. J. B. Effect of non-rational factors on inductive reasoning. *J. exp. Psychol.*, 1944, 34, 159-168.
20. Morton, J. T. The distortion of syllogistic reasoning produced by personal convictions. Unpublished Ph.D. dissertation, Northwestern Univ., 1942.
21. Oseas, L. An exploratory study of the effects of distribution of practice on the attainment of concepts. Unpublished Master's thesis, Northwestern Univ., 1951.
22. Reed, H. B. The learning and retention of concepts: IV. The influence of complexity of stimuli. *J. exp. Psychol.*, 1946, 36, 252-261.
23. Seashore, R. H. Experimental and theoretical analysis of fine motor skills. *Amer. J. Psychol.*, 1940, 53, 86-98.
24. Thistlethwaite, D. Attitude and structure as factors in the distortion of reasoning. *J. abnorm. soc. Psychol.*, 1950, 45, 442-458.
25. Thune, L. E., & Underwood, B. J. Retroactive inhibition as a function of degree of interpolated learning. *J. exp. Psychol.*, 1943, 32, 185-200.
26. Underwood, B. J. *Experimental psychology.* New York: Appleton-Century-Crofts, 1949.
27. Welch, L. A behavioristic explanation of concept formation. *J. genet. Psychol.*, 1947, 71, 201-222.
28. ——. The transition from simple to complex forms of learning. *J. genet. Psychol.*, 1947, 71, 223-252.
29. Wertheimer, M. *Productive thinking.* New York: Harper, 1945.
30. Woodworth, R. S., & Sells, S. B. An atmosphere effect in formal syllogistic reasoning. *J. exp. Psychol.*, 1935, 18, 451-460.

Effect of Distributed Practice on Paired-Associate Learning

This monograph is concerned with the effect of varying length of intertrial interval after each learning trial on the acquisition of paired-associate (PA) lists. If the interval is short (0–4 sec.) it is called massed practice (MP), if longer than 4 sec., distributed practice (DP). The basic purpose of the present report is to assess the empirical status of the effects of DP on PA learning. There are two means by which this will be accomplished. First, in summary form, the results of 25 previously unpublished experiments performed during the past 6 yr. in the Northwestern laboratories will be reported. Second, the procedures and results of a further major experiment will be described. This experiment manipulated several variables believed to interact with DP in PA learning. These two devices, along with the results of a few studies done in other laboratories, should make summary statements possible. It will be useful initially to provide some background to the problem.

In 1960 a theory of the mechanisms involved in facilitation by DP had been worked out, a theory which was published a year later (Underwood, 1961). It is not of moment to detail the theory other than to note that it held that DP will be most likely to facilitate the learning of verbal lists when certain highly specific conditions obtained. One of these conditions was that some minimum level of interference must be present in response-term integration. Thus, response terms of low meaningfulness or high intralist similarity, or both, would be most likely to provide a necessary condition for facilitation by DP. Since serial learning does not allow a clear separation of stimulus and response functions, the experimental work which followed the development of the theory made use almost exclusively of PA lists. Of the studies done during the past 6 yr., only one report has been published (Underwood, Ekstrand, & Keppel,

---

Benton J. Underwood and Bruce R. Ekstrand, "Effect of Distributed Practice on Paired-Associate Learning," *Journal of Experimental Psychology Monograph Supplement Number 1* 73 Part 2 of No. 4 (1967): 1–21. Reprinted with permission. Copyright 1967 by the American Psychological Association.

This work was done under Contract Nonr-1228 (15), Project 154–057, between Northwestern University and the Office of Naval Research. Reproduction in whole or in part is permitted for any purpose by the United States Government.

Miscellaneous 219

1964). This lack of publication was in part due to rather consistent negative findings of each experiment considered separately, and in part due to replication failures for a few positive findings, thus representing a failure to develop a situation in which DP had a predictable effect of such magnitude that the manipulation of other variables (to study interactions predicted by the theory) could be expected to achieve success. These statements will be subsequently documented. It may also be noted that insofar as the data have been able to test the theoretical notions outlined in 1961, it has not received much support. At the same time, however, the results may raise a question as to whether or not there is a phenomenon of sufficient reliability and magnitude to have a theory about.

SINGLE-LIST EXPERIMENTS[1]

In this section the results of 16 experiments in which S learned a single PA list within the experiment will be reported. The materials (lists) and essential conditions are shown for each experiment in Table 5.1. Only four different intertrial intervals were involved in these experiments, namely, 4, 15, 30, and 60 sec., and in most, only the 4-sec. and 30-sec. intervals were used (see Table 5.2). The MP interval was usually 4 sec. but sometimes 3 sec. or 3.5 sec. when rates of presentation deviated from that most commonly used (2:2 sec.). It will be noted that Exp. I–VI all used bigrams as response terms, Exp. VII–XIV, trigrams. The DP intervals were always filled with a cancellation task.

No purpose will be served by giving a rationale for each experiment. Some were dictated by theory; some were simply replication attempts; some were concerned with the effect of DP when different types of interfering associations obtained within the lists; some were tests of the use of naive Ss; all of them had been designed with the belief that some interference within the list would be a favorable condition for DP to influence learning. Many earlier studies (e.g, Underwood, 1961) indicated that words, in which response integration is minimal, cannot be expected to produce a task which will be facilitated by DP. Recent work from other laboratories (Baker & Noble, 1965) continue to support this conclusion. Thus, when words

---

[1]Most of the supervision of the data collection for the experiments summarized here, and for some of those summarized in the following section, was the responsibility of Geoffrey Keppel. Both G. Keppel and R. W. Schulz were also involved in the data analysis of some of these studies.

Table 5.1 Materials and Essential Conditions in 16 Experiments on the Effect of Massed and Distributed Practice in Paired-Associate Learning

Experiment	Materials and Conditions
I	List 1: JH, XV, EY, RZ, CF, MK, QW, DS; List 2: RQ, YF, OC, MX, AJ, PN, TK, HS; Stimuli, No. 2-9; Two rates, 2:1 sec., 2:2 sec.; 16 groups, 12 Ss; 15 trials.
II	List same as List 1, Exp. I; 4 groups, 30 Ss: 12 trials
III	List same as List 1, Exp. I; Two rates, 1.5:2 sec., 2:2 sec.; 4 groups, 20 Ss; 12 trials
IV	List: QX, MF, BW, GV, RZ, HK, DS; Stimuli, names of colors; Anticipation and study-recall method each used with MP and DP; 4 groups, 11 Ss, 12 trials
V	List same as List 1, Exp. I; Instructions to minimize or maximize overt errors each used with MP and DP; 4 groups, 20 Ss; 15 trials
VI	List 1: KB, RD, JH, ZG, FX, LV, MU; List 2: WB, ND, QH, SG, CX, PV, AU; List 3: BK, DR, HJ, GZ, XF, VL, UM; List 4: BW, DN, HQ, GS, XC, VP; UA; Color names stimuli for Lists 1 and 3, animal names for Lists 2 and 4; 8 groups, 12 Ss; 10 trials
VII	List 1: OCZ, AJU, YFV, HSW, TKD, RQL, PNB, MXG; List 2: HDU, BPC, XEW, IJF, RNL, TVZ, MGK, YSA; Stimuli, No. 2-9; 8 groups, 33 Ss; 25 trials
VIII	List: XKV, VFK, FVK, KXF; Stimuli, names of colors; 4 groups, 20 Ss; 20 trials
IX	List: DSU, RZL, CFY, XBN, IGW, TPM, OVJ, KHQ; Stimuli, adjectives; 2 groups, 18 Ss; 20 trials
X	List same as the Exp. IX; 2 groups, 18 Ss; 20 trials
XI	List: HFG, BVA, XPL, IWD, RZQ, TJU, MKC, YSN; Stimuli, No. 2-9; Two rates, 2:1 sec., and 2:2 sec.; 4 groups, 12 Ss, 20 trials
XII	List: IRB, IZR, FZI, FBZ, RIF, LFI, BFL, ZIR; Stimuli, two-syllable words; 2 groups, 20 Ss; 20 trials
XIII	List same as Exp. IX; 2 groups, 20 Ss; 20 trials
XIV	Stimuli: VHX, XKH, HVK, KHQ, XQV, VKQ. Responses, No. 2-7; 2 groups, 22 Ss; 20 trials
XV	List 1: Oak-Bob, Oak-Cow, Oak-Waltz, Oak-Ant, Dog-Elm, Dog-Bill, Dog-Bean, Dog-Head, Joe-Cat, Joe-Fir, Joe-Trout, Joe-Iron; List 2: double-word response units of List 1 reversed, e.g., Oak-Bob became Bob-Oak; Stimuli, names of dwellings; 4 groups, 24 Ss; 15 trials
XVI	8 pairs as follows: COF-JUL, DAP-BEV, HEB-JUL, GOS-VOR, KAL-BER, CAS-JUL, PID-BEV, LIB-VOR, VIK-JUL; 2 groups, 20 Ss; 15 trials.

Note.—Materials refer to response terms unless noted otherwise; intertrial intervals used appear in Table 5.2.

were used in lists they were arranged in such a way as to produce interference to hinder integration among words (Exp. XV).

The results for each condition of each experiment, given as the mean total correct responses produced over all trials, are shown in Table 5.2. When evaluated separately, only 2 of the 16 experiments (I and IX) showed a statistically significant effect in favor of DP. In addition, in 2 other experiments (III and VII), DP would be said to have facilitated if scores on the last trial only were used. However, considering the 16 experiments as a whole, there are 43 possible comparisons between MP and DP; that is, 43 comparisons may be made in which the only difference in conditions was length of intertrial interval. Of the 43, 37 numerically favor DP, 6 favor MP. If, when there is more than one DP condition for a list, an average of them is obtained, 27 comparisons may be made between MP and DP. Of these, 23 numerically favor DP, 4 favor MP. By a sign test on these values it must be concluded that DP has a facilitating effect on learning PA lists. However, apparently the true magnitude of the effect is so small that within any given experiment the likelihood of obtaining a statistically significant effect is low.

In all instances in which MP was numerically superior to DP, the response units were bigrams. For the first 6 experiments there are 25 possible comparisons between MP and DP for the bigram lists. Of these, 19 numerically favor DP, 6 favor MP. According to a sign test (Siegel, 1956), this split is significant at the .014 level. However, if multiple DP conditions within an experiment are averaged and compared with the MP condition, 15 comparisons remain and these are split 11 for DP, 4 for MP, which is not significant statistically (.118). Thus, for the bigram lists of Exp. I–VI, DP may be expected to have little, if any, facilitating effect.

In Exp. VII–XIII there are seven instances in which a list with trigrams as response terms may be compared on MP and DP (30 sec.). If these seven instances are summed, the total number of Ss is 176 each for MP and DP. The mean total correct responses are 64.44 for MP, 72.12 for DP. The evidence indicates that DP will facilitate the learning of lists in which trigrams are response terms but the amount of facilitation is, in an absolute sense, quite small. Taken separately by experiment, for these trigram lists the effect has been statistically significant for only 1 (Exp. IX).

Two experiences of failure to replicate statistically significant effects of DP will be mentioned as further evidence for the evanescence of the phenomenon under question. The theory mentioned earlier made critical use of the results of an experiment in which

Table 5.2 Mean Total Correct Responses as a Function of Intertrial Interval for Experiments Outlined in Table 5.1

	Intertrial Interval (sec.)			
Experiment	4	15	30	60
I				
List 1				
2:1	38.17	51.58	41.92	54.17
2:2	60.92	63.17	50.33	70.50
List 2				
2:1	46.50	51.58	54.58	63.67
2:2	63.17	78.50	70.83	81.42
II	41.37	39.27	43.60	37.67
III				
1.5:2	33.65		40.70	
2:2	43.35		49.40	
IV				
Anticipation	48.91		55.72	
Study-Recall	49.64		55.72	
V				
Minimum Errors	59.45		52.60	
Maximum Errors	52.30		55.50	
VI				
List 1	43.92		44.08	
List 2	47.50		40.42	
List 3	46.58		46.08	
List 4	43.75		47.67	
VII				
List 1	93.21	98.55	95.36	105.33
List 2	98.15	111.52	111.55	115.73
VIII	20.75	26.95	24.35	29.65
IX	37.28		68.72	
X	57.00		60.06	
XI	52.92		53.00	
XII	35.30		41.25	
XIII	72.95		73.95	
XIV	54.59		57.27	
XV				
List 1	92.20		93.95	
List 2	88.90		94.05	
XVI	78.85		81.45	

bigrams were response terms (Underwood & Schulz, 1961b). This report included a replication which produced almost exactly the same as those found initially. In both instances a 30-sec. DP interval was shown to facilitate learning and the effect was statistically significant. The list in question is List 1, Exp. I, as shown in Table 5.1. It will be noted in Table 5.2 that in a further experiment (Exp. I) MP was actually superior to DP (30 sec.) for this list presented at the 2:2 sec. rate, the rate used in the earlier studies. A further attempt to reproduce the original findings (Exp. II) also failed. Jung (1966) was also unable to find a significant DP effect for this list.

One of the earlier experiments completed was Exp. IX, in which trigrams were response terms. The difference between MP and DP was in an absolute sense large, and, statistically, highly significant. Experiments X and XII were essentially replications, and while DP is superior in both, it is a very small effect.

There was, of course, every reason to believe initially that such failures to replicate could be traced to specific variables. The attempts in this direction have been unsuccessful. At the present time it appears that the most appropriate conclusion for the results of the experiments as shown in Table 5.2 is that DP does have a small positive effect and that the data for the 16 experiments represent deviations above and below the true means for the DP and MP conditions.

MULTIPLE-LIST EFFECTS

In this section the results of nine experiments will be summarized; all nine show that DP inhibits learning. In each experiment S learned four successive lists. The first three lists were learned by MP, with half of the Ss given the fourth list by MP and the other half by DP. These procedures were primarily designed to study the influence of DP in reducing proactive inhibition in the recall of the fourth list (e.g., Underwood, Keppel, & Schulz, 1962) and it may be noted parenthetically that in eight of the nine possible comparisons, forgetting of the fourth list was slower following DP than following MP. Because these experiments were directed primarily toward the study of forgetting of the fourth list due to proactive interference, a number of different paradigms were used, paradigms reflecting, presumably, varying degrees of interlist interference. These paradigms will now be noted.

Experiment I. The lists consisted of eight paired two-syllable adjectives and across the four lists conformed to an A-B, C-D paradigm. This is to say, there were no repeated units.

Experiment II. The materials were the same as for Exp. I, but the four lists conformed to an A-B, C-B paradigm. That is, the response terms in the four lists were identical, the stimuli differed from list to list.

Experiment III. Three-letter words were used as both stimuli and responses, and the lists fit the A-B, A-C paradigm; the stimuli were the same across the four lists, the response terms differed.

Experiment IV. The paradigm of interest held only *within* the response terms of the four lists, and may be identified as A-B, C-B. Each response consisted of a compound of two three-letter words. Across the four lists, the first element differed, the second was identical. The stimulus terms for each list represented different classes of materials. Four pairs may be given as illustration:

YELLOW-gas box   OF-sky box
B-hen box   3-arm box

The S always responded with the two words when the appropriate stimulus was presented.

Experiment V. As in Exp. IV, two three-letter words were used as response terms. The paradigm was A-B, A-C, i.e., across the four lists the first word in each response compound was identical, the second varied.

Experiments VI and VII. The materials were exactly the same as Exp. IV and V.

Experiments VIII and IX. The response terms were the same as in Exp. IV and V. However, all four lists had the same stimulus terms (single-digit numbers).

There were nine pairs in all lists in Exp. III–IX. The intertrial interval defining DP was 60 sec. in all experiments except IV and V, where it was 30 sec. Massed practice always involved a 4-sec. intertrial interval and the rate was always 2:2 sec. Seven anticipated trials were given on the fourth list in Exp. I and II, eight in Exp. III, and 10 in the remaining ones. For the nine experiments in order, the number of Ss assigned to each group was: 30, 30, 36, 24, 24, 36, 36, 33, 33.

The mean total correct responses given on the fourth list under MP and DP conditions are shown in Table 5.3. Without exception, numerically poorer performance occurred under DP than under MP. As was true with the experiments reported in Table 5.2, the differ-

Table 5.3 Mean Total Correct Responses on the Fourth List as a Function of Massed Practice and Distributed Practice for Nine Experiments[a]

Experiment	Massing	Distribution
I	44.20	37.93
II	46.37	45.23
III	54.58	53.86
IV	47.00	38.96
V	49.33	47.17
VI	48.11	45.67
VII	51.50	49.75
VIII	65.70	58.24
IX	59.94	51.61

[a]Described in text.

ence between MP and DP when considered separately for each experiment was sometimes statistically significant, sometimes not. Considering all experiments together there is no doubt that DP has a small but consistent inhibiting effect. Across the nine experiments, MP has a mean total of 52.22 correct, DP, 48.09. It is known from other work (Keppel, 1964; Underwood et al., 1962) that increasing the length of the DP interval beyond the longest (60 sec.) used here will result in a still greater inhibitory effect, at least early in the learning.

The data of Table 5.3 suggest that when S learns a number of lists, at some point in the sequence of lists DP will inhibit acquisition, or at least performance. Here again, however, in spite of the unanimity of the data in Table 5.3, there are published instances in which DP performance was quite superior to MP performance on a fourth-learned PA list (Underwood & Schulz, 1961a). There are, furthermore, cases where it appeared that DP produced better performance than MP with nonnaive Ss (those who had served in other verbal-learning experiments), but not with naive Ss (e.g., Underwood et al., 1964). Therefore, it does not seem possible to arrive at a consistent generalization relating previous experiences of S and the role DP will play in acquisition. The evidence suggests again the brittleness of the phenomenon involved. Nevertheless, it appeared necessary to make at least one more effort to see if a critical condition or a cluster of critical conditions which result in a positive effect of DP could be identified experimentally. The immediate background of this effort may now be given.

BACKGROUND OF THE PRESENT EXPERIMENT

The first decision made in planning the present experiment was that only naive Ss would be used. As noted above, while the data are not clear or consistent concerning the role of experienced Ss in producing a positive DP effect, the use of naive Ss at least allows the conclusions reached to be tied unequivocally to the conditions of the experiment and removes any ambiguity which may be occasioned by an interaction between the conditions and previous experimental experience of Ss.

In a previous experiment (Underwood et al., 1964) it was shown that if Ss were given free-learning (FL) trials on trigrams of low similarity before these trigams became response terms in PA lists, DP facilitated the learning of the PA lists. The FL trials must almost inevitably result in an increase in the level of integration of each trigram. In a manner of speaking, varying the number of FL trials varies the meaningfulness of the trigrams. Of course, FL trials may have other consequences which may be responsible for the DP effect in PA learning; for example, insofar as learning-to-learn transfers from FL to PA learning, following FL S is no longer a naive S. In any event, included in the present experiment are conditions in which the amount of FL is varied prior to learning a PA list in which DP is introduced.

Without detailing the evidence, it can be said that most of the previous work indicates that in some manner the level of formal similarity is tied to a DP effect. In planning the present experiment, therefore, three different levels of formal similarity were included in the design. However, it was necessary to confound similarity with length of list. It was known (e.g., Exp. VIII, Tables 5.1 and 5.2) that when high formal similarity obtains among the response terms of a PA list it presents a learning task of formidable difficulty. With only four pairs, learning proceeds at a very slow pace. If, on the other hand, the formal similarity is zero (no repeated letters among the trigrams), four pairs become a relatively simple task for S. All considerations recommended that the number of pairs be confounded with similarity. It will not be possible, therefore, to make direct comparisons of the results for the different levels of similarity so each will be analyzed and reported separately.

Most of the experiments summarized in Table 5.1 were concerned with characteristics of the response terms; the stimulus terms were normally neutral in the thinking which preceded the experiments. However, Marshall and Runquist (1962) have presented evidence indicating that formal similarity among stimulus terms interacts with MP-DP. A subsequent experiment (Exp. XIV in Tables 5.1 and 5.2), using a list with high formal stimulus similarity, failed to produce a DP effect of appreciable magnitude. Nevertheless, it seemed clear that the role of the variables manipulated must be evaluated when these roles may be attributed to stimulus properties and functions as well as to response properties and functions. Therefore, each experiment is symmetrical; all variables are manipulated among stimulus terms and also among response terms.

Finally, the choice of intertrial intervals depended upon a number of considerations. In most previous studies, the MP interval has been 4 sec. To maximize the potential for obtaining a difference, a zero intertrial interval should be used. In the present study, therefore, the MP condition is essentially a form of continuous learning.

Two DP intervals were employed, 15 sec. and 45 sec. It can be argued on the basis of the data in Table 5.2 that a positive effect of DP is most likely to emerge with relatively long DP intervals. If the results of the experiments where several intervals were used are combined, the 60-sec. interval is numerically superior to the shorter intervals. Perhaps a 2- or 3-min. interval would enhance the effect. Other considerations, however, essentially denied the use of such intervals unless a radical change in procedure was instituted. With lists of trigrams of high formal similarity, learning proceeds very slowly so that many trials are required. If long DP intervals were employed (e.g., 3 min.) so few trials could be given within a single session that little, if any, learning would occur. A radical change would be to have S appear on successive days in learning a single list under DP. This procedure, however, introduces complications because of the known differences in retention which occur over long intervals between MP and DP. The two DP intervals chosen eliminated the scheduling and fatigue problems which occur when S must serve continuously for more than 1 hr. on a given day and yet they are representative of the intervals used in many of the previous experiments.

METHOD

Design.—Each of the three experiments investigated the effect of DP on PA learning (word-trigram or trigram-word pairs) following various amounts of FL of the trigrams. The three experiments represent the manipulation of three levels of formal similarity among the trigrams. In Exp. I, representing low formal similarity, lists of six pairs were employed; in Exp. II (medium similarity), there were five pairs in a list; and, in Exp. III (high similarity), four pairs were learned. The three experiments were run concurrently.

The design of each experiment was the same, although the use of different numbers of items for the different levels of similarity necessitated giving different numbers of trials (both in FL and PA learning) in the three experiments. Each design was a 3 × 3 × 2 × 2 factorial. There were three levels or degrees of FL (none, medium, or high degree), and there were two sets of trigrams (Set I and Set II). Following the prescribed amount of FL of the trigrams, Ss learned a PA list of either trigram-word (T-W) pairs or word-trigram (W-T) pairs. The fourth variable in each experiment was intertrial interval, the three levels being 0 sec. (MP) and two DP levels, 15 and 45 sec.

Pilot work determined the number of trials to be given on FL and PA learning. The values were chosen such that rough equality in terms of percentage correct would be obtained across the three experiments. The numbers of trials given on FL in the three experiments to attain a moderate or a high degree of FL are shown in the left portion of Table 5.4. There was, of course, another set of groups that received no FL training. For PA learning, it was determined that 15 trials would be given in all three experiments to those Ss learning T-W lists. In W-T conditions, different numbers of PA trials were given to the various groups, the exact number depending upon the degree of prior FL training and the level of similarity. These values are shown in the right portion of Table 5.4.

Lists.—The two sets of lists used in each experiment are presented in Table 5.5. The three experiments represent different levels of formal similarity among the trigrams in a list. The alternate

Table 5.4 Numbers of Trials Given During FL and PA Learning for the Three Experiments

Experiment	Number FL Trials		PA Trials on W-T Conditions[a] Degree of FL		
	Medium	High	None	Medium	High
I	10	30	30	30	20
II	20	40	30	30	20
III	20	40	40	30	20

[a]T-W conditions in all three experiments involved 15 PA trials.

Table 5.5 Lists

Experiment	Set I	Set II
Exp. I		
	BQL-arm	CNG-arm
	RDP-end	MSX-end
	HSX-sea	PFB-sea
	MKC-lip	JZH-lip
	JNW-box	LQK-box
	FZV-car	TDV-car
Mean GMV	1.50	1.58
Exp. II		
	ZGV-box	ZMJ-box
	FVK-car	SBM-car
	GQZ-sea	DKB-sea
	CFQ-arm	HSK-arm
	MKC-lip	JZH-lip
Mean GMV	1.80	1.30
Exp. III		
	KXF-sea	HQJ-sea
	XKV-lip	JZH-lip
	FVK-car	ZJQ-car
	VFX-arm	QHZ-arm
Mean GMV	1.87	1.75

Note.—The lists are presented in the T-W form. For W-T conditions the pairs were reversed, with the words as stimuli and trigrams as responses.

member of each pair was a high-frequency three-letter word. The six trigrams used in each list of Exp. I had low intralist formal similarity. Each list was made up from a set of 18 different letters so that no letter was repeated. The mean generated meaningfulness value (GMV) was determined for each list according to the Underwood and Schulz (1960) tables. The GMV for a trigram is determined by adding together the response frequency of the second letter given the first letter as a stimulus (e.g., how many Ss responded with Q to the stimulus B) and the response frequency of the last letter given the first two letters as a stimulus (e.g., the frequency of the response L given the stimulus BQ). The mean GMV for each of the lists is also presented in Table 5.5. It will be noted that the meaningfulness of all trigrams was quite low.

The five trigrams used in each list of Exp. II had medium formal intralist similarity. Eight different letters were used to make each list, seven of the letters occurring in two different trigrams. The four trigrams used in each list of Exp. III had a high formal intralist similarity. Only four different letters were used to make each list, each letter occurring in three of the four trigrams.

Procedure: Free learning.—Free learning of the trigrams was given by a paced procedure (Ekstrand & Underwood, 1963) for the specified number of trials. Alternate study and test trials were employed. On study trials, each trigram was presented along with a set of three asterisks while on test trials only the sets of asterisks were presented, one set for each trigram in the list. As each set of asterisks appeared on the memory drum, *S* was to try to spell one of the trigrams he had seen on the study trial. The *S*s were fully instructed that the trigrams had to be spelled correctly, but that the order in which the trigrams were emitted was not important.

There were four different random study orders of the six trigrams in Exp. I, five different random study orders of the five trigrams in Exp. II, and six different random study orders of the four trigrams in Exp. III. All trigrams were typed in capital letters on the memory-drum tape. The lists were presented on a Stowe memory drum at a 2-sec. rate during study and test trials, with a 2-sec. intertrial interval between every trial.

Procedure: PA learning.—Following the prescribed FL, *S*s learned a PA list consisting of the trigrams paired with the three-letter words. If *S* was in a condition calling for no FL the PA list was his first learning task. Half the *S*s learned lists with the trigrams as stimuli and words as responses (T-W) and half learned word-trigram pairs (W-T). The units in the stimulus position were typed in lower case letters, those serving as responses in capitals. All responses were spelled, including the words.

The PA learning was by the anticipation method at a 2:2-sec. rate on a Stowe memory drum. Again, there were four random orders of the six pairs in the low similarity experiment, five orders of the five pairs in the medium similarity experiment, and six orders of the four pairs in the high similarity experiment. These random orders were different from those employed during FL. The intertrial interval was either 0, 15, or 45 sec. The *S*s in the 15-sec. and 45-sec. conditions performed a symbol cancellation task during the intertrial interval.

In order to have a 0-sec. intertrial interval, it was necessary to prepare different memory-drum tapes for the MP and DP groups. The DP tapes (used for the 15- and 45-sec. conditions) had a strip of masking tape separating each random order of the list. While these *S*s were cancelling symbols the tape was in the window. The

0-sec. or MP tapes, however, did not have a strip of tape separating each order of the list. The last item from one order was followed immediately by the first item of the next order. There was, however, one strip of tape separating the last random order and the first random order. This tape was in the window of the memory drum while E read S the instructions for the 0-sec. condition. Once the drum was started there was no intertrial interval until a complete cycle of the list had been presented at which time the tape would reappear. Thus, the 0-sec. conditions actually involved a 4-sec. intertrial interval after every four, five, or six trials in Exp. I, II, and III, respectively.

With no tape to signal Ss in the 0-sec. conditions that a trial had been completed, one might expect these Ss to be at some disadvantage as compared to Ss in the 15- and 45-sec. conditions. To provide Ss in the 0-sec. conditions with this information, an asterisk was printed after the response term of the last pair in each random order and he was informed of its meaning. This asterisk was also printed on the tapes used in the DP conditions.

Following the prescribed number of PA learning trials, certain retention conditions were introduced. Since the results of these retention comparisons will not be presented, the procedures for them will not be detailed.

Subjects.—In each experiment there were 36 conditions: 2(W-T or T-W) × 2(Set I or II) × 3(level of FL) × 3(intertrial interval). Each condition was represented by a group of 18 Ss, undergraduate students at Northwestern University. Each experiment thus required 648 Ss. All Ss were naive to verbal-learning experiments and served in the experiment to fulfill a course requirement.

All three experiments were run concurrently over a period of 2 yr. In order to facilitate the running of Ss, blocks of 12 conditions were made up. All 12 conditions in a given block represented the same level of similarity and the same degree of FL. The 12 conditions in each block represented the factorial combination of list set (I or II), trigram position (T-W or W-T), and intertrial interval during PA learning (0, 15, or 45 sec.). The order of the 12 conditions in a block was random. With a total of 1,944 Ss, 162 blocks were required. The 162 blocks were printed, each on a separate page, and then the 162 pages were randomized. The blocks were then assigned to Es according to this randomization. The Ss were assigned to a particular condition in a block according to their order of appearance at the laboratory.

RESULTS

Experiment I

Free Learning

There were 432 Ss who had a minimum of 10 trials of FL, 216 on each list. An analysis of variance showed that the performance of these 24 groups did not differ ($F < 1$). This means that the two lists did not differ in difficulty and that the differences in the performance levels of the groups were well within the range expected by sampling variation.

There were 108 Ss who were given 30 trials on each list of the six low-similarity trigrams. The performance on selected trials is shown in Fig. 5.1. It can be seen that groups given 10 FL trials will have achieved, on the average, slightly less than four correct re-

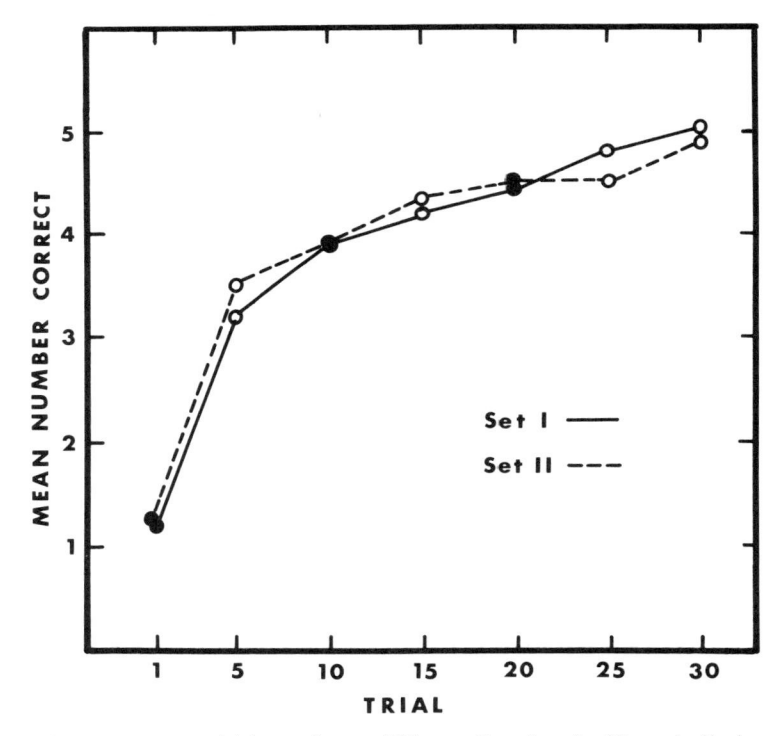

Figure 5.1 Acquisition of two different lists (sets) of low-similarity trigrams by free-learning procedure.

sponses on the tenth trial, those given 30 trials, five correct responses on the thirtieth. The essential equality in the difficulty of the two lists is apparent in Fig. 5.1.

Paired-Associate Learning

The nature of the analyses of PA learning to be used for all experiments will be described. The basic statistical tests will involve three variables, namely, level of FL, intertrial interval, and trigram sets. Certain considerations recommended against including the trigram-position variable (T-W vs. W-T) as a fourth variable in these analyses. In all experiments the learning of the T-W lists proceeded at a far more rapid rate than it did for the W-T lists. As will be seen, certain differences in the learning of the W-T lists emerge beyond 15 trials. This is to say that including T-W and W-T as a variable in the analyses means that comparisons between them would be made at quite different levels of learning and this did not seem appropriate. Furthermore, the variances associated with the W-T scores were much greater than those associated with the T-W scores. Finally, it appeared that any sizeable differences in the effects of the variables on W-T and T-W would be apparent without the need for statistical support.

As noted above, the effects of a variable need not necessarily be manifest on the initial trials of a task. It is possible that an interaction may occur between trials and a given variable. Using blocks of five trials as the unit, all acquisition curves have been plotted and when these plots suggest an interaction between a variable and trials, it will be discussed at the appropriate point in the exposition.

It will be remembered that for the W-T lists the groups differing on amount of FL were not all given the same number of PA trials. The number actually given was determined by data from pilot Ss, the intent being to achieve a final level of learning that was roughly equivalent for all groups. It is possible, therefore, to ask about the effect of intertrial interval on the final stage of PA learning when performance level is much the same for all groups despite differences in the number of PA trials required to reach that level. For such analyses, performance on the last five trials will be used.

Finally, it should be said that some conservatism seems warranted in reaching conclusions about the effect of the intertrial-interval variable; it seems warranted because of the data presented earlier which seemed to demonstrate the brittle nature of the DP effect. Generally speaking, unless a given finding occurs for both lists, it will not be given much weight.

Trigrams words.—The mean total correct over 15 trials on the low-similarity lists for both sets combined is shown in the upper panel of Fig. 5.2. It would appear that only level of FL has influenced performance. This is confirmed by the statistical analysis presented in Table 5.6. This table represents the basic form of the statistical tests made for all experiments; by presenting this table the degrees of freedom to be used in all subsequent tests will be available so that further tables will be unnecessary. The conclusion from Fig. 5.2 and Table 5.6 is clear; intertrial interval does not influence the learning of these lists.

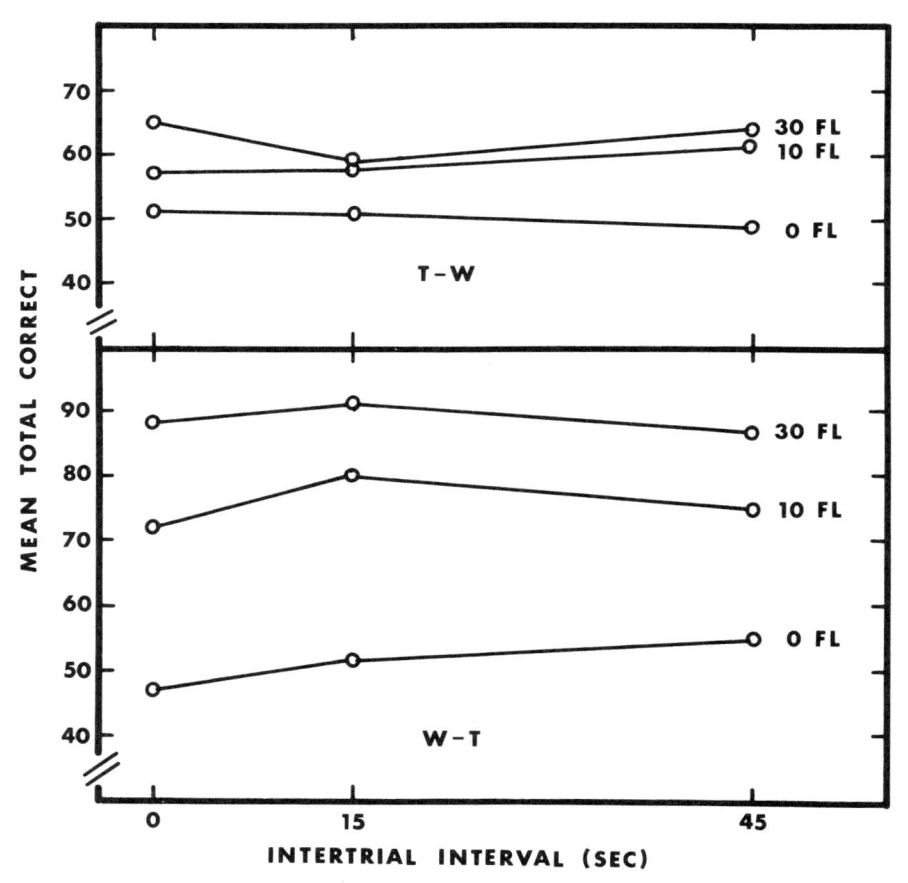

Figure 5.2 Paired-associate learning of trigram-word (T-W) and word-trigram (W-T) lists of low similarity as a function of intertrial interval and degree of prior free learning (FL).

Table 5.6 Analysis of Variance for the T-W Lists of Exp. I

Source	df	MS	F
Intertrial Interval (II)	2	202.43	—
Free Learning (FL)	2	4369.56	13.45
Set (S)	1	420.25	1.29
II × FL	4	189.62	—
II × S	2	43.46	—
FL × S	2	247.96	—
II × FL × S	4	296.52	—
Within	306	324.83	

Words trigrams.—The mean total correct responses produced in 20 anticipation trials are shown in the lower panel of Fig. 5.2 for the W-T lists. As with the T-W lists, degree of free learning is a highly significant variable ($F = 66.46$), but no other source of variance approaches statistical significance. However, it may be noted that there are six different comparisons which may be made between MP and DP, and five of these numerically favor DP. The groups having 0 and 10 FL trials were given 30 PA trials; the values in Fig. 5.2 are based only on the first 20 PA trials since this was the total given the group having 30 FL trials. Following 0 FL, the acquisition curves for Set II were essentially indistinguishable for the three different intertrial intervals. For Set I, on the other hand, the curves were separated and ordered 0, 15, and 45 sec. However, statistically the differences were far from significant. The learning of neither set, therefore, can be said to have been influenced appreciably by differences in length of intertrial interval.

With 10 FL trials, the 0- and 15-sec. conditions are essentially equivalent across all learning trials for Set I, but the 45-sec. condition is distinctly superior to both. For Set II, the positions of the 15- and 45-sec. conditions are exactly reversed from those shown for Set I. Yet, in neither case can statistical support be found for the effect of intertrial interval. Set I was used in a previous experiment (Underwood et al., 1964) and there was a significant DP effect following 15 FL trials. In the present case the relationships for 0, 15, and 45 sec. are almost identical to those found in the previous experiment; the difference is that there is a lack of statistical significance in the present case. In addition, Set II does not replicate the results found for Set I. An analysis of the scores for the last five acquisition trials (disregarding number of trials given) shows that FL is not a significant source of variance ($F = 2.28$) and the $F < 1$ for intertrial interval. It is concluded that PA learning of the W-T lists in the present study is not influenced to a statistically significant level whether preceded by FL of the trigrams or not.

Overt errors.—The frequency of overt errors made in the T-W conditions in all experiments was essentially inversely correlated with the number of correct responses and thus adds no new information of relevance. For the W-T lists, however, it was possible to ask about the effect of the variables on integrative errors when such errors are expressed as a proportion of total errors made. An integrative error was defined as the giving of a single-letter response if no trigram had that letter in the initial position, or any two- or three-letter sequence which did not occur in that order in any trigram in the list. The means for the 20 PA trials are plotted in Fig. 5.3. The proportion of integrative errors clearly decreases as the number of FL trials increases. Since the variances of the distributions were not significantly heterogeneous, no transformation was made prior to the statistical analysis (of the same type as shown in Table 5.6).

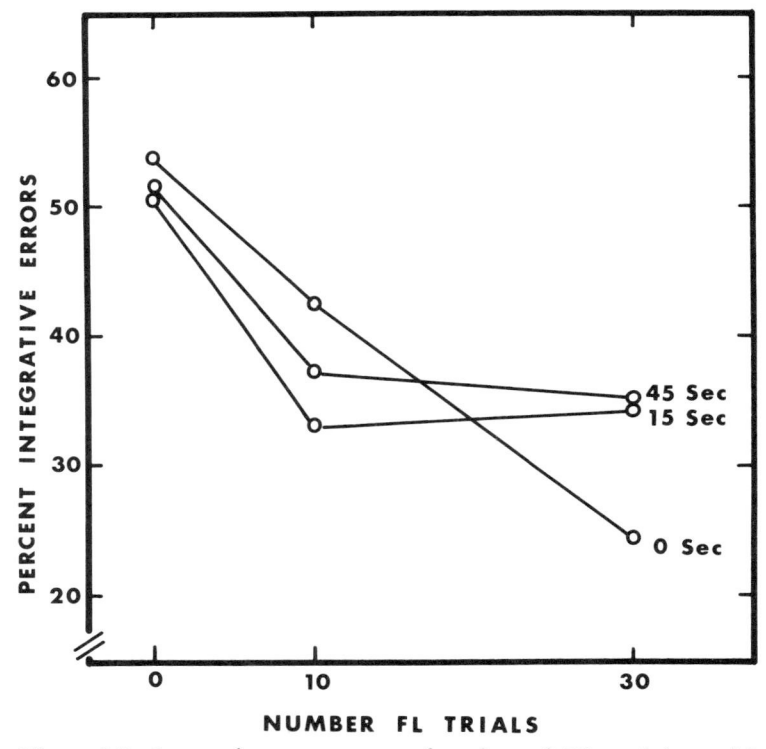

Figure 5.3 Integrative errors as a function of FL and intertrial interval in learning paired-associate lists of low similarity.

Miscellaneous 237

The only significant source of variance was FL ($F = 16.22$). It is quite reasonable to expect integrative errors to decrease as FL increases; FL should take S through a portion of the response learning which must occur in PA learning when PA learning is not preceded by FL.

Experiment II

Free Learning

This experiment dealt with the five-item lists representing medium similarity. There were 108 Ss given 40 FL trials on each set and the scores from selected trials are plotted in Fig. 5.4. Differences in the difficulty of the two sets of five items are obvious. Groups within each set, however, did not differ on performance.

Paired-Associate Learning

Trigrams words.—The mean total correct responses across 15 PA trials for the combined T-W lists are shown in the upper panel of

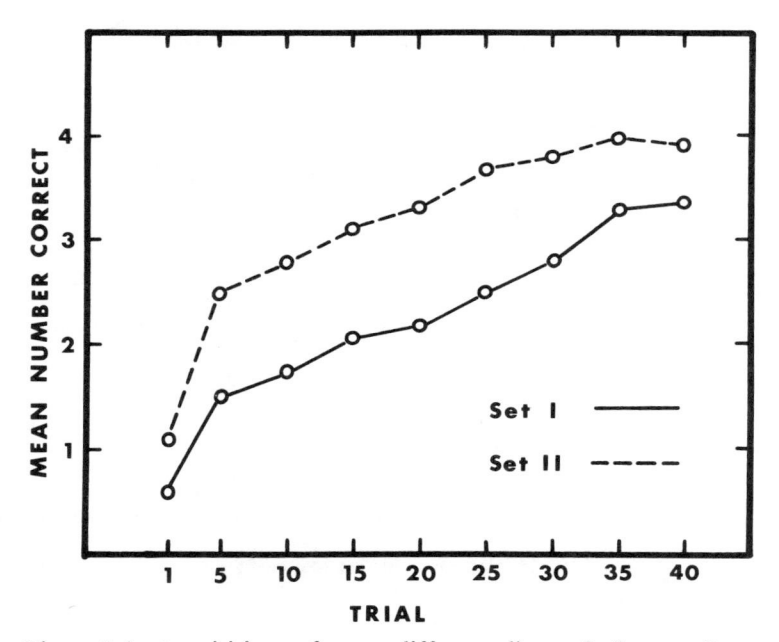

Figure 5.4 Acquisition of two different lists of five medium-similarity trigrams by free-learning procedure.

Fig. 5.5. As in Exp. I, the only obvious differences in performance are related to differences in number of FL trials. An analysis shows that the effect of FL is significant ($F = 19.95$) but that no other term attains the 5% significance level. It will be remembered from Fig. 5.4 that the two sets of trigrams differed widely in difficulty in FL. In the T-W situation the means for the two lists across all conditions were almost identical, and this was also true when no FL was involved. This indicates that whatever it is that makes the two sets different in difficulty for FL is not a relevant factor when the trigrams become stimulus terms. If FL integrates trigrams, it must follow that the integration of these trigrams is not necessarily responsible for the FL effect in the T-W lists; otherwise, it would appear that a difference in the sets should have been observed in PA learning. However this may be, the conclusion concerning the

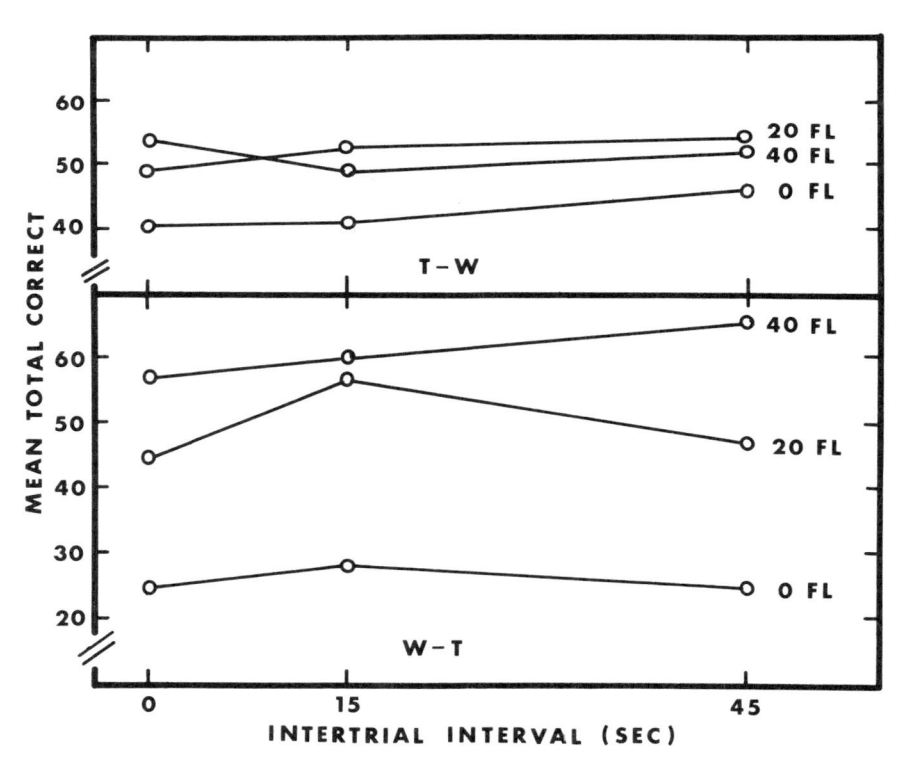

Figure 5.5 Paired-associate learning of T-W and W-T lists of medium similarity as a function of intertrial interval and degree of prior FL.

effect of intertrial interval is clear; there is no effect in learning these medium-similarity lists.

Words trigrams.—The lower panel of Fig. 5.5 displays the results for the combined W-T lists. The values are the mean total correct over 20 trials. The statistical analysis shows that Set ($F = 26.67$) and FL ($F = 117.47$) are both significant beyond the 1% level, and that intertrial interval ($F = 3.45$) achieves the 5% level of significance. For every level of FL, the two DP conditions exceed the MP condition. Because the optimal interval appears to differ as a function of degree of FL, it might be expected that the interaction between FL and interval would be significant. Its value ($F = 2.16$), however, does not meet the 5% significance level. None of the other interactions approaches significance.

An examination of the acquisition curves for the 0 FL and 20 FL groups over 30 trials provides no additional information. The plots do indicate that the DP effect is greater in Set I than in Set II. If only these two levels of FL are entered into an analysis of variance, however, none of the interactions is significant and the effect of intertrial interval achieves the 1% level of significance. An analysis of the performance on the last five trials for all conditions showed that intertrial interval was significant ($F = 6.16$), but none of the interaction terms approached significance. It must be concluded that for these lists DP has a small positive effect that is independent of the degree of FL and of the sets.

Overt errors.—A plot of the integrative errors presents a picture very similar to that shown in Fig. 5.3 for Exp. I. The statistical analysis shows FL ($F = 11.54$) and Set ($F = 14.06$) both to be significant. With regard to the differences in sets, the greater number of integrative errors was made on Set I which, it will be seen in Fig. 5.4, was the more difficult set in FL.

Experiment III

Free Learning

The maximum level of FL given was 40 trials, and this amount was given to 108 Ss assigned to each set. The acquisition curves are shown in Fig. 5.6. The extreme difficulty of these high-similarity lists of only four trigrams each becomes apparent upon inspection of Fig. 5.6. After 40 trials the mean number correct was approximately 2.2 for each list. The two sets differed in difficulty ($F = 29.38$) but there was no other source of variance which was significant.

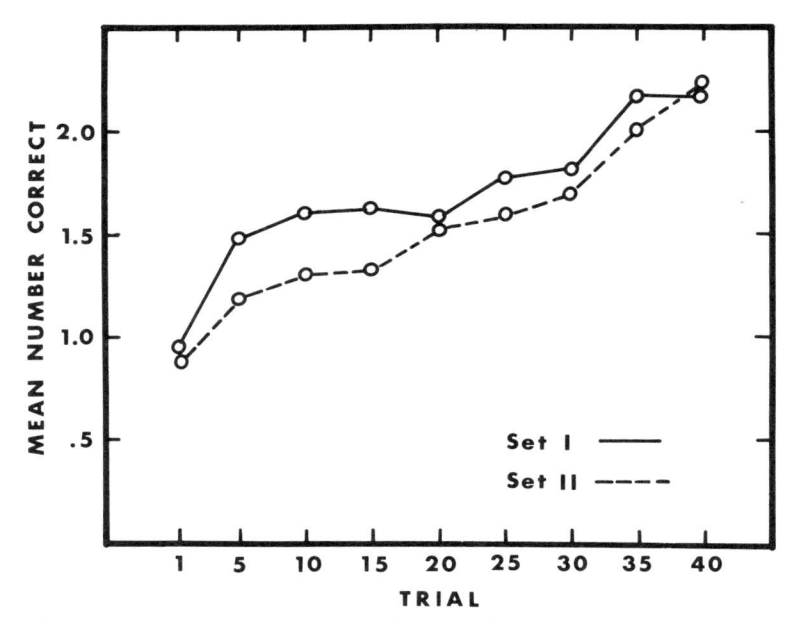

Figure 5.6 Acquisition of two different lists of four high-similarity trigrams by free-learning procedure.

Paired-Associate Learning

Trigram words.—The mean numbers of correct anticipations produced over 15 trials of PA learning for the T-W lists are shown in the upper section of Fig. 5.7. As intertrial interval increases, performance increases, this being most apparent after 40 FL and 20 FL trials. The F for intertrial interval (4.47) is significant beyond the 5% level, with the effect of FL significant beyond the 1% level ($F = 10.60$). Although it appears that there is an interaction between FL and intertrial interval the $F < 1$ for this term. Thus, the data indicate that DP facilitates acquisition of these lists having high-similarity stimuli and whether or not FL was given on the trigrams is irrelevant for this facilitation.

The response terms in these four-pair lists were common three-letter words. Undoubtedly S knew these words after a trial or two, i.e., response availability must have been high. Given this situation, it seems apparent that S might develop a guessing strategy on each trial, and such a strategy might increase performance, at least on the initial trials. Assuming that S knows the four response terms and that on a given trial he remembers the ones that have been shown him, guessing would give him probabilities of being correct

Miscellaneous

of .25, .33, .50, and 1.00 for the four positions in order. Two questions have been asked about such a guessing strategy. First, did it occur? The answer is "yes." If guessing were not used, the fourth item across all orders should contribute one-fourth of the total correct responses. However, across conditions and sets the mean percentage the fourth item *did* contribute varied between 31% and

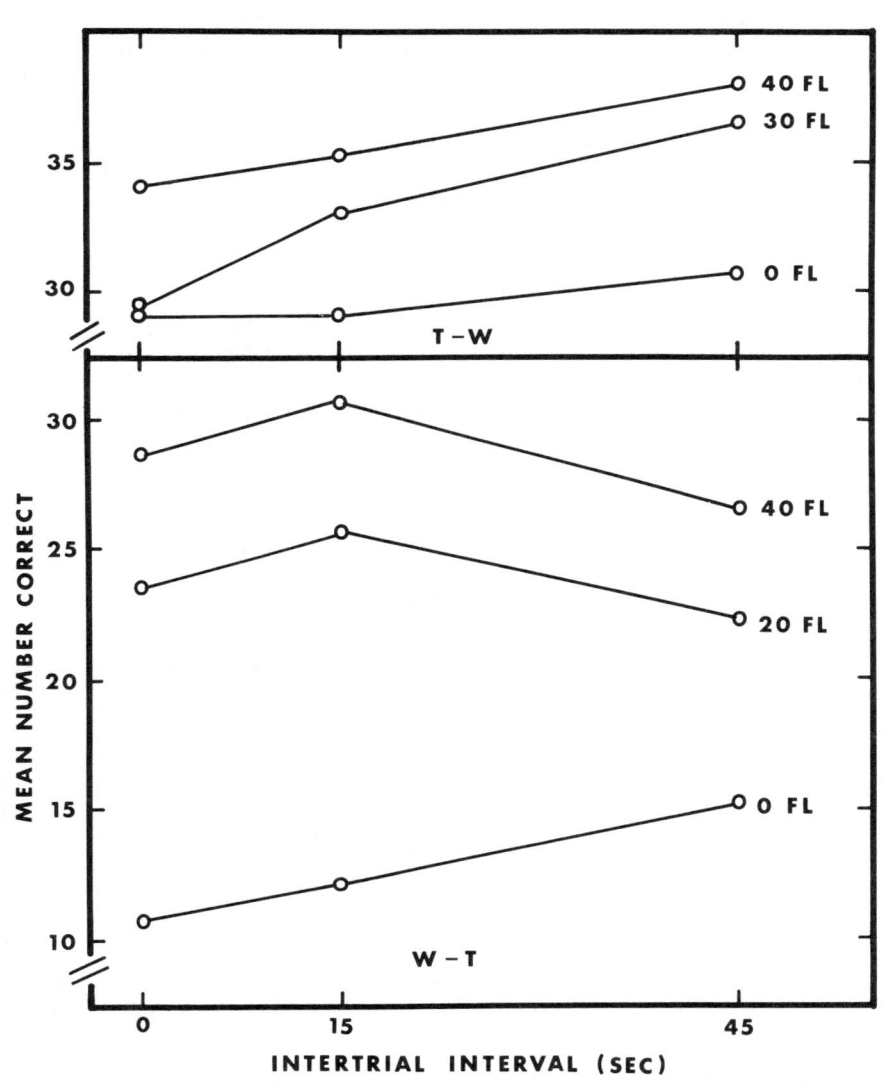

Figure 5.7 Paired-associate learning of T-W and W-T lists of high similarity as a function of intertrial interval and degree of prior FL.

37%. While these values indicate that guessing was not a prominent factor in performance, they do indicate that it contributed.

The second question is whether or not guessing was in some way responsible for the DP effect. The answer to this question appears to be negative. Although there was some slight evidence that guessing was used more frequently with DP than with MP, when Ss were selected in such a way as to equalize the guessing index for intertrial intervals, the superiority of DP over MP was still quite evident.

The acquisition curves, plotted in three blocks of five trials each, were examined for any possible interactions with trials. With neither 0 FL nor 20 FL trials were interactions of any magnitude apparent. With 40 FL trials, however, for Set II the performance under the DP intervals, distinctly superior to the MP on the first two blocks, was inferior on the third. This interaction with trials was significant at the 1% level. However, the comparable interaction for Set I was not present, $F < 1$. The failure to replicate, therefore, must question the reliability of the Trial × Interval interaction.

Words trigrams.—The mean number of correct responses over 20 PA trials for the W-T lists are plotted in the lower section of Fig. 5.7. An analysis shows that the only F greater than one was associated with FL ($F = 33.58$). Thus, the differences in difficulty of the two lists as shown in FL is not carried over to PA learning.

It may be noted in Fig. 5.7 that with no FL there is a regular increase in performance as intertrial interval increases. An examination of performance on the trials beyond 20 is obviously in order for these groups as well as for those having 20 FL trials. Following 20 FL trials, 30 PA trials were given. In the last block of five trials, the DP groups were slightly ahead of MP for both sets but there was no statistical support for a conclusion that DP facilitated acquisition. However, performance was not high in an absolute sense; across all conditions the mean number correct per trial on Trials 26–30 was 1.8 out of a possible 4.0. Therefore, it is possible that had additional trials been given, a further separation might have occurred between the MP and DP curves. Only the curves for Set II suggest (by extrapolation) that this is a reasonable possibility.

The acquisition curves over the 40 trials are plotted in Fig. 5.8 for the groups whose PA learning was not preceded by FL. Both lists are combined for this figure. It is apparent that DP produced a positive effect. For total correct responses across 40 trials the F for interval was 6.76, which, with 2 and 102 *df,* is significant beyond the 1% level. Both lists showed about the same separation between the curves for 0 sec. and 45 sec. For Set I, the performance with 15 sec. was about midway between that shown for 0 and 45 sec; for Set

Miscellaneous

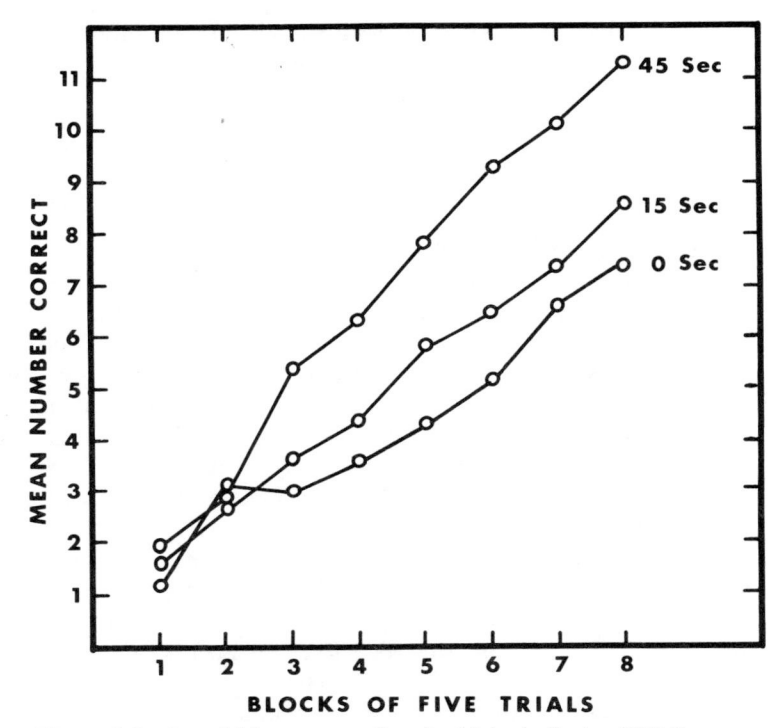

Figure 5.8 Acquisition curves for the high-similarity W-T lists over 40 trials as a function of intertrial interval.

II, the performance under 15 sec. was only slightly ahead of that under 0 sec.

The large effects of DP noted in Fig. 5.8 late in learning, taken in conjunction with the small differences noted earlier for the 20-FL and 40-FL conditions, suggest that there might be an interaction between intertrial interval and FL for performance on the late trials. However, an analysis of variance on the scores for the last five trials of all groups does not support the expectation. Although the F for intertrial interval is significant ($F = 3.71$), the interaction with FL is not ($F = 2.19$). Since the F for FL was less than one, the analysis was made when performance levels did not differ as a function of number of FL trials.

An evaluation of integrative errors showed that only FL ($F = 3.18$) and Set ($F = 5.10$) attained the 5% significance level, the former being of such magnitude that it just reached the 5% level. This analysis includes only the first 20 trials. It is reasonable to ask about integrative errors on later trials for the conditions without prior FL since it was on these conditions that DP facilitated performance. For Trials 21–30 the percentages of integrative errors for 0, 15, and 45 sec. were 68%, 74%, and 70% for Set I, and 46%, 59%, and 68% for Set II. These data do not indicate that DP facilitated because it reduced the elicitation of integrative errors.

FURTHER EVALUATION AND INTERPRETATION

The results of the three experiments may now be summarized with respect to the role of intertrial interval, a summary based upon rather conservative statistical analyses of the data. With low formal similarity, DP facilitates neither the learning of the W-T nor T-W lists. With medium similarity, learning of the W-T lists is facilitated, the T-W is not. With high similarity, the learning of both types of lists is enhanced by DP, although for W-T lists the facilitation develops slowly across trials.

The data across all three experiments may now be examined for the numerical superiority of DP over MP without regard to statistical significance. If the 15-sec. and 45-sec. intervals are considered independent tests of the role of DP, for each level of FL for a given level of similarity there are four comparisons which may be made, two involving each set of lists. For each type of list (W-T or T-W) for a given level of similarity, therefore, there are 12 possible comparisons between MP and DP when summed across all FL levels. The results viewed in this manner are summarized in Table 5.7. Total correct across all trials given was used to determine numerical superiority. The bottom row of this table represents the percentage of times that DP was superior to MP, each percentage being based on the 12 comparisons possible. It will be seen that for the T-W lists the values are 25%, 50%, and 92% for low, medium, and high

Table 5.7 Summary of the No. of Cases in Which DP Performance Was Numerically Superior to MP Performance

	Trigrams-Words			*Words-Trigrams*		
	LS	MS	HS	LS	MS	HS
0 FL	1	3	3	4	3	4
Medium FL	1	3	4	3	4	3
High FL	1	0	4	2	4	3
Totals	3	6	11	9	11	10
Percent	25	50	92	75	92	83

similarity (LS, MS, HS), respectively. The corresponding values for the W-T lists are 75%, 92%, and 83%. Clearly, for the T-W lists, facilitation by DP cannot be expected unless stimulus-term similarity is high. For the W-T lists, on the other hand, the most unfavorable case is low similarity but even here DP may be expected to facilitate learning three times out of four. Taken by itself, this value is not impressive, but when viewed in conjunction with the data from earlier experiments (Table 5.2) in which similarity among trigrams was low, it seems reasonable to conclude that a chance effect is not involved; on the average DP will produce a mean performance level that is slightly above the mean performance level for MP. With medium and high similarity, the probability of numerical facilitation by DP becomes somewhat greater.

The above conclusions involving comparisons across levels of similarity must be accepted with full knowledge that numbers of items in the lists and similarity are confounded. However, it seems improbable that DP will be more likely to facilitate learning merely because the list becomes shorter. In fact, for serial learning, quite the opposite is true (Hovland, 1940). It does not seem unreasonable to proceed as if formal similarity is the critical variable running across the three experiments.

The role of free learning.—For all experiments there was a fairly direct relationship between amount of FL and performance on PA learning. The nature of the design of the experiments does not allow specific conclusions concerning the factors involved in the transfer effect. The nonassociative factors of learning-to-learn and warm-up may contribute. For the T-W lists, FL may increase the likelihood of stimulus selection in PA learning (see later). The FL may provide S with a more stable representational response to the trigram so that the learning of the T-W lists is facilitated. For the W-T lists, it would seem that FL contributed heavily to the response learning necessary in such lists. The reduction in integrative errors following FL is quite consistent with this conclusion. Nevertheless, there is no way from the present data to determine the contribution made by the various factors. It is only clear that FL preceding the PA learning results in a marked increase in the rate of PA learning.

It was expected that FL would interact with intertrial interval. The statistical analysis failed to demonstrate this interaction in any experiment for either type of list. If the rows in Table 5.7 are summed it will be also seen that FL is not appreciably related to facilitation by DP. For the W-T lists the data indicated that FL results in response-term integration. The theory mentioned in the introduction (Underwood, 1961) made level of response-term integration a critical factor in determining whether or not DP would facilitate learning. The conclusion must be that response-term integration is not critically involved, at least not response-term integration as developed in the laboratory. Such a conclusion is also recommended by the fact that DP facilitated the learning of the T-W lists when stimulus similarity was high, and these are lists where response-term integration cannot be involved.

Length of DP interval.—For the W-T lists the experiments give no consistent picture with regard to length of intertrial interval most favorable for obtaining a DP effect. This is true if only the two experiments are considered in which intertrial interval was a statistically significant variable (Exp. II and III; Fig. 5.5 and 5.7). For the T-W lists with high similarity (where DP facilitated learning) the 45-sec. condition is superior to the 15-sec. condition in every comparison. This may suggest that given longer DP intervals than used here, performance might have been further facilitated.

Similarity.—It was pointed out earlier that the overall results appear to make formal similarity a critical factor in producing a DP effect. Since data obtained in previous experiments may also be used in support of this conclusion (Underwood & Richardson, 1957; Underwood & Schulz, 1959), it must constitute the major empirical finding from the present experiments. For W-T lists, the probability of getting a DP effect is higher with medium and high similarity than with low. For the T-W lists, facilitation by DP may be expected only if the stimuli have very high formal similarity. Similarity among both stimuli and responses, such as obtained in an earlier experiment (Underwood & Richardson, 1957), appears to make the task optimal for obtaining a DP effect.

Stimulus selection.—When low-meaningful units of low similarity are used as stimulus terms in PA learning the possibility of stimulus selection is always present. The lists used in all three experiments were constructed so that none of the first letters of the trigrams within a list was duplicated. Insofar as selection of the first letter as the functional stimulus is likely to prevail if stimulus selection occurs (Jenkins, 1963), the possibility for stimulus selection is equivalent across all levels of similarity. There is no conclusive way to tell from the present data whether or not stimulus selection occurred. The most compelling argument against there having been much selection lies in the learning rates. If stimulus selection occurred promptly at the beginning of acquisition for the T-W lists, learning should have been very rapid because the lists are reduced to single-letter stimuli and common words as responses. The rapid rate of learning should be most apparent in the four-pair lists used for high similarity and the most rapid learning of these lists took place following 40 FL trials. However, of the 108 Ss given 40 FL trials, 18 failed to give all four responses correct on a single trial within the 15 PA trials administered. If these Ss are assigned a score of 16 as the number of trials required to reach a perfect recitation, the mean for the 108 Ss is 9.42 trials. Even so, this value is probably reduced somewhat by guessing (as discussed earlier). It seems unlikely that this task could have been so difficult if stimulus selection were occurring with appreciable frequency.

Because the evidence against stimulus selection is not entirely convincing, however, it may be asked whether or not the DP effect observed with the high similarity T-W lists could in some way be a consequence of stimulus selection. Assuming that stimulus selection would facilitate the learning of these lists, it would mean that selection was more likely to occur under DP than under MP. In addition to a lack of apparent reasons why DP should be related to stimulus selection, the fact remains that DP facilitated only with high similarity and there is no reason to believe that it should not have occurred at all levels of similarity if stimulus selection is involved.

EXPLANATORY POSSIBILITIES

The purpose of this final section is to discuss some explanatory notions, some of which do *not* seem appropriate for handling a DP effect, and some of which may be appropriate.

The theory that asserts that DP will facilitate PA learning only when some level of interference occurs in response-term integration (Underwood, 1961) cannot be maintained. The major reasons why the theory is inadequate may be reviewed and extended. (*a*) If it is assumed that FL increases response-term integration, variation in the number of FL trials should have interacted with intertrial interval in PA learning. Although some of the plots suggested such interactions, in no case did the interaction between the two variables approach statistical significance. (*b*) The occurrence of a DP effect with high similarity among the stimulus terms found in the present study, as well as in an earlier study by Marshall and Runquist (1962), argues against interference in response-term integration as the necessary condition for the DP effect. It is possible, of course, to have the DP effect produced by one set of mechanisms when response-term integration is involved and quite a different set when stimulus-term similarity is the variable, but it seems prudent to avoid such multiplicity of explanatory notions until it is clear that they are required. (c) In an earlier study (Underwood et al., 1964) it was found that FL of difficult trigrams was not influenced by DP, and FL of such units might be considered a rather pure test of the notion that DP will influence learning only when interference obtains in response-term integration. (d) In the Underwood et al. (1964) study, interference in response-term integration in PA learning was experimentally induced but still DP had no influence. At best, then, the theory survives only in a general sense, the sense that similarity (hence, presumably interference) is in some way critical for maximizing a DP effect.

Periodically the idea that the DP effect may result from a performance inhibition (e.g., reactive inhibition) must be reviewed. It would not seem unreasonable to assume that manipulations of similarity could vary the amount of inhibition developed and that DP allows for the dissipation of the inhibition. A direct test of this, made in an earlier study (Underwood, 1957), failed to give support to the performance-inhibition explanation. Nevertheless, conditions were arranged in the present experiment to provide a further test. For all Ss having FL prior to PA learning, a 3-min. rest interval was given following the last PA learning trial, and this interval was followed in turn by five additional acquisition trials. If a performance inhibition is involved, the scores following MP should increase over the 3-min. interval more than following DP, or should decrease less. There was absolutely no indication of such changes, and this was true whether DP had facilitated learning or not. It does not seem proper to hold to a performance-inhibition explanation of a DP effect in verbal learning.

A very inelegant explanation of the DP effect is that Ss rehearse during the DP rest interval. Although it is not possible to eliminate rehearsal as a factor, it is difficult to relate rehearsal to the critical variable, i.e., to similarity. Furthermore, it is difficult to reconcile rehearsal with instances in which DP rather consistently inhibits performance (Table 5.3). It is also possible that MP produces fatigue when the learning period is extended. The gradual separation over trials of the MP and DP curves for the high-similarity W-T lists might suggest that fatigue was involved. On the other hand, the effect of DP on the high-similarity T-W lists was immediate, and surely fatigue was not involved in this instance. Again, however, there is no way in which fatigue as a factor can be eliminated completely as an explanatory possibility. Thus, the suggestion by Brown and Huda (1961) that because of fatigue under MP the nature of the learning differs from that under DP, remains as one alternative, albeit a remote one.

In an earlier paper (Underwood & Schulz, 1961a) it was suggested that a DP effect might be mediated by a true associative inhibition, that is, by an inhibition which retards or slows the growth of associate strength. Such an inhibition would dissipate during the DP rest interval. At the present time, such an explanatory notion seems to not only be the most parsimonious one but also to be capable of incorporating the bulk of the experimental findings. The critical condition for the most rapid development of such an inhibition must, of course, be tied to similarity as a manipulable variable. This requirement may indicate that the inhibition is interference produced.

The problem in refining such a theory lies in the difficulty of understanding the nature of the interference which produces the inhibition. There are a number of studies (summarized in Underwood, 1961) reporting heavy interference in word lists but in which no DP effect was found. And, as shown in Table 5.3, DP may actually result in slower learning than MP when interlist interference becomes high. Generally speaking, a DP effect is most likely to be found if the interference is produced by formal similarity among nonword units, and this is true for both serial and PA learning. This in turn may suggest that the associative inhibition assumed to be responsible for the DP effect is developed maximally when associations must be learned among perceptually similar items. It seems necessary to assume that the inhibition develops maximally in the process of forming associations among perceptually similar items since (a) no DP effect is observed in verbal-discrimination learning even with high formal similarity (Underwood & Archer, 1955) and (b) little facilitation is observed in FL even with high formal similarity (Underwood et al., 1964). It is not implied that the inhibition does not develop at all for materials with low formal similarity. The accumulated evidence reviewed earlier indicates that with no repeated letters among trigrams as response terms in a PA list a small but consistent DP effect has been noted. The data, therefore, indicate that formal similarity merely maximizes the development of the inhibition, and it is presumed that the inhibition is in some way interference produced. Nevertheless, just why interference among words rarely results in a DP effect is unclear. The presence of other counteracting factors is the most likely possibility.

The idea that a DP effect is produced by an associative inhibition which retards the growth of associative strength is not far removed from the thinking of other investigators. It seems similar to the theory recently advanced by Dey (1966). Brown and Huda (1961) have shown that latency of response is slower under MP than under

DP and this could be expected for items in the threshold region if the associative inhibition is greater under MP than DP. Greeno (1964) varied the number of other pairs falling between repetitions of a given pair and concluded that little if any learning of a pair occurred as a consequence of a second repetition when an item was repeated very soon after its initial presentation. Greeno suggests that MP retards the development of differentiation or discrimination among pairs, but this could be a by-product of the development of an associative inhibition. However, it should be noted that Greeno's method (varying DP and MP for items within a single list, and not in terms of length of interval between trials) would require that the inhibition be specific to items. Such specificity is not implied by the notion of associative inhibition advanced here. The Greeno phenomenon may be based on quite a different set of mechanisms.

Finally, it may be noted again that with PA learning the DP effect is one of small absolute magnitude. It is most likely to occur with high formal similarity but even under optimal conditions there is not much "room" to work with it experimentally, i.e., to study the influence of other potential interacting variables. In many ways, intertrial interval is a most unsatisfying variable with which to deal experimentally, and no further studies are contemplated with it in the immediate future in the Northwestern laboratories.

REFERENCES

Baker, B. L., & Noble, C. L. Effects of time factors in paired-associate verbal learning. *J. verbal Learn. verbal Behav.*, 1965, 4, 437–445.

Brown, J., & Huda, M. Response latencies produced by massed and spaced learning of a paired-associate list. *J. exp. Psychol.*, 1961, 61, 360–364.

Dey, M. K. An explanation of distributed practice efficacy in paired-associate learning. *J. gen. Psychol.*, 1966, 74, 61–75.

Ekstrand, B., & Underwood, B. J. Paced versus unpaced recall in free learning. *J. verbal Learn. verbal Behav.*, 1963, 2, 288–290.

Greeno, J. G. Paired-associate learning with massed and distributed items. *J. exp. Psychol.*, 1964, 67, 286–295.

Hovland, C. I. Experimental studies in rote-learning theory: VII. Distribution of practice with varying lengths of list. *J. exp. Psychol.*, 1940, 27, 271–284.

Jenkins, J. J. Stimulus "fractionation" in paired-associate learning. *Psychol. Rep.*, 1963, 13, 409–410.

Jung, J. A test of Underwood's theory of distributed practice. *J. exp. Psychol.*, 1966, 71, 778–780.

Keppel, G. Facilitation in short- and long-term retention of paired associates following distributed practice in learning. *J. verbal Learn. verbal Behav.*, 1964, 3, 91–111.

Marshall, M. A., & Runquist, W. N. Facilitation in paired-associate learning by distributed practice. *J. verbal Learn. verbal Behav.,* 1962, 1, 258-263.

Siegel, S. *Nonparametric statistics.* New York: McGraw-Hill, 1956.

Underwood, B. J. Studies of distributed practice: XVI. Some evidence on the nature of the inhibition involved in massed learning of verbal materials. *J. exp. Psychol.,* 1957, 54, 139-143.

Underwood, B. J. Ten years of massed practice on distributed practice. *Psychol. Rev.,* 1961, 68, 229-247.

Underwood, B. J., & Archer, E. J. Studies of distributed practice: XIV. Intralist similarity and presentation rate in verbal-discrimination learning of consonant syllables. *J. exp. Pscyhol.,* 1955, 50, 120-124.

Underwood, B. J., Ekstrand, B. R., & Keppel, G. Studies of distributed practice: XXIII. Variations in response-term interference. *J. exp. Psychol.,* 1964, 68, 201-212.

Underwood, B. J., Keppel, G., & Schulz, R. W. Studies of distributed practice: XXII. Some conditions which enhance retention. *J. exp. Psychol.,* 1962, 64, 355-363.

Underwood, B. J., & Richardson, J. Studies of distributed practice: XVII. Interlist interference and the retention of paired consonant syllables. *J. exp. Psychol.,* 1957, 54, 274-279.

Underwood, B. J., & Schulz, R. W. Studies of distributed practice: XIX. The influence of intralist similarity with lists of low meaningfulness. *J. exp. Psychol.,* 1959, 58, 106-110.

Underwood, B. J., & Schulz, R. W. *Meaningfulness and verbal learning.* Philadelphia: Lippincott, 1960.

Underwood, B. J., & Schulz, R. W. Studies of distributed practice: XX. Sources of interference associated with differences in learning and retention. *J. exp. Psychol.,* 1961, 61, 228-235. (a)

Underwood, B. J., & Schulz, R. W. Studies of distributed practice: XXI. Effect of interference from language habits. *J. exp. Psychol.,* 1961, 62, 571-575. (b)

Attributes of Memory

Of what does a memory consist? The theme of the present article is that a memory is composed of a number of attributes, and the central purpose of this paper is to identify these attributes. A memory is an organism's record of an event. We infer this record when, by any of a variety of measures, the organism responds in a manner he would not have responded had the event not occurred. An event has no size limits other than those imposed arbitrarily for classification purposes. Much of the evidence on memory deals with very limited events, primarily memory for verbal units. In appealing to the empirical for the evidence on attributes, it is necessary, therefore, to look primarily at the data from the verbal learning laboratory.

It is quite common to speak of the *encoding* of material by the subject (S) as it is presented for learning. In the context of the present discussion, encoding represents the process by which the attributes of a memory are established, although no assumption is made about the necessary intentionality on the part of S in these processes. When a memory is conceptualized as consisting of an ensemble of attributes, memory for an event per se has no psychological meaning because a memory without attributes is incapable of being remembered (retrieved). There is no "corpus" which can be recalled directly. Furthermore, differences in the attributes for different memories are fundamental for discriminating or differentiating memories, hence are fundamental for understanding the failure of S to perform perfectly on a retention test, that is, for understanding forgetting. Implications of these assumptions will emerge gradually as the discussion progresses.

As will be seen, some of the attributes may be positively correlated in some situations. This is of no moment for the overall conception being presented, but it is of some importance if one wishes to study experimentally the effect of each attribute. Therefore, some attention will be paid to this matter at appropriate points.

The attributes may be classed into one of two broad categories,

---

Benton J. Underwood, "Attributes of Memory," *Psychological Review* 76 (1969): 559–573. Reprinted with permission. Copyright 1969 by the American Psychological Association.

This work was supported by Contract Nonr-1228 (15), Project NR 154–057, between Northwestern University and the Office of Naval Research. Appreciation is due Leo Postman for his very critical reading of an early draft of this paper.

namely, those which are independent of the task presented for learning, and those which are task dependent. The listing will begin with the former class. However, it should be clear that this is not a literature review; studies are cited only to illustrate the probable operation of a given attribute.

TEMPORAL ATTRIBUTE

The perception of an event occurs at a given point in time and the memory of the event may carry a temporal attribute, an attribute that is unique, since no other memory was established at exactly the same point in time. Yet, a given point in time can have no memorial representation except by the events which occurred; the temporal attribute of a memory must consist of a contiguous event which refers in some way to a point in time or to a time range. In the simplest case, the temporal attribute may identify one event as having occurred before or after another event, or as first or last. It is not clear how dependent a temporal attribute is on standard dimensions for measuring time, for example, days of the week, although some evidence (discussion will follow) may suggest that a temporal attribute may take such forms.

Although acceptance of the temporal attribute must rest ultimately on convincing data, there are certain logical problems which cannot be skirted. A memory may be said to grow weaker with time—it is forgotten. Further, it might be asserted that because of forgetting we are able to orient ourselves in time. A "weak" memory may lead to the inference that the memory was established at an earlier point in time than was the memory for another event which is now "strong." Therefore, it could be argued that the so-called temporal attribute is contingent on forgetting and that a memory does not carry independent temporal information.

In terms of the present orientation, the above argument would not be accepted as a general case. Rather, it is assumed that the strength of a memory has no meaning except as it can be referred to the attributes of the memory. In other words, strength, so-called, is a by-product of the attributes, of which the temporal attribute is only one. Furthermore, if orientation in time is produced only by comparative strengths of memories, considerable disorientation would be present. Some older memories are much stronger than recent ones and yet they are also identified as older, indicating the presence of a discriminating attribute which counteracts a discrimination based on comparative judgments of strength. Nevertheless, if a discrimination of the strength of a memory can be made without reference to the attributes (contrary to the assumptions of the present paper), it will follow that in certain situations the inference of a temporal attribute is not justified. Such situations will now be examined and will be referred to as within-task situations as opposed to between-task situations.

Within Tasks

Yntema and Trask (1963) presented S a series of words, one at a time. Occasionally, two words which had been presented previously were shown, and S was asked to judge which one of the two had appeared earlier in the series. The greater the discrepancy in the age of the members of a pair, the greater the accuracy in identifying the older one. These investigators suggested the possibility that a memory carries a "time tag." However, as Morton (1968) has pointed out, if it is assumed that the strength of the trace of the memory for a word decays with time, and if S makes a judgment on the basis of the strength, the Yntema-Trask data could be accounted for without appeal to a temporal attribute. Morton's approach was to vary strength by presenting an item (digit) more than once. Thus, the older item was presented twice and the younger item once, and then S was asked to make an age judgment between the two. The expectation was that under these conditions the older item would be stronger at the time of the judgment and S would, if judging age by comparative strengths, be in error. The data give support, albeit slight, to the expectation. However, when each item was presented once, judgments were at a chance level indicating that age discriminations based either on strength or a temporal attribute were quite impossible. Furthermore, Ss reported that they felt they were responding randomly. It is quite likely that in the 2:1 case, Ss, having no temporal discrimination, responded on the basis of frequency differences (discussion will follow). It is probably difficult to establish a fine discriminative temporal attribute during a short run of homogeneous events.

Some data gathered by the present writer will be examined next, these data not having been previously published. When S is asked to remember a series of words presented auditorially, and is then asked to identify the position of each word in the series, a temporal judgment would seem to be required. In this study a long list of words was presented, some being presented for 10 seconds, some 15 seconds, and some 20 seconds. During these intervals, S heard the word being repeated each 2.5 seconds. Recall increased directly as a function of the length of the study period and by almost any conception, the recall measure may be used as a two-category measure of strength (strong enough to be recalled and not strong enough to be recalled). Thus, the longer the presentation interval, the "stronger" the word. Following recall, all words were presented and S was asked to identify the position by assigning a number (1 for first position, 2 for the second, and so on). Judgments of position showed significant correlations with true position but these judgments did not vary systematically with recall (study time), hence with strength.

In the same study there was a large number of words presented for 5 seconds each. There was no relationship between the frequency with which a word was recalled and its position within the list. Nevertheless, position judgments were significantly related to true position. Given the word, S could identify the position with some accuracy although on an absolute basis this temporal knowledge was poor. If words which are recalled are said to be stronger than those which are not, it does not appear that these position judgments could have been based on strength.

In the above studies, temporal knowledge was incidental in that the Ss did not know at the time of list presentation that they would be requested to make position judgments. In a further unpublished study, 100 Ss were presented a 25-word list, auditorially, each word for 5 seconds, under instructions that their memory for position would be tested, that is, they were told that following a single presentation of the list, they would be given the words in random order and they were to assign a number from 1 to 25 for each word to identify the position it held. The percentage of Ss correctly identifying the position of each word was determined. This curve was quite comparable to the usual free recall curve, having clear primacy and recency effects. Thus, while it may be inferred that position knowledge in this case would be highly correlated with recall, it must also be inferred that position knowledge is not automatically inferred from the strength of a trace. If this were the case, for example, words in the initial positions of the list should be assigned positions at the end of the list. Thus, it appears that position (temporal) knowledge can exist as an attribute and is independent of so-called trace strength based on recency.

An earlier point must be repeated. There is no intent to argue that the temporal attribute of a memory exists independently of other events occurring in time. A word in a list may be associated with a verbal time-tag (early, late, firstness, and so on). It is remotely possible that when S is presented a list auditorially, he projects or imagines a linear spatial dimension (as on a sheet of paper) along which words are ordered, and, therefore, a spatial attribute is involved (discussion will follow). Berlyne (1966) has suggested that position knowledge of two events in a series may be mediated by the number of other events falling between them. As will be seen, the assimilation of event frequency is such as to make this interpretation quite plausible.

Between Tasks

In a recent study of proactive inhibition (Underwood & Freund, 1968a), evidence was presented which indicated that temporal discrimination may drastically reduce the interference between two lists. Paired-associate lists were used in which the paradigm between the two lists was A-B, A-C. One group of Ss had the two lists in immediate succession on a Thursday, followed by recall of the second list on Friday. Another group had the first list on Monday, the second list on Thursday, and recall of the second list on Friday. For the second group, recall of the second list was 65% correct, for the first group, 38%. That the differentiation is in some way based on a temporal discrimination is suggested by the results of further conditions in which some of the pairs of the first list were carried over intact into the second list. Under these conditions, the Monday-Thursday group showed heavy proactive interference for the pairs not carried over. It was as if this procedure destroyed the temporal discrimination; the time-tag lost its validity.

The above study indicates that the integrity of two sets of responses associated to a common set of stimulus terms can be maintained given a sufficient separation in time of the acquisition of the two sets. However, the length of the interval between the two tasks may not be the only important factor. It may be that any distinctive event occurring between the learning of the two lists could serve to establish a temporal discrimination (before and after) and thereby reduce the interaction between the two tasks. This possibility is suggested by Zavortink's (1968) findings. A number of studies (e.g., Bilodeau & Schlosberg, 1951) have shown that retroactive inhibition is reduced if the two interfering lists are learned in distinctly different physical contexts. Zavortink replicated this finding but included a control group in which the Ss, during the interval between the learning of the two lists, left the room, moved down the hall to a drinking fountain, and then returned to the same room to learn the second list. Thus, the activity involved was essentially the same as that given the group which changed physical locations. Zavortink found that retroactive inhibition was reduced equally in both groups, suggesting that the critical factor was not the change in physical context for the learning of the two lists, but the activity of S between the learning of the interfering lists. In a manner of speaking, the trip down the hall to the water fountain provided a point of reference for a before-after discrimination between the two lists.

SPATIAL ATTRIBUTE

In ancient days, memory systems were developed as a necessity by public figures who had to deliver long speeches. Without paper for making notes, some technique was needed for remembering the points of the speech and the order in which the points were to be delivered. The memory systems which arose frequently included a spatial dimension (Yates, 1966). A common procedure was to use various positions or loci in a building as one went from one room to the next—a column, a dark corner, a vase, a statue, and so on. The ideas of the speech to be remembered were then associated with these focal points and ordered by the spatial relationships of the objects, so that in delivering the address the orator strolled through the building (in his mind's eye), summoning up each successive point as required.

Incidental observations would support the notion of a spatial attribute. It is not unusual to hear a person remark that he doesn't remember a certain aspect of an event about which he has read but does remember that it was "described near the bottom of a right-hand page." The reliability of such reports is unknown, but, if reliable, they indicate a spatial attribute of memory. The experimental evidence confirms the reliability of such observations.

When a serial list is presented auditorially, it can be thought of as being ordered along a temporal dimension, the relationship with a spatial dimension being minimal unless S in some way projects it spatially (see previous discussion). However, when a serial list is presented visually by a tape which is pulled by steps into S's vision, both the temporal and spatial dimensions may be involved, and we often speak of a spatial-temporal dimension. In presenting a paired-associate list, we intentionally negate the correlation with the spatial-temporal dimension found in serial learning; we do this by presenting the pairs in different orders on each trial. Obviously, the experimental problem is to arrange a situation in which there is a lack of correlation between the spatial and temporal attribute.

Ebenholtz (1963) devised a paired-associate task in which the stimulus "terms" held different positions on a memory-drum tape, the particular position for a given response term being indicated by a red patch. On successive trials the order in which the red patches occurred (each patch in a different position) was varied. Learning, it appears, could only occur if position could serve as a differentiating cue. The results show that learning was just as rapid as when usual serial learning procedures were used and where, as already noted, the spatial and temporal attributes are confounded. Slamecka (1967) presented items in different positions but in the same temporal order on each trial. However, in producing the items, S was required to order them according to the spatial position and not by the temporal order. Learning was as rapid as by the usual serial learning method. Asch, Hay, and Diamond (1960) used various spatial configurations with the verbal units (nonsense syllables) placed at various places on these configurations. Type of configuration was a significant variable in the serial learning of the syllables. In general, learning was somewhat more rapid when different positions were used for the items than when the same position was used for all. Thus, although the spatial and temporal attributes were confounded in all of the conditions, the fact that learning differed for the various spatial configurations must be attributed to differences in spatial discriminability associated with the configurations. In an incidental learning procedure, Berlyne (1966) produced evidence indicating that a spatial attribute adds to or supports a temporal attribute in memory for position in a series, and Monty (1968) has shown that if four different stimuli are presented consistently in spatially different locations, frequency information is more accurate than if all four are presented in the same spatial location.

The evidence indicates that a spatial attribute may be a part of a memory. It would be expected, therefore, that two memories which might be expected to interfere with each other would do so to a lesser extent if different spatial attributes were involved. It is not apparent that an adequate test of this proposition has been made. In one study (Underwood, 1950), two interfering lists were learned either on the same side of the memory drum or on opposite sides. Differences in retroactive inhibition were slight, but it is not at all clear that the spatial differences were sufficiently different psychologically to expect a difference. Probably the most convincing data on a common spatial attribute as a source of interference come from the short-term memory studies of intrusions in the learning and recall of difficult letter sequences (e.g., Smith, 1966).

FREQUENCY ATTRIBUTE

Frequency is a major manipulable variable underlying learning; the greater the frequency, the better the learning. Further, the better the learning, the better the retention. Frequency is normally assumed to be associated with strength of learning, with strength inferred from probability of response. The intent of this section is to suggest the existence of a frequency attribute of memory which is in some instances separable from a strength concept. It will be useful again to discuss these notions for within-task situations and between-task situations, independently.

Within Tasks

It may be shown that the ability to assimilate event frequency is a highly developed skill, the assessment being made from the ability to judge relative frequency of events. No attempt is made here to summarize this evidence, evidence which stems from judgments of event frequency manipulated in the laboratory (e.g., Erlick, 1964), and from judgments of event frequency for events which have occurred outside the laboratory (e.g., Attneave, 1953). How are such judgments mediated? If an S is asked which letter, q or s, occurs most frequently in words, the reply is rapid and correct. Is s stronger than q? It is not easy to conceptualize strength in this situation. To say that one is more familiar than the other seems to do no more than substitute familiarity for frequency and does not change anything. The position taken here is that a frequency attribute can exist as a component of memory and may be independent of any so-called strength measure.

The evidence to support this position is by no means convincing and must be bolstered in part by the problems involved in conceptualizing what strength means in certain situations. Strength is given clear conceptual meaning only when referred to as associative strength—when the probability of B following a specific event A can be shown to increase as a function of frequency. But what, for example, can be specified about associative strength when S is presented a very long list of words for a single trial under free recall instructions? There are possible answers to this question. Words within the long list may develop associative relationships so that if one is recalled the other will also be. To "obtain" recall of the first word in such a pair, as well as isolated words, we sometimes say that words are associated with the context. Indeed, some may assert that it is impossible to conceive of a word from such a list being recalled without it having entered into some sort of an associative relationship. If so, the problem is to discover the nature and source of these associations. This matter is not pursued further here, for such a pursuit would require a thorough evaluation of the nature of an association and that is not the central purpose of the paper. It must be admitted that it may be quite possible to tie frequency to an associative relationship, and as already noted, the meaning of strength can be made quite clear in such situations, at least up to the point where the probability of a response becomes unity. Given this situation, therefore, the best that can be done is to present data where strength and frequency do achieve some independence.

In one study (Underwood, 1969), Ss were presented a long list of words under instructions that their memory for the words would be tested. Within the list, some of the words occurred as many as four times. Following the presentation of the list, half of the Ss were presented the words and made judgments of the frequency with which each had occurred. The other half recalled the words. The results show that the greater the frequency of presentation, the higher the mean frequency judgments and the higher the recall. However, a number of the words were presented only once, and it is to these words that attention is turned in order to break the correlation between frequency and strength (as inferred from recall). Words presented once which occurred in the early and late portions of the list were recalled far more frequently than were words presented once within the body of the list. However, the mean frequency judgments were almost identical for the two classes of words. If recall is used as an index of strength, and if the frequency attribute reflects only strength, the frequency judgments should have been higher for the words occurring at the beginning and end of the list than for those occurring in the body of the list.

The above data are not definitive. Other attributes of memory may have been involved in the better recall of the words at the ends of the list than of those in the body. Better recall might not have resulted from higher associative strength involving these attributes, but from a unique combination of the attributes. To be convincing, evidence on the converse case should be available; that is, evidence showing that differential frequency was correctly perceived but where recall or strength was equivalent. To the writer's knowledge, no such evidence is available.

Between Tasks

Winograd (1968) studied differentiation between two lists of 25 nouns each. The critical variable was the trial frequency on each list. When a list was presented for more than one trial, the order of the words differed from trial to trial. Following the presentation of the two lists, the 50 words were intermingled, forming a single list. This list was presented, one word at a time for 8 seconds each, and *S* was asked to judge in which list the word had occurred and also to provide a confidence rating for the judgment. The correct list identification and the confidence ratings produced essentially the same findings, namely, that identification was more accurate when the two lists differed in number of learning trials than when the number of learning trials was equivalent. This was true only when the number of trials given under the equality condition was three. With six trials on both lists, identification was better than in the conditions where number of trials differed, but where the absolute number was six or less. Winograd believes that with the higher number of trials, other factors come into play to aid the differentiation between lists.

As already noted, when fewer, equal, or more trials were given around three trials as an anchor, list-membership knowledge was better when the number of trials on the two lists differed. Winograd was able to show that it was quite unlikely that a temporal attribute (recency) was responsible for this discrimination, but it is not possible to eliminate strength associated with frequency as a factor. That is, *S* could sort all strong words into one list, all weak words into another. When trials are equivalent, this discrimination is not possible. While admittedly ambiguous, therefore, the data are consonant with the notion that a frequency attribute is directly involved in the judgments.

One study goes a little farther toward breaking the strength-frequency correlation (Underwood & Ekstrand, 1968). All *S*s learned four paired-associate lists, with the fourth list being recalled after 24 hours. The lists had an A-B, A-C, A-D, A-E relationship. For two groups (E1 and E2) the response terms to each stimulus term in the first three lists were associates of the stimulus term they were paired with. For example, across the three lists, *S* "learned" TABLE-*chair*, TABLE-*floor*, TABLE-*food*. There were 15 pairs in each list. The fourth list did not contain associates. A third group (a control) had the same paradigm, but the response terms were *not* associates of the stimuli. The fourth list, the list recalled, was the same for all groups and was presented for six trials for all groups. The number of anticipation trials on each list, with the percentage of four-list items recalled, were as follows:

Group	A-B	A-C	A-D	A-E	Recall Percentage
E1	1	1	1	6	68
E2	5	5	5	6	22
C	5	5	5	6	27

It should be noted that the only difference in the treatments of E1 and E2 was the number of trials given on the first three lists. The results show that this had a profound influence on the recall of the fourth list. When the interfering lists had about the same number of trials as the list to be recalled, recall was markedly reduced—proactive inhibition was much greater. Is this due to a higher degree of learning, hence more interference? There is no way to eliminate this possibility completely. However, in the case of associates, the different degrees of learning is a difficult one to conceptualize, since the learning has primarily occurred before S came into the laboratory. After a single study trial, Ss averaged 13 of the 15 correct. This is to say, therefore, that learning was nearly perfect after a single trial. Furthermore, it is known from other studies (e.g., Underwood & Ekstrand, 1966) that continued learning beyond this level has very little influence on the amount of proactive inhibition. The preferred interpretation, therefore, is that the trial frequency difference between the interfering lists and the list to be recalled is the discriminative attribute which markedly reduced the interference in Group E1.

MODALITY ATTRIBUTE

Material may be presented for learning by auditory signals or by visual signals. Procedurally, this can be done in rather pure form. However, at least with young adults, it is not clear that the signal remains pure. When a visual stimulus (a word) is presented, S may whisper it to himself and thus provide something approximating an auditory signal. It seems less probable that the reverse is true, that an auditory signal is transformed into a visual signal, although even this may be possible. The S with good visual imagery may in fact "see" the printed word when it is presented auditorially.

The question of whether learning rate differs as a function of input modality is not a point at issue here. Rather, the question is whether a memory can carry a modality attribute which may serve to discriminate this memory from a memory carrying an attribute signifying a different modality. Evidence from the older literature (e.g., Nagge, 1935), as well as recent studies (e.g., Inoue, 1968), gives an affirmative answer. Retroactive inhibition is reduced if the original and interpolated tasks are presented via different modalities than if presented through a common modality. Inoue, in fact, in some of his conditions, used the cutaneous modality by having blind *S*s learn by the Braille method. Retroactive inhibition for free recall of nonsense syllables was much reduced if the modalities for two successive lists were cutaneous-auditory as compared to cutaneous-cutaneous.

The nature of the modality attribute associated with a memory is not clear. Murdock (1968) has concluded that the storage systems are different for visually and auditorially presented material. If this is true, a memory may carry a modality tag which leads to the appropriate system. Admittedly, this is not very satisfactory. Yet, there are common expressions which reflect such a distinction. A question may arise concerning a certain fact and we say, as we try to retrieve this fact: "I heard X report on this at the MPA convention," or "I know I read about that somewhere." Whether these modality-specific statements lead to different search processes is not known. In any event, the evidence indicates that memories can be said to have some degree of modality specificity, and it is assumed that there is an attribute which reflects this. At the same time, this matter should not be overemphasized. In the case of the visual and auditory modalities at least, there is a great deal of interchange. Studies show that retroactive inhibition may be reduced a little by using different modalities for the two tasks, but it is by no means eliminated.

ORTHOGRAPHIC ATTRIBUTES

In this and the following sections the concern is with attributes associated with the task or material. As will become more apparent in later discussion, these attributes are so much a part of the memory that it becomes to a large extent a manner of speaking to distinguish between a target memory and its attributes.

It is of some moment to recognize that a subjective belief that a memory *has* been established has some validity (Hart, 1967). Hart initially asked *S*s some general information questions. For those questions for which answers could not be recalled, S indicated whether he did or did not have a feeling of knowing the answer. Subsequently, on a multiple-choice recognition test, S was more often correct for questions for which he had originally indicated a feeling of knowing than for questions for which he had not had this feeling. In terms of the present analysis, the feeling of knowing is mediated by attributes of the memory, attributes which are faint or weak.

With regard to memory for words, Brown and McNeil (1966) have evaluated a phenomenon similar to the feeling of knowing, a phenomenon they call "tip of the tongue." The portion of their analysis of interest here has to do with what may be called the orthographic attributes of the memory for a word. In their study, Brown and McNeil read definitions of low-frequency words to Ss. Their interest was in words which S felt he knew (it was on the tip of his tongue), but which he could not produce immediately. When S signaled he was in this "state," he was asked to characterize the word he was trying to recall. More particularly, he was asked to give the number of syllables, the initial letter of the word, and words that had similar sounds. When the data were analyzed and compared with the attributes of the target word, it was found that all three attributes had validity. Thus, even though S could not recall the word, he was quite accurate in identifying the number of syllables it had, and his guess of the initial letter was correct 57% of the time. Further, by comparing the words written by S with the target word, it was shown that there was some degree of accuracy for letters beyond the first.

The Brown-McNeil data indicate that a memory for a word may include orthographic attributes. That these attributes are not irrelevant for retrieval of a word was shown by Horowitz, White, and Atwood (1968). Furthermore, the work of Marchbanks and Levin (1965) indicates that with young children the first letter of words is the predominant attribute for recognizing a word.

The orthographic attributes may not be independent of other attributes. One possibility is that some of the orthographic attributes of a word could be reduced to the spatial-temporal attributes associated with the letters within the word. Viewing a word as a serial list of letters is not entirely unreasonable when the comparability of the phenomena associated with the serial learning of a list of words and those associated with the spelling of a word are noted, as was done by Brown and McNeil. Such reduction assumes that spatial-temporal attributes are fundamental parts of the memory for a serial list.

The orthographic attributes may also be reducible to nonverbal associative attributes, a topic to which attention is now turned.

ASSOCIATIVE ATTRIBUTES: NONVERBAL

Earlier, evidence was presented for the existence of attributes associated with different modalities. Nonverbal associative attributes are identified here in part as attributes distinguishing memories within a modality.

Acoustic

Each letter, or a set of letters forming a syllable within a language, has a particular sound spectrum when pronounced. The memory for the letter, syllable, word, or series of words may carry an acoustic attribute. Indeed, it might be argued that for the normal person this attribute is inevitably present. That a memory can exist without this attribute, however, is evident in the congenitally deaf. For the normal person, perhaps, the question is not whether an acoustic attribute exists as a part of the memory for verbal material, but rather, whether or not it plays a discriminative role for the memory. The evidence available allows a reasonable characterization of this role. The more that verbal associates dominate the attributes (discussion will follow), the less the role played by the acoustic attribute. Roughly, the greater the meaningfulness of the material being stored as a memory, the greater the dominance of the verbal associative attribute; hence, the less prominent the role of the acoustic attribute.

Work in short-term memory (e.g., Conrad, 1964; Wickelgren, 1965) clearly shows a relationship between acoustic similarity and errors in recall of letters and digits. This suggests a prominent role for the acoustic attribute with relatively low-meaningful material, or at least for material presented very rapidly for learning (as in memory-span procedures). With common words, however, the acoustic properties appear to play a very minor role under procedures normally used for either free recall learning (Underwood & Freund, 1968b) or for short-term memory studies (Wickens & Eckler, 1968). Only if attributes other than the acoustic attribute are minimized at the time the material is presented for learning does it appear that the acoustic attribute plays a dominant role in memory.

Two further points should be made about the acoustic attribute. First, it is not a unitary attribute; it may be broken down into subattributes, and it has been suggested (Wickelgren, 1966) that these subattributes may be forgotten at different rates. Second, the evidence does not allow a conclusion that the acoustic attributes are independent of attributes in other modalities. For example, Hintzman (1967) presents data indicating that interference produced by acoustic similarity in short-term memory can be referred to the kinesthetic modality, at least for some attributes. Thus again, no definitive statements can be made about the independence of the attributes being listed.

It can be seen that orthographic attributes might be "deduced" from the acoustic attribute. If S remembers a sound pattern, he might reconstruct the orthographic features of a word with some degree of accuracy. It might seem that this is unreasonable in the memory for words if, as already stated, the acoustic attribute is dominated by other attributes in the memory for words. However, it may be that these other attributes are forgotten more rapidly than is the acoustic attribute. There is simply no evidence available to mediate these issues.

Visual

The visual attribute of a memory consists of images. If S learns a list of concrete nouns, each may be represented by an image of the object symbolized by the word. A group of words expressing an idea may also be reflected by an image. That visual imagery may be absent or minimal for some people is of no moment in that individual differences for all attributes may be expected. The evidence (e.g., Paivio & Madigan, 1968) is quite clear in showing that visual images may be present during learning and thus become attributes. It is also possible that some of the orthographic attributes are carried by visual images.

Affective

Words may be associated with certain affective responses which are nonverbal in nature. This does not imply that words cannot be used to describe these responses; rather, it means only that an affective response may be aroused by an event and this is not dependent on the arousal of a verbal description. A memory, therefore, may consist in part of a nonverbal associative affective attribute.

The older studies on the role of the pleasant-unpleasant dimension of words on memory for the words would give scant support to the idea that an affective attribute can serve as a discriminative attribute for a memory (McGeoch & Irion, 1952). Recent work, however, has changed this conclusion. When the affective attribute is defined by the major dimensions of the semantic differential, effects on memory are experimentally demonstrable. Turvey (1968) has shown that the amount of proactive interference in short-term memory for word triads is related to some extent to common affective connotation. Assuming that no other attribute of memory is correlated with the affective scales of the semantic differential, it must be concluded that the affective attribute can serve as a discriminative attribute for memory. There is, furthermore, some evidence that the affective attribute may be remembered even when the particular word with which it is associated cannot be remembered (Yavuz & Bousfield, 1959).

Context

A memory may carry with it certain information about the context in which that memory was established, hence a contextual attribute. Again, such attributes may not be independent. For example, it was noted earlier that reduced retroactive inhibition resulting from learning two tasks in different contexts may reflect the indirect operation of a temporal discrimination mediated by the context cues. But, this need not necessarily be true; and, until such potential relationships are better understood, the possibility should be kept open that context cues per se may serve directly as discriminative attributes of a memory.

There is an enormous number of ways in which contextual attributes may be manipulated. To discover if such an attribute influences memory, the basic technique is to determine if interference in retention changes when context cues for the learning of the two tasks are the same or different. Although there are some positive instances in the literature (e.g., Goggin, 1967; Gottlieb & Lindauer, 1967), positive in the sense that interference was reduced by different contexts, it is not possible at this time to educe any general principles as to when and when not the contextual attribute will influence memory for an event.

ASSOCIATIVE ATTRIBUTES: VERBAL

When words make up a task to be learned, other associated words, words which are not a part of the task, may be elicited implicitly. Such implicitly elicited words are attributes of the memory for the task. For a specific word in the task, the attribute is usually identified as the overt response produced in word association procedures. Thus, the verbal attribute might consist of an antonym, or a synonym, or a category name, although sometimes a phrase may be elicited. Any given learning task may result in the production of one class of attributes more frequently than those of another. For example, if a number of words in a free recall task are names of objects which all belong to the same category, the category name may predominate as the attribute for all words in the category. In general, it may be said that the immediate recall of words in a free recall task is influenced positively by the verbal attribute when the same categorical attribute is elicited by more than one word, or when the verbal attribute for a given word is, in addition, a word in the list. However, the verbal attribute may, in certain situations, decrease the accuracy of a memory. This may occur, for example, whenever the memory test requires a discrimination between the word to be remembered and its verbal attribute (e.g., Anisfeld & Knapp, 1968). It must be clear, therefore, that like the other attributes, the verbal attributes may be sources of interference as well as providing bases for distinguishing one memory from another.

In the usual paired-associate task, unrelated words are paired and several such pairs make up the task. In a sense, the learning consists of developing an artificial associative attribute (the response term) for the stimulus word of each pair. Learning is said to have occurred when S can produce the response term when the stimulus term is presented. When we present an A-B, A-C transfer paradigm, we are changing the attribute in learning the second list, or giving the stimulus term a second artificial attribute. When we present an A-B, C-B paradigm, we are using the same attribute for two different stimulus words. However, considering the bidirectional nature of associations (Ekstrand, 1966), the word in a pair to be called the attribute is quite arbitrary; in effect, each becomes an artificial attribute of the other.

As a consequence of prior learning, the stimulus term in a paired-associate task has associative attributes prior to learning the paired-associate task. The same is true of the response term. Many reports indicate that these attributes may serve as mediators between the stimulus term and the response term so that the establishment of the so-called artificial attribute may be indirect.

Class Attributes

A memory may carry with it information concerning the class of events involved. If a paired-associate list has numbers as response terms, this information will undoubtedly be retained even if S is unable to provide the appropriate number for each stimulus term. If the response terms are three-letter words, it would be rare for S on a retention test to produce words with more or less than three letters. If a list of nonsense syllables makes up a free recall task, a retention test will rarely show three-letter words appearing. Now, in fact, this attribute probably plays a minor role in most laboratory studies of memory because the experimenter (E) usually specifies to S the class of events involved. The E tells him to recall as many appropriate numbers as possible; E tells him to recall as many nonsense syllables as he can. Only when class boundaries are seemingly unimportant or nondiscriminative is E likely to omit such information on the retention test. Even in less structured situations, the search among memories for a particular memory does not take place without "instruction" concerning the class attribute. In searching our memory for a particular technical term, we normally do not search for it among the names of acquaintances.

SOME IMPLICATIONS AND SPECULATIONS

Retention Tests

Within the conception just outlined, it becomes apparent that when measuring memory, two considerations are essential in interpreting the measurements. The first is the nature of the attributes making up a memory, and the second is the attributes emphasized by the retention test. The more consonant these are, the higher will be the retention. Thus, if a memory consists of associative attributes A and B, with B the target, the presentation of A on a recall test should yield a higher retention score than if A is not presented. On the other hand, given the same situation and a recognition test, correct recognition of B will be higher if C and B are presented for a binary choice than if A and B are presented for such a choice.

It appears that certain of the attributes serve primarily as discriminative attributes, others primarily as retrieval attributes. The pure case of a discriminative attribute is frequency. There does not seem to be any way by which frequency per se can serve as a retrieval attribute for a target event. The temporal, spatial, and modality attributes also appear to emphasize the discriminative function over the retrieval function, with retrieval being the primary role of the associative attributes. However, these different functions are by no means clear at the present time. Only in the case of frequency does the discriminative function seem clear and unique. Frequency differences, it is believed, are primarily responsible for the discriminations involved in recognition memory. Given a single acquisition trial on a long list of common words, recognition performance measured by binary choices may be as high as 90% correct (Shepard, 1967). That recognition performance is normally much higher than recall after a single trial is accounted for by two factors. First, a single trial is sufficient to establish a discriminable frequency difference between words presented for study and those not presented, whereas, and this is the second factor, more trials (or study time) are necessary to establish the associative attributes which will produce correct recall. Further, for the associative attributes at least, there is some evidence that a search for a particular target word in a recall test will not occur unless the associative attribute presented at recall is first recognized as being an attribute of the target word (e.g., Martin, 1967). Indeed, concerning the associative attributes, it is worth repeating that a particular target event and its attributes are undifferentiated except for their function at any moment of attempted recall. That one word, for example, is recognized as the target word and another as the attribute rests on a discrimination produced by other attributes. When these other attributes fail to provide a discrimination between the target word and its associative attribute or attributes, intrusions in free recall (e.g., Deese, 1959) or errors in recognition (e.g., Anisfeld & Knapp, 1968) will occur with relatively high frequency.

Studies of incidental versus intentional learning may be viewed as studies in which the attributes of memory are investigated. Postman (1964) has long maintained that a major difference between intentional and incidental Ss is in the occurrence of verbal associative attributes, these being more predominant for the former Ss. The incidental S, on the other hand, may predominate on other attributes, such as the acoustic attribute (Wallace, 1968). Without knowing the nature of the task, and the nature of the memory test, it is not possible to predict the relative retention of incidental and intentional Ss.

Multiple Attributes

Whenever one or more attributes are a part of two or more different target memories, interference may occur in recall attempts. The greater the number of different attributes making up a memory, and the less these attributes are parts of other memories, the less the interference, hence, the less the forgetting. In unlearning, the attribute (or attributes) of one memory is displaced to another. During A-C learning in the A-B, A-C paradigm, C replaces B as the associative attribute of A so that A cannot directly serve as an attribute in the recall of B. That unlearning is seldom complete suggests that other attributes, specific to the A-B pairs, do not become unlearned during A-C acquisition. Just what these other attributes are is not known.

However, it does not seem unreasonable to suggest that A-B as a memory unit may include an attribute which is distinctly different from any of those included in A-C as a unit. Such differential attributes would most likely develop when number of trials on a task is high. Multiple attributes always allow more than one route to a target memory. Most have had the experience of being unable to recall a name, or a term, only to have it suddenly "pop into mind" at a later time. It may be presumed that an attribute, not previously present, was elicited by the changed situation and that this attribute was responsible for the recall.

Development and Forgetting of Attributes

As S learns a task, it is presumed that certain attributes are developing which not only allow him to perform the task at the moment, but also to constitute the long-term memory of the task. Undoubtedly, not all reactions produced by a learning situation remain as attributes; some drop out and some are stored as the permanent memory. If S is given a paired-associate list of high intralist similarity, attributes which are normally evoked in a learning situation may be inappropriate as discriminative attributes, and to master the task, their occurrence must be eliminated in some manner, or truly discriminative attributes developed to a stronger level. Once learning has occurred, attributes may be forgotten at different rates. Some attributes may be forgotten more rapidly than others because they become a part of other memories, hence are displaced as a part of the original memory. Other attributes, which are satisfactory for discrimination purposes at the time of learning, may cease to be so after a lapse of time. For example, a temporal discrimination that is based on a relatively short difference in time during learning may be quite inadequate for such discrimination after a retention interval of a week. Yet, in fact, little is known about the differential development and forgetting of attributes, but if forgetting is to be understood, and if the present orientation is appropriate for developing this understanding, an experimental attack on these problems will be necessary. There are already some beginnings; for example, Baddeley and Dale (1966) have suggested that acoustic attributes are of primary importance in short-term memory, whereas verbal associative attributes are of primary importance in long-term memory.

Developmental Changes

The attributes which are established as a memory during learning may differ as a function of the developmental stage. In a very young child, the associative attributes may be subordinate to other attributes, particularly the acoustic and spatial. If there are primordial attributes, the acoustic and spatial are the most likely ones. It sometimes seems that when a learning task made up of difficult letter sequences (e.g., consonant syllables) is imposed on adult Ss, these Ss are forced to revert to the more primordial attributes to master the task because these materials do not elicit the attributes commonly produced by more meaningful material.

As a child ages, and particularly as he concomitantly is exposed to successive learning experiences in the school systems, the primary attributes developed in learning may change, with the associative verbal attributes becoming more and more common. At the far extreme, senility, where new learning is minimal (or forgetting very rapid), it appears that few if any attributes are established at the time an event occurs. There is some evidence that the retardate is less likely to establish associative verbal attributes than is the normal (e.g., Wallace & Underwood, 1964). But again, whether retention will differ for normals and retardates depends in part at least on the nature of the memory test (Wallace, 1967).

It cannot be expected that all young adults will, as a consequence of their experiences, develop the same attributes in a given learning situation. This is merely to say that there are individual differences in the preferred or dominant attributes. Therefore, it cannot be expected that the correlation in learning across tasks, tasks which emphasize different attributes, will be particularly high. It would seem that the study of individual differences in learning might begin with a study of the dominant attributes which S may bring to tasks in general, and, in addition, the ease with which he can shift attributes when the dominant ones are inappropriate for a task.

CONCLUSION

The conception developed in this paper views the memory for an event as consisting of a collection of attributes. The notions advanced are not incompatible with statements about memory traces as long as the plural is emphasized. The conception is neutral with regard to the topography of memory. It can accommodate the memory of an idea or relationship as well as the memory for a more discrete event, such as a word. It has emphasized the multiattribute characteristic of a memory in the belief that understanding of interference among attributes will be ultimately enhanced thereby, because various tasks and procedures used in the learning laboratory must lead to the development of different attributive hierarchies.

The notion that the multidimensional nature of a memory must be recognized is not new. Wallach and Averbach (1955) made a similar proposal; Wickelgren's (1966) distinctive-feature analysis emphasizes subattributes within the acoustic stimulus; Bower (1967) has proposed a multicomponent theory of memory. The present article merely expands the number of attributes with which we must be concerned, but even so, no claim of comprehensiveness is intended.

REFERENCES

Anisfeld, M., & Knapp, M. Association, synonymity, and directionality in false recognition. *Journal of Experimental Psychology*, 1968, 77, 171-179.

Asch, S. E., Hay, J., & Diamond, R. M. Perceptual organization in serial rote-learning. *American Journal of Psychology*, 1960, 73, 177-198.

Attneave, F. Psychological probability as a function of experienced frequency. *Journal of Experimental Psychology*, 1953, 46, 81-86.

Baddeley, A. D., & Dale, H. C. A. The effect of semantic similarity on retroactive interference in long- and short-term memory. *Journal of Verbal Learning and Verbal Behavior*, 1966, 5, 417-420.

Berlyne, D. E. Effects of spatial order and interitem interval on recall of temporal order. *Psychonomic Science*, 1966, 6, 375-376.

Bilodeau, I. M., & Schlosberg, H. Similarity in stimulating conditions as a variable in retroactive inhibition. *Journal of Experimental Psychology*, 1951, 41, 199-204.

Bower, G. A multicomponent theory of the memory trace. In K. W. Spence & J. T. Spence (Eds.), *The psychology of learning and motivation*. Vol. 1. New York: Academic Press, 1967.

Brown, R., & McNeil, D. The "tip of the tongue" phenomenon. *Journal of Verbal Learning and Verbal Behavior*, 1966, 5, 325-337.

Conrad, R. Acoustic confusions in immediate memory. *British Journal of Psychology*, 1964, 55, 75-84.

Deese, J. On the prediction of occurrence of particular verbal intrusions in immediate recall. *Journal of Experimental Psychology*, 1959, 58, 17-22.

Ebenholtz, S. M. Position mediated transfer between serial learning and a spatial discrimination task. *Journal of Experimental Psychology*, 1963, 65, 603-608.

Ekstrand, B. Backward associations. *Psychological Bulletin*, 1966, 65, 50-64.

Erlick, D. E. Absolute judgments of discrete quantities randomly distributed over time. *Journal of Experimental Psychology*, 1964, 67, 475-482.

Goggin, J. First-list recall as a function of second-list learning method. *Journal of Verbal Learning and Verbal Behavior*, 1967, 6, 423-427.

Gottlieb, W., & Lindauer, M. S. The effect of contextual stimuli on retroactive inhibition. *Psychonomic Science*, 1967, 9, 331-332.

Hart, J. T. Second-try recall, recognition, and the memory-monitoring process. *Journal of Educational Psychology*, 1967, 58, 193-197.

Hintzman, D. L. Articulatory coding in short-term memory. *Journal of Verbal Learning and Verbal Behavior,* 1967, 6, 312–316.
Horowitz, L. M., White, M. A., & Atwood, D. W. Word fragments as aids to recall: The organization of a word. *Journal of Experimental Psychology,* 1968, 76, 219–226.
Inoue, K. A study on interaction among sense modalities in memory. *Journal of Child Development,* 1968, 4, 28–37.
McGeoch, J. A., & Irion, A. L. *The psychology of human learning.* New York: Longmans, 1952.
Marchbanks, G., & Levin, H. Cues by which children recognize words. *Journal of Educational Psychology,* 1965, 56, 57–61.
Martin, E. Relation between stimulus recognition and paired-associate learning. *Journal of Experimental Psychology,* 1967, 74, 500–505.
Monty, R. A. Spatial encoding strategies in sequential short-term memory. *Journal of Experimental Psychology,* 1968, 77, 506–508.
Morton, J. Repeated items and decay in memory. *Psychonomic Science,* 1968, 10, 219–220.
Murdock, B. B., Jr. Modality effects in short-term memory: Storage or retrieval? *Journal of Experimental Psychology,* 1968, 77, 79–86.
Nagge, J. An experimental test of the theory of associative interference. *Journal of Experimental Psychology,* 1935, 18, 663–682.
Paivio, A., & Madigan, S. A. Imagery and association value in paired-associate learning. *Journal of Experimental Psychology,* 1968, 76, 35–39.
Postman, L. Short-term memory and incidental learning. In A. W. Melton (Ed.), *Categories of human learning.* New York: Academic Press, 1964.
Shepard, R. N. Recognition memory for words, sentences, and pictures. *Journal of Verbal Learning and Verbal Behavior,* 1967, 6, 156–163.
Slamecka, N. J. Serial learning and order information. *Journal of Experimental Psychology,* 1967, 74, 62–66.
Smith, K. H. Grammatical intrusions in the recall of structured letter pairs: Mediated transfer or position learning? *Journal of Experimental Psychology,* 1966, 72, 580–588.
Turvey, M. T. Analysis of augmented recall in short-term memory following a shift in connotation. *British Journal of Psychology,* 1968, 59, 131–137.
Underwood, B. J. Retroactive inhibition with increased recall time. *American Journal of Psychology,* 1950, 63, 67–77.
Underwood, B. J. Some correlates of item repetition in free-recall learning. *Journal of Verbal Learning and Verbal Behavior,* 1969, 8, 83–94.
Underwood, B. J., & Ekstrand, B. R. An analysis of some shortcomings in the interference theory of forgetting. *Psychological Review,* 1966, 73, 540–549.
Underwood, B. J., & Ekstrand, B. R. Linguistic associations and retention. *Journal of Verbal Learning and Verbal Behavior,* 1968, 7, 162–171.
Underwood, B. J., & Freund, J. S. Effect of temporal separation of two tasks on proactive inhibition. *Journal of Experimental Psychology,* 1968, 78, 50–54. (a)
Underwood, B. J., & Freund, J. S. Errors in recognition learning and retention. *Journal of Experimental Psychology,* 1968, 78, 55–63. (b)

Wallace, W. P. Implicit associative response occurrence in learning with retarded subjects: A supplementary report. *Journal of Educational Psychology,* 1967, 58, 110–114.

Wallace, W. P. Incidental learning: The influence of associative similarity and formal similarity in producing false recognitions. *Journal of Verbal Learning and Verbal Behavior,* 1968, 7, 50–54.

Wallace, W. P., & Underwood, B. J. Implicit responses and the role of intralist similarity in verbal learning by normal and retarded subjects. *Journal of Educational Psychology,* 1964, 55, 362–370.

Wallach, H., & Averbach, E. On memory modalities. *American Journal of Psychology,* 1955, 68, 249–257.

Wickelgren, W. A. Acoustic similarity and intrusion errors in short-term memory. *Journal of Experimental Psychology,* 1965, 70, 102–108.

Wickelgren, W. A. Distinctive features and errors in short-term memory for English consonants. *Journal of the Acoustical Society of America,* 1966, 39, 388–398.

Wickens, D. D., & Eckler, G. R. Semantic as opposed to acoustic encoding in STM. *Psychonomic Science,* 1968, 12, 63.

Winograd, E. List differentiation as a function of frequency and retention interval. *Journal of Experimental Psychology Monograph Supplement,* 1968, 76(2, Pt. 2).

Yates, F. A. *The art of memory.* Chicago: University of Chicago Press, 1966.

Yavuz, H. S., & Bousfield, W. A. Recall of connotative meaning. *Psychological Reports,* 1959, 5, 319–320.

Yntema, D. B., & Trask, F. P. Recall as a search process. *Journal of Verbal Learning and Verbal Behavior,* 1963, 2, 65–74.

Zavortink, B. L. Retroactive inhibition in free-recall learning of conceptually related words as a function of change of context and interlist similarity. Unpublished doctoral dissertation, University of California, 1968.

6
Current Perspectives

In this concluding chapter I will attempt to describe the current status of the areas of research taken up in the earlier chapters. In some cases this can be done quickly; in others, extended discussion is required. In addition, I will comment on related topics if I have had direct research contact with them. It seems likely that certain pronouncements will inevitably infiltrate this final chapter, although I will do what I can to avoid them.

PROACTIVE INHIBITION

By the late 1950s it appeared that PI must be central in developing theories to account for long-term forgetting that occurs outside the laboratory. We knew that both RI and PI could produce very heavy forgetting when studied entirely within the laboratory. In the sense that McGeoch (1932) held up RI as a model for all forgetting, it seemed that we could hold up both RI and PI as models, but with the emphasis on PI. In describing these developments it will be useful to keep several stages separate.

Interference Outside the Laboratory

There may be certain phenomena that require such a unique set of conditions for their occurrence that they might be referred to as laboratory curios. Some of the visual illusions, such as the Muller-Lyer illusion, might be placed in this category, although researchers in perception would probably disagree. However, it was unthinkable to conceive of RI and PI as laboratory curios because they occurred under such a broad range of conditions. It seemed necessary to conceive of them as having representation in our everyday forgetting—

forgetting that occurs outside the laboratory. It seemed to me that the issues might be subsumed in a simple question, namely, how to account for the forgetting that is observed when a naive subject learns a single list in the laboratory and is then tested for retention 24 hours later. Roughly speaking, a loss of 20 percent would be expected. My orientation leads me to assert that this loss must be attributed to interference, both PI and RI; but because no interfering list was acquired in the laboratory, the source of RI and PI must lie outside the laboratory. Furthermore, it seemed reasonable to assume that it was very probable that the source of interference would be PI rather than RI. The PI could arise from any of the enormous number of associations learned over the past years, whereas RI could come only from associations learned outside the laboratory during the 24-hour retention interval.

A formalized version of this thinking was published in 1960 (Underwood, 1960, 2). In this theory we assumed that during the learning of the single list in the laboratory by the naive subject, the associations required in learning the list would be to some degree in conflict with associations previously learned outside the laboratory. Or, in PI terms, the associations learned previously constituted A-B, those of the single list learned in the laboratory, A-D. Conflicting associations such as this would result in the unlearning of A-B, but these associations would spontaneously recover with time, and PI would be produced at recall. We viewed this theory as one in which laboratory phenomena (such as unlearning) were assumed to occur outside the laboratory. In other words, the theoretical "action" was isomorphic to observed laboratory action.

This theory made some very explicit predictions. We believed we knew enough about the verbal repertoire of our college-student subjects to construct lists that varied in the degree to which they were in conflict with already established associations. The greater the amount of conflict, the greater the ultimate interference at the time of recall. In other words, we developed lists that appeared to differ in the likelihood that the associations required in learning would be antithetical in some way to the association the subjects had learned previously outside the laboratory. Different groups of naive subjects, then, learn the lists, which differ in the degree to which the associations conflict with previous learning. The prediction is that the forgetting rate will be directly related to the amount of conflict between the associations required in learning the list and associations already acquired. To simplify somewhat, if the association to be learned in the laboratory was *cup-wall,* that association would be in conflict with *cup-saucer* and *cup-coffee.* Therefore, forgetting should have been greater if the task involved the learning of *cup-wall* than if it involved the learning of *cup-saucer.*

A variety of tests of this theory were made, both by its originators and by other more disinterested parties. Fortunately, there was almost complete agreement in assessing the theory in light of the findings; the theory simply was not supported. Among other things, this conclusion shows that the elegance and integrity of a theory have nothing to do with its value. But it is to the "other things" that our attention must be directed. Two of these will be examined.

Tests of the theory essentially required an examination of forgetting as a function of the meaningfulness of the material, and these tests showed that meaningfulness was not a pertinent variable in producing different rates of forgetting. In a more general sense, the research over the past two decades or so has shown that task variables (such as meaningfulness, intralist similarity, concreteness) that may produce very large differences in the rate of learning have little if any influence on the rate of forgetting. It seems that as researchers we must accept the idea of finite causality, the idea that not every event in the world can influence every other event. In the case of learning, one might sometimes believe that this assumption is in error because we keep discovering more and more variables that do influence learning. In the case of forgetting, however, the research has led to the opposite conclusion; forgetting is influenced by fewer variables than originally believed.

The second point concerns the theory per se. Where did the theory go wrong? We have no firm answer to this question, although some evidence indicates that linguistic associations of long standing do not interfere appreciably with so-called conflicting associations being learned in the laboratory (Underwood, 1966, 5). This may well be another instance of the interference paradox discussed in Chapter 1. Our attempt to build a theoretical bridge from the laboratory to real life was unsuccessful, but I am more firmly convinced than ever that we were on the right track. That is, I cannot yet accept the proposition that RI and PI are of no consequence to the forgetting we observe outside the laboratory. I remain steadfast in my belief that the problem is not with the basic approach. Rather, there must be an error in the translation. Sooner or later the correct translation will occur to someone.

Further Turbulence

The failure of the foregoing theory, as well as some disenchantment with the details of interference production, led to some critical reappraisals of interference theory and some rather sharp criticisms of it. I will not cover these issues in detail, but I do want to point out some of the problems. More extensive discussion may be found in Underwood (1973, 4) and the references given therein.

The two-factor theory of RI was based on two components—competition at recall and the unlearning of the first-list associations because of the learning of the second, interfering task. One could proceed with this theory by viewing unlearning as a hypothetical construct, but from the beginning it seemed worthwhile to try to devise a set of operations that would allow direct measurement of the presumed phenomenon. The crucial aspect of any such operation was that the loss due to unlearning must not include any of the loss due to competition. One way this might have been done at an early stage in our understanding was by using amount of PI as an index of forgetting due to competition, and the difference between RI and PI as the amount due to unlearning. The trouble with these equations was that it was known that over time RI and PI became equivalent in amount (Underwood, 1948, 1). Perhaps one should eliminate unlearning from the theory. But such a step could not be justified because RI was greater than PI when retention intervals were short. Something had to be left in the theory to fill in the gap. One possibility was to treat unlearning as if it were an extinction process as observed in the conditioning laboratory. The extinction, then, might be followed by spontaneous recovery (Underwood, 1948, 2). This would certainly fill in the gap. Still, there remained a felt need for a direct measure of unlearning if one could be found.

A direct measure of unlearning was offered in 1959 (Underwood, 1959, 2). The procedure was simple. The subjects learned A-B followed by A-D, and then on the test they were given the A terms and were asked to provide both of the response terms that had been learned to each stimulus term. Essentially unlimited time was allowed. Because the subjects were to try to give both response terms, there was a belief that interference could not, or at least would not, occur. The technique came to be known as MMFR for reasons that need not be reported here. The results of the experiment showed that the subjects could produce only about half of the B response terms. It appeared that the other response terms had indeed been unlearned or extinguished; the subjects apparently simply could not find them. Given this outcome, it now appeared that unlearning could rightfully take its place in the two-factor theory as an empirical concept. Things looked promising.

The history of unlearning over the past twenty years is an exceedingly complex one, and I will not follow it in detail here. Numerous experiments were conducted to determine what is lost when unlearning occurs, how the loss is related to various transfer paradigms, and whether or not the loss differs in amount as a function of type of materials. At the same time, many tests were made to determine whether spontaneous recovery of the extinguished or unlearned associations could be detected.

In the original study using the MMFR technique, as well as in many others that followed, the recall of the second-list items was essentially perfect when the tests were made immediately after learning A-D. This could be taken as further evidence that competition was not involved in the leisurely recall procedures of the MMFR. However, some disquieting reports began to be heard to the effect that the MMFR was not free from competition. This, if true, would be a serious disruption in the development of forgetting theory. How does one tell whether there is competition in the MMFR? Perhaps the best way is to find out if PI occurs in MMFR. That is, if the recall of A-D under MMFR is less than the recall of A-D for a control (not having A-B), it must represent competition because A-D could not have been unlearned. Of course, reports of competition in MMFR were limited to studies wherein tests were made sometime after the learning of A-D. Such reports came from several different laboratories, and I also found severe competition in MMFR when appropriate tests were made (Underwood, 1977, 1, Experiment 6).

That the MMFR may allow competition has two implications. First, the analytical power thought to be inherent in MMFR is lost. Second, and more important, there is the possibility that no unlearning occurs. The basic observation indicating unlearning comes when A-B and A-D are learned in immediate succession and the MMFR administered at once. The basic observation is that recall of A-B is less than when A-D is not learned (control). It is possible that this loss is due to competition from A-D associations that block some of the A-B associations. However, even if this is not true in its entirety, there is the very real possibility that some of the loss of A-B attributed to unlearning is actually due to competition. This relates back to the first point, that the MMFR may have lost its usefulness as a means of separating decrements due to competition from decrements due to unlearning. There is no replacement in sight.

Current Assessment

My current belief is that PI may be understood in its entirety by relating the competition (which produces PI) to list differentiation or list discrimination. Notions of spontaneous recovery of interfering tasks are really not essential in accounting for PI, although if it turns out that spontaneous recovery cannot be ignored, it can probably be accommodated in terms of its role in determining list discrimination.

First, I want to describe a case in which list discrimination was perhaps completely destroyed (Underwood, 1968, 3). In this study the subjects learned two 12-pair lists having the A-B, A-D relationship. In one of the conditions six of the A-B pairs were retained in the A-D list. That is, six of the A-B pairs, learned in the first list, occurred without change in the second list. Thus there were only six of the pairs that truly formed interference paradigms. The idea was that by carrying over half the pairs intact from the first to the second list, the subjects could be deprived of temporal cues that normally would be used to differentiate the two lists. The two lists were learned in immediate succession with recall of the second list being taken after 24 hours. Scoring of recall was based only on the six items that had formed the A-B, A-D paradigm. The paced recall attempts showed 73 correct responses for the 30 subjects, and 66 intrusions from the first list. Essentially, the subjects could not discriminate between the first and second lists. This is what I mean when I say that there is a complete loss of list discrimination.

At the other extreme, we have devised procedures that essentially make discrimination between A-B and A-D perfect (Underwood, 1968, 3). This was done by having the A-B learning and A-D learning widely separated in time. In our study the separation was three days. Recall of the A-D took place 24 hours after learning. The recall of A-D was 65 percent correct when three days separated the learning of A-B and A-D, and was 38 percent correct when the two lists were learned in immediate succession. The three-day separation essentially eliminated PI. I must hasten to add that these findings, although quite replicable, are in some way related to the type of materials making up the lists (Underwood, 1977, 1). I was not able to confirm the aforementioned differences when the list materials were inadvertently changed. This failure to replicate with changed materials does not deny the previous findings because they have been replicated. It seems that there are certain unknown task characteristics that interact with temporal separation; at present I do not know what these critical task characteristics are. One could presume, however, that even with the materials that failed to reduce PI, the amount of PI could be varied by lengthening the time between the learning of the two tasks and by shortening the length of the retention interval. Beyond this, it has become obvious that we need a series of studies on the relationships between task variables and list differentiation. In addition to asking about the effect of the word characteristics on list differentiation (and hence on PI), we need to know about the influence of various encoding operations. For example, depth-of-processing manipulations influence recall in a striking manner. Therefore, they might be expected to influence list discriminations.

The importance of list discrimination in varying the amount of PI has been illustrated in a quite different way in our very recent research. We have been conducting more or less exploratory studies using what we call *simultaneous learning.* In simultaneous learning the subjects are given two or more lists to learn at once. Thus far we have always used items in the two or more lists that are clearly discriminable. If two lists are involved, for example, one might consist of animal names, the other of vegetable names. On the study trials the subjects are shown two words at a time, one an animal name, the other a vegetable name. Then another pair is shown (a second animal name and a second vegetable name), and so on down through the list. Memory is tested separately for the two lists.

In one study using simultaneous learning (Underwood, 1979, 2), the subjects acquired three lists, and recall was taken after 24 hours. The recall of one of these lists was compared with its recall after being learned singly. Recall was 38 percent better following simultaneous learning than following single-list learning. On the surface it would seem that interference would be greater on the recall of one of the lists when the three lists had been learned than when a single list was learned. As indicated by the results, this was not the case. The results suggest that simultaneous learning increased the discrimination between the lists and other sources of interference. I believe these other sources to be of a proactive nature, but they have not yet been identified. Needless to say, we are carrying out further work using simultaneous learning. We know thus far that recall is enhanced by simultaneous learning regardless of the types of lists (free recall, serial, paired associate) that are learned (Underwood, 1980, 2).

Although the amount of PI and the amount of list differentiation seem to be reasonable correlates, there are some situations that produce interpretive problems. Consider a study done by Keppel, Postman, and Zavortink (1968). Their subjects learned and recalled 36 successive paired-associate lists made up of 10 pairs of common words. The learning was carried to a criterion of one perfect recitation, and recall was taken after 48 hours. A second list was then learned, and it too was recalled after 48 hours. This continued for 36 lists. It should be emphasized that the words in the lists were unrelated except insofar as high-frequency words will be interassociated. These investigators found recall to decrease with each successive list; the recall of the first list was 70 percent, the recall of the 36th list was 4 percent. This appears to be indicative of a PI phenomenon and might also seem to fit in with the general notion that PI results from a loss of list discrimination.

The list-discrimination interpretation may be correct, but there is a problem of specifying the particular nature of the interfering associations. Each word in the Keppel et al. study occurred in only one list. On recall the subject was shown each stimulus term for 3 seconds, during which time the subject attempted to produce the response term paired with it during learning. Since each stimulus word was unique, whence did the interference arise? We noted that high-frequency words are interassociated by cultural usage, and we might suspect that this is responsible for the buildup in PI. However, other research has shown that the buildup is not related to word frequency (Underwood, 1967, 4). Another possible source of interference could be the formal similarity among the words. Such similarity is seen most clearly in prefixes and suffixes, which are almost inevitably repeated across a large number of words; but the formal similarity may also obtain within the body of words. Essentially, then, interference could increase across lists because of an increase in both visual and acoustical similarity. I believe that these souces of PI are most probably responsible for the massive PI buildup observed in the Keppel et al. study.

In Chapter 1 I pointed out that PI in short-term memory (using the Brown-Peterson procedures) was based on the same sort of interference as was the PI in list-learning procedures with relatively long retention intervals. It can also be argued that the amount of interference that occurs in short-term memory is related to discrimination between successive items. For example, if the time interval between successive trials (presenting and recalling a single unit) is increased, PI decreases, suggesting that a temporal discrimination is enhanced, thereby reducing interference.

I now think it unlikely that the interference mechanisms involved in the PI buildup in short-term and long-term memory are parallel. In the long-term situation, the acquisition of the two or more interfering lists is carried to the same level of learning. In the short-term studies no such equation in learning occurs. Thus the decrease in recall with each successive item tested in short-term memory may indicate only that less and less learning occurred with each successive item. It is quite possible that the so-called PI buildup in short-term memory procedures represents an increase in negative transfer comparable to the negative transfer observed in list learning of A-D following the learning of A-B. This issue has been discussed by many investigators over the years, and there have been a number of attempts to make empirical determinations of whether the PI buildup in short-term memory is a storage effect or a retrieval effect. Such attempts have not been convincing (see Radtke & Grove, 1977, for a comprehensive discussion of the issues involved). What is needed is a way to make the learning of each successive item equivalent in the Brown-Peterson procedure. Then PI could be studied as a function of the number of prior items learned. Given this solution, the short-term techniques might come to give us the benefits that seemed likely when these techniques were first developed. Hours and days (necessary to study PI in long-term studies) might be reduced to seconds and minutes, thereby producing a far more efficient use of time and other resources. The potential of the short-term technique has not been fully realized for the study of PI because of the ambiguity associated with the so-called PI buildup.

What Happened to RI?

My concentration on PI here came about because of the papers reprinted on that topic. Of course, if my reasoning is correct, when relatively short retention intervals are used, the thinking that makes RI and PI the models of interference must emphasize PI. Laboratory-produced RI and PI become roughly equivalent in amount within 24–48 hours following learning; but if theoretical attention is directed toward forgetting which occurs outside of the laboratory, the interference potential is much greater from PI sources than from RI sources. Nevertheless, I do not want to conclude that RI should be ignored. When retention intervals are long, RI must be due in part to a loss of list differentiation, just as in the case of PI. Studies of list differentiation, ostensibly directed toward an understanding of PI, will also have direct application to RI. Furthermore, if someone can invent a technique for sorting out unlearning from competition, we might again direct our attention to RI more than to PI.

IMPLICIT ASSOCIATIVE RESPONSES

As discussed earlier, it is a straightforward matter to implicate implicit associative responses (IARs) in an interference-producing situation. An intrusion from an interfering list indicates a case in which the IAR got above some type of threshold, perhaps a threshold of belief in the correctness of the response tendency. The identification of IARs with interference might lead one to ask how it is possible to get away from interference. How are we able, in a relatively short period of time, to set aside or in some way avoid the IAR and hence the interference. I will discuss some failures in IAR theory as a means of opening up this issue.

Failures of IAR Theory

We recently published a paper reporting a factor analysis of a number of verbal-learning tasks (Underwood, 1978, 2). Among the tasks was one using running recognition, set up to obtain false-recognition responses produced (we assumed) by IARs induced earlier in the sequence. Because we wanted to have a measure of the reliability of false recognitions, we gave the subjects two independent running-recognition tests. The results for the first test provided the usual false-alarm effect, but on the second test there was no effect. One might suspect that this was a statistical fluke of some kind but for the fact that at least one other case has been reported of the failure of the false alarms for the experimental items to be greater than those for the control items (Toglia & Kimble, 1976). Furthermore, it is likely that other investigators have failed to find the effect but that, as often happens, negative results are not reported. Furthermore, if one examines the data in the second reprinted article in Chapter 3, it will be seen that not all types of items (presuming to produce predictable IARs) showed an IAR effect. These various instances seem to indicate that some shielding process may occur so that the subjects are not completely dependent on the IARs, yet may use them when it is to their advantage to do so. To these instances of the failure of IARs to lead to their expected effect, we may add other failures associated with IARs and frequency theory.

Frequency theory, as originally formulated, made provisions for adding IAR frequency to situational frequency, and some evidence was found to support this idea. However, since that time the evidence has been generally negative in the sense that predictions based on IAR-produced frequency have not been supported. Some of these predictions may be illustrated. Suppose that the pairs of words in a verbal-discrimination task all consisted of high associates, such as *king-queen, up-down,* and so on. A strict interpretation of IAR and frequency theory would say that a list composed of such pairs could not be learned. Each word in the pair would elicit the other implicitly, so that there would be no way for the correct word to gain a superiority in frequency. Suppose that *king* and *queen* were not paired but were both correct words in their pairs. The IARs in this case should facilitate learning because they would increase the frequency of the correct word in the pairs. One may also vary conceptually related words and expect IARs to influence the frequency relationship in a specified way.

Experiments testing the various expectations of IARs in verbal-discrimination learning have been essentially negative, both in our laboratory and in others (for example, Kanak, Cole, & Eckert, 1972; Underwood, 1973, 5). Generally speaking, it has been found that subjects proceed to learn as if there were no related words in the lists. However, the failure of IARs to operate as expected does not in any way work detrimentally on frequency theory as based on direct situational frequency differences of items in the list. The inclusion of IAR frequency as an addition to situational frequency just does not seem to work in verbal-discrimination learning, despite the fact that it meets expectations in some types of recognition tasks (for example, Bach, 1974).

The foregoing illustrations are said to represent a failure of IAR theory, but the failure involved in these cases may represent control of the memory system to a degree not previously recognized. I interpret the evidence to indicate that two things may be happening in the cases discussed previously and others like them. First, the subject (by some unknown means) may prevent the IARs from occurring. Second, the IARs may occur, but the subjects may be capable of keeping these implicit responses in some neutral corner of the memory system. Keeping the responses in a neutral zone might be dependent on the subject recognizing that to allow them to enter actively into performance would be counterproductive.

I believe there are cases in which the subject essentially turns off the IARs, thereby effectively preventing them from becoming a part of the memories being formed. This must be true in the cases wherein IAR expectations have not been supported in verbal-discrimination learning. I have no reason to believe that IARs *always* occur to common words during the learning of a task, but I do not know the conditions under which IARs are likely to occur and those under which they are unlikely to occur. It appears that subjects have some control over this matter and that by some means they prevent IARs from occurring under some conditions.

The other possibility noted earlier is that subjects maintain different types of information in memory but only use a given type when appropriate. Galbraith (1975) has shown that subjects can keep frequency information and associative information quite separate and not let one type interfere with performance based on the other type.

I should not overemphasize the failures of IAR theory, for in fact it has had numerous successes. It is a theory well worth keeping at the present time.

Acquisition of Associations

Many mnemonic systems require the use of already established associations. In a sense, we build new associative relationships on top of old ones. But sooner or later in the study of verbal learning we must at least ask again how associations are formed initially. It seems to me that we must accept as fact the existence of an enormous number of associations among the words we have stored in memory. How were these associations established? How are associations we learn today established?

The sheer number of associations existing in our memories makes it seem unlikely that all were established as a result of intentional learning, wherein one says, in effect, "I am going to learn that." In fact, I think that very few associations are established in this manner. I also choose to believe that notions of reinforcement have no place in attempts to understand how the human organism establishes associations between words. The mechanisms that are required to produce associations must be automatic to some degree, but they must also be selective so that everything will not be associated with everything else. As far as I can tell, only the concept of *temporal contiguity* will satisfy the two requirements. This hoary concept has been around for centuries, but its age cannot be used to deny that it has a fundamental role to play. The question is what sort of role it does play.

Some may reject entirely the idea that contiguity plays a role in the establishment of associations between verbal units, but I doubt it. In fact, many might say that contiguity is a necessary condition. What is denied is that contiguity is a sufficient condition for the formation of associations. It is possible to cite studies that apparently demonstrate that contiguity per se is not a sufficient condition for associative formation (for example, Thorndike, 1932). There are also studies from my laboratory that concluded that contiguity is a sufficient condition (Underwood, 1964, 10; 1980, 1).

When the conclusion is reached that contiguity is not a sufficient condition for verbal-associative formation, the issue remains of what other factor or condition must be added to temporal contiguity in order for learning to occur. Thorndike (1932) used the concept of *belonging*, but most who deny that contiguity is a sufficient condition are hard pressed to suggest other factors that must be implicated before learning occurs. I do not think it is possible to show that contiguity per se has no effect. There is the obvious variable of the frequency of contiguous occurrences as an auxiliary variable, and it is always possible that learning would have been observed had more trials been given. This is an underhanded argument, which I dislike, but it is not an irrelevant one. In a recent study by Glenberg and Bradley (1979), the conclusion was reached that mere contiguity had little if any effect on associative formation in recall, although the data did indicate an effect when measured by recognition. I am convinced that when a subject is actively trying to learn a task, associations will develop between contiguously presented words even if the associations so established are not necessary for the performance of the task. We need a principle such as contiguity to account for fundamental properties of the associative memory system, and I have no reluctance in simply postulating contiguity as a fundamental mechanism if the data are judged too weak to support the concept as an empirical one.

FREQUENCY THEORY

It will be remembered that frequency theory was formulated originally to account only for verbal-discrimination learning. During the period 1965-1975 the theory as applied to verbal-discrimination learning was actively tested in several laboratories. As a result of this work I gradually reached the conclusion that the theory was correct. The fact that very little work testing the theory further has taken place in recent years may seem to support the conclusion that the theory is correct. This is a state of affairs that has seldom occurred in psychology. Theories are often discarded or proved incorrect or not tested, but it is rare to find a theory with considerable empirical support that is just left alone. What happens to a theory under such circumstances? Will it be forgotten? Will someone propose an alternative theory, thereby reopening the whole theoretical interpretation of verbal-discrimination learning? It is true that frequency theory as applied to verbal-discrimination learning reached its present status without a serious competing theory. Perhaps such a theory is yet to come. Or perhaps the theory will be kept active by the fact that, when applied to classical recognition, it does in fact have competition.

I said earlier that frequency theory is no longer goading investigators of verbal-discrimination learning, leading to the inference that the theory is judged to be sound. This matter needs further discussion.

Is the Theory Correct?

Two topics in verbal-discrimination learning have yielded results that are not in sympathy with the theory as originally formulated. One area has to do with IARs, as discussed earlier. The conclusion reached on this matter was that failure to support the theory with respect to IAR functioning is not a serious problem for the theory. In a sense the IAR part of the theory is an adjunct, and failure to support the IAR expectations does not negate the basic idea that decisions by the subjects in verbal-discrimination learning are based on directly accrued situational frequency differences.

The second topic of contradiction cannot be handled so easily. This topic has to do with transfer effects. Several slightly different procedures have been used in experiments, but the simplest is the reversal case. The subject learns a verbal-discrimination list until the level of learning is relatively high. Then the correct-incorrect functions of the items are reversed. For example, if A was initially correct and B incorrect, then a reversal makes A incorrect and B correct. The subject is fully informed about the reversal. Evidence from a variety of studies shows that on the initial reversal trials the subjects perform very well, some perhaps perfectly. The theory indicates, however, that as reversal trials continue, performance should deteriorate because the frequencies of the correct and incorrect items become closer and closer together. Strictly speaking, the theory would predict that performance would revert to a chance level at the point during the reversal trials where frequency differences will no longer mediate correct responding. However, the fact is that peformance does not deteriorate seriously.

I have come to believe that we should not consider this a serious problem for the theory. We assume that frequency differences will be used as a general rule for governing item choice; but when the frequency differences break down as a basis for discrimination, the subject will search for other attributes to provide a basis for new rules. The data seem to indicate that the subject had a difficult time finding a new rule when frequency differences no longer appeared to be valid. There are other cases in which the theory does not handle the data with precision. For example, the study reprinted as the second article in Chapter 4 is not completely in accord with the theory because, according to the theory, the performance level for the two middle groups should have been reversed for the conditions in which the frequency of the incorrect words was varied.

The history of psychology has provided us with a pointed lesson about the durability of theories. This lesson is that the theory should not be changed and additions should not be made to it to try to accommodate each empirical finding that is not strictly in accord with the theory. If the theorist does bow to each minor divergence by adding a further assumption or providing a new postulate, the theory soon gets top heavy and too detailed to have much value as a general set of interpretive ideas. I do not mean that the theorist should ignore the divergent data; but unless various sets of discrepant data can be handled by a simple addition to the theory, I think the theory should not be changed. Perhaps it is better to have a theory that gives roughly correct predictions from simple premises than to have one that gives more precise predictions from very complicated premises. In the present state of theoretical psychology, the former has a much better chance of survival than the latter; and it serves an organizing function for the time being that many can understand.

Alternative Possibilities

If one were to propose alternatives to frequency theory, three possibilities might be raised. When one learns a verbal-discrimination list, associations between the words in the pairs develop quite readily (for example, Underwood, 1969, 7). A correlation always presents the possibility of being interpreted as a cause-effect relationship. If associations develop as verbal-discrimination learning proceeds, perhaps the associations are in some way responsible for the learning. However, two lines of evidence argue against this idea.

Frequency theory predicts that in learning the verbal-discrimination list, the pairings of the right and wrong words from trial to trial need not be constant. Studies show that if the subjects are informed that the pairings will not be constant, performance is as good when they are not constant as when they are constant (Underwood, 1972, 8). This seems to indicate that the associations that normally develop when pairings are constant are not necessary for the acquisition of the discriminations. Of course, it is possible that the association is important in the constant-pairing lists, whereas some other factor leads to the learning when the items are re-paired from trial to trial; but this is the sort of theoretical complication discussed previously that I think we should try to avoid.

In a further study (Underwood, 1976, 2) the subjects learned a paired-associate list and a verbal-discrimination task simultaneously, using the same pairs for both types of lists. The subjects had bi-directional paired-associate learning in which each word in each pair was used half the time as a stimulus term and half the time as a response term. In addition, one member of each pair was underlined (as in a verbal-discrimination task), and the subjects knew they were to learn which word in each pair was underlined. Thus the subjects were instructed to learn associations between the words in the pairs and to learn also which word in each pair was underlined. Alternate study and test trials were given. The results showed that over trials the paired-associate learning progressed rapidly but that the subjects were unable to make headway in identifying which word in each pair was underlined. Thus associative learning was not correlated at all with verbal-discrimination learning. I think the evidence must be interpreted to mean that verbal-discrimination learning is not based on the acquisition of associations between the words in the pairs.

Another possible interpretation for verbal-discrimination learning is associative strength of the individual items. It could be assumed that associative strength to the situation or context is directly related to frequency of presentation of the items. Therefore, in making decisions about the right and wrong items in the pairs, the subject chooses the stronger of the two. Thus strength differences, not frequency differences, could be said to become the crucial attribute for decision making. As far as I can tell, a strength position would (for most variables) lead to exactly the same predictions as does frequency theory. As long as a perfect correlation between frequency and strength is assumed, there is no way to distinguish experimentally between the two. However, one might be able to construct conditions that would violate the assumption. It seems that it would be possible to separate frequency and strength experimentally, although to the best of my knowledge this has not been done. Frequency judgments are very little influenced by duration of exposure (Hintzman, 1970), whereas strength obviously is. An experiment might be carried out along the following lines. In one case the correct and incorrect items would each be presented for one second, whereas in a second case the correct item would be presented for one second, the incorrect for two seconds. If strength is crucial, verbal-discrimination performance should be poorer in the second case than in the first since the incorrect item will be about as strong as the correct item, and discrimination should be impossible. On the other hand, if frequency is crucial, learning should be equivalent in the two cases because frequency is not influenced by exposure duration. Until such a study shows clearly that strength of association provides a better interpretation than does frequency, I will stick to the frequency approach.

A third possibility for interpreting verbal-discrimination learning using assumptions different from those of frequency theory could revolve around what I call a *two-category classification task*. Essentially, this task represents disjunctive concept formation with two categories. The subject is presented with a long list of words, one at a time, with half the words underlined. The subject's task is to learn which words are underlined and which are not. One could view the verbal-discrimination task as a two-category classification task in which the subject learns which words are called correct, and which incorrect. Another way to view the two-category task is as a paired-associate list with only two response terms; the words are stimulus terms, and the two categories are the response terms. The learning of such tasks takes place at a surprisingly rapid rate (Ghatala, Levin, & Subkoviak, 1975), so that the usual rapid learning of the verbal-discrimination task could be handled quite readily.

The two-category classification task as a model for verbal-discrimination runs into some data problems. For example, there is no reason that the two types of lists used in the study reported in the second article in Chapter 4 should produce a difference in learning the lists as two-category classification tasks. Also, several studies in verbal discrimination show the operation of Weber's Law, which holds for frequency discriminations. Weber's Law would seem to have no counterpart in two-category classification learning. Thus it seems to me that classification learning is not a serious threat to frequency theory, although I have sometimes speculated that when frequency breaks down as a discriminative cue, two-category classification learning may be substituted. Of course, to say that verbal-discrimination learning is merely a special case of two-category classification learning explains nothing unless there is a theory to account for the classification learning, and there appears to be no such theory.

I do not consider any of the three alternatives a serious alternative to frequency theory. In concluding this section, however, I do want to make a few more comments about associative information and frequency information. Part of my reason for concern about any role that associative information might play in verbal-discrimination learning is that I take the position that association and frequency information play quite different roles in rote learning. I mentioned this earlier in pointing out the reasons for writing the article reprinted as the last article in Chapter 5. We immediately are led to a consideration of the relationship between recall and recognition, and it must be apparent that I believe that recall and recognition are mediated by quite different attributes. This issue has been discussed at great length by many authors (see Brown, 1976), and I will not repeat their arguments here. However, I do want to mention certain data that I believe have been generally overlooked in the discussions. These data have to do with the role of overt errors in learning.

We are sometimes told that our learning tasks should be programmed so as to prevent the subject from making overt errors or at least so as to minimize the number made. Frequency theory tells us exactly why such advice is of great importance in recognition performance. In both verbal-discrimination learning and classical recognition tasks, error production is inimical to good performance because it decreases the frequency differences between correct and incorrect items. On the other hand, in the case of recall tasks (such as the paired-associate task), it is quite irrelevant for overall learning whether subjects make many or few overt errors (for example, Underwood, 1954, 5). Within a group of subjects the correlation of overt-error rate and rate of learning is usually close to zero. Further, if subjects are instructed to make many overt errors, they do so quite willingly but with no influence on the rate of learning. Such evidence seems to indicate that frequency theory deals with a distinctly different area within verbal learning than does learning that requires the recall of items. Thus, whether frequency theory is correct or not, it does seem that theories cannot ignore the differences between recall and recognition that exist at many different levels. The apparent differences in the role of frequency information and associative information probably will have to be reflected in theories if the data are to be a guide.

CONCEPT LEARNING AND UTILIZATION

The first reprinted article in Chapter 5 deals with a wide range of behavior representing the higher mental processes. My own work in this field has been primarily restricted to concept utilization involving word lists, although, as indicated earlier, I have not carried out a systematic series of studies on issues relating to concept formation and utilization. My primary interest has been in demonstrating in a variety of ways that concept activation enters into many verbal-learning studies and that concept learning in turn may be understood in part by referring to verbal-learning principles.

In thinking about the relationship between concept learning and verbal learning, it will be useful initially to restrict attention to paired-associate lists in which the number of response terms is varied. If there are fewer response terms than stimulus terms, the potential for concept learning is present in that more than one response term must be associated with a single stimulus term. In a simple, symmetrical list, we might have sixteen different stimulus terms and four different response terms, with each response term assigned to four different stimulus terms. Such a list is an amplification of the A-B, C-B transfer paradigm but is manipulated within a list. Disjunctive concept learning is involved if there is no relationship among the four stimulus terms paired with a single response term (the concept name). If, however, there is some characteristic common to the four stimuli paired with a response term that is not common to the four stimuli paired with a different response term, them we have conjunctive concept learning. When we have used such lists for disjunctive concept learning (lists that could be learned in a rote fashion), we have found evidence that conceptual learning was indeed involved (Underwood, 1969, 6). Hence it is not very daring to suggest this model as a combined verbal-learning and concept-learning model.

There are two other phenomena that tend toward joining verbal learning and concept learning in my mind. The first is referred to commonly as backward associations. The first reprinted article in Chapter 5 made use of the notion of contiguity, but it also required the utilization of backward associations if the contiguity was to be effective in relating two or more stimulus terms. At the time that paper was written, there was no literature at all on backward associations. The term *backward association* refers to the fact that following the learning of A-B, it can be shown that B will elicit A with a fairly high probability. A graduate student (Thomas Thornton) and I carried out a study of paired-associate learning to see whether or not backward associations existed. If they did, then the theory discussed in Chapter 5 became quite feasible. This study was never published because it was a demonstration, not an experiment. It showed that after a subject learned a paired-associate list, 83 percent of the response terms would elicit the appropriate stimulus terms. In a very few years a sizable literature grew up on backward associations, focusing on the fact that backward associations were not at the same level of strength as were forward associations.

A second phenomenon with ties to both verbal learning and concept learning is *stimulus selection.* Conjunctive concept learning requires stimulus selection in the sense that the subject must find a common property for a group of stimuli; and, of course, in order to make the task challenging for the subject, stimulus properties that are irrelevant to the concept are also present. In verbal learning it was found that when compound stimuli are used in a paired-associate list, the subjects may select for a functional stimulus some part of the nominal stimulus (Underwood, 1962, 1). Thus, in this experiment, when consonant syllables used as stimulus terms were printed on distinctly different colors, the subjects ignored the syllables and selected the colors as the functional stimuli. If only the consonant syllables are used as the nominal stimulus terms, the subjects may select only the first letters as the functional stimulus terms. Again, an extensive literature is available on stimulus selection in verbal learning, but very little work is being done on the phenomenon at present.

Conceptual Organization and Long-Term Retention

I discussed earlier how a theory of forgetting of the single list based on interference from language habits was not supported by the results of many appropriate experiments. The basic idea of the theory, however, would not go away. I kept thinking that, given the right situation, it would be shown to be correct. The idea that organization of the material learned is intimately involved in memory functioning could be said to be a basic belief of many researchers who have become involved in verbal-learning research in the past two decades. Conceptual relations assuredly must represent a prime basis of organization. I therefore considered the possibility that long-term retention was firmly bound up with organization. It would seem that if level of organization was used as an independent variable, differences in retention of the single list might occur, providing us with new leads for developing forgetting theory.

My research made use of serial lists of words. Sometimes the words were numbered in sequence; but since this had no notable effect on the learning, we may talk in terms of traditional serial learning. At one extreme the words were organized in a three-level hierarchy, whereas at the other extreme the same words were ordered randomly (Underwood, 1974, 5). The most highly organized list consisted of the following words: *robin, owl, bobolink, trout, guppy, sturgeon, apple, lemon, fig, rose, lilac, marigold, beer, rum, sherry, milk, soda, cocoa, diamond, opal, sapphire, iron, brass, tungsten.* As can be seen, at the lowest level of structure or organization, this list consists of three instances of each of eight concepts. At a higher level, four concepts are involved (animals, plants, beverages, minerals) with six instances of each; and at the highest level, the distinction between animate and inanimate divides the list in half. Whether this organizational scheme has behavioral relevance or not depends on a demonstration that the rate of learning is a function of the level of organization. In fact, another study demonstrated that although the largest influence on learning came from the lowest conceptual level (about 80 percent), both of the two higher levels contributed to the remaining 20 percent (Underwood, 1975, 6). We will consider here only the two extreme cases of organization, namely, the one just given and, at the other extreme, the case in which the same 24 words are randomly positioned in the serial list.

It will be remembered that the basic idea of the theory that related forgetting to linguistic habits assumed that if the associations required in the task were congruent with already established habits, forgetting would be less than if they were not congruent. In the same sense, we could say that if the ordering of the items in the list were congruent with already established habits of organization, retention should be better than if the required habits were not congruent. Specifically, the organized list should be better retained than the random list of the same words.

The experiments showed that lists with appropriate conceptual ordering of the words were learned more rapidly than were the lists with the words randomized. However, 24-hour recall did not differ for the two lists when the criterion for learning was the same for both lists. These null findings merely extend the results from other experiments in showing that task variables (such as meaningfulness or intralist similarity), though producing large differences in rate of learning, do not influence forgetting. This general conclusion appears particularly convincing in the case of the two lists involved because not only should the conceptual hierarchy reduce forgetting, but the random list of the same items might also be expected to pick up interference from conceptual IARs. It seems beyond doubt that the subjects given the random list recognized that there were several instances of each of several concepts, which means that conceptual IARs were produced. As discussed earlier, however, the subjects appeared to have ways of setting these potentially interfering associates aside when they were judged to be inappropriate for the task. The overt errors gave no indication that interference resulted from the conceptual IARs produced by the items in the random list.

One further matter must be mentioned with regard to the use of organized lists. The fact that forgetting over 24 hours did not differ for the structured and random lists could lead to the inference that both types of lists would be equally subject to interference produced in the laboratory. We tested this general idea (Underwood, 1976, 5) and found that an interpolated learning task involving classical interference paradigms produced heavy retroactive inhibition of the original structured list, and that the amount of interference was independent of the structure of the interpolated list. That is, a highly structured interpolated list and a nonstructured interpolated list produced the same loss for a highly structured list.

Overall, the evidence seems to lead to the conclusion that the use of conceptual organization in acquiring a serial list does not protect the associations acquired from interference.

MP-DP EFFECT

When I terminated our seemingly interminable series of studies on the MP-DP effect with the publication reprinted in Chapter 5, I had no intention of returning to the topic. Good riddance, I thought. Let other investigators have a go at bringing a fresh outlook and new approaches. At least one did (Izawa, 1971). We were excited about frequency theory and chose to channel our energies in that direction. But in so doing I found myself once again involved with an MP-DP effect, in the following manner.

At Northwestern, as at most universities, the subjects in our experiments are students enrolled in the introductory psychology course. Usually the students are required to serve as subjects for a given number of sessions. In the fall of 1966 I had a new research assistant, and I did not want to overload him with work in setting up experiments, assigning experimenters, and so on during the initial quarter. Thus I had planned to initiate only a few experiments. Consequently, we were not drawing heavily on the subject pool. It also happened that my colleagues and their graduate students had less than the usual amount of research underway. Further, enrollment in the introductory course was higher than normal. As a consequence of these several factors, the students in the elementary course soon began to complain about the lack of different experiments in which they might serve. They indicated that unless more experiments became available, they could not be expected to meet the requirement. Their position was unassailable.

Most researchers keep a notebook in which they jot down various ideas for research that they hope to accomplish sooner or later. As a consequence of need for experiments during this particular school quarter, many faculty members consulted their notebooks for ideas. A high priority in my notebook was the idea of obtaining basic data on the judgment of situational frequency of words. Because such a study could be done using group testing, it seemed to be an ideal topic for the situation. In making up the lists, I scheduled items to occur 1, 2, 3, or 4 times. But a problem arose in putting the words in positions in the list. If a word was to be presented two or more times, it was possible to distribute the occurrences widely in the list or to present them in successive positions. I decided to do both so that some items having multiple occurrences would be widely spaced throughout the list, whereas others occurring with the same frequency occupied adjacent positions. The plan was to have the subjects listen to the tape on which the words were recorded, after which they would be asked to make absolute frequency judgments for all words occurring in the list in addition to a few items that did not occur in the list.

At this point I remembered all those subjects pounding at the laboratory doors and thought how nice it would be to have evidence on the recall of such long, free-recall lists. So the materials were then used in an experiment in which recall was the response measure. The findings led to more and more recall studies, with the frequency judgments becoming a secondary matter. The data were showing that recall for the widely spaced items was much better than for the items repeated in adjacent positions (massed items). A quantitative result that was found, and that I have since replicated, was that a word presented twice by distributed practice was recalled with about the same frequency as a word presented four times in a massed schedule. In both cases the recall was about 42 percent. Unwittingly, then, I was back with an MP-DP effect, but in this case an effect that was hearty and consistent. I then discovered that several other investigators had also found this type of MP-DP effect, and very quickly a sizable literature developed. The work persisted at a rather high level until the late 1970s, when the published reports diminished sharply.

This MP-DP effect (or, as it is often called, the *spacing effect*) occurs for a wide variety of materials and for subjects of all ages, and is larger and larger the greater the frequency of presentation of the items being memorized. The phenomenon occurs in paired-associate learning but is most often studied using a free-recall procedure. It might seem that, in view of the high consistency of the results and the large magnitude of the phenomenon, the theoretical trimmings ought to be formulated quite readily. However, it seems that the very fact that the spacing effect does occur under such a wide variety of conditions is an impediment to theory building. If we could find conditions under which no spacing effect occurred, the theories might be formulated more readily or at least tested more readily.

This is not the place to go into the various theories that have been offered and the tests which have been made of them. However, because one of the theories originated in my laboratory, I will mention it here. The theory is quite simple. It assumes that massed presentation causes the subjects to attenuate attention to the massed items so that the full study time is not used for encoding or rehearsal. This theory leads to several expectations, three of which will be mentioned here. All have empirical backing from the references given.

1. Frequency judgments of MP items should be lower than the frequency judgments for DP items (Underwood, 1969, 2).
2. The greater the frequency of presentation, the greater the difference between the recall of MP and the recall of DP items (Underwood, 1970, 1).
3. If subjects pace themselves through a list, they spend less time studying the MP items than studying the DP items (Underwood, 1972, 4).

As I noted earlier, work on this MP-DP effect has declined; but I believe, for two reasons, that this does mean that the area will become dead. First, I know that some investigators feel there are other theoretical approaches that are better than the one guided by the attenuation-of-attention theory; this will keep some active. The second reason that MP-DP effect will not be forgotten is that it provides one of the few genuine cases in which laboratory work has uncovered a phenomenon so large and so consistent that it necessarily has applied value. In any institutional situation in which verbal materials are to be learned, the spacing effect should be considered carefully in programming the materials to be learned.

ATTRIBUTES

Generally speaking, I still find the orientation given in the last reprinted paper in Chapter 5 a useful one. When we say we learn something new, it means that we are establishing a unique set of attributes and, therefore, that the memory is in some way distinguishable from all other memories. The purpose of theory under this orientation is to propose how the various attributes contribute to the establishment of memories and their functioning. Thus I have talked about the role of frequency in recognition performance, about the role of temporal attribute in proactive inhibition, and so on.

In thinking about memory functioning in terms of the constituent attributes, it has become more and more important to distinguish between the attributes that constitute a memory and which of those attributes are used in performing the memory tests we use in the laboratory. This is to say that a given memory may consist of attributes, among which there are some that do not determine the performance in the experiment. This is essentially a repetition of something I said earlier in discussing experiments in which IAR expectations were not borne out. Subjects can choose from among the attributes constituting a memory, and these chosen attributes are those that will determine performance in an experiment.

We are likely to overestimate the role of word meaning or the semantics of words in accounting for various verbal-learning phenomena. I will describe two such cases with which I have been involved. In studying alternative theories to frequency theory (to account for word recognition), I found that it was a rather common belief that word meaning was the major type of information used in making recognition decisions. Not much evidence was cited for this belief; it was almost taken as a given. However, when we evaluated the available data and did some experiments of our own, we found that word meaning was a very minor factor in making recognition decisions (Underwood, 1979, 1). This did not mean that the meaning of the words was not a part of the memory for the list of words, but it does mean that word meaning is not heavily involved in the recognition decisions.

I will describe another situation in which word meaning might be expected to play a major role but in which it did not (Underwood, 1980, 3). A study involved learning as a function of intralist similarity. The subjects' task was to learn to assemble eight word triads, in which each word consisted of three letters. After being shown the eight triads on a study trial, they then tried to assemble the triads on the test. They were given the twenty-four words used in all triads and were expected to put the words into eight triads, with the order of the words within triads being part of the memory test. In one set of conditions, intralist similarity was increased by increasing the number of repeated words in the triads. In a second set of conditions, homonyms were used so that in mimicking the increase in similarity in the first set of conditions, the number of pairs of homonyms was increased, with their positions in the triads being the same as that of the repeated words in the other conditions. Viewed in the abstract, the use of homonyms need not influence learning at all because each has a distinctly different meaning. That is, the formal similarity produced by the homonyms could be irrelevant if learning to assemble the triads was based primarily on word meaning.

The results of the study showed that an increase in the number of homonym pairs used has as great a decremental effect on learning as did an increase in the corresponding number of repeated words. It appeared that the learning that occurred did not result from discriminations made on the basis of semantic attributes; other attributes must have been heavily implicated in the learning that was observed. Again, I believe that the subjects carried word meaning as part of the memory for the task but that it simply did not enter into the associative-recognition performance.

These two cases against meaningfulness as a dominant attribute in recognition memory must not be overemphasized. There are many cases in recall learning in which meaningful similarity among words in a list will impede learning. This must mean that meaning attributes are entering into the learning endeavor and influencing performance. It might suggest that meaning is a dominant attribute in performing tasks for which recall is required. Thus again we see the recall-recognition bifurcation to be of potential value. In any event, these considerations seem to underline the work that needs to be done in identifying the roles of the various attributes in memory functioning. They perhaps also emphasize that preexperimental predilections about memory functioning should be borne very lightly. I think there is every reason to press on with the attribute approach, which stresses that a major job is that of identifying the function of the attributes. This work may be faciliated by articulate theories, but I do not consider the theory a prerequisite for such work.

PUZZLES AND PROBLEMS

In this section I will go beyond the topics as represented in the reprinted articles and will discuss three puzzles or problems that have arisen in our research.

Stimulus Differentiation

It was fairly typical of verbal-learning research of the last twenty years for investigators to view the tasks as consisting of subtasks or subprocesses, some of which might be studied independently. For example, the paired-associate task might be viewed as consisting initially of response learning and the learning of an association between the stimulus and response terms. Further subprocesses could be identified, including stimulus learning and, perhaps separately, stimulus differentiation. It seems absolutely necessary that the stimulus terms of a paired-associate list elicit differentiating implicit responses if the response terms are to be elicited consistently by the stimulus terms. When intralist stimulus similarity is manipulated, the time necessary to establish the differentiating responses increases directly as the similarity increases.

This conception of stimulus differentiation leads to certain expectations for transfer studies. Suppose we use the A-B, A-D transfer paradigm, along with the control (A-B, C-D). If the establishment of stimulus differentiation is necessary in learning A-B (which, as noted earlier, seems necessary by almost any conception), that should produce a positive component in the transfer from A-B to A-D. The amount of the positive effect would be reflected by the time taken to establish differentiating responses to the A stimulus terms during A-B learning. Because the time taken to establish the differentiation increases as intralist similarity increases, the amount of positive transfer from this source should increase directly as intralist stimulus similarity increases. Of course, we gauge this by using the control paradigm as a base, because there can be no positive transfer in the control paradigm from this source because the stimulus terms are different in the two lists.

The foregoing considerations lead to some striking predictions. For example, it would be predicted that transfer performance on A-D (in the A-B, A-D paradigm) would actually be better than the performance on C-D for the control paradigm when intralist stimulus similarity is high. The so-called negative transfer paradigm would turn into a positive transfer paradigm.

We tested this prediction (Underwood, 1968, 1). The stimulus terms were consonant syllables, and the response terms were three-letter words. Similarity was either very low (little letter duplication) or high (many letters duplicated). The prediction was not supported. The findings indicated that for the A-B, A-D paradigm, when the subjects started to learn A-D, it was as if they had never had anything to do with the stimulus terms before. How could this be? The subjects spent approximately thirty-five anticipation trials learning A-B when stimulus similarity was high, but when they were given A-D to learn they behaved as if they had had no experience with the A terms before.

Undoubtedly the solution to this puzzle lies in the nature of the differentiating responses to the stimulus terms that are developed in learning A-B. One possibility is that the differentiating response that is ultimately used is in some way dependent on the response term.

Given this dependency, if the response term of A-B is taken away when A-D is to be learned, the subject must start again to develop a dependency between a differentiating response to the stimulus term and the response term. We tested this possibility and were able to find at best only weak support for the idea (Underwood, 1968, 5), and I still find the lack of positive transfer from A-B to A-D when intralist stimulus similarity is high to be a devilish puzzle.

Formal Intralist Similarity

One could bring together a great deal of evidence to support the general statement that the rate of learning of lists decreases as formal intralist similarity increases. This evidence would consist largely of studies in which only low and high levels of similarity were used. Under certain circumstances the relationship between formal similarity and learning is not a simple, direct one. Two studies will be cited.

In the first study (Underwood, 1968, 7) seven different levels of formal similarity were used. The items were CCCs, and at one extreme there were no repeated letters in the list; then, with each successive list, 2, 4, 6, 8, 10, different letters were repeated. For the seventh list six letters were used twice each, and three letters three times each. These seven lists were used in three different tasks. Two of the tasks were paired-associate lists in which the seven syllables were paired with the numbers 1 through 7. In one case the syllables were stimulus terms, in the other they were response terms. The third task was a free-recall list of seven CCCs.

The results showed that with syllables as response terms in paired-associate learning, and with free recall, learning was a decreasing linear function of intralist similarity. However, with the CCCs as stimulus terms, the relationship was complex: learning first increased and then decreased as stimulus similarity increased. Thus, when the task required the recall of the CCCs, performance decreased regularly as similarity increased; but when stimulus recognition was required for the CCCs (when they were stimulus terms), a complex relationship was discovered.

In the foregoing study we used three different sets of CCC lists, so that it seemed unlikely that we were dealing with some fluke that produced the complex relationship when the CCCs were stimulus terms. But even this remote possibility was discarded when we recently found another instance of the same complex relationship (Underwood, 1980, 3). This study was mentioned earlier in conjunction with another matter. Subjects learned eight word triads. On the study trials the eight triads were shown, and on test trials the 24 words were provided and the subjects attempted to assemble the triads correctly. Intralist similarity was manipulated by varying the number of repeated words in the eight triads. The results were again complex; performance first increased and then decreased as formal similarity increased. Because the assembly of the triads does not require recall of the components, it is similar to the first experiment in which stimulus similarity was varied for the paired-associate lists. It appears that recognition memory is emphasized in both cases, but we have not yet developed an optimistic hypothesis to account for the findings.

Task Variables

A number of years ago Rudy Schulz and I set out to give an empirical and theoretical characterization of the effect of meaningfulness of verbal units on learning (Underwood, 1960, 3). We may have done a fair job in meeting our first goal, but we certainly did not succeed in the second. Our attempts to develop a theory consisted of trying to find a single underlying force that was basic to the whole variety of techniques used to scale meaningfulness (taking meaningfulness only as a generic term). I think the problems we encountered can be best illustrated by a subsequent study that I carried out (Underwood, 1966, 2).

I brought together 27 trigrams representing a wide range of item difficulty, from CCCs to common three-letter words. The 27 items were scaled for ease of learning, ease of pronouncing, and number of associates elicited (association value). Other subjects learned the list by free recall. The data indicated that the lowest correlation among the variables was .85. This high correlation means that it is essentially impossible to carry out experiments to try to determine which characteristic or factor is basic to the learning. For example, in this study the correlation between ease of pronouncing and association value was .88. To do the needed experiment, we should hold one of these variables constant and manipulate the other. However, with correlations of this magnitude it is impossible to do this; one could not find items that were constant on one measure but differed appreciably on the other. In effect, then, a characteristic such as meaningfulness (in the general sense) does not allow analysis leading to cause-effect statements.

A second illustration will be given of the difficulties that arise when we try to analyze the underlying properties of task variables. I recently carried out an experiment to collect data for teaching purposes. More particularly, I wanted basic data on the role of concreteness of words on learning. From available norms (Paivio, Yuille, & Madigan, 1968) I put together two lists of 16 items each that varied widely on concreteness but were equivalent on meaningfulness and frequency. The 16 words in each list were paired with the numbers 1-16. Half the subjects learned a paired-associate list in which the words were stimulus terms, and half learned such lists when the words were response terms.

There are two expectations from such an experiment (Paivio, 1971). First, when the words are stimulus terms, the lists with the concrete words should be learned more rapidly than the corresponding lists having abstract words. Second, when the words are response terms, the difference in learning as a function of concreteness should be less than when the words are stimulus terms. The results of my experiment supported neither of these expectations. Learning was a little faster with the lists having the concrete words, but the difference was far from reliable statistically. This small, insignificant effect was essentially identical for both types of lists.

I report this experiment in order to sensitize us to a problem. I do not think the results of my little experiment should shake the structure of concreteness and imagery that has been erected as a result of many, many other experiments. Still, I do think my findings raise some questions. The items of low and high concreteness were matched item by item on meaningfulness and frequency. This would seem to neutralize two competing characteristics, particularly meaningfulness. I do not know what I did wrong that prevented me from obtaining the effects of concreteness, and I do not propose to find out because any attempt to do so would lead me into another quagmire. Hence my message is that words differ on many, many characteristics, some very highly correlated. When we scale words along one dimension and find that lists constructed from different levels of the scaled characteristic are learned at different rates, we must not conclude that the differences in learning are caused by this characteristic. There are probably many correlated dimensions, and it is impossible to determine which one (or ones) is responsible for the relationship between it and learning.

WHAT IS AHEAD?

Returning to Figure 1.1, it can be seen that the peak year for publications was 1969, followed by a decline in the number in 1970 and 1971. Statistically speaking, this fall may not be reliable; furthermore, it may be a consequence of new journals siphoning away articles that normally would have been published in the *Journal of Experimental Psychology*. However that may be, it is probably true now, ten years later, that the outflow of articles in the more or less classical area of verbal learning and memory is sharply reduced. There are several likely reasons for this. Younger researchers have moved on, opening up other fields of verbal learning as identified by the use of sentences and prose material. Others have moved in another direction, toward research on very short-term memories, where the units are letters, single words, or very short lists and the response measure often latency of responding. Thus the field of human learning and memory has in fact expanded far beyond that field with which I am identified and which was used as a criterion to include the article in the statistics in Figure 1.1.

It is no secret that the universities are not appointing many new faculty members in experimental psychology. As a consequence of this lack of job opportunities, the number of outstanding students seeking training in learning and memory has been severely reduced, so that in recent years we are not getting the infusion of energy that is always important to keep a field humming. It is also probably true that research funding of the classical areas has been reduced. On the evidence, we can expect still fewer active researchers in the area in the coming years.

This is a regrettable conclusion. There are many intriguing problems to be solved and many old ideas to be rid of. Still, there will surely be a small group of people who find it both interesting and important to try to remove the enigma associated with serial learning, to find out what the basic mechanisms are that underlie proactive inhibition, or to develop a theory that makes sense out of the differences between recognition and recall.

REFERENCES

Bach, M. J. Implicit response frequency and recognition memory over time. *Journal of Experimental Psychology*, 1974, *103*, 675-679.

Brown, J. *Recall and recognition*. New York: Wiley, 1976.

Galbraith, R. C. On the independence of attributes of memory. *Journal of Experimental Psychology: Human Learning and Memory*, 1975, *104*, 23-30.

Ghatala, E. S., Levin, J. R., & Subkoviak, M. J. Rehearsal strategy effects in children's discrimination learning: Confronting the crucible. *Journal of Verbal Learning and Verbal Behavior*, 1975, *14*, 398-407.

Glenberg, A. M., & Bradley, M. M. Mental contiguity. *Journal of Experimental Psychology: Human Learning and Memory*, 1979, *5*, 88-97.

Hintzman, D. L. Effects of repetition and exposure duration on memory. *Journal of Experimental Psychology,* 1970, *83,* 435–444.

Izawa, C. Massed and spaced practice in paired-associate learning: List versus item distributions. *Journal of Experimental Psychology,* 1971, *89,* 10–21.

Kanak, N. J., Cole, L. E., & Eckert, E. Implicit associative responses in verbal discrimination learning. *Journal of Experimental Psychology,* 1972, *93,* 309–319.

Keppel, G., Postman, L., & Zavortink, B. Studies of learning to learn: VIII. The influence of massive amounts of training upon the learning and retention of paired-associate lists. *Journal of Verbal Learning and Verbal Behavior,* 1968, *7,* 790–796.

McGeoch, J. A. Forgetting and the law of disuse. *Psychological Review,* 1932, *39,* 352–370.

Paivio, A. *Imagery and verbal processes.* New York: Holt, Rinehart & Winston, 1971.

Paivio, A., Yuille, J. C., & Madigan, S. A. Concreteness, imagery, and meaningfulness values for 925 nouns. *Journal of Experimental Psychology Monograph,* 1968, *76* (1, Pt. 2).

Radtke, R. C., & Grove, E. K. Proactive inhibition in short-term memory: Availability or accessibility? *Journal of Experimental Psychology: Human Learning and Memory,* 1977, *3,* 78–91.

Thorndike, E. L. *The fundamentals of learning.* Bureau of Publications, Teachers College, Columbia University, 1932.

Toglia, M. P., & Kimble, G. A. Recall and use of serial position information. *Journal of Experimental Psychology: Human Learning and Memory,* 1976, *2,* 431–445.

7
Biographical Sketch

Benton J. Underwood was born in Center Point, Iowa, on February 28, 1915. He attended primary and secondary schools in Albion, Iowa, and pursued his undergraduate studies at Cornell College in Mount Vernon, where he earned a B.A. degree in 1936 and qualified as an athletic coach. After working for three years as a high school teacher and coach, Underwood began his graduate studies at the University of Oregon in the summer of 1939, transferring that fall to the University of Missouri in Columbia, where he received an M.A. in psychology in 1940.

Underwood's lifelong interest in learning and memory was kindled in the University of Missouri Psychology Department, chaired at that time by Arthur Melton. These interests were further nurtured when Underwood became a research assistant to John A. McGeoch at the University of Iowa in 1940 and entered the doctoral program in experimental psychology. Influenced by McGeoch and Kenneth Spence, Underwood began a series of investigations of retroactive and proactive inhibition, which culminated in a dozen studies that he published on these topics during the next decade.

Upon obtaining his Ph.D. from Iowa in December of 1942, Underwood was immediately commissioned in the U.S. Navy, and he served during the war years as a Naval Aviation Psychologist. In 1946 he joined the faculty at Northwestern University with an appointment as assistant professor of psychology. The academic climate at Northwestern and the stimulation provided by such distinguished colleagues as William A. Hunt, Carl P. Duncan, and Donald T. Campbell have no doubt contributed to his tenure on the Evanston campus over the past thirty-five years.

Prepared by the Series general editor based on information provided by the author.

Professor Underwood's association with the U.S. Navy has also continued over the past three decades through the support he has received from the Office of Naval Research for his research on human learning and memory. His current research, on the mechanisms involved in discrimination among memories, is supported by a grant from the National Institutes of Health.

Through dedicated leadership in professional organizations and service on government boards and panels, Professor Underwood has made many important contributions to the discipline of psychology. The offices he has held include: president of the Midwestern Psychological Association; president of two American Psychological Association divisions (experimental psychology and general psychology); and chair of the psychology sections for both the National Academy of Sciences and the American Association for the Advancement of Science. He has also served on the Psychobiology Review Panel for the National Institute of Mental Health, the Department of Defense's Advisory Panel on Personnel and Training, the National Research Council's Committee on Naval Medical Education and panel for screening NSF fellowship applications, and the Illinois State Certification Board for Psychology.

Professor Underwood has also contributed to scientific psychology through his work as editor of the *American Journal of Psychology* and his service as a member of the editorial board of three major APA journals: the *Psychological Bulletin,* the *Journal of Experimental Psychology,* and the *Journal of Educational Psychology.* Together with Leo Postman he was instrumental in founding the *Journal of Verbal Learning and Verbal Behavior,* and he has served continuously as a consulting editor of this journal for nearly two decades.

During his productive career, Professor Underwood has always placed a high value on the education and training of the graduate students who have worked with him, and many have been leading contributors to psychological science in their own right, including: E. James Archer, Bruce R. Ekstrand, Joel S. Freund, Geoffrey Keppel, Jack Richardson, R. W. Schulz, E. A. Schwenn, J. J. Shaughnessey, Slater Newman, R. K. Young, W. N. Runquist, John Jung, William P. Wallace, E. B. Zechmeister, Eva Ferguson, and Sarnoff Mednick and R. A. Gardner.

In addition to teaching, research, and intensive work with his graduate students, Underwood has served as chairman of the Northwestern University Psychology Department. In recognition of his service to the university and his scholarly contributions to the discipline of psychology, he was appointed Stanley G. Harris Professor of Social Science in 1976. His distinguished contributions to psychology and society have also been recognized by his receipt of an honorary Doctor of Science degree from Cornell College in 1966 and of the Warren Medal given by the Society of Experimental Psychologists in 1964; by his election to the National Academy of Sciences in 1970; and by his receipt of the Distinguished Scientific Contributions Award from the American Psychological Association in 1973. The citation for the APA award recognizes the broad range and significance of Professor Underwood's many contributions to psychological science (*American Psychologist,* 1974, pp. 38-39):

> For his massive contributions to the experimental and theoretical analysis of verbal learning and memory. A master of experimental design, he has been a recognized leader in the development of a modern and sophisticated methodology in his field of research. For more than a quarter of a century his wide-ranging investigations have focused on the fundamental processes of acquisition and retention. The substantive areas in which his work has yielded new theoretical insights and basic empirical findings are too numerous to list. Among the highlights are his systematic explorations of the effects of distribution of practice, the principles of transfer, the mechanisms of interference in retention, and the role of discriminative processes in recognition. While firmly rooted in the traditions of his discipline, he has throughout his career been an innovator and a pacesetter in a rapidly growing and changing domain of research.

Publications:
A Comprehensive Bibliography

1941

1. The effects of punishment in serial verbal learning. *Proceedings of the Iowa Academy of Science,* 1941, *48,* 349–352.

1942

1. Three comparisons of retroactive and proactive inhibition. *Proceedings of the Iowa Academy of Science,* 1942, *49,* 425–429.

1943

1. With J. A. McGeoch. Tests of the two-factor theory of retroactive inhibition. *Journal of Experimental Psychology,* 1943, *32,* 1–16.
2. With L. E. Thune. Retroactive inhibition as a function of degree of interpolated learning. *Journal of Experimental Psychology,* 1943, *32,* 185–200.

1944

1. Associative inhibition in the learning of successive paired-associate lists. *Journal of Experimental Psychology,* 1944, *34,* 127–135.

1945

1. The effect of successive interpolations on retroactive and proactive inhibition. *Psychological Monographs,* 1945, *59* (3, Whole No. 273).

1948

1. Retroactive and proactive inhibition after five and forty-eight hours. *Journal of Experimental Psychology,* 1948, *38,* 29–38.
2. "Spontaneous recovery" of verbal associations. *Journal of Experimental Psychology,* 1948, *38,* 429–439.
3. With H. H. Kendler. The role of reward in conditioning theory. *Psychological Review,* 1948, *55,* 209–215.

1949

1. *Experimental psychology.* New York: Appleton-Century-Crofts, 1949.
2. Proactive inhibition as a function of time and degree of prior learning. *Journal of Experimental Psychology,* 1949, *39,* 24–34.

1950

1. Proactive inhibition with increased recall-time. *The American Journal of Psychology*, 1950, *63*, 594-599.
2. Retroactive inhibition with increased recall-time. *The American Journal of Psychology*, 1950, *63*, 67-77.
3. With R. Greenberg. Retention as a function of stage of practice. *Journal of Experimental Psychology*, 1950, *40*, 452-457.
4. With R. H. Hughes. Gradients of generalized verbal responses. *The American Journal of Psychology*, 1950, *63*, 422-430.
5. With R. L. Morgan. Proactive inhibition as a function of response similarity. *Journal of Experimental Psychology*, 1950, *40*, 592-603.
6. With A. Ribback. An empirical explanation of the skewness of the bowed serial position curve. *Journal of Experimental Psychology*, 1950, *40*, 329-335.

1951

1. Associative transfer in verbal learning as a function of response similarity and degree of first-list learning. *Journal of Experimental Psychology*, 1951, *42*, 44-53.
2. Studies of distributed practice: II. Learning and retention of paired-adjective lists with two levels of intralist similarity. *Journal of Experimental Psychology*, 1951, *42*, 153-161.
3. Studies of distributed practice: III. The influence of stage of practice in serial learning. *Journal of Experimental Psychology*. 1951, *42*, 291-295.
4. With E. J. Archer. Retroactive inhibition of verbal associations as a multiple function of temporal point of interpolation and degree of interpolated learning. *Journal of Experimental Psychology*, 1951, *42*, 283-290.
5. With D. Goad. Studies of distributed practice: I. The influence of intralist similarity in serial learning. *Journal of Experimental Psychology*, 1951, *42*, 125-134.
6. With R. O. Viterna. Studies of distributed practice: IV. The effect of similarity and rate of presentation in verbal-discrimination learning. *Journal of Experimental Psychology*, 1951, *42*, 296-299.

1952

1. An orientation for research on thinking. *Psychological Review*, 1952, *59*, 209-220.
2. Studies of distributed practice: VI. The influence of rest-interval activity in serial learning. *Journal of Experimental Psychology*, 1952, *43*, 329-340.
3. Studies of distributed practice: VII. Learning and retention of serial nonsense lists as a function of intralist similarity. *Journal of Experimental Psychology*, 1952, *44*, 80-87.
4. With D. E. Ellis & V. Montgomery. Reminiscence in a manipulative task as a

function of work-surface height, prerest practice, and interpolated rest. *Journal of Experimental Psychology*, 1952, *44*, 420-427.
5. With L. Oseas. Studies of distributed practice: V. Learning and retention of concepts. *Journal of Experimental Psychology*, 1952, *43*, 143-148.

1953

1. Learning. *Annual Review of Psychology*, 1953, *4*, 31-58.
2. Studies of distributed practice: VIII. Learning and retention of paired nonsense syllables as a function of intralist similarity. *Journal of Experimental Psychology*, 1953, *45*, 133-142.
3. Studies of distributed practice: IX. Learning and retention of paired adjectives as a function of intralist similarity. *Journal of Experimental Psychology*, 1953, *45*, 143-149.
4. Studies of distributed practice: X. The influence of intralist similarity on learning and retention of serial adjective lists. *Journal of Experimental Psychology*, 1953, *45*, 253-259.
5. Studies of distributed practice: XI. An attempt to resolve conflicting facts on retention of serial nonsense lists. *Journal of Experimental Psychology*, 1953, *45*, 355-359.
6. With C. P. Duncan. Retention of transfer in motor learning after twenty-four hours and after fourteen months. *Journal of Experimental Psychology*, 1953, *46*, 445-452.

1954

1. With C. P. Duncan, J. T. Spence, & J. W. Cotton. *Elementary statistics.* New York: Appleton-Century-Crofts, 1954.
2. Intralist similarity in verbal learning and retention. *Psychological Review*, 1954, *61*, 160-166.
3. Speed of learning and amount retained: A consideration of methodology. *Psychological Bulletin*, 1954, *51*, 276-282.
4. Studies of distributed practice: XII. Retention following varying degrees of original learning. *Journal of Experimental Psychology*, 1954, *47*, 294-300.
5. With H. Scheible. The role of overt errors in serial rote learning. *Journal of Experimental Psychology*, 1954, *47*, 160-162.
6. With R. K. Young. Transfer in verbal materials with dissimilar stimuli and response similarity varied. *Journal of Experimental Psychology*, 1954, *47*, 153-159.

1955

1. With E. J. Archer. Studies of distributed practice: XIV. Intralist similarity and presentation rate in verbal-discrimination learning of consonant syllables. *Journal of Experimental Psychology*, 1955, *50*, 120-124.
2. With J. Richardson. Studies of distributed practice. XIII. Interlist interference and the retention of serial nonsense lists. *Journal of Experimental Psychology*, 1955, *50*, 39-46.

1956

1. With J. Richardson. The influence of meaningfulness, intralist similarity, and serial position on retention. *Journal of Experimental Psychology*, 1956, 52, 119-126.
2. With J. Richardson. Some verbal materials for the study of concept formation. *Psychological Bulletin*, 1956, 53, 84-95.
3. With J. Richardson. Verbal concept learning as a function of instructions and dominance level. *Journal of Experimental Psychology*, 1956, 51, 229-238.

1957

1. *Psychological research*. New York: Appleton-Century-Crofts, 1957.
2. A graphical description of rote learning. *Psychological Review*, 1957, 64, 119-122.
3. Interference and forgetting. *Psychological Review*, 1957, 64, 49-60.
4. Studies of distributed practice: XV. Verbal concept learning as a function of intralist interference. *Journal of Experimental Psychology*, 1957, 54, 33-40.
5. Studies of distributed practice: XVI. Some evidence on the nature of the inhibition involved in massed learning of verbal materials. *Journal of Experimental Psychology*, 1957, 54, 139-143.
6. With S. M. Feldman. Stimulus recall following paired-associate learning. *Journal of Experimental Psychology*, 1957, 53, 11-15.
7. With J. Richardson. Comparing retention of verbal lists after different rates of acquisition. *The Journal of General Psychology*, 1957, 56, 187-192.
8. With J. Richardson. Studies of distributed practice: XVII. Interlist interference and the retention of paired consonant syllables. *Journal of Experimental Psychology*, 1957, 54, 274-279.

1958

1. With E. M. Jantz. R-S learning as a function of meaningfulness and degree of S-R learning. *Journal of Experimental Psychology*, 1958, 56, 174-179.
2. With J. Richardson. Studies of distributed practice: XVIII. The influence of meaningfulness and intralist similarity of serial nonsense lists. *Journal of Experimental Psychology*, 1958, 56, 213-219.
3. With J. Richardson. Supplementary report: Interlist interference and the retention of paired consonant syllables. *Journal of Experimental Psychology*, 1958, 55, 95-96.

1959

1. Verbal learning in the educative processes. *Harvard Educational Review*, 1959, 29, 107-117.
2. With J. M. Barnes. "Fate" of first-list associations in transfer theory. *Journal of Experimental Psychology*, 1959, 58, 97-105.

3. With W. N. Runquist & R. W. Schulz. Response learning in paired-associate lists as a function of intralist similarity. *Journal of Experimental Psychology,* 1959, *58,* 70-78.
4. With R. W. Schulz. Studies of distributed practice: XIX. The influence of intralist similarity with lists of low meaningfulness. *Journal of Experimental Psychology,* 1959, *58,* 106-110.
5. With H. M. Twedt. Mixed vs. unmixed lists in transfer studies. *Journal of Experimental Psychology,* 1959, *58,* 111-116.

1960

1. Verbal learning. In *McGraw-Hill Encyclopedia of Science and Technology,* 1960, 301-305.
2. With L. Postman. Extraexperimental sources of interference in forgetting. *Psychological Review,* 1960, *67,* 73-95.
3. With R. W. Schulz. *Meaningfulness and verbal learning.* Philadelphia: Lippincott, 1960.
4. With R. W. Schulz. Response dominance and rate of learning paired associates. *Journal of General Psychology,* 1960, *62,* 153-158.

1961

1. Distributed practice on the Tsai-Partington numbers test. *Perceptual and Motor Skills,* 1961, *12,* 325-326.
2. An evaluation of the Gibson theory of verbal learning. In C. N. Cofer (Ed.), *Verbal Learning and Verbal Behavior.* New York: McGraw-Hill, 1961.
3. Ten years of massed practice on distributed practice. *Psychological Review,* 1961, *68,* 229-247.
4. With R. W. Schulz. Studies of distributed practice: XX. Sources of interference associated with differences in learning and retention. *Journal of Experimental Psychology,* 1961, *61,* 228-235.
5. With R. W. Schulz. Studies of distributed practice: XXI. Effect of interference from language habits. *Journal of Experimental Psychology,* 1961, *62,* 571-575.

1962

1. With M. Ham & B. R. Ekstrand. Cue selection in paired-associate learning. *Journal of Experimental Psychology,* 1962, *64,* 405-409.
2. With G. Keppel. An evaluation of two problems of method in the study of retention. *American Journal of Psychology,* 1962, *75,* 1-17.
3. With G. Keppel. One-trial learning? *Journal of Verbal Learning and Verbal Behavior,* 1962, *1,* 1-13.
4. With G. Keppel. Proactive inhibition in short-term retention of single items. *Journal of Verbal Learning and Verbal Behavior,* 1962, *1,* 153-161.
5. With G. Keppel. Retroactive inhibition of R-S associations. *Journal of Experimental Psychology,* 1962, *64,* 400-404.

6. With G. Keppel & R. W. Schulz. Studies of distributed practice: XXII. Some conditions which enhance retention. *Journal of Experimental Psychology,* 1962, *64,* 355-363.
7. With R. Rehula & G. Keppel. Item-selection in paired-associate learning. *American Journal of Psychology,* 1962, *75,* 353-371.

1963

1. Stimulus selection in verbal learning. In C. N. Cofer & B. S. Musgrave (Eds.), *Verbal Behavior and Learning: Problems and Processes.* New York: McGraw-Hill, 1963.
2. With B. R. Ekstrand. Paced versus unpaced recall in free learning. *Journal of Verbal Learning and Verbal Behavior,* 1963, *2,* 288-290.
3. With G. Keppel. Bidirectional paired-associate learning. *American Journal of Psychology,* 1963, *76,* 470-474.
4. With G. Keppel. Coding processes in verbal learning. *Journal of Verbal Learning and Verbal Behavior,* 1963, *1,* 250-257.
5. With G. Keppel. Retention as a function of degree of learning and letter-sequence interference. *Psychological Monographs,* 1963, 77 (4, Whole No. 567).

1964

1. Articulation in verbal learning. *Journal of Verbal Learning and Verbal Behavior,* 1964, *3,* 146-149.
2. Degree of learning and the measurement of forgetting. *Journal of Verbal Learning and Verbal Behavior,* 1964, *3,* 112-129.
3. Forgetting. *Scientific American,* 1964, *210* (3), 91-99.
4. Laboratory studies of verbal learning. In E. R. Hilgard (Ed.), *Theories of Learning and Instruction.* Chicago: University of Chicago Press, 1964.
5. The representativeness of rote verbal learning. In A. W. Melton (Ed.), *Categories of Human Learning.* New York: Academic Press, 1964.
6. With B. R. Ekstrand & G. Keppel. Studies of distributed practice: XXIII. Variations in response-term interference. *Journal of Experimental Psychology,* 1964, *68,* 201-212.
7. With F. Jesse & B. R. Ekstrand. Knowledge of rights and wrongs in verbal-discrimination learning. *Journal of Verbal Learning and Verbal Behavior,* 1964, *3,* 183-186.
8. With W. H. Saufley, Jr. Cue-selection interference in paired-associate learning. *Journal of Verbal Learning and Verbal Behavior,* 1964, *3,* 474-479.
9. With E. Schwenn & G. Keppel. Verbal learning as related to point of time in the school term. *Journal of Verbal Learning and Verbal Behavior,* 1964, *3,* 222-225.
10. With N. E. Spear & B. R. Ekstrand. Association by continguity. *Journal of Experimental Psychology,* 1964, *67,* 151-161.
11. With W. P. Wallace. Implicit responses and the role of intralist similarity in verbal learning by normal and retarded subjects. *Journal of Educational Psychology,* 1964, *55,* 362-370.

1965

1. False recognition produced by implicit verbal responses. *Journal of Experimental Psychology*, 1965, 70, 122-129.
2. The language repertoire and some problems in verbal learning. In S. Rosenberg (Ed.), *Directions in Psycholinguistics*. New York: Macmillan, 1965.
3. With B. R. Ekstrand. Free learning and recall as a function of unit-sequence and letter-sequence interference. *Journal of Verbal Learning and Verbal Behavior*, 1965, 4, 390-396.
4. With B. R. Ekstrand & G. Keppel. An analysis of intralist similarity in verbal learning with experiments on conceptual similarity. *Journal of Verbal Learning and Verbal Behavior*, 1965, 4, 447-462.
5. With A. H. Erlebacher. Studies of coding in verbal learning. *Psychological Monographs*, 1965, 79 (13, Whole No. 606).
6. With E. Schwenn. Simulated similarity and mediation time in transfer. *Journal of Verbal Learning and Verbal Behavior*, 1965, 4, 476-483.

1966

1. *Experimental psychology* (Second Edition). New York: Appleton-Century-Crofts, 1966.
2. Individual and group predictions of item difficulty for free learning. *Journal of Experimental Psychology*, 1966, 71, 673-679.
3. Motor-skills learning and verbal learning: Some observations. In E. A. Bilodeau (Ed.), *Acquisition of Skill*. New York: Academic Press, 1966.
4. Some relationships between concept learning and verbal learning. In H. J. Klausmeier & C. W. Harris (Eds.), *Analyses of Concept Learning*. New York: Academic Press, 1966.
5. With B. R. Ekstrand. An analysis of some shortcomings in the interference theory of forgetting. *Psychological Review*, 1966, 73, 540-549.
6. With B. R. Ekstrand & W. P. Wallace. A frequency theory of verbal-discrimination learning. *Psychological Review*, 1966, 73, 566-578.

1967

1. With B. R. Ekstrand. Effect of distributed practice on paired-associate learning. *Journal of Experimental Psychology Monograph*, 1967, 73 (4, Pt. 2.)
2. With B. R. Ekstrand. Response-term integration. *Journal of Verbal Learning and Verbal Behavior*, 1967, 6, 432-438.
3. With B. R. Ekstrand. Studies of distributed practice: XXIV. Differentiation and proactive inhibition. *Journal of Experimental Psychology*, 1967, 74, 574-580.
4. With B. R. Ekstrand. Word frequency and accumulative proactive inhibition. *Journal of Experimental Psychology*, 1967, 74, 193-198.
5. With G. Keppel. Reminiscence in the short-term retention of paired-associate lists. *Journal of Verbal Learning and Verbal Behavior*, 1967, 6, 375-382.
6. With G. Wood. Implicit responses and conceptual similarity. *Journal of Verbal Learning and Verbal Behavior*, 1967, 6, 1-10.

1968

1. With B. R. Ekstrand. Differentiation among stimuli as a factor in transfer performance. *Journal of Verbal Learning and Verbal Behavior*, 1968, 7, 172-175.
2. With B. R. Ekstrand. Linguistic associations and retention. *Journal of Verbal Learning and Verbal Behavior*, 1968, 7, 162-171.
3. With J. S. Freund. Effect of temporal separation of two tasks on proactive inhibition. *Journal of Experimental Psychology*, 1968, 78, 50-54.
4. With J. S. Freund. Errors in recognition learning and retention. *Journal of Experimental Psychology*, 1968, 78, 55-63.
5. With J. S. Freund. Transfer of stimulus discrimination: Can response terms be used to differentiate stimulus terms? *Journal of Verbal Learning and Verbal Behavior*, 1968, 7, 825-830.
6. With J. S. Freund. Two tests of a theory of verbal-discrimination learning. *Canadian Journal of Psychology*, 1968, 22, 96-104.
7. With E. A. Schwenn. The effect of formal and associative similarity on paired-associate and free-recall learning. *Journal of Verbal Learning and Verbal Behavior*, 1968, 7, 817-824.
8. With J. T. Spence, C. P. Duncan, & J. W. Cotton. *Elementary statistics* (Second Edition). New York: Appleton-Century-Crofts, 1968.
9. With J. Zimmerman. Ordinal position knowledge within and across lists as a function of instructions in free-recall learning. *Journal of General Psychology*, 1968, 79, 301-307.

1969

1. Attributes of memory. *Psychological Review*, 1969, 76, 559-573.
2. Some correlates of item repetition in free-recall learning. *Journal of Verbal Learning and Verbal Behavior*, 1969, 8, 83-94.
3. With J. S. Freund. Further studies on conceptual similarity in free-recall learning. *Journal of Verbal Learning and Verbal Behavior*, 1969, 8, 30-35.
4. With J. S. Freund. Storage and retrieval cues in free recall learning. *Journal of Experimental Psychology*, 1969, 81, 49-53.
5. With J. S. Freund. Verbal-discrimination learning with varying numbers of right and wrong terms. *American Journal of Psychology*, 1969, 82, 198-202.
6. With J. S. Freund & N. H. Jurca. The influence of number of response terms on paired-associate learning, transfer, and proactive inhibition. *Journal of Verbal Learning and Verbal Behavior*, 1969, 8, 369-377.
7. With E. B. Zechmeister. Acquisition of items and associations in verbal discrimination learning as a function of level of practice. *Journal of Experimental Psychology*, 1969, 81, 355-359.
8. With E. B. Zechmeister & D. W. Biers. Bidirectional unlearning. *Journal of Verbal Learning and Verbal Behavior*, 1969, 8, 54-58.

1970

1. A breakdown of the total-time law in free-recall learning. *Journal of Verbal Learning and Verbal Behavior*, 1970, 9, 573-580.

2. With M. J. Bach. Developmental changes in memory attributes. *Journal of Educational Psychology*, 1970, *61*, 292-296.
3. With J. S. Freund. Relative frequency judgments and verbal discrimination learning. *Journal of Experimental Psychology*, 1970, *83*, 279-285.
4. With J. S. Freund. Restricted associates as cues in free recall. *Journal of Verbal Learning and Verbal Behavior*, 1970, *9*, 136-141.
5. With J. S. Freund. Retention of a verbal discrimination. *Journal of Experimental Psychology*, 1970, *84*, 1-14.
6. With J. S. Freund. Testing effects in the recognition of words. *Journal of Verbal Learning and Verbal Behavior*, 1970, *9*, 117-125.
7. With J. S. Freund. Word frequency and short-term recognition memory. *American Journal of Psychology*, 1970, *83*, 343-351.
8. With R. F. Williams. Encoding variability: Tests of the Martin hypothesis. *Journal of Experimental Psychology*, 1970, *86*, 317-324.

1971

1. Recognition memory. In H. H. Kendler & J. T. Spence (Eds.), *Essays in Neobehaviorism*. New York: Appleton-Century-Crofts, 1971.
2. With J. Zimmerman & J. S. Freund. Retention of frequency information with observations on recognition and recall. *Journal of Experimental Psychology*, 1971, *87*, 149-162.

1972

1. Are we overloading memory? In A. W. Melton & E. Martin (Eds.), *Coding Processes in Human Memory*. Washington, D.C.: V. H. Winston & Sons, Inc., 1972.
2. Word recognition memory and frequency information. *Journal of Experimental Psychology*, 1972, *94*, 276-283.
3. With M. Patterson & J. S. Freund. Recognition and number of incorrect alternatives presented during learning. *Journal of Educational Psychology*, 1972, *63*, 1-7.
4. With J. J. Shaughnessy & J. Zimmerman. Further evidence on the MP-DP effect in free-recall learning. *Journal of Verbal Learning and Verbal Behavior*, 1972, *11*, 1-12.
5. With J. J. Shaughnessy & J. Zimmerman. Learning-to-learn verbal-discrimination lists. *Journal of Verbal Learning and Verbal Behavior*, 1972, *11*, 96-104.
6. With J. J. Shaughnessy & J. Zimmerman. List length and method of presentation in verbal discrimination learning with further evidence on retroaction. *Journal of Experimental Psychology*, 1972, *93*, 181-187.
7. With B. S. Uehling. Transfer as a function of stimulus, response and simultaneous stimulus and response similarity. *Journal of Experimental Psychology*, 1972, *95*, 375-381.
8. With J. Zimmerman & J. J. Shaughnessy. The role of associations in verbal-discrimination learning. *The American Journal of Psychology*, 1972, *85*, 499-518.

1973

1. With P. K. Broder & J. Zimmerman. Associative matching and cumulative proactive inhibition. *Bulletin of the Psychonomic Society*, 1973, *1*(1A), 48.
2. With P. K. Broder & J. Zimmerman. Retention of verbal discrimination lists as a function of number of prior lists, word frequency, and type of list. *Journal of Experimental Psychology*, 1973, *100*, 101-105.
3. With R. C. Galbraith. Perceived frequency of concrete and abstract words. *Memory and Cognition*, 1973, *1*, 56-60.
4. With L. Postman. Critical issues in interference theory. *Memory and Cognition*, 1973, *1*, 19-40.
5. With C. S. Reichardt & J. Zimmerman. Conceptual associations and verbal-discrimination learning. *American Journal of Psychology*, 1973, *86*, 613-615.
6. With J. J. Shaughnessy. The retention of frequency information for categorized lists. *Journal of Verbal Learning and Verbal Behavior*, 1973, *12*, 99-107.
7. With J. Zimmerman. Serial retention as a function of hierarchical structure. *Journal of Experimental Psychology*, 1973, *99*, 236-242.
8. With J. Zimmerman. The syllable as a source of error in multisyllable word recognition. *Journal of Verbal Learning and Verbal Behavior*, 1973, *12*, 701-706.

1974

1. Memory: Retention and forgetting. From the 15th Edition of *Encylopedia Britannica*, 891-895, 1974.
2. The role of the association in recognition memory. *Journal of Experimental Psychology Monograph*, 1974, *102*, 917-939.
3. With A. S. Brown, Verbal context shifts and free recall. *Journal of Experimental Psychology*, 1974, *102*, 133-141.
4. With L. V. Esrov. Effects of context and length of interpolated list on retroactive inhibition in free recall. *Canadian Journal of Psychology*, 1974, *28*, 426-437.
5. With J. J. Shaughnessy & J. Zimmerman. The locus of the retention differences associated with degree of hierarchical conceptual structure. *Journal of Experimental Psychology*, 1974, *102*, 850-862.
6. With J. J. Shaughnessy & J. Zimmerman. The spacing effect in the learning of word pairs and the components of word pairs. *Memory & Cognition*, 1974, *2*, 742-748.
7. With J. Zimmerman. A comparison of the effects of formal similarity among trigrams and among word triads. *Memory & Cognition*, 1974, *2*, 283-288.

1975

1. The first course in experimental psychology: Goals and methods. *Teaching of Psychology*, 1975, *2*, 163-165.
2. Individual differences as a crucible in theory construction. *American Psychologist*, 1975, *30*, 128-134.

3. With A. S. Brown. Interference in recognition memory: A replication. *Bulletin of the Psychonomic Society*, 1975, *5*, 263-264.
4. With C. S. Reichardt. Contingent associations and the double-function, verbal-discrimination task. *Memory & Cognition*, 1975, *3*, 311-314.
5. With C. S. Reichardt. Implicit associational responses produced by words in pairs of unrelated words. *Memory & Cognition*, 1975, *3*, 405-408.
6. With C. S. Reichardt & R. A. Malmi. Sources of facilitation in learning conceptually structured paired-associate lists. *Journal of Experimental Psychology*, 1975, *2*, 160-166.
7. With J. J. Shaughnessy. *Experimentation in psychology*. New York: John Wiley & Sons, Inc., 1975.

1976

1. Recognition memory for pairs of words as a function of associative context. *Journal of Experimental Psychology: Human Learning and Memory*, 1976, *2*, 404-412.
2. With E. A. Boulay. Simultaneous paired associate and verbal discrimination learning as a simulation of the double-function list. *Memory & Cognition*, 1976, *4*, 298-301.
3. With S. M. Kapelak & R. A. Malmi. Integration of discrete verbal units in recognition memory. *Journal of Experimental Psychology: Human Learning and Memory*, 1976, *2*, 293-300.
4. With S. M. Kapelak & R. A. Malmi. The spacing effect: Additions to the theoretical and empirical puzzles. *Memory & Cognition*, 1976, *4*, 391-400.
5. With J. L. Rogers, Jr. Retroactive inhibition as a function of the conceptual structure of original and interpolated lists. *Memory & Cognition*, 1976, *4*, 109-116.

1977

1. *Temporal codes for memories: Issues and problems*. Hillsdale, N.J.: L. Erlbaum Associates, 1977.
2. With J. Zimmerman, P. Broder, & J. J. Shaughnessy. A recognition test of vocabulary using signal-detection measures, and some correlates of word and nonword recognition. *Intelligence*, 1977, *1*, 5-31.

1978

1. Recognition memory as a function of length of study list. *Bulletin of the Psychonomic Society*, 1978, *12*, 89-91.
2. With R. F. Boruch & R. A. Malmi. Composition of episodic memory. *Journal of Experimental Psychology: General*, 1978, *107*, 393-419.
3. With A. M. Lund & R. A. Malmi. The recency principle in the temporal coding of memories. *American Journal of Psychology*, 1978, *91*, 563-573.
4. With R. A. Malmi. An evaluation of measures used in studying temporal codes for words within a list. *Journal of Verbal Learning and Verbal Behavior*, 1978, *17*, 279-293.

5. With R. A. Malmi. The simultaneous acquisition of multiple memories. In G. Bower (Ed.), *The Psychology of Learning and Motivation* (Vol. 12). New York: Academic Press, 1978.
6. With R. A. Malmi. Transfer from recency learning to corresponding two-category classification learning. *Bulletin of the Psychonomic Society*, 1978, *11*, 200-202.
7. With R. A. Malmi & A. M. Lund. Recency judgments as measures of temporal coding. *Bulletin of the Psychonomic Society*, 1978, *12*, 67-68.

1979

1. With M. Humphreys. Context change and the role of meaning in word recognition. *American Journal of Psychology*, 1979, *92*, 577-609.
2. With A. M. Lund. Retention differences as a function of number of verbal lists learned simultaneously. *Journal of Experimental Psychology: Human Learning and Memory*, 1979, *5*, 151-159.
3. With R. A. Malmi & J. B. Carroll. The interrelationships among some associative learning tasks. *Bulletin of the Psychonomic Society*, 1979, *13*, 121-123.

1980

1. With A. M. Lund. Incidental development of associations in simultaneous learning. *Bulletin of the Psychonomic Society*, 1980, *16*, 411-413.
2. With A. M. Lund. Process similarity and the simultaneous acquisition retention phenomenon. *Bulletin of the Psychonomic Society*, 1980, *16*, 325-328.
3. With A. M. Lund. Semantic encoding and the effects of formal intralist similarity. *American Journal of Psychology*, 1980, *93*, 235-245.
4. With A. M. Lund. Transfer effects from single-task learning to simultaneous learning. *Bulletin of the Psychonomic Society*, 1980, *16*, 391-393.

Author Index

Anisfeld, M., 268, 270, 273
Archer, E. J., 38, 39, 48, 67n, 145, 146, 150, 249, 251, 310, 313, 314
Asch, S. E., 258, 273
Attneave, F., 181, 188, 259, 273
Atwood, D. W., 264, 274
Ausubel, D. P., 69, 92
Averbach, E., 273, 275

Bach, M. J., 14, 30, 287, 307, 320
Baddeley, A. D., 271, 273
Baker, B. L., 219, 250
Barnes, J. M., 315
Bartlett, F. C., 48
Battig, W. F., 145, 149
Belmont, L., 40, 48
Berlyne, D. E., 256, 258, 273
Biers, D. W., 319
Billings, M. L., 204, 216
Bilodeau, E. A., 318
Bilodeau, I. M., 48, 256, 273
Birch, H. G., 40, 48
Blankenship, A. B., 5, 6, 30, 31
Boruch, R. F., 322
Boulay, E. A., 322
Bourne, L. E., Jr., 17, 30, 94, 105, 116, 117, 128
Bousfield, W. A., 94, 96, 105, 106, 108, 114, 115, 116, 128, 134, 136, 149, 267, 275
Bower, G. H., 188, 273
Brackett, H. R., 145, 149
Bradley, M. M., 289, 307
Bransford, J. D., 187, 188
Briggs, G. E., 48, 53, 66
Broadbent, D. E., 190, 199
Broder, P. K., 321, 322
Brown, A. S., 321, 322
Brown, J., 6, 30, 248, 249, 250, 294, 307

Brown, R., 264, 273
Burack, B., 216
Buss, A. H., 211, 216

Carroll, J.B., 323
Cheng, N. Y., 36, 40, 49
Cofer, C. N., 316, 317
Cohen, B. H., 96, 105, 108, 115
Cole, L. E., 287, 308
Conrad, R., 265, 273
Cotton, J. W., 314, 319

Dale, H. C. A., 271, 273
Dallenbach, K. M., 42, 49
Dallett, K. M., 121, 128
Danick, J. J., 94, 105, 106, 115, 116, 128, 134, 149
DaPolito, F. J., 9, 30
Deese, J., 14, 30, 113, 115, 146, 149, 270, 273
Dey, M. K., 249, 250
Diamond, R. M., 258, 273
Dollard, J., 206n, 216, 217
Duncan, C. P., 49, 143, 309, 314, 319
Duncker, K., 203, 216

Ebbinghaus, H., 1, 9, 30, 34, 35, 36, 44, 49
Ebenholtz, S. M., 258, 273
Eckert, E., 287, 308
Eckler, G. R., 265, 275
Edwards, A. L., 143, 144n, 149
Ekstrand, B. R., 14, 30, 67n, 94, 105, 116, 128, 132, 132n, 150, 151n, 191, 199, 218, 218n, 230, 250, 251, 261, 262, 268, 273, 274, 310, 316, 317, 318, 319
Ellis, D. E., 313
Erlebacher, A. H., 318
Erlick, D. E., 259, 273
Esrov, L. V., 321

325

Feldman, S. M., 315
Fitch, F. B., 31
Franks, J. J., 187, 188
Freund, J. S., 151n, 157n, 168, 169, 170, 170n, 180, 183, 188, 256, 265, 274, 310, 319, 320

Gagné, R. M., 190, 199, 208, 216
Galbraith, R. C., 287, 307, 321
Ghatala, E. S., 293, 307
Gibson, E. J., 23, 24, 30, 40, 41, 49, 211, 216
Glenberg, A. M., 289, 307
Goad, D., 313
Goggin, J., 267, 273
Gottlieb, W., 267, 273
Greenberg, R., 6, 36, 39, 49, 313
Greeno, J. G., 9, 30, 250
Greitzer, F. L., 13, 30
Griffith, B. C., 95, 105
Grove, E. K., 285, 308
Guilford, J. P., 216

Haagen, C. H., 212, 216
Hall, M., 31
Ham, M., 316
Harris, C. W., 318
Hart, J. T., 263, 273
Hay, J., 258, 273
Heidbreder, E., 213, 216
Hiew, C. C., 30
Hilgard, E. R., 317
Hintzman, D. L., 172, 180, 265-266, 274, 292, 308
Horowitz, L. M., 264, 274
Hovland, C. I., 23, 26, 30, 31, 36, 40, 49, 245, 250
Huda, M., 248, 249, 250
Hughes, R. H., 313
Hull, C. L., 2, 18, 23, 31, 216
Humphreys, M., 323

Inoue, K., 263, 274
Irion, A. L., 49, 266, 274
Irwin, J. M., 2, 31, 149
Izawa, C., 298, 308

Jacoby, L., 17, 31
James, C. T., 9, 30
Jantz, E. M., 315
Jenkins, J. G., 42, 49
Jenkins, J. J., 108, 115, 140, 149, 246, 250
Jensen, A. R., 95, 105
Jesse, F., 132, 150, 317
Johnson, L. M., 40, 49
Jung, J., 223, 250, 310
Jurca, N. H., 319

Kaess, W., 173, 174, 179, 180
Kanak, N. J., 287, 308
Kapelak, S. M., 322
Katona, G., 49
Kellogg, R. T., 30
Kendler, H. H., 312, 320
Keppel, G., 7, 28, 31, 51n, 67n, 68, 75, 80, 81, 82, 92, 126, 129, 146, 149, 218, 219n, 223, 225, 250, 251, 283, 284, 308, 310, 316, 317, 318
Kimble, G. A., 286, 308
Kincaid, W. D., 108, 115
Klausmeier, H. J., 318
Knapp, M., 268, 270, 273
Kothurkar, V. K., 68, 92
Krueger, W. C. F., 36, 40, 49

Lefford, A., 213, 216
Lester, O. P., 36, 40, 49
Levin, H., 264, 274
Levin, J. R., 293, 307
Lindauer, M. S., 267, 273
Lipman, R. S., 95, 105
Lorge, I., 98, 105, 117, 158, 169, 174, 180, 183
Lovallo, W. R., 30
Luchins, A. S., 213, 216
Luchins, E. H., 216
Luh, C. W., 36, 40, 49
Lund, A. M., 322, 323

Madigan, S. A., 266, 274, 306, 308
Maier, N. R. F., 18, 203, 204, 208n, 210, 213, 216, 217

Author Index

Malmi, R. A., 322, 323
Marchbanks, G., 264, 274
Margolius, G., 40, 50
Marshall, M. A., 226, 247, 251
Martin, E., 270, 274, 320
McGeoch, J. A., 1, 2, 5, 6, 8, 22, 23, 25, 31, 35, 36, 49, 266, 274, 277, 308, 309, 312
McNeil, D., 264, 273
Melton, A. W., 1, 2, 8, 31, 53, 54, 66, 89, 90, 91, 92, 149, 309, 317, 320
Miller, N. E., 206n, 216, 217
Mink, W. D., 114, 115
Montgomery, V., 313
Monty, R. A., 258, 274
Morgan, J. J. B., 213, 217
Morgan, R. L., 210n, 313
Morton, J. T., 213, 217, 254, 274
Murdock, B. B., Jr., 51, 66, 88, 89, 90, 92, 120, 128, 179, 180, 263, 274
Musgrave, B.S., 317

Nagge, J., 263, 274
Noble, C. L., 219, 250
Norman, D. A., 160, 169

Oldfield, R. C., 11, 31
Oseas, L., 211, 217, 314
Osgood, C. E., 45, 49

Paivio, A., 266, 274, 306, 308
Palermo, D. S., 140, 149
Parker, B. K., 94, 105, 116, 117, 128
Patterson, M., 170n, 320
Peixotto, H. E., 160, 169
Perkins, D. T., 31
Peterson, L. R., 6, 7, 31, 51, 52, 53, 54, 55, 56, 62, 66, 88, 92
Peterson, M. J., 6, 7, 31, 51, 52, 53, 54, 55, 56, 62, 66, 88, 92
Polson, P. G., 9, 30
Postman, L., 10, 31, 52, 54, 66, 80, 82, 92, 146, 148, 149, 162n, 270, 274, 283, 308, 316, 321

Radtke, R. C., 17, 31, 285, 308
Rapaport, D., 49
Reed, H. B., 211, 217
Reichardt, C. S., 321, 322
Rehula, R., 317
Reitman, J. S., 188
Ribback, A., 313
Richardson, J., 17, 40, 50, 67n, 68, 72, 73, 77, 80, 92, 109, 115, 117, 118, 129, 246, 251, 310, 314, 315
Rieber, M., 95, 105
Riley, D. A., 52, 66
Robinson, E. S., 8, 31
Rockway, M. R., 49
Rogers, J. L., Jr., 322
Rohwer, W. D., 95, 105
Rosenberg, S., 318
Ross, R. T., 31
Runquist, W. N., 43, 49, 67n, 86, 92, 226, 247, 251, 310, 316
Russell, W. A., 49, 108, 115, 140, 149

Saufley, W. H., Jr., 317
Scheible, H., 314
Schlosberg, H., 48, 256, 273
Schulz, R. W., 56, 66, 67n, 73, 82, 92, 95, 105, 148, 150, 219n, 223, 225, 229, 246, 249, 251, 305, 310, 316, 317
Schwenn, E. A., 126, 129, 148, 149, 310, 317, 318, 319
Seashore, R. H., 217
Sells, S. B., 212, 217
Shapiro, B. J., 181, 188
Shaughnessey, J. J., 310, 320, 321, 322
Shepard, R. N., 107, 115, 270, 274
Siegel, S., 221, 251
Slamecka, N. J., 258, 274
Smith, K. H., 258, 274
Spear, N. E., 317
Spence, J. T., 314, 319, 320
Spence, Kenneth W., 2, 8, 18, 309
Spitz, H. H., 95, 105
Stark, K., 148, 149
Sturges, P. T., 179, 180
Subkoviak, M. J., 293, 307

Teghtsoonian, M., 107, 115
Thistlethwaite, D., 213, 217
Thorndike, E. L., 98, 105, 117, 158, 169, 174, 180, 183, 288, 289, 308
Thune, L. E., 217, 312
Toglia, M. P., 286, 308
Trask, F. P., 254, 275
Turvey, M. T., 266, 274
Twedt, H. M., 316

Uehling, B. S., 320
Underwood, B. J., 6, 11, 13, 17, 18, 21, 22, 23, 24, 25, 26, 27, 28, 34n, 40, 48, 49, 50, 51n, 52, 53, 56, 65, 66, 67n, 68, 72, 73, 75, 77, 80, 81, 82, 85, 92, 94, 94n, 95, 103, 105, 106n, 109, 115, 116, 116n, 117, 118, 126, 128, 129, 132, 132n, 133, 134, 136, 137, 138, 145, 146, 147, 148, 149, 150, 151n, 157n, 168, 169, 170, 170n, 180, 181, 181n, 182, 183, 188, 189n, 191, 199, 202n, 217, 218, 218n, 219, 223, 225, 226, 229, 230, 235, 245, 246, 247, 248, 249, 250, 251, 252n, 256, 258, 260, 261, 262, 265, 272, 274, 275, 278, 279, 280, 281, 282, 283, 284, 286, 287, 288, 291, 294, 295, 296, 297, 298, 300, 301, 303, 304, 305, 309, 310, 311, 312-323

Viterna, R. O., 145, 150, 313

Wallace, W. P., 12, 14, 31, 94n, 132n, 151n, 191, 199, 270, 272, 275, 310, 317, 318
Wallach, H., 273, 275
Ward, L. B., 42, 50
Waugh, N. C., 160, 169
Weiss, W., 40, 50
Welch, L., 211, 217
Wertheimer, M., 203, 217
White, M. A., 264, 274
Whitely, P. L., 5, 6, 30, 31
Whitmarsh, G. A., 94, 96, 105, 106, 108, 108-109, 115, 116, 128, 134, 149
Wickelgren, W. A., 265, 273, 275
Wickens, D.D., 265, 275
Williams, M., 40, 50
Williams, R. F., 320
Wilson, J. T., 24, 25, 31
Winograd, E., 261, 275
Wood, G., 13, 116n, 318
Woodworth, R. S., 1, 212, 217

Yaroush, R. A., 30
Yates, F. A., 257, 275
Yavuz, H. S., 267, 275
Yntema, D. B., 254, 275
Young, R. K., 310, 314
Youtz, A. C., 36, 39, 40, 42, 50
Yuille, J. C., 306, 308

Zavortink, B. L., 256, 275, 283, 308
Zeaman, D., 173, 174, 179, 180
Zechmeister, E. B., 310, 319
Zeller, A. F., 50
Zimmerman, J., 181n, 319, 320, 321, 322

Subject Index

Associationism, 8, 29
Associations,
 backward, 116
 competing, 2
 strength of, 10
Association formation, 27, 288
Associative attributes, 265-269
 acoustic, 265
 affective, 266
 class, 268
 context, 267
 nonverbal, 265
 verbal, 267
 visual, 266
Associative inhibition, 249
Associative repertoire, 11
Atmosphere effect, 212
Attenuation-of-attention theory, 300
Attributes of memory, 29-30, 158
  252-273, 300-302.
 associative, 265
 developmental changes in, 271
 forgetting of, 271
 frequency, 259
 modality, 262
 multiple, 270
 orthographic, 263
 spatial, 257
 temporal, 253

Backward association, 116, 295
Belonging, 289
Biases in thinking, 212

Clustering, 103, 120-123
Color naming, 22
Competition, 2, 280
Concept learning, 17-18, 202-216
 conjunctive, 295
 disjunctive, 295

Conceptual associations, 94-128
Conceptual organization, 296
 effect on long-term memory, 296
 retroactive inhibition with, 298
Contiguity,
 associative learning by, 28
 role in thinking, 206
Converging associations, 108
Creativity, 202

Decay, 2
Differential-forgetting theory, 22
Difficulty hypothesis, 26
Distributed practice, 19-29, 218-250
 and formal similarity, 226
 in thinking, 215
 with multiple lists, 223-225
Disuse, 2
Double-function lists, 17
Dynamic psychology, 1

Einstellung, 213
Encoding, 252

False alarms in recognition, 110-115
Finite causality, 47
Forgetting
 measurement problems, 7, 67
 theory, 34, 68
 role of: affectivity, 46; degree of
  learning, 45, 52; distribution of
  practice, 45; individual differences,
  45, 52; meaningfulness, 45; number of interfering associations, 52;
  similarity, 45; sleep, 42; warmup,
  47
Formal similarity, 188
Frequency
 abstractive nature of, 181
 attribute, 157, 259

329

background, 16, 181
discriminations of, 15
situational, 14, 151
Frequency attribute, 259-262
and strength, 259
between tasks, 261
within tasks, 259
Frequency theory, 14-17, 131-188, 289-294
associative learning, 291, 293
choice rules, 14, 135
concept recognition, 17
overt errors, 294
role of: implicit associative responses, 138; intralist similarity, 145; presentation rate, 147; rehearsal, 135; strength of associations, 292
transfer effects, 133, 290
Functionalism, 1, 2

Generalization, 23, 114
Generated meaningfulness values, 229
Gibson theory, 23, 211

Hierarchy of responses, 209
Higher mental processes, 1, 202-216, 294-298

Implicit associative responses (IARs), 8-14, 94-129, 285-289
and frequency theory, 136
conceptual, 9, 13
failures of theory, 286
production by retardates, 12, 94
theory, 8, 93
Incidental learning, 270
Individual differences
forgetting, 74
recognition, 113
theory usage, 16, 189
Information processing, 1
Interference
intralist, 27
paradigms, 4
paradox, 11
role of: conceptual similarity, 95; degree of learning, 52; extraexperimental sources, 277; number of associations, 52; retention interval, 53
Interference theory, 34-66
two-factor theory, 2, 280
Intervening processes, 193
interaction between, 194
Intralist similarity
conceptual, 94, 116
formal, 27, 145
meaningful, 21
Intrusions, 14, 64-65, 113, 148-149

Jost's laws, 39, 45

Learning-to-learn, 6, 53
Learning-to-recall, 6, 37
List differentiation, 261
and proactive interference, 281
loss of, 282

Massed practice, 19-29, 218-250
associative inhibition in, 249-250
multiple lists, 223
performance inhibition in, 248
Memories
continuity between, 43
discrimination among, 252
fallibility of, 209
Modality attribute, 262-263
Model building, 190
Meaningfulness, 145
MMFR, 280
competition in, 281
MP-DP effect, 19-29, 218-250, 298-300
difficulty hypothesis for, 26
interference in, 28
multiple-list, 223
overt errors in, 236, 239, 243
stage of practice in, 25
theory of, 300
Multiple-choice tests, 179
Multiple-entry projection, 85-88

Orthographic attributes, 263-264

Subject Index

Overt errors, 102, 236, 239, 243

Performance-inhibition theory, 23, 248
Proactive inhibition, 4-7, 34-66, 271-285
 as model of forgetting, 285
 buildup, 37, 283
 in short-term memory, 51, 284
 temporal discrimination in, 256, 281
 using within-subject designs, 6, 7, 41
Problem solving, 202
Pronunciation response, 134-137
Reasoning, 202
Recognition
 forced choice, 15, 158
 role of: context, 165; formal similarity, 188; number of alternatives, 170; testing, 15, 158, 183
 running, 2, 107
 versus recall, 294
Representational response, 94, 106, 116, 134
Response dominance, 210
Response integration, 27-28
Rest-interval activity, 23
Retroactive inhibition, 2, 4, 34-48
 as model of forgetting, 2, 5, 277, 285
 modality discrimination in, 263
 temporal discrimination in, 256
 two-factor theory of, 2, 280
Rote learning, 1

Schemata, 196
Second-order habits, 9
Selector mechanism, 148
Semantic memory, 10
Sense impressions, 109, 117
Short-term memory, 6, 51-66
 contrasted with long-term, 51, 63
 practice effects in, 54

role of degree of learning, 88
Similarity
 conceptual, 94, 116
 formal, 27, 226, 304
 meaningful, 21
 role in thinking, 211
Simultaneous learning, 283
Single-entry projections, 70-81
 asymptotic probabilities, 75
 biases in, 74
 variations on, 80
Spacing effect, see MP-DP effect
Spatial attribute, 257-259
Spontaneous recovery, 53, 281
Stimulus differentiation, 302-304
Stimulus selection, 246-247, 295
Syllogistic reasoning, 212

Task variables, 305-306
Temporal attribute, 253-257
 between tasks, 256
 position judgments, 255
 within tasks, 254
Testing effects, 157-168, 183-188
Thinking, 17-18, 202-216
 biases in, 212
 number of stimuli, 210
 practice in, 214
 similarity among stimuli, 211
Time tags for memories, 254
Tip-of-the-tongue phenomenon, 264
Two-category classification task, 293
Two-stage experiment, 67

Unlearning, 2, 280-281
 measure of, 280

Verbal repertoire, 10-11
Visual images, 266

Warmup, 47
Weber's law, 145, 293